Seeing Things

SOUTH ASIA ACROSS THE DISCIPLINES

Edited by Muzaffar Alam, Robert Goldman, and Gauri Viswanathan

Dipesh Chakrabarty, Sheldon Pollock, and Sanjay Subrahmanyam, Founding Editors

Funded by a grant from the Andrew W. Mellon Foundation and jointly published by the University of California Press, the University of Chicago Press, and Columbia University Press

For a list of books in the series, see page 283.

• • • • •

The publisher and the University of California Press Foundation gratefully acknowledge the generous support of the Ahmanson Foundation Endowment Fund in Humanities.

Seeing Things

SPECTRAL MATERIALITIES
OF BOMBAY HORROR

Kartik Nair

UNIVERSITY OF CALIFORNIA PRESS

University of California Press
Oakland, California

© 2024 by Kartik Nair

Library of Congress Cataloging-in-Publication Data

Names: Nair, Kartik, 1985– author.
Title: Seeing things : spectral materialities of Bombay horror / Kartik Nair.
Other titles: South Asia across the disciplines.
Description: Oakland, California : University of California Press, [2024] | Series: South Asia across the disciplines | Includes bibliographical references and index.
Identifiers: LCCN 2023019898 (print) | LCCN 2023019899 (ebook) | ISBN 9780520392274 (cloth) | ISBN 9780520392281 (paperback) | ISBN 9780520392298 (ebook)
Subjects: LCSH: Horror films—India—Mumbai—20th century. | Artists' materials—India—Mumbai. | Horror films—Production and direction—India—Mumbai. | Cinematography—Special effects—20th century.
Classification: LCC PN1995.9.H6 N325 2024 (print) | LCC PN1995.9.H6 (ebook) | DDC 791.43/61640954792—dc23/eng/20230802
LC record available at https://lccn.loc.gov/2023019898
LC ebook record available at https://lccn.loc.gov/2023019899

33 32 31 30 29 28 27 26 25 24
10 9 8 7 6 5 4 3 2 1

For my parents, Anu and Govind

Contents

Acknowledgments   ix

Introduction: Accidental Exposures   1

1. Paper Cuts: Inside the Bureaucratic Encounter with *Darwaza*   43
2. Celluloid Splatter: The Graphic Violence of *Jaani Dushman*   79
3. Unsettling Design: Built Atmosphere in *Purana Mandir*   111
4. Making Monsters: *Veerana* and the Craft of Excess   149
5. Hidden Circuits: *Kabrastan* from Film to Videotape   181

Epilogue: An Archive of Failures   211

Notes   219
Bibliography   243
Index   277

Acknowledgments

This book began as a research project in the School of Arts and Aesthetics at Jawaharlal Nehru University (JNU), where Ranjani Mazumdar and Ira Bhaskar have established a peerless cinema studies program. After supervising a dissertation on the Ramsay Brothers, Ranjani served on my doctoral dissertation committee and as a reader in a manuscript workshop focused on the book. In other words, Ranjani has helped make the many iterations of this project (and of my life since) possible. From her, I am still learning how to channel intense cinephilia and political commitment into the "invisible work" of reading, writing, and teaching, though it is her generosity that I most wish to emulate.

In the Department of Cinema Studies at New York University, Richard Allen was my dissertation adviser and strongest advocate. For their mentorship then and ongoing support now, I thank Tejaswini Ganti, Anna McCarthy, Antonia Lant, Dana Polan, and Dan Streible. I am grateful for the continued presence of friends from within and across cohorts, including Neta Alexander, Bruno Guaraná, Linnéa Hussein, Laliv Melamed, and Jaap Verheul. Early financial support for dissertation research came from the Corrigan Fellowship at NYU, followed by a Junior Research Fellowship from the American Institute of Indian Studies. I was hired by the

School of Film and Media Studies at Purchase College while still a graduate student. Teaching alongside Paula Halperin, Shaka McGlotten, Anne Kern, Michelle Stewart, Agustin Zarzosa, and Ling Zhang, I came to understand the labor of pedagogy even as I fell in love with the classroom. My teaching and research have been inseparable since.

At Temple University, I thank my colleagues in the screen studies program. Nora Alter unreservedly welcomed me into her home as a colleague and friend, and Chris Cagle has been the kindest mentor I could have hoped for. I am deeply appreciative of the collegiality of Warren Bass, Rod Coover, Peter D'Agostino, Sarah Drury, LeAnn Erickson, Michael Kuetemeyer, Afia Nathaniel, Eran Preis, Elisabeth Subrin, Rea Tajiri, and Lauren Wolkstein. The administration of a large research university is no easy task, and I am grateful to the chair of my department, Chet Pancake, former chairs Paul Swann and Jeff Rush, as well as Alison Crouse, Meag Jae Kaman, Sammip Parikh, and (the now-retired) Rita Kozen for the work they do to ensure that the Department of Film and Media Arts thrives. At the Center for Performing and Cinematic Arts, Dean Robert Stroker, Beth Bolton, Sue Alcedo, and Jason Horst have supported my career on the tenure track. An invaluable yearlong sabbatical from teaching and service allowed me to draft the manuscript in timely fashion, while a daylong manuscript workshop allowed me to improve it in revision. The Vice Provost for the Arts Grant and Summer Research Awards enabled me to return to India to complete archival research and pay for production services on the book. The Center for the Humanities, under director Kimberly Williams, provided a yearlong fellowship; its salutary benefits included a course release and the company of junior faculty across the humanities at Temple. As I write these acknowledgments, Temple faculty are set to enter negotiations with the university over the terms of their contract. I thank TAUP for fighting the important fight.

The story I tell in this book came into sharper focus every time I shared it, and I was fortunate to receive generous speaking invitations from the School of Arts and Aesthetics, JNU; the Cinema Studies Colloquium at the University of Pennsylvania; the Department of Cinema Studies at the University of Toronto; the Moving Image Workshop conducted by the film studies program at Michigan State University; the Department of Film and Media Studies at Colorado College; and the Film and Media Studies

Speaker Series at Lafayette College. Many devoted precious time and energy to reading (and sometimes, rereading) drafts of the book. For their immense contributions, I thank Arielle Xena Alterwaite, Nicholas Baer, Piyali Bhattacharya, Bud Bynack, Manuela Coppola, Pardis Dabashi, Kirsty Dootson, Sahana Ghosh, Justin Gifford, Nitin Govil, Radhika Govindarajan, Monica Hahn, Rebeca L. Hey-Colón, Lotte Hoek, Kathleen Karlyn, Suvir Kaul, Ranjani Mazumdar, Laliv Melamed, Debashree Mukherjee, Emily Neumeier, Jess Marie Newman, Pallavi Pinakin, Francis Russo, Terenjit Sevea, Samhita Sunya, and Kuhu Tanvir.

After talks, during walks, and over meals, at conference panels and in between them, comments, questions, and reading suggestions from the following individuals decisively improved the manuscript and my day: Pritika Agarwal, Alexander Alberro, Kaveh Askari, Harry Benshoff, Debjani Bhattacharya, Kaushik Bhaumik, Tupur Chatterjee, Iftikhar Dadi, Neal Dhand, James Leo Cahill, Iggy Cortez, Jennifer Fay, Marc Francis, Smita Gandotra, Sabeena Gadihoke, Nicola Gentili, Shohini Ghosh, Michael Gillespie, Sangita Gopal, Lalitha Gopalan, Veena Hariharan, Maggie Hennefeld, Priya Jaikumar, Kajri Jain, Shikha Jhingan, Carolyn Kane, Scott Krzych, Lawrence Liang, Bliss Cua Lim, Rich Lizardo, Ania Loomba, Rochona Majumdar, Neepa Majumdar, Meta Mazaj, Ellen McCallum, Monika Mehta, Cain Miller, Justin Morris, Madhuja Mukherjee, Rahul Mukherjee, Mike Phillips, Swarnavel Eswaran Pillai, Brian Price, Karen Redrobe, Meghan Romano, Kate Russell, Jeff Scheible, Jordan Schonig, Joshua Schulze, Meheli Sen, Shaunak Sen, Megha Sharma Sehdev, Anooradha Iyer Siddiqi, Kyle Stevens, Ravi Sundaram, Mayur Suresh, Ishita Tiwary, Jean-Thomas Tremblay, Julie Turnock, and Elizabeth Wijaya. I thank the organizers and audiences of the annual conference of the Society for Cinema and Media Studies and the Conference on South Asia, two events from which I derive so much intellectual and social sustenance. Hat tip to the conveners of the De-Westernizing Horror Conference at King's College—Iain Robert Smith, Zubair Shafiq, and Alice Haylett—as well as Jessamyn Abel and Leo Coleman, who organized the Global Asias Summer Institute on Infrastructure. Students at NYU, SUNY, and JNU, as well as those attending guest lectures at Delhi University, Jamia Millia Islamia, and Boston University, have proved the most reliable sounding boards for my ideas in their exploratory phase. I owe a debt to all my students, but especially those in The Horror Film (2022), who energized me with their love of the genre.

Several libraries and archives enabled the writing of this book, including the National Film Archive of India in Pune, the Nehru Memorial Museum & Library and Soochna Bhawan in Delhi, the New York Public Library and Elmer Holmes Bobst Library in New York City, and the Charles Library at Temple University in Philadelphia. I recognize the hard work done by archivists and librarians at these institutions, including Aruna Magier and Brian Boling.

I feel so very lucky to have published my first book with University of California Press. Since she heard the pitch, my editor Raina Polivka has guided the project with enthusiasm and care. Editorial assistants Madison Wetzell and Sam Warren shepherded the book in and out of review. Jeff Anderson and Jon Dertien ensured a smooth production process. Sharon Langworthy's painstaking copyedits have made this a better read, and the comprehensive index at the end of the book is the singular work of Sarah Osment. I am honored that *Seeing Things* appears in the illustrious South Asia Across the Disciplines series, and I thank series editors Gauri Viswanathan and Robert Goldman for their words of support. Francis Russo designed that sumptuous cover, giving stylish expression to the book's argument on a tight timeline. For their advocacy of the manuscript in various ways, I am indebted to Usha Iyer, Sudhir Mahadevan, Cecilia Sayad, Robert Spadoni, and Caetlin Benson-Allott. Caetlin's championing of junior scholars and editorial labor while at JCMS provide a model of service to the field. Over the years, I have become especially grateful to those whose camaraderie has made it easier for me to come into my own: Nick, Harry, Chris, Iggy, Marc, Daniel Howell, Kareem Khubchandani, David Lugowski, Jeff, Kyle, and Jaap.

This book is about the making of horror films in 1980s Bombay and centers on a small but influential group of filmmakers. I give thanks to some of the most recognizable names in the horror business for taking the time to speak to me, including the late Tulsi Ramsay, Mohan Bhakri, and Vinod Talwar. As this book came together in its final stages, research queries and production questions were answered with help from the ever-reliable Aditya Basu, as well as Aseem Chandaver, Brian Collins, Shamya Dasgupta, Neal Dhand, Nadia Hironaka and Matthew Suib, Erica Jones,

Aditi Sen, Deborah Stoiber, Anand Theraney, Rosie Thomas, Aparna Subramanian, Balbir Ward, and Kyle Westphal. For a typically revelatory reading that rescued the book's introduction at a crucial stage (and for everything before then), I thank Nitin Govil.

In the midst of the demands of the book, Friday morning meetings with my fellow *BioScope* editors kindled happiness in the hard work that is putting every issue together. It has been a privilege to work at *BioScope* for the past decade, alongside Ravi Vasudevan, Rosie Thomas, S. V. Srinivas, Lotte Hoek, Salma Siddique, Vebhuti Duggal, and Debashree Mukherjee.

Piyali Bhattacharya is living proof of the nicest surprise a peripatetic life such as this can bring: new places will become home because of old friends. Piyali, Tariq Thachil, Kasturi Sen, Nazia Kazi, Neesha Shah, Ania Loomba, Suvir Kaul, and Chris Devine are some of the best things about living in Philadelphia. In New York, I found home because of Nilanjana Bose, Jakub Ciupiński, Josh Kaplan, Rasha Dalbah, Amit Bhatia, the Ganti family, Maryam Jahanshahi, Anthony Miler, and the Center on 13th Street. Since they've moved to Boston, I have missed Manuela Coppola and Teren Sevea dearly. When I'm in Delhi, Arunoday Mukharji and Neha Poonia make me wish I lived closer. College friends who, happily, have become college professors too— Sahana Ghosh, Kuhu Tanvir, Aliya Rao, Dwai Banerjee, Gaurav Khanna, and Aditi Saraf—are reliable sources of sagacity and levity. Debashree Mukherjee shows me how to live with intellectual and ethical conviction, while the sheer silliness of our phone calls lightens my life. There is no one like her.

Members of my family have made the process of writing a little less lonely. I am astonished by the unending hospitality of Nirmal Rajagopalan; Gita, Maitri, and Jagdish Dore; Valeria Roasio and Giuseppe Pissinis (grazie Beppe!). Lara Chandni accompanied me on one final research trip to an old palace on the sea, but she has been with me every step of the way even when she was halfway around the world. I met Bhavya Dore twenty years ago, and we have been the very best of friends since—a researcher second to none, she has saved the book many times, and me many times more.

In the years leading up to the publication of this book, my family weathered major health challenges. I celebrate my mother for her resilience and for always supporting my interest in this thing called "film studies." My father set an early example of following one's passion, and I marvel at a former fighter pilot who remains the very image of calm. Gayatri Nair is an older sister in every sense of that word: it feels good to have her as a mutual witness to this life and to know I will grow older still with her watching. The best man I know has moved across countries and between continents when I couldn't and stilled my frantic heart with his hazel eyes, fine Italian cuisine, and brilliant writing advice. The book is done now, Andrea: let's swim into the ocean and watch the sun set.

An earlier version of chapter 4 appeared as "Unfinished Bodies: The Sticky Materiality of Prosthetic Effects," in *Journal of Cinema and Media Studies* (formerly *Cinema Journal*), 60, no. 3 (Spring 2021): 104–128. An earlier version of chapter 1 appeared in *A Companion to Indian Cinema* (edited by Neepa Majumdar and Ranjani Mazumdar) as "Scenes of Horror: Reading the Documents of Indian Film Censorship" (Wiley Blackwell, 2022, 170–195).

Introduction

ACCIDENTAL EXPOSURES

As the sun sets and night falls, a vampire rises from his crypt. Emerging from a cave deep inside the mountains, the *shaitan* (demon) is desperate to quench his thirst for human blood. His eyes are red, and his fangs are sharp. The vampire looks out over the dark valley that lies before him and takes flight into the night (see figure 1). So begins the Ramsay Brothers' *Bandh Darwaza* (Closed door, 1990), one entry in a cycle of Hindi-language horror films made in India between the late 1970s and the early 1990s. During this time, a few filmmakers shot dozens of horror films in the decrepit colonial mansions and empty industrial mills of Bombay and in the forested hills and seaside palaces surrounding the city. Foremost among these filmmakers were the seven siblings known as the Ramsay Brothers, who made "India's First Horror Film," *Darwaza* (Door, 1978). Working with enthusiastic actors and skilled technicians, the Ramsay Brothers and their contemporaries produced a wave of horror movies about soul-sucking witches, knife-wielding psychopaths, and dark-caped vampires. Thrilled audiences turned some of these films into box office hits, but critics routinely disparaged the films as "second-hand imitations of third-grade foreign horror movies," while the Indian government censored them for their graphic violence.[1] As the Bombay film business transformed into Bollywood, a global

Figure 1. Vampire surveying the darkness: detail from *Bandh Darwaza* (1990). *Source:* Ramsay Pictures.

culture industry known for lavish melodramas, the horror wave dissipated, and the Ramsay Brothers disbanded.

The films they made have not been forgotten. A modest hit when it first opened in a few theaters in Bombay, *Bandh Darwaza* has since then traveled far beyond the city (renamed Mumbai in 1995) via successive releases on videotape, disc, and online. In 2023 a new transfer of the film from the original negative was released on Blu-ray by the cult film label Mondo Macabro, while on YouTube, different versions of the film have collectively tallied more than one hundred million views. Meanwhile, contemporary directors who came of age watching 1980s horror films seek to evoke in their own work the atmosphere that makes them effective. Horror films often immerse us in faraway worlds and distant pasts in order to induce terror, anxiety, discomfort, disorientation, and disgust—the syndrome of responses with which the genre is identified. *Bandh Darwaza* accomplishes its aim by accumulating small details: the milky fog that envelops the mountains; the deep silence into which the vampire's coffin creaks open; and the long, gnarled fingers of the vampire as he crawls out from inside the crypt. Such details make the nightmare feel real: like we are deep inside the dark cave, able to touch the vampire's body and be touched by him.

Consider, however, another detail: as the vampire awakens in the murkiness of night, we are shown the territory he will hunt. Surveying what the stentorian voiceover describes as a land shrouded in the "darkness of

Figure 2. Daylit hills: detail from *Bandh Darwaza* (1990). *Source:* Ramsay Pictures.

death," we see rolling hills, their green valleys brightly dappled in daylight (see figure 2). This daylight doesn't destroy the vampire, though it does somewhat upset the illusion. Erupting into the nocturnal mood *Bandh Darwaza* conjures from so many textured images and sounds, the daylight exemplifies a second class of details frequently encountered in Bombay horror: *failures*. A film may suddenly lose resolution or fill with noise; feature a continuity error or celluloid damage; or betray a botched special effect, incomplete makeup, or lame performance. Such failures may be fleetingly visible, but they encourage us to see things a bit differently.

It is a convention of Bombay horror that all strange visions must first be dismissed. Because what they see—a flitting shadow, a reflection in a mirror, a face in the window—pressures the limits of temporal and spatial presence, the protagonists of Bombay horror must weather a duration of uncertainty in which friends, family, and the film's viewers wonder if they are in the grip of a *vehem* (superstition), *sapna* (dream), or *paagalpan* (madness). But they persist, trying to close the gap between what they have seen and what they can say about it (see figure 3). For the heroines of horror films, as Bliss Cua Lim has written, space turns out to be a "spectral surface of only limited opacity, behind which other times and places are poignantly apparent."[2] Slowly, seeing gives way to doing: examining old photographs, asking questions, and undertaking journeys. When they return to the site of haunting with aging witnesses, yellowing newspapers, or just a sledgehammer, their progressive investment in the past pays off with a public

Figure 3. Seeing with the visionary heroines of Bombay horror (*Dahshat*, 1981).
Source: Author's collection.

exhumation of something buried: hidden acts of violation, murder, and dismemberment so traumatic they spawned ghosts to possess the present.

This book follows the intrepid ghost hunters and paranormal mediums of horror films. Ghost stories have something to teach historians: to "see the past in the shape of something odd" and "stake their historical claims on it."[3] The failures of Bombay horror are reminders and remainders of the mundane resources from which the fantastic was secured onscreen. *Seeing Things* reads failures as historiographic clues—to the conditions in which the films were once made, censored, and seen—and as aesthetic cues—in my experience of horrific story worlds. What I call the *spectral materialities* of Bombay horror are both sensuous and significant, because they mark the spectral presence of cinema's material pasts at the scene of horror. Like the phantom in *Jadu Tona* (Black magic, Ravikant Nagaich, 1978) or the living corpse in *Khooni Panja* (Killer claw, Vinod Talwar, 1991), the spectral materialities of Bombay horror too exist at the edges of ordinary perception and encourage imaginative explanations of their origins. The ghosts I hunt in this book thrive in the corners of frames and lurk between reels: a man is seen crouched above a monster's lair, positioning a spotlight, or an inexplicable jump cut suddenly reorders the lair's layout. Seeing things in scenes of horror reveals that creators of the films reused latex masks and props till they fell apart, that state censors destroyed some images entirely while mangling others visibly, and that viewers handled the films as junk prints and worn-out videocassette copies. In this way, *Seeing Things* tracks the felt physicality that informs the genre's globally familiar conventions and gives visceral force to our experience of horror's possessed bodies, gothic landscapes, and graphic violence. Combining close analysis with extensive archival research and original interviews, the book reveals the material histories encrypted within the genre's spectral visions. Following Priya Jaikumar's suggestion to read visual space as sites "where histories reside," *Seeing Things* brings into view the tactile practices of production, regulation, and circulation that have shaped the world's largest film culture.[4]

BOMBAY HORROR

By 1980, India was the largest producer of films in the world: approximately 1,000 films were released that year alone, among them 150 from the Bombay film industry. In a "vast country like India, where 80 percent of the population cannot even read," declared a government report, cinema exerts an "exceptionally powerful hold on the Indian public."[5] Yet the report noted that cinema "continues to be treated almost as a subculture" by members of the cultural intelligentsia, critics in the quality press, and the state.[6] The report was prepared in the shadow of *Sholay* (Embers, Ramesh Sippy, 1975), an exhilarating, big-budget revenge picture. By the time the report was published in 1980, the film had become the biggest hit in the history of Indian cinema. Audiences returned for multiple viewings, memorizing lines of dialogue, the lyrics of its songs, and body language of its stars. In the wake of *Sholay*'s success, the production of "masala" genre films exploded. Aiming to replicate *Sholay*'s canny combination of a familiar menu—action, romance, comedy, and song and dance—with conventions of the Western, these producers found success repackaging other globally circulating genres in films like the spy thriller *Agent Vinod* (Deepak Bahry, 1977), the dance film *Disco Dancer* (Babbar Subhash, 1982), and the gangster film *Parinda* (Bird, Vidhu Vinod Chopra, 1989).

Advertised as "India's First Horror Film" (see figure 4), *Darwaza* (*Door*, Shyam and Tulsi Ramsay, 1978) begins when a cruel *thakur* (baron) murders a peasant devotee of the goddess Kali for fomenting resistance to his exploitative regime. Setting the young man on fire before the drought-stricken farmers whose crop he commands, the baron's cruelty in turn draws a curse from the martyr's mother: "Oh, Thakur, the way you've set my child on fire, I wish extinction on your family!" The curse cast by a powerless woman haunts the baron's son. As he comes of age, the son has nightmares of a woman's wail, a cobwebbed cave, of lightning striking in the dead of night—all beckoning him to return to the maw of ancestral violence and open the *haveli* (mansion) door behind which a cursed monster lurks.

That ancestral haveli supplies *Darwaza*'s opening shot: an establishing view of the mansion at night. The shot draws me in to the here and now of its storyworld (this house, this night) but it is also an opening into other times. In films such as Bombay Talkies's *Mahal* (Palace, Kamal Amrohi, 1949), *Madhumati* (Bimal Roy, 1958), *Kohraa* (Fog, Biren Nag, 1964), and *Woh Kaun Thi?* (Who was she?, Raj Khosla, 1964), protagonists and viewers were likewise lured to rural mansions. Through sensuous sound

Figure 4. Publicity for *Darwaza* (1978). Source: *Times of India*, 23 February 1978.

and gorgeous black-and-white photography, such films exercised the "mesmeric lure of the ghost story."[7] Pulled into the gravitational orbit of a lush and decrepit haveli, the viewer accompanied the hero on a journey back to a placeless, timeless world of curses, cobwebs, shadows, and siren songs. *Darwaza*'s establishing shot is thus a generic image of the past, an unremembered memory of gothic thrillers made during the "golden age" of Bombay cinema. While in the older films monsters and ghosts were usually revealed as actors, plots and illusions staged to avenge crimes of violence and greed committed in the haveli long ago, similar misdeeds unleash a very real monster in *Darwaza*. With an opening shot that sweeps us (back) into the haveli, this time in color—where a blood-red chandelier sways above and a claw-footed monster roams below—*Darwaza* is better understood as the first horror film for a new generation of moviegoers.

Darwaza was quickly followed by *Haiwan* (Monster, Ram Rano, 1978), *Jadu Tona, Aur Kaun* (Who else?, 1979, Shyam and Tulsi Ramsay; see figure 5), and *Jaani Dushman* (Mortal enemy, Rajkumar Kohli, 1979). The Ramsay Brothers gained early control of the theatrical market with loyal distributors and exhibitors, but viable competitors arose after their box office smash *Purana Mandir* (Old temple, Shyam and Tulsi Ramsay, 1984): director-producers like Mohan Bhakri, starting with *Cheekh* (Scream, 1985), and Vinod Talwar, with *Raat Ke Andhere Mein* (In the dark of the night, 1987). An issue of the industry periodical *Trade Guide* from 1985 indicates the frenzied rate of production: full-page advertisements for *Saamri*, a sequel to *Purana Mandir* ("From the Only Genuine Makers of Horror Films in India") jostle with notices for Joginder Shelly's *Pyasa Shaitan* (Thirsty demon) and Mohan Bhakri's *Cheekh* and *Khooni Mahal* (Bloody palace)—"Our Next Venture Now on the Sets," declares an advertisement for the latter film (see figure 6).[8]

Despite the intensity of audience interest, the longevity of the genre was uncertain. Every year may have brought a film advertised as "The Final Horror," as was the case with 1985's *Tahkhana* (Dungeon, Shyam and Tulsi Ramsay).[9] In a 1987 article, *Filmfare* wryly commented on the "fast-multiplying clan of Ramsays," a school of producers adept at imitating the "Ramsay Brothers' time-worn strategy of scaring people for a fast buck."[10] *Saat Saal Baad* (Seven years later, S. U. Syed, 1987) was followed in 1988 by *Bees Saal Baad* (Twenty years later, Rajkumar Kohli), and in

Figure 5. Song booklet for *Aur Kaun* (1979), an early entry in the Bombay horror cycle. *Source:* National Film Archive of India, Pune.

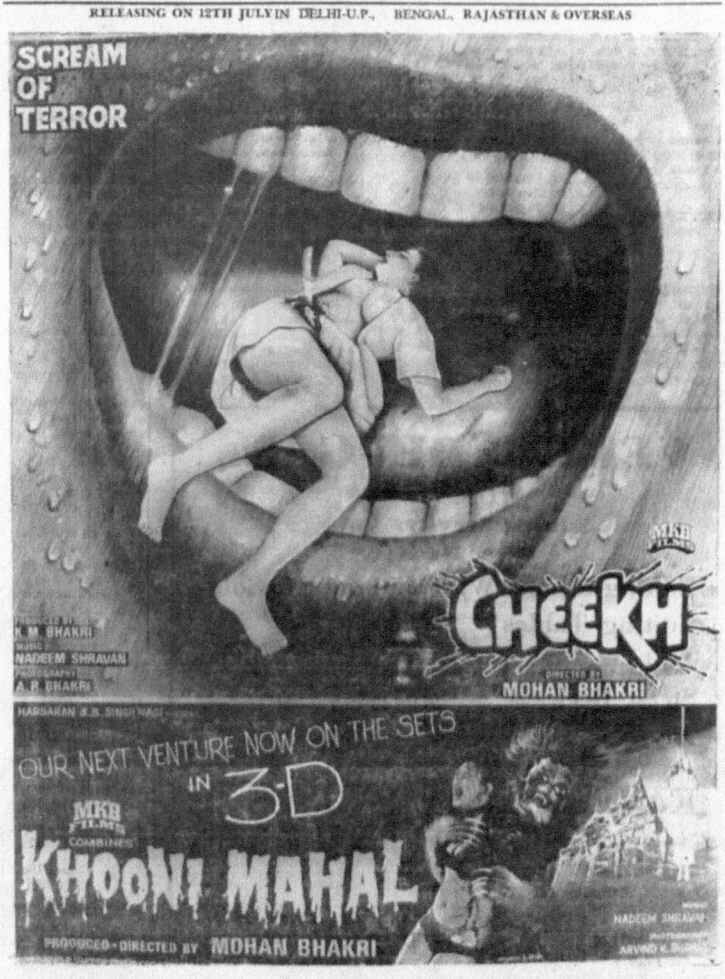

Figure 6. "Our Next Venture Now on the Sets": horror booms in the mid-1980s. *Source: Trade Guide*, 6 July 1985.

1989 by *Sau Saal Baad* (Hundred years later, Mohan Bhakri). Perhaps predictably, audience appetite was depleted by film after film, and the life of the genre began to resemble a cycle that could be "financially viable for only five to ten years."[11] The end of Bombay horror was coming, with films like the prophetically titled *Aakhri Cheekh* (The last scream, 1991, Kiran Ramsay). Talwar and Bhakri moved out of horror films, while a few of the Ramsay Brothers parlayed their film career into a move to television. On the *Zee Horror Show* (1993–97), Shyam and Tulsi Ramsay reused many of the same props and locations first seen in their films and devised multi-episode narratives that resembled their films. Gangu Ramsay, who had served as cinematographer on *Bandh Darwaza*, took his skills outside the family studio, while Kiran Ramsay became a significant sound designer of the 1990s.

Between *Darwaza* and *Bandh Darwaza*, approximately fifty horror films were made in Bombay. These were, effectively, what the horror film was in 1980s India. The most successful of them shared thematic, stylistic, and narrative characteristics. At the source of haunting lies a decadent feudal order, at the top of which sits a thakur. The depredations of this land-owning caste are visited upon helpless peasants and young village women in the film's prologue and reverberate down the thakur's family line and follow it to the city. In returning to the ancestral palace, the horror hero explicitly acknowledges the sins of his father. By vanquishing whatever cave-dwelling monster or black magic the thakur's misdeeds caused to exist, our hero also clears cobwebs and renews the feudal order. Benign yet righteously violent climaxes follow, in which a monster is fatally pierced with a holy *trishul* (trident) or a *chudail* (witch) is hanged in the village square. These conventions recur in many of the films, though there are significant variations: in the bloody slasher film *Jaani Dushman*, a werewolf kills women in a mountain valley; in *Cheekh*, a gloved serial killer attacks while heroes and heroines shimmy at the discotheque; in *Kabrastan* (Graveyard, Mohan Bhakri, 1988), a television screen and a Sony Walkman beam messages from the beyond, eventually possessing the body of their user.

The horror film's "countless scenes of violence, cruelty and horror," the state-run censor board once warned, "would offend the sensibilities of an average citizen."[12] As Bombay's first horror films were reaching their audiences, the Ministry of Information and Broadcasting revised the censorship code for the first time in almost two decades; a new category, "scenes of horror," moved to the proscriptive fore. Many horror films were "banned," or refused clearance to release; others were released with disclaimers appended about the fictionality of ghosts and monsters. Along with the 1980s' cycle of rape-revenge thrillers such as *Insaf Ka Tarazu* (The scales of justice, B. R. Chopra, 1980) and *Zakhmi Aurat* (Wounded woman, Avtar Bhogal, 1988), the horror film was one of the most surveilled genres at the Bombay office of the censor board.

The veteran film critic Khalid Mohammed decried how strictly horror films were being regulated. The censors, he wrote, "evidently do not care a whit about the new concerns or the shifting styles of international cinema. To them, horror is dirty business. And that's it."[13] "What do they expect?" Mohammed asked exasperatedly. "A song by the lakeside or mealy-mouthed sermons in the tradition of Rajshri Pictures?"[14] Like the Ramsay Brothers, Rajshri Pictures was a family-run studio that had been commissioning thrifty genre films: the spy film *Agent Vinod*, the religious devotional film *Gopal Krishna* (Vijay Sharma, 1979), and the domestic drama *Saaransh* (Gist, Mahesh Bhatt, 1984). By the end of the 1980s, however, the studio was responsible for what became the highest-grossing release of the decade: the romantic melodrama *Maine Pyar Kiya* (I have loved, 1989, Sooraj Barjatya). The film's gargantuan success predicted an array of expensive song-and-dance spectaculars centered on family, love, and marriage, such as *Hum Aapke Hain Koun!* (Who am I to you?, Sooraj Barjatya, 1994) and *Dilwale Dulhania Le Jayenge* (The braveheart will take the bride, Aditya Chopra, 1995). Like these films, Bombay's horror films too featured lakeside songs and sermons, but privileged the disruptive shocks and unsettling ambience afforded by horror. In *Saat Saal Baad*, for example, the lake is where the film's undead killer surfaces from, upturning boats and dragging victims down with him.

The final victim in *Saat Saal Baad* was played by Sharmila Tagore, now past her reign as the darling of Bombay romances of the 1960s, and almost three decades after she debuted in Satyajit Ray's *Apur Sansar* (Apu's World, 1959). At the peak of Bombay horror's popularity, marquee names appeared in the films. Mithun Chakraborty starred in *Bees Saal Baad* in 1988, by which time his *Disco Dancer* had outstripped *Sholay* to become the highest grossing Indian film of all time, setting box office records in the Soviet Union and China. But Chakraborty and Tagore were outliers in a genre that was minting its own stars. The pinup-friendly Hemant Birje, who had a buff start in *Adventures of Tarzan* (Babbar Subhash, 1985), was a principal in the Ramsays' *Veerana* and *Tahkhana*, as well as Bhakri's *Kabrastan* and *Sau Saal Baad*. Tina Ghai was cast in *Veerana*, *Sau Saal Baad*, and then *Khooni Murda* (Killer corpse, Mohan Bhakri, 1989), in which her head is smashed into a television screen by the ghost of a serial killer. Madhu Malhotra acted in *Cheekh* and the Ramsays' *Telephone* (1985) after she appeared in *Pyasa Shaitan*, in the opening minutes of which she is trapped in the woods and raped by the vines of a demonic tree.

These images might recall memories of other 1980s horror movies like *Evil Dead* (Sam Raimi, 1981), *Friday the 13th* (Sean Cunningham, 1981), and *Nightmare on Elm Street: Dream Warriors* (Chuck Russell, 1987). Bombay horror had little investment in producing a folk form; instead, filmmakers deliberately alluded to other horror films from Bombay and around the world, alternately paying tribute to or subtly undermining their contemporaries and competition. *Bandh Darwaza*, for example, limns a "visual genealogy of transnationalism," evoking vampire films shot in and around Berlin, Los Angeles, London, Rome, Lahore, and Mexico City over the decades.[15] These films span the canon of horror, from foundational texts such as the German expressionist *Nosferatu* (F. W Murnau, 1922) and Hollywood studio film *Dracula* (Tod Browning, 1931) to the British *Horror of Dracula* (Terence Fisher, 1958), Italian *Mask of Satan* (Mario Bava, 1960), Pakistani *Zinda Laash* (Living corpse, Khwaja Sarfraz, 1967), and Mexican *Alucarda* (Juan López Moctezuma, 1977). Writing about the "semiotic osmosis" of *Bandh Darwaza*, Usha Iyer has noted how the film blends the global trappings of the cinematic vampire with Indian cinema's popular iconography of tantrism.[16] Tulsi Ramsay himself made no secret of having watched videotape after videotape for "ideas aur gadgets" ("ideas and gadgets"), in the process ensuring that Bombay's horror films blended repetition and variation in the way that audiences of genre films enjoy.[17]

Yet the charge of plagiarism aggressively stalked the films, and film critics and industry insiders have long referred to Bombay horror as "spurious desi by-products," "second-hand imitations," and "bad copies" of foreign horror films.[18] In fact, the films are reminders that the horror film was different things in different places at different times. Bombay horror generates the states of fear, anxiety, and disgust associated with horror but also induces the pathos of melodrama, the amorousness of romance, and the levity of comedy—it moves viewers through a cycle of feelings over two hours in which horror is produced by juxtaposition. *Bandh Darwaza* features a bloodthirsty vampire, but also other attractions: action, such as when the hero comes to fisticuffs with the vampire's henchmen; song-and-dance romance, such as the number "Bheega Bheega Mausam Tadpaye"; and slapstick comedy, courtesy of the house servant, played by Johnny Lever. Such combinations could leave viewers cold or confused. A "veritable hotchpotch in search of a genre" is how a critic in the trade journal *Screen* dismissed *Purana Mandir* in 1984.[19] But an essay published the following year in a different *Screen* might have helped the critic make sense of what they saw.

In her 1985 essay, "Indian Cinema: Pleasures and Popularity," in the academic journal of film studies *Screen*, Rosie Thomas focused on the flexible assemblage of masala films, which she cautioned made "Hollywood genre classification quite inappropriate to Hindi cinema."[20] Arguing that a carefully "ordered succession of modes of affect" constitutes masala cinema, Thomas helped lay the foundation of Indian film studies as an academic subfield.[21] Since then, scholars seeking to understand what makes Indian popular cinema distinctive have historicized, contextualized, and theorized its "interrupted," "omnibus," and "disaggregated" format as a meaningful and pleasurable mélange born of South Asian performance traditions, financial speculation, and state imperatives.[22] "Horror appeared late in the history of Indian cinema, and when it did so," writes Sangita Gopal, "it was not as a full-blown genre but as a variation on the dominant *masala* format."[23]

As Bombay horror, Gopal concludes, horror was "incomplete," the genre not yet having "found its true form" in Hindi cinema.[24] That "true form," she suggests, arrived in the 1990s with "new horror," beginning with *Raat* (Night, Ram Gopal Varma, 1991): the performance of an international style of horror addressed to a cosmopolitan consumer class in India's rapidly transforming cities.[25] Ditching song-and-dance routines while adopting digital special effects, new horror films of the 1990s and afterward target audiences in upscale multiplex theaters: ghosts haunt cellphone screens and chic apartments, surfacing "anxieties buried in the delirium of middle-class consumerism, globalization, and the new media sensorium."[26] The gentrification of horror continues into the contemporary era, with landmarks extending from the theatrical hit *Bhoot* (Ghost, Ram Gopal Varma, 2003) to *Bulbbul* (Songbird, Anvita Dutt, 2020), a glossy horror film produced and distributed globally by the streaming service Netflix.

In other parts of the internet, something else brews. A "wave of cinephiliac B-movie desire has erupted across social media platforms," writes Vibhushan Subba, in which the "universe of the low-budget Bombay film runs silent, runs deep."[27] Viewers are discovering what Bombay cinema once was (and could still be): "avenging amazons in leopard print leotards," "wild jungle fantasies with stuffed tigers," "violated men in cheap Halloween costumes," and "draculas with Styrofoam wings."[28] Where the films are lost, posters, song booklets, and other "scraps" of films like the sea monster movie *Gogola* (Balwant Dave, 1966) have become collector's items.[29] The fascination is shared by film scholars, who are publishing "revisionist historiographies" of Bombay cinema's first century.[30] Stunt films of the 1920s, 1930s magic films, 1940s adventure films, 1960s wrestling films, and 1970s devotional films—these genres, their makers, and their audiences are indications of diverse histories missed by a focus on the respectable genres of the mythological, the social, or the family melodrama.[31] The academic study of Indian popular cinema has been visibly remade by an inverted "axis of taste," in which "cinematic value" and "scholarly value" are reciprocally related: "the lower-brow the object" from Bombay cinema's past, the "more interesting it is as an object of study" for film scholars working across institutional and geographical locations.[32] Horror films too help expose the hierarchies of taste, which regulate the ranks of the respectable genres of Bombay film history.

Seeing Things focuses on films that have been eclipsed in the industrial, journalistic, and scholarly focus on Bollywood—a big-budget, star-driven cinema of song-and-dance spectacle in frictionless circulation around the world. Bombay cinema of the 1980s remains, in Tejaswini Ganti's words, "emblematic of Hindi cinema's uncool past."[33] During her interviews with filmmakers in the Bombay film industry of the 1990s and after, Ganti observed the persistence of a discourse that figured the 1980s as "a particularly dreadful period of filmmaking, in contrast with both earlier and later periods of Hindi cinema."[34] Neither like the politically incandescent hits that established Amitabh Bachchan as an "angry young man" in the 1970s nor like the flossy romantic blockbusters of the 1990s associated with Bollywood, the popular films of the 1980s were from the beginning deemed largely unworthy.[35]

In a booklet accompanying the state-sponsored Film Utsav of 1985, film critic Iqbal Masood lamented the state of affairs. Action films like director K. Bapaiah's *Mawaali* (Rascal, 1983) and *Maqsad* (Aim, 1984) were differentiated from other films only in degree: they were "high kitsch," compared to the "lower" kitsch of mythological and horror films, the "former usually on a level with the roadside stage performances during the Ganapati festival and the latter frequently more hideous than frightening."[36] Masood's anxiety about a new and "rampant lowbrow cinema" emerging in the wake of Bombay's studio system was generally displaced onto the "sub-grade producers who make horror films," and from them onto the "goo and monsters" of such films.[37]

The blooper that besieges the start of *Bandh Darwaza* would not have surprised most film critics. Journalistic, governmental, and industrial discourses from the 1980s link a rapid decline in film "quality" with multiple, interconnected crises in film production, censorship, and circulation. What emerges from these discourses is a view of Bombay cinema in the 1980s as an industrial, aesthetic, and even moral failure. Bombay horror was the failure within this failure, so that its moments of failure doubly metonymize the seemingly unprecedented crises of Bombay cinema during the 1980s. But the failures explored in this book are not just arbitrary imprints of a chaotic reality; they are the inscriptions—both evidence and effect—of the struggles to wrangle that reality into film. These struggles come into view via the failures of Bombay horror. By glitching the conventions of a genre, Bombay horror generated traces through which we can experience and interpret the material past at the scene of horror.[38]

A MATERIALIST AESTHETICS OF BOMBAY HORROR

Like nightmares, horror films bid viewers to unscramble the meaning hidden in their symbolic representations. As viewers, we understand the spaces, bodies, and stories on-screen to be displaced versions of our reality, somehow coded into the conventions of horror. That encoding, which installs the gap between history and fantasy, between cultural past and cinematic presence, elicits reading. It calls on us to fill the gap between the bizarre worlds of the genre and the everyday world we inhabit. Accordingly, scholars of horror have understood the fearsome visions of horror as our collective unconscious—as "monsters from the id"—returning in fiendish forms.[39]

"The true subject of the horror genre," Robin Wood proposed in an important 1979 essay, "is the struggle for recognition of all that our civilization represses."[40] Wood's foundational analytic for the horror film—"normality is threatened by the monster"—reveals the construction of a social order as normality, of difference as horrific, and of the violent destruction of the monster as peacekeeping.[41] The genre is therefore a "site of ideological contradiction": horror films may depict attacks on our reality, but it is often reality itself that is truly the problem.[42] A model of symptomatic reading in film studies, Wood's understanding of the horror film has endured because it is a psychoanalytic theory that is also responsive to cultural history. The repressed always returns, but because what is repressed can change with time and place, so can the thematic, narrative, and iconographic preoccupations of horror films. This has been a highly influential—and redemptive—reading strategy for horror film studies. It has helped filmgoers and critics get past the "blood-soaked façade" of some of the "most degraded works of mass culture."[43] In the process the most disdained of popular film genres has become the most written about over the last few decades.

What "unconscious material" returns in Bombay horror?[44] The films resurface ways of thinking and knowing rendered beyond the pale by scientific rationality in colonial and postcolonial India; Meraj Mubarki argues that the magic spells, chanting priests, and haunted feudal mansions within the films figure the persistence of what modernity says we have long left behind.[45] Bodies and desires stigmatized by caste and patriarchal supremacy, Mithuraaj Dhusiya offers, are reflected in stories of witchcraft and vampirism in Indian horror films.[46] The films also are, in Meheli Sen's words, a "symptom of the frayed and unraveling political fabric of the 1970s and 1980s."[47] Sen posits that the state-sanctioned "lawlessness, crime, and violence" pervading India in the 1970s and 1980s are addressed by the genre's "symbolic ruses."[48] In the wake of such substantial scholarship on the supernatural genres of Indian cinema and the cultural histories they signify, *Seeing Things* offers a slightly different perspective on Bombay horror.[49]

My argument is also premised on the idea that images signify, but that they do so *in their materiality*. For the repressed to return on-screen in horror films, that repressed must first be expressed: *in, as, and through the cinematic medium*. *Bandh Darwaza*'s visual and aural forms comprise the perceptual surface that we read as an allegory of monstrous otherness. But these forms ought not to be entirely vaporized by symbolic reading. "Criticism of the horror film," argues Jonathan Crane, will often "willfully deny the [genre's] gruesome spectacle."[50] "In this act of intentional blindness," Crane claims, "looking past what carries a brutal charge, horror imagery is treated as a particularly bloody variation of insubstantial and inconsequential *maya*."[51] Crane is, broadly speaking, correct, but there has been an important current in horror film scholarship that is attentive to what is on-screen. "What we see is what we see," Steven Shaviro writes, adding that "the figures that unroll before us cannot be regarded merely as arbitrary representations or conventional signs."[52] Challenging conceptualizations of cinema as imaginary signifier, ideological illusion, or empty simulacrum, Shaviro asks not what horror films hide but what they show: "nothing but images," "composed only of flickering lights, evanescent noises, and insubstantial figures."[53] This line of thinking shifts our understanding of the content of a horror film. *Bandh Darwaza* is horrific not only for what its images mean, but for what they are: an atmospheric assemblage in which darkness swallows the frame and sound is silenced. Meaning emerges from the coordinated assault of filmic elements, rather than being a prior set of values expressed in film style.

While it draws attention to how form creates horror, the notion of film style somewhat abstracts the dimensional texture of horror images into programmatic considerations of "line and color."[54] The vampire's cape, his creaking coffin: these are formal entities in a patterned arrangement—visual shapes and sonic intensities—but these details have an unfolding presence that takes up space and time onscreen. Such an approach sees the "materiality of cinema . . . wielding an expressive force" beyond what can be paraphrased about a film.[55] For Adrian Martin, these are the "millions of atomic details" by which a film makes its "moves" on us: how a film can "change its temperature, shift its focus, raise its stakes, modulate its mood, thicken its atmosphere, or scramble its hitherto established premises."[56] Because "we take in all these details," tracking film's expressive materiality requires switching between scales of close reading—from the synoptic to the granular—and adjusting "definitions of what constitutes the minimum identifiable unit for analysis."[57]

"Close reading," Eugenie Brinkema writes, "begins with a serious, rigorous, careful interpretation of textual specificity."[58] In film, she clarifies, "that means attending to framing, montage, *mise en scène*, color and light, rhythm, texture, sound," while "bracket[ing] entirely things like production history and context" and "the long and many forms of reception theory."[59] What I found, however, was something else. Staring at *Bandh Darwaza*'s display of verdant valleys, I was confronted with an instance of what seemed like a daytime shoot that was insufficiently incorporated into the fiction. I could not quite list this as an instance of "montage" or "mise-en-scène" or "point-of-view shot": seams had opened up in how I had learned to segment film style. The closeup of the vampire's face gazing off-screen did not fit with what I saw next, a panning camera widely composing a sun-bathed mountain range. A difficulty arose in the reading. *Bandh Darwaza*'s sunlit slopes may appear to be neither symbol nor style, but they are there all the same. When confronted with what seemingly exceeds signification and stylization, representational and formal readings should expand out and zoom in, switching in and out of disciplinary scales of reading. The closer I got to the textured density of the film, the more I felt the text's many contexts unbracketing themselves—the stronger I perceived histories of production and reception pressing on the film.

Seeing Things proposes that we need a stronger, sharper vocabulary to understand the role of this materiality in our experience of film: how the materiality of the medium shapes our aesthetic apprehension of cinematic storytelling. Across the humanities, researchers dissatisfied with the narrow range of what could be studied as communication—as discourse, signification, representation—continue to navigate the "material turn."[60] They argue that the history of human expression cannot be understood without heeding the means of expression: the stuff through, in, and as which ideas, thoughts, and feelings are expressed. Consequently, the material cultures of the past are not only deposits of but determinants of symbolic cultures. Advancing insights from art history, anthropology, and archaeology, film and media scholars have excavated the material cultures of film production and circulation to write new film histories.[61] While the insights of this material turn are vast and varied, one of its consequences is a better appreciation of what Caetlin Benson-Allott calls the "significance of apparatus in the creation of affect."[62]

This is a materialist approach that advances from the "old" materialisms, which focused on how the means of production determined aesthetic forms. What I have in mind here is closer to strains in film and media theory which emphasize how symbolic differences originate in the physical differences between inscriptive media. The meaning of a representation, after all, is inseparable from its means; this inseparability paves the way for what Hannah Frank has called a "materialist aesthetics."[63] *Seeing Things* explores how the properties of celluloid, uses of paper, affordances of latex, and limits of plastic shaped Bombay horror. Horror films seek to evoke otherworldly places and beings, but to do so they must draw on the resources available in this world. In order to exploit our common fears, horror filmmakers have developed formal conventions by mastering the medium's affordances, what it can and cannot do. A materialist aesthetics can be better attuned to how the medium's limits productively determine the genre's affective power. The failures of Bombay horror provide just such an opening.

FAILURES OF HORROR

The materiality of Bombay horror is more present to us now than ever before—in the "very moment that 'things,' at least the way we thought we once knew them, appear to be on their way out."[64] Haunting the contemporary dream of immateriality, the seemingly obsolete physicalities of film stock, Foley sound effects, monster makeup, or celluloid film projection become more visible to us with each passing day. Consequently, cinematic storytelling of the twentieth century too comes into view as "a set of conventions" derived from the "material conditions of a given technical support."[65] These conventions are the result of filmmakers grappling with the "enabling impediment" of film's photographic limits, its framing enclosure, its flickering movements.[66] Mary Ann Doane argues that this process of reckoning with the resistance of the medium has been productive, for in "its very resistance, matter generates the forms and modes of aesthetic apprehension."[67] Rather than boundlessness, Doane suggests, it is the bounded medium of celluloid that brought artists and audiences together to complete the illusion. How a camera can (and cannot) move; how sound and image can (and cannot) be combined; how filmstrips can (and cannot be) joined: these have driven the aesthetic form of the genre, shaping the way we know the world in the horror film. For example, it is an affordance of the medium that exposure to light will cause an image to form on film. Multiple images can thus be formed on the same film by repeatedly exposing it to light, yet each exposure will also degrade pictorial clarity. We see this (in)capacity exploited in *Bandh Darwaza*, which overlays the vampire's face and a flying bat to create stutteringly eerie views of magic metamorphosis. The sensational promise of the genre is entirely reliant on the skill with which the form of film is mastered (a theme I take up in greater detail in the first chapter).

The history of horror, writes Adam Charles Hart, is a "history of artists figuring out how to use the formal possibilities of their medium."[68] This history is long, dating back to the origins of cinema. From the start, cinema's uncanny capacity to capture the invisible world—to break habituated perception via time-lapse or close-up—was allegorized in stories of strange bodies, time travel, and waking dreams, as well as the "special effects" that summoned them.[69] In her account of the films of the 1890s and early twentieth century, Stacey Abbott notes a "preoccupation with the fantastic as a means of showcasing the spectral nature of film."[70] From the use of negative images to jump cuts, Abbott chronicles the centrality of film's photochemical and physical properties in early evocations of a favorite figure: the vampire.

Writing about 1922's *Nosferatu*, Abbott argues that the film's use of a "slow dissolve to suggest the vampire's disintegration in the rays of the sun" heralded a "new convention in the first major vampire film," one "strongly linked to the fact that light is the essence of cinema."[71] As she goes on to explain: "It is light that burns an image onto film and then projects that image onto a screen. Orlok, a creature of the night, fades away in the sunlight in the same manner that a photograph or the image on a strip of celluloid fades into nothingness when overexposed."[72] For Abbott, this "suggests that the vampire is made up of similar properties as film itself."[73] A materialist aesthetics is therefore attuned to the "specific ways in which sound and imaging technologies physically manifest themselves to the participating viewer in the event of the encounter."[74] The "uncanny body" of 1931's *Dracula*, Robert Spadoni has argued, was shaped by the limited ability to synchronize the sight of speaking screen characters with the sound of their voices, helping generate horror in early sound film.[75] Especially in moments of historical transition—such as the arrival of sound or color film stock, digital filmmaking, or streaming technologies—the materiality of the apparatus is perceptible in the narrative and visual conventions of films.[76]

Take, for example, our fear of the dark. This fear may be culturally learned, biologically hardwired, or "biocultural"; whatever the case, horror films have consistently explored the abyssal darkness of the night, of dim recesses, and obscure depths.[77] In Bombay's horror films, darkness and its denizens multiply. In *Jaani Dushman*, a monster pounces on wedding processions at dusk. In *Purana Mandir*, a curse strikes childbearing women as lightning splits open the night sky. In *Khooni Murda*, a serial killer strikes during a love song. In *Hatyarin* (Murderess, Vinod Talwar, 1991), a man lifts the veil on his bride to discover an evil crone awaiting him on his *suhaag raat* (wedding night). These are the moments in which the horror of Bombay horror is most palpable; the films come alive in the transgression of Bombay cinema's long-reigning fantasies of musical romance and familial bliss.

In order to film the dark, however, makers of horror have had to confront a fundamental limit of the medium. Light triggers the photochemical reaction in which whatever is before the camera is captured on celluloid film. Because many film stocks respond poorly to the absence of light, filmmakers have learned to create darkness onscreen by shooting in daylight and then darkly tinting the footage in development. This innovation, known as day-for-night shooting, indicates how one seemingly abstract convention of horror—the night—is the product of a material practice. But horror films are comprised of many such conventions. Genre films, as Edward Buscombe states, are "composed of an outer form consisting of a certain number of visual conventions": "guns, cars, clothes" constitute gangster films, while "castles, coffins, and teeth" constitute horror films.[78] For filmmakers working outside genre, it may very well be the "subject matter that determines the outer form, not the other way round.... [T]he thing the director wants to say will decide the form he or she uses."[79] As Buscombe draws our attention to the iconography of genre films, we note that the outer form of genre is a "thing" as well: castles, coffins, and teeth—the constitutive shorthand of a film like *Bandh Darwaza*—have to be located, fabricated, and photographed. Conventions must be realized for each shot, scene, or film; the form of horror must be *performed* for the camera. The repetitive reproduction of a convention generates production expertise and audience familiarity, but each performance of the convention is also a risk. The performative instant creates an opening, as filmmaking enters a zone of possible failure in front of the lens. Indeed, it is by analyzing the resultant "fractures of signification"—in this case, what we see on film rather than what the film may want to show us—that a kind of truth about cinema comes into view.[80]

Watching Bombay horror today, I feel the globally familiar conventions of horror films sputter in the flux of actualization, as hairy beasts, cursed objects, and sticky gore come to be riddled with small disappointments. In *Khooni Mahal*, a man transforms into a vampire before my eyes: I see him grow fangs. Yet the angle and duration of the close-up permit me to perceive the actor pushing fake fangs out of his mouth. Similar fiascos have impressed themselves on other critics, viewers, and scholars. Sangita Gopal writes that the "entire Ramsay oeuvre (and that of its imitators) is unmistakably B-movie," featuring "garish and unconvincing sets" and "monsters that veered to the side of kitsch."[81] Similarly, Rachel Dwyer describes the films of the Ramsay Brothers as "often (bad) copies of western films" that had "very basic special effects."[82] Meheli Sen notes that they contain "horror set pieces involving burly monsters in old mansions," "tacky prosthetic makeup," "patently fake blood and gore," and "rudimentary special effects."[83] These are, as she puts it, the results of "abysmal production values," further exposed by "flimsy, often utterly inchoate plots" and "inept performances."[84] These descriptions get at an ambient accidental quality that also characterizes my experience of Bombay horror. Because the films solicit my attention most when they are at their most conventionally horrific, I find myself rapt by such moments—and their malfunctioning minutiae.

Since failures are often felt in horror, science fiction, and action films, genres with long histories of low-budget production in many parts of the world, the "excess of visibility" may be connected to an impression of lack.[85] The genres' fantastical stories trade in and tolerate what would be considered failures of editing, lighting, performance, or storytelling according to standards set by realism. Still, the feeling that an element of the film—such as the daylight of *Bandh Darwaza*—is attracting *too much* attention prompts judgment that *not enough* expertise, energy, or economic resources were invested in integrating it into the film's "smooth perceptual cues."[86] Roughness at crucial moments of cinematic spectacle makes transparent not only the materiality on which the spectacle depends but also the aggressively enthusiastic drive to summon it on a budget.[87]

Some of the most iconic horror films of all time were low-budget productions. To give two examples: *Night of the Living Dead* (George Romero, 1968) and *The Texas Chainsaw Massacre* (Tobe Hooper, 1974) were made on a shoestring by American independent producers after the collapse of the studio system in Hollywood. Indeed, the collapse of the studio system ushered in a new age of horror; films of the 1960s, 1970s, and 1980s evidence an "overwhelming sense of weirdness," without "striv[ing] above all for expediency"—for the "perfect match of signifying device and (usually narrative) signified."[88] Instead, they are lauded for their "pragmatic aesthetics," "in which budgetary and technical compromises are made to work aesthetically," that is, to "serve" the story.[89] But sometimes things may not quite "work": the "cinematic tools" used may, to use Thomas Sipos's term, "sabotage" the story.[90] Failures are judged to have happened when we perceive that the "intentionality of authorship and narrative requirement" has come "into conflict with the strategies of execution and the primarily budgetary limitations placed upon them."[91] Typically, when something on-screen fails—when it is more or less *there* than we think it should be—viewers assume it was not given enough time, craft, or money to be smoothly incorporated into the film's fiction and move on. What if viewers did not move on?

When scholars scrutinize images for breakdown, seams, and mismatches, such as when Anand Pandian chronicles the "failure of actors and equipment to act and react as they should" in his ethnography of

Tamil film production, they also call on us to be mindful of the fertility of failure in jamming the punitive and painful regulation of conventions.[92] Human beings are in their mere materiality often judged to be failing a normative ideal—some social or cultural convention—that is correctly embodied by someone else, somewhere else.[93] Failure, then, reveals the political valence of aesthetic judgment, or how our differently racialized, gendered, classed, or sexualized bodies may be judged to be failing in their very physical existence. Likewise, the "ruptured body" of films made for tertiary circuits and audiences—films derisively termed grindhouse, exploitation, or "B movies"—are frequently seen to be "lacking the kind of integrity commonly attributed to popular narrative cinema."[94] Ruptures can bring viewers back to reality, so that "the spectator is brought abruptly back to discontinuity—that is, to the body, to the technical apparatus which he had forgotten."[95] There is joy for some scholars in lack, signaling an attack on the hegemony of "well made" films and reminding us that film is a "performative production."[96] A mutual measure of "failed seriousness" or camp is activated, an attitude that revels in "love of the unnatural: of artifice and exaggeration" by drawing attention to the constructedness of a convention or observing it in breakdown.[97]

For example, one might be able to see that the monster in *Curse of the Swamp Creature* (Larry Buchanan, 1968), though "intended to be a startling and menacing cinematic revelation," is "simply an overweight actor standing in weeds with ping-pong balls attached to his eyes on a hot day in Dallas in 1966."[98] Akin to the distancing effects of avant-garde or experimental film, screen failures, Becky Bartlett suggests, "obliterate" disbelief and thereby "dismantle the illusory potential of cinema."[99] So-called bad films are valuable to cult audiences because they can "reveal modes of production that are otherwise concealed in 'good' films."[100] In "moments of impoverished excess," concludes Jeffrey Sconce, the "diegesis becomes the thin and final veil that is the indexical mark" of "the film's construction."[101]

This book grapples with that thin, final veil and the divergent desires it sparks. When failures happen at the scene of horror, they don't always break the spell. Film may be a ghostly medium, but its images of the past are also "material ghosts."[102] These sights and sounds take up space and time—they matter—on-screen, but they also move through our space and time: they matter to us as viewers. Sometimes the failures of Bombay horror deepen the disturbance, putting the materiality of filmmaking into play as constitutive of cinematic conventions and their effects. In such cases, *Seeing Things* sticks close to the veil, even when it is at its most distractingly diaphanous or disruptively depleted: by incorporating the impoverished excess on-screen into my experience of the story world (what Sconce calls the "diegesis").

When the veil falls, I can read visible failure as an automatic imprint (what Sconce terms an "indexical mark") of the film's historical creation, tinging the expressive materiality of horror's otherworldly fantasy with an evidentiary materiality of the recent past. *Indexicality*, in film studies, usually refers to the automatic inscriptions of physical reality generated by the photochemical reaction of exposed film to light, such that what is on film is said to point back to its referent, the "profilmic" reality that was once in front of the camera. When a contingent performance in front of the lens is registered by the machinic performance of the camera, the result is a photographic image. The photograph, as Roland Barthes wrote, "mechanically repeats what could never be repeated existentially," forever stamped with an adhesive referentiality that brings the past into the present.[103] Because of this indexical capacity, film has been likened to a "ghostly medium" that shows us what was once before the camera and is no more; a medium that can reveal physical reality to us better than our senses can.[104] The indexical marks of Bombay horror range from ostensibly accidental elements of the filmed image—continuity errors, bad acting, clumsy effects—to what can more properly be called sonic or "avisual" elements of the film—jarring splices, changeover cues, and electronic noise.[105] For these traces to matter as indices of the past, I developed a materialist historiography of Bombay horror.

A MATERIALIST HISTORIOGRAPHY OF BOMBAY HORROR

Things have lives in Bombay horror. Doors open and close by themselves. Portraits look back at their owners. Statues shift, instantiating a pervasive trope of horror films more generally: objects in horror are seemingly possessed of an agency independent of the human beings who purchased, found, stole, or inherited them (and who must, as so often happens at the end of horror films, destroy them).¹⁰⁶ Before such things are destroyed, however, they are made: by someone exhaling a dying breath, desperate incantation, or vengeful curse. In *Bandh Darwaza*, the vampire can only be vanquished when a totemic *putla* (miniature) is destroyed: a wooden sculpture of a bat that must be set on fire. The vampire's *naapak shakti* (profane power) inheres in this object, but that power was placed there by his own magic touch. This is the lesson taught by horror film after horror film. Things *do*, because something was *done to* them. They are things touched by human history, even when they appear to be beyond human control. They have lives because they were shaped by living hands. The failures of Bombay horror too are visionary intimations of filmmaking history, traces of how the films were produced, regulated, and circulated.

The traces may appear to be too minor or idiosyncratic to be of general significance: a prismatic play of color over the story world or sounds of vehicular traffic during an intimate conversation. But paying attention to insignificant details is a core practice for cinephiles, who watch films repeatedly while engaging their "panoramic perception" of "peripheral details."¹⁰⁷ Such details are typically stylistic elements that exceed—in duration, design, display, or other aspects of "treatment"—the demands of a film's narrative. Unassimilated into the "system of representation," a camera movement or frame composition might appear possessed of a "metafictional edge that operates as an indirect/oblique commentary on representation."¹⁰⁸ That commentary is attributed to the film's director, the auteur who leaves inside the repetitive, industrialized work of genre film production their personal signature in stylistic flourishes like so many secrets. The details in Bombay horror that occupy me did not seem to have been *put* into the scene intentionally by anyone, popping up instead as inconsequential trifles. Nonetheless, they were like the "moments of intense yet inscrutable audiovisual pleasure" devoured by cinephiles and served as a "spark" for what Rashna Wadia Richards labels a "materialist film historiography."¹⁰⁹ A materialist film historiography treats what is on-screen as the momentary instantiation of a material world, a networked materiality under arrest: emulsion leaking from a film print or a film being dubbed inside a moving van.¹¹⁰ For the traces of Bombay horror to matter, I had to shift from seeing them as one-off mistakes to seeing them as the routinized output of systems of filmmaking.

Contemporary techno-culture and capitalist innovation champion planned obsolescence: "failing fast, failing often." Haunting this euphoria of nonstop progress toward an imminent future of cybernetic transcendence is the obstinate wreckage of development: whether as toxic landfill or circulating scrap, the past remains present, the very materiality of human history presenting as a failure to become immaterial. In order to make "visible what is actually present," scholars in philosophy, literature, sociology, anthropology, architecture, and cultural studies have led a "spectral turn" to center ghostly traces, suppressed memories, and occult logics that challenge the drive to modern transparency, linear time, developmental progress, economic rationality, and written history.[111] Ghosts "indicate that beneath the surface of received history, there lurks another narrative, an untold story."[112] To tell that story, write Maria del Pilar Blanco and Esther Peeren, "requires a perspective combining a materialist with an affective, sensuous dimension."[113] An emergent counteraesthetics of glitch, noise, and trash contests the prevailing rhetoric of endless perfectibility and seamless capture, preserving errors as "meaningful symbols of a broader human struggle."[114] Bombay horror offers an accidental archive of such struggle, of how the world's largest film culture has endured state control, production scarcity, and circulatory challenges. The spectral materialities of Bombay horror were generated when small acts of urban *jugaad* (improvisation), labor mobilization, subaltern circulation, and transgressive imagination collided with the forces of labor informalization, bureaucratic control, violent policing, and moral panic. These contexts have implicitly informed much scholarship on the genre, but they remain underrepresented, underresearched and undertheorized. Widening my scope beyond what I have previously termed the Ramsay Brothers' "cottage industry of terror," *Seeing Things* investigates the industrial production, institutional regulation, and public circulation of Bombay horror across the 1980s.[115]

This book began as a project to understand how the horror films of 1980s Bombay were made and seen. Accordingly, archival research and ethnographic fieldwork—not close analysis—were the privileged methodological instruments for tapping the historical circuits of production and circulation. I found that documentary records of the period were plentiful, scattered across Delhi, Mumbai, and Pune: trade magazines like *Film Information*, *Trade Guide*, *Variety*, and *Screen*; reportage in Hindi- and

English-language newspapers and magazines including *Times of India, Hindustan Times, Manushi, Madhuri, Stardust, Cine Blitz, Filmfare,* and *India Today*; government files and film publicity preserved at the National Film Archive; and censorship records and court orders published in the *Gazette of India*. Yet these archives presented the challenge of how to retrieve stories of thrilling images (that were deleted), creative work (that was devalued), and popular films (that were ignored). I gathered interviews for more than a decade, amassing dozens of oral narratives by speaking to directors including Tulsi Ramsay, Mohan Bhakri, and Vinod Talwar, as well as the actors, makeup artists, optical effects artists, stunt directors, distributors, and exhibitors they worked with. During many of these interviews, questions about specific scenes or films routinely generated blank stares and long silences from actors and actresses, film directors and producers, costume launderers, and stunt performers, many of whom I had sought out precisely because they had worked on these films. Bombay's horror films, I realized, were partly condemned to the same oblivion that shrouds much of the 1980s Bombay film industry.

Bombay horror is an example of the "upside down," a cinema in which performers, audiences, and genres sidelined by blockbuster cinema ruled.[116] An account of this "upside down" cinema also pushes something else to the top: the physical realities of filmmaking. While advising the need to "crack open the category of 'popular' cinema to reveal the diversity within," Lotte Hoek warns that "peculiarly lopsided case selections in cinema and film culture push from view the prevalence of flop films featuring B actors, failing equipment in studios and theaters, plagiarizing scriptwriters, or frayed third-run movies spliced beyond recognition in dilapidated tin-roofed rural cinemas."[117] Hoek's sturdy itemization of images, circuits, and practices implies that different films invite (or incite) differently material histories, and that canon formation and film historiography regulate the degree to which materiality matters. Within her itemization, we can also detect a dialectic that is central to this book: the dialectic of material crisis and material creativity.

Crisis has been a durable drumbeat in the "melodrama of Bollywood as a culture industry."[118] As Nitin Govil reminds us, crisis talk permeates discourses of film production, censorship, and circulation, whether in the 1960s or the 2000s.[119] What is missed in this "historiography of crisis" is *how* the film industry "reemerges in the face of predation and dire odds," how the "permanence of crisis" is the "engine" of "innovation."[120] *Seeing Things* argues that the failures of Bombay horror don't simply index the widespread and undifferentiated chaos of filmmaking; rather, they register how specific crises were navigated, managed, and contained by the practices of filmmaking.

Practice, as Debashree Mukherjee writes, is a "repetitive activity oriented to a future."[121] The movies remembered those practices, extending my reach into the past. Where institutional, industrial, and individual memories have faded or fallen short, films remembered in their very failure to represent. The close analysis of films was transformed by the sensitivity to *stuff*, filling the breach where my archival and ethnographic endeavors failed. I began treating the finished film as a series of production stills, working as I was with a paucity of behind-the-scenes documentation or production stills typically generated for promotion or posterity.[122] When I could not get my hands on a court file or be admitted inside a nineteenth-century palace that served as a filming location, I returned to the films. The speculative reorientation of the textual trace has been an important methodological innovation within film studies, a response to the geopolitics of preservation wherein the past must be accessed differently for histories of difference.[123] Bringing materialist analysis and sensuous appreciation together in close reading, *Seeing Things* brings film back into the fold with the archives of a new cinema history, casting the mise-en-scène of Bombay horror as a field in which to do research and a formal force to contend with.

While Bombay horror's representations are an "important index of an especially turbulent period in India's history," the films' failures are symptoms of the turbulent history of filmmaking during the same period.[124] The failures of Bombay horror allow us to glimpse the dynamics that shape the materialities of filmmaking, the decisions that were made in order to create irrational worlds within a fundamentally rational, if slightly unpredictable, medium. The materialities of filmmaking convert cultural past into cinematic presence, but these materialities are themselves social, political, and historical things that are encoded into light and sound. After observing something on-screen—for instance, the foam mattress supporting an ancient sarcophagus—I moved outward to find out more, following the film's networks of human labor, energy, finance, and resources along which things are displaced till they reach their resting place before the camera and become visual images. Following Bombay horror's spectral materialities like crumbs back into a lost world, the book reconstructs the force field of technology, finance, creativity, and moral panic that enmeshed the films. How an actor wore a mask, when a prop was moved, when a censor objected most to a film—these are things that happened and what happened to things, on film sets, in laboratories, courtrooms, government offices, movie theaters, and video parlors.

Seeing Things conceives of filmmaking corporeally, as a series of tactile encounters in which humans, machines, and environments were incipiently instantiated as embodied presences (and then disembodied as they receded from those encounters). As I use the term here, *corporeality* names the relational experience of *becoming body*. Recently, Usha Iyer has explored the potential of a "corporeal history" of film bodies, one that makes visible bodies that are embedded in the production process but erased from visual legibility by a film's fictional and press discourses.[125] Corporeal history is a methodology that reveals the onscreen body as a "composite" assemblage made up of other bodies, such as the on-screen dancing body, as made up of backup dancers, doubles, and dance teachers. I too expand corporeal history beyond the visible to include bodies that were never in front of the camera or even, properly speaking, human. In its pursuit of bodies that touched props, filmstrips, masks, and projection reels, *Seeing Things* discovered the embodied practices of creative excitement, anxious unease, and desirous cinephilia that made, managed, and moved films inscribed in the scene of horror: how performers, machines, and their environments may have mutually interacted and materialized in the process of generating moving images.

What I found was that before the "unconscious material" of classed, gendered, and sexual anxieties could "return" on-screen, these anxieties marked the conscious materialization of images in the work of film making. Bombay horror was, after all, an industrial art form, the behind-the-scenes reality of which was shaped by the same historical forces that acquired allegorical form in on-screen fictions. For example, the opening of *Bandh Darwaza* indicates how the tools of continuity editing, including shot/reverse shot and eyeline matching, operated to link elements of studio photography (the vampire's lair) and location filming (the hills). The daylight helps bring into view what that location was—the Western Ghats outside Bombay—but it also raises new questions about why the cinematic geography of Bombay horror took the particular shape it did. I answer these questions later in the book, arguing that the cost and volatility of filming in Bombay's studios propelled innovations in the iconography of horror: that we can "see" in the films' forbidden, faraway places a solution to the lightning strikes called by below-the-line workers in the city's studios. The atmosphere of horror thus compresses the social, political, and historical materiality of film making, but this materiality, typically encoded into the oneiric landscapes of horror, only swims into view in moments of failure. If there had been no daylight between me and the film, I may never have thought to even ask these questions, let alone look for answers.

CRISIS AND CREATIVITY IN THE 1980S BOMBAY FILM INDUSTRY

Seeing Things tracks the cycle of Bombay horror from its origins to its end, from the late 1970s to the early 1990s. It also tracks the lifecycle of films from production to circulation, with a caveat: the book explores the censorship of horror films (in the late 1970s) before examining the making of horror films (in the mid-1980s). This inversion challenges the priority of industrial practices over state control, instead showing how governmental censorship received, revised, and remade—effectively, produced—the first horror films and so influenced the shape of the cycle to come.

Originating with the colonial administrations of the British Raj, film censorship remains the most prominent instance of cultural regulation by the Indian state. Whatever reasons the censors have had for censoring a film—such as obscenity, subversion, and criminal incitement—scholars of Indian film censorship have revealed the reasons beneath those reasons: paternalism, elitism, the anxieties of an old colonial order, the aspirations of a new nation-state, pressures from the mob, and pressures from the market.[126] This disciplinary drive increasingly impinges on the freedom of expression enshrined in the nation's constitution, as autocratic intercession of democratic expression in India is extended by pressure groups whipping up moral panics over cinema. "Anxiety about the filmic image" has manifested in the Indian state's "continuous effort to discipline and regulate films, filmmaking, and filmmakers."[127] *Seeing Things* tracks the materiality of the effort to regulate the origins of Bombay horror in the late 1970s, enhancing the picture of ideological and affective control with a focus on filmstrip editing and bureaucratic paperwork. Close attention to the physical practices of censorship—*how* censors censor—textures our understanding of what was censored and why.

In the summer of 1975, Prime Minister Indira Gandhi had a state of "internal emergency" declared to quell opposition from trade, student, and government unions (and to remain in power after a court conviction over electoral misconduct.)[128] For the next twenty-one months, blackouts descended on printing presses, journalists were detained en masse, public assembly was curtailed, civil disobedience movements were banned, and dissenting news stories were killed. When film producers complained of increased oversight of the film capital by the Ministry of Information and Broadcasting in the nation's political capital, the minister of information and broadcasting was said to be "furious" and "ordered the Censor Board not to pass films, to make more and more cuts, and generally to harass the producers."[129] When the Emergency ended in 1977, the state invested in increasing bureaucratization as the path to procedural transparency, while filmmakers and viewers became keenly aware of censorship's power to make images (and films) disappear. If, as Meheli Sen has argued, "the Ramsay film emblematically captures the zeitgeist of Emergency and post-Emergency India," reconstructing the material terrain of censorship allows us to see how the politics of this transitional period are registered in paper files and celluloid damage.[130]

Chapter 1 chronicles the censorship of "India's First Horror Film," *Darwaza*, by reconstructing the paper trail of the film's regulation by the Bombay censors. What the censors describe as "scenes of horror," I argue, reveals their corporeal response to the physical affordances of film—its manipulability via looping, dissolves, and stop-motion effects—by which *Darwaza* surfaced a spectral time on-screen. They may be causes of despair to filmmakers, but state documents can give film scholars a peek into the bureaucratic world of film censorship as its own "scene of horror." The chapter's engagement with the phantom touch that haunts the medium of film sets the stage for the spectral materialities explored in the subsequent chapters.

Chapter 2 moves from "behind the scenes" and into the scene by examining scratches, leaks, and other visual damage in *Jaani Dushman*. Before the film was released, "lingering details" of horror were purged under an order from the Bombay High Court. The chapter probes the effect of this intervention on the film's style and story world, giving us a tactile sense that censorship is what censorship does. While a werewolf hunts young brides in the valley, celluloid splatters in sequences of abduction, murder, and dismemberment as masking tape and cutting blade tear through the film's haunted frames and color film stock. The state's regulatory effort infects the body of Bombay horror, thickening the genre's motifs of strange belief, graphic violence, and blocked vision.

The origins of Bombay horror offer a privileged point of entry into the material cultures of film censorship. "To censors the world over," Mark Kermode has remarked, horror films "present an insurmountable problem: How to make acceptable a brand of filmmaking which strives to be thoroughly unacceptable?"[131] This effort to make Bombay horror acceptable unfolded slowly, generating a wealth of objects including workprints, cuts, paperwork, and informal meetings over weeks, then months, and finally years. At the same time, filmmakers navigated the structures and strictures of censorship through a range of informal tactics, including exploiting the inefficiencies of government bureaucracy and devising cinematic strategies to ward off scrutiny.[132] Files, censor scripts, application letters, official memoranda, cut pieces of footage, and censor certificates are the props by which I reconstruct a dramaturgy of censorship. Far from being proof of total ideological control or affective containment, these things disclose a censorship machine that worked and broke, failed and overheated when exposed to cinematic horror: paperwork logs feelings that are felt, or a cut was too clumsily visible.[133] In the process, disclaimers are scribbled and celluloid is disfigured—censorship transformed the aesthetic experience of Bombay's first horror films and eventually the stylistic preferences and production practices of those making horror films.

By the mid-1980s the strict surveillance of screen violence by the Indian government forced filmmakers to redirect the widespread preference for showing over telling that was making the horror genre more graphic in other parts of the world.[134] Instead, filmmakers expended effort to generate horror by other means: Bombay horror's affective lures would be gothic spaces, haunted objects, and creaturely transformations—and these had to be produced quickly. Following the box office success of the Ramsay Brothers' *Purana Mandir*, a dozen horror films were in development, postproduction, or release at the same time. *Seeing Things* explores the atmospheric and mechanical craft of horror at the peak of the genre's popularity: how surreal atmospheres and grotesque monsters produce the horror of Bombay horror, and how these spaces and bodies themselves were produced behind the scenes.

In her discussion of popular genre pictures of the Hindi film industry, Valentina Vitali has documented the "economic pressures that generated the films as commodities and which, in so doing, left the marks of their interests in the body of the texts."[135] Vitali capaciously reads the gestures, conventions, and even accidents of stunt figures on-screen—their varied "efforts"— in a mimetic relationship to the Hindi film industry's efforts to industrialize and stabilize its production economy and circulation networks. In more recent and related work, Vitali has argued that the horror film emerged when it did in Bombay because speculative finance, or what she terms "radical capital," until then "contained by the Indian government's economic policies," was unleashed in the late 1970s.[136] These large reserves of undeclared cash had to circulate quickly, leading to the overproduction of films. "India once again tops in film production," the trade journal *Screen* noted in 1982, including 150 Hindi films from Bombay in its annual count of 1,000 films made across the country that sold an estimated four hundred million tickets.[137]

Following the government's centralization of credit, a new type of financier emerged in the film business, looking to launder "black" money into "white." This parallel economy, which grew as India's official economy shrank, needed low-budget films that could move quickly through production and exhibition pipelines. The horror films of the Ramsay Brothers, Vitali argues, transcribe these considerations as narrative and mise-en-scène: in the "ruthless financial speculation" they often depict as setting off stories of dispossession, violation, and haunting, as well as in the "imploded frontality" and unstable views of the action.[138] Vitali sees correspondences between economic base and ephemeral images, with the base determining features of the images, as "no more and no less than an indexical registration of the collapse of the apparatus that had, until then, sustained the ideological legitimacy of the Indian state."[139]

The economic and political history Vitali outlines forms the backdrop to *Seeing Things*, which fleshes out a world of filmmaking during the 1980s by spotlighting production design and special effects in Bombay horror. Scholars of Hindi cinema, including Clare Wilkinson, have tracked the collaborative practices between a film's director and its cinematographer, choreographer, costumer, and production designer that have produced the visual worlds of big-budget romances, studio-era social films, and period dramas.[140] To this complex terrain of production cultures, *Seeing Things* adds the practices of set designers, below-the-line crew, and makeup artists of Bombay horror.[141] Zooming into the "historical materialist" forces invariably determining the film style, close attention to the aesthetic and design practice of the Ramsay Brothers as a film studio reveals how they tamed the financial and material crises of the "post-studio" era into a practice of house style.[142]

Film historians have long sought to situate films in relation to the circumstances of their social, economic, and technological production. Moving past delineating modes of production in monolithic terms, new film histories illuminate the "pulsating traffic—of actors, performers, authors, technicians, technologies, genres, styles" through which the moving image is concretized.[143] The precise nature of chemical accidents and poor performances on film also reveals the classed and gendered dimensions of film production as a "hustle" in the churn of the fast, ingenious, and dangerous—and an "ecology" consisting not only of skilled personnel but also of the technological processes and profilmic accidents they wrestled with.[144] In such accidents, the assemblages, technologies, and practices of filmmaking also become visible, as accidents, improvisation, and chances taken—in short, contingencies—in the creative process of filmmaking are virtually embossed in the image.

Chapter 3 tracks how the Ramsay Brothers transformed existing buildings and locations into "forbidden places" for *Purana Mandir*. Situating the iconography of the faraway, haunted haveli as an economic solution to the rising costs of shooting inside studios—and away from a politically activated below-the-line workforce—I show how the atmosphere of horror derives from reused locations, depleted extras, and rogue props. Chapter 4 unveils the art of prosthetic special effects. Bringing creative personnel into contact with exciting and expressive materials, prosthetics were responsible for the arresting images at the heart of every Bombay horror film. A focus on this craft shows how the grotesque bodies of witches, vampires, and other monsters—visual ideologies of gendered and sexualized excess—were engineered. Yet prosthetic effects also exposed human bodies to the unstable properties of rubber and latex—and special effects sometimes exceeded craft in on-set accidents. A mask was botched during *Veerana* and filmed as it had unexpectedly latched itself onto the sweaty skin of its young star, transforming her into a monstrous materiality that lurches toward her victims. Narrated to me by a hairdresser who worked on the film, an anecdote of the accident discloses the gendered ideologies of disgust operative in makeup work and a material world beyond the masculine control of its makeup artists.

My goal is to reacquaint readers with the expressivity and materiality of film form—with the art of bodies, spaces, and objects that have for decades weathered elite disdain for the booming low-budget film culture of the 1980s. The fantastical visual worlds of Bombay horror were, according to a critic in India's leading film magazine, *Filmfare*, "nowhere near the awesome technical masterpieces that [American filmmaker Steven] Spielberg's creations are."[145] ("We don't aspire to be Steven Spielberg," Tulsi Ramsay once said. "We are quite happy the way we are.")[146] Against narratives of industrial failure, the visual worlds of Bombay horror reopen a different history of work, one remarkable for being so accomplished in conditions marked by exploitation, scarcity, and precarity.[147] Those visual worlds quickly became iconic of the genre, widely displayed on hoardings and posters, captivating onlookers and drawing them into theaters.

One of the oft-repeated truths about Bombay's horror films is that they catered to male, working-class, or rural audiences residing in small towns and villages, who watched the films in rundown theaters of the "B" or "C" circuit. Rather than reinforcing affective affinity between Bombay horror and its classed and gendered audiences, chapter 5 thinks tangibly about film circulation, or the paths that films take (and are given) in order to realize value. "The paucity of permanent movie theaters," writes Sudhir Mahadevan, "has been a persistent backdrop to the history of movie exhibition [in India]."[148] The nearly six thousand built theaters in operation at the start of the 1980s (against a population of over six hundred million) were heavily monopolized, and Bombay horror's producers struggled within this scarcity-driven and stratified filmmaking economy. "Film Industry Faces Problem of Boom" declared one industry headline—a problem because, given the immense scarcity of theaters in India, there were not enough screens for films to recoup their cost.[149] Enter video. Often considered the cause of a "crisis" for the film industry—for the "fading glitter" of Hindi cinema "brought on by new technologies"—commercial video was, at least for a while, a source of financial sustenance and aesthetic possibility for filmmakers including Mohan Bhakri and Vinod Talwar.[150] This brief window has left its mark on the films, in their stylistic strategies and in the static that strikes their images. Chapter 5 examines the transforming circuits of Bombay horror's distribution, exhibition, and circulation across the arrival of commercial video cassettes in 1980s India. Along the way, the films have picked up the marks of projection damage, videotape degradation, and virtual circulation.

The marks of a film's consumption across media, formats, platforms, and eras are also marks of value extraction—by producers, audiences, and scholars. Since its theatrical release, *Bandh Darwaza* has been seen in various forms: as celluloid; as videocassette; as television broadcast; as video compact disc; as DVD; and now online, as streaming media. In the process, the first prints of the film, projected in a few theaters in Bombay, have been transformed into digital files, which circulate online in illicit form. On our computer screens, it becomes easy to pause or pore over a frame, possible to see film objects as fractal relics. The twentieth century grows ever more remote—as does the original moment of the films I am studying—but the films come closer to me than ever before. In the epilogue, I reflect on the perpetual reanimation of Bombay horror and the temporality of failure, such as when I return to *Bandh Darwaza* to find that its daylight has turned back into night.

THE HORROR OF FAILURE

Failure is a function of time. Things betray their thingness they "stop *working* for us," writes Bill Brown, underscoring how things betray their essence when they refuse their assigned roles or proper place.[151] Connoted in his description is also another sense: things reveal their thingness when they stop working for *us*—historical beings situated in a particular time or place. Conventions fall out of favor, and histories are forgotten: by us. The perception of something on-screen failing can sharpen with the passage of time and the arrival of new viewers to old images.

Seeing Things is the product of a widening historical gulf: between the past and the present of Bombay horror, between the films' original viewers and me. This gulf also separates the film's commercial audiences from scholars trained on a "Eurocentric set of references," in a discipline for which American horror films have been "normalized as a route to theorizing horror film per se."[152] By judging a Bombay horror film to have failed, I also court failure in my reading of it. It is often a *perceived* failure that forces the intention into view: viewers discern "the appearance of intention" from the very scene that is felt to fail it.[153] Viewers are actively parsing not only what is on-screen, but what is intended; without this interpretation of a film's intention, the film cannot be said to have failed the illusion.

For much of its history, after all, popular Hindi cinema has not been illusionistic in the way popular American or European films are. Unlike films that "hide the fact that they are films, a Hindi film does not pretend that it is presenting an unmediated view of reality."[154] Yet the terms on which that reality is allowed to be visible—or forces itself into visibility—deserve engagement. Films are never solely "frozen in the time of their production or the hierarchy of someone else's value system"; hermeneutic investments change, and there are revolutions in reading.[155] Theories of horror may not have been developed with Bombay horror's failures in mind, but theory can "be and remain conjectural, even tentative." Theory is "creative," Kyle Stevens asserts, because it "creates new ways of seeing things."[156] By indicating a materiality that may or may not have been intentionally included, failure can serve as a prompt for what makes horror films so disturbing.

What conception of horror emerges from the uncanon of Bombay horror? Moving between two orders of moving image materiality (the material presence of cinematic sounds and images on-screen, and their material past, when those images and sounds were forged off-screen), *Seeing Things* links the immersions of cinematic fantasy with the illuminations of film history. Mediating this link between an aesthetics of horror and an account of behind-the-scenes practices is the felt materiality of a body genre. In Linda Williams's important coinage, horror films are one of the "body genres" that aim to collapse the distance between bodies on-screen and the bodies of those watching the film.[157] A character's scream, sweating skin, pounding heartbeat, clammy hands, and nervous excitement may elicit the spectator's own. Horror films have been favored objects for phenomenologists exploring the film experience or film as a perceptual event that mutually implicates and mimetically generates sensation and cognition. Scholars of horror have helped recover the cinematic experience as normatively "carnal," "corporeal," "haptic," "sensuous," and "tactile," all terms used to belatedly give sensory perception back to the theoretical spectator.[158] As Angela Ndalianis argues, for example, a scene of "bodily destruction" that is "depicted onscreen unrelentingly weaves its way offscreen and onto the body of the spectator," who "extracts meaning from the body."[159] Bombay horror is replete with scenes of bodily destruction: a mother dying in the throes of labor because of a curse, a living man packed into plaster struggling to breathe, a vampire slitting open a wrist to feed. Yet these are also compelling scenes of creation. I am watching actors in writhing intensity or sweating under plaster, or the viscosity of synthetic blood pumping through tubes.

These scenes introduce the certainty of a real, historical *touch*—of very close contact between blades and film prints, faces and masks, workers and props, projectionists and reels—into the surreal story worlds of Bombay horror. That touch mediates between the bloodshot eyes of the deadly vampire and the nocturnal landscape he surveys: our sense of a tactile encounter involving a cameraperson, the device that is the camera, the photochemical substance that is film, land and light. Disturbing the illusory bond between the vampire and his line of sight, a fugitive feeling forms. There must have been other presences in the vampire's cave in *Bandh Darwaza*. I see human skin peeping out from under latex makeup and scratches that break out over the images. Perhaps a fog machine was blowing into the cave, which is why those clouds lie close to the floor; an actor was moving under a spotlight; a sound track was layered with looped musical cues, Foley effects, and dubbed voices in distinct tracks that do not quite cohere. But I can never quite be sure.

A history of human interventions has created the film, but what is actually present are indexical marks that do not quite amount to infallible wisdom. Pressuring a revelationist definition of the documentary index, failures force us to see things without disclosing much more about them. If, as Robin Wood proclaimed, the "true subject" of horror films is a "struggle for recognition," Bombay's horror films also incite a struggle *to* recognize.[160] They leave us suspended in the stretchy, liberatory possibilities of what Katherine Groo calls "bad film history": speculation, uncertainty, and best guesses about the felt touch traced on-screen.[161]

Whose eyes are we seeing through when we see the daylit hills? Horror films often present us with situations in which we sense someone seeing without being seen: we are forced to share the perspectives of monsters and masked killers, fostering a creepy dynamic of identification that is broken with the revelation of the seeing body and its destruction. No such revelation attends the point-of-view shot of the daylit hills, which cannot ever be attributed to a seeing subject within the film. This is what a materialist aesthetics can help us understand about the genre. The scratched surfaces, faded images, and unfinished bodies of Bombay horror indicate the multiple paths by which the affective impact of low-budget horror is achieved. Bombay horror prompts a different phenomenology of the horror film experience, cultivating the capacity for embodied viewing to feel an *other* material world encrypted in spectral forms on-screen.[162] Film phenomenology—which has principally centered on the experiential bond between the projected image and my viewing body—can also cultivate a feeling for the embodied world of filmmaking, for how performers, machines, and their environments may have mutually interacted and materialized in the process of generating moving images. Scenes of horror fitfully expose us to technologies and objects that constitute the material world of film but also to the anonymous performers, censors, and audiences who were transforming that world into moving images. Something of this collective effort remains on display, charging the mise-en-scène with traces of human bodies who worked on these films and so inhere in this body genre.

Horror, writes Erin Huang, is not only a set of narrative or visual conventions in films. If we do not define horror solely as a "scripted and commodified feeling," horror "opens up" as a "historical mode of perception arising when the perceived external reality exceeds one's internal frame of comprehension."[163] The spectral touch I sense is not reducible to the brute facts of what once happened behind the scenes. The processes and personnel I investigate historically are separate from, and ultimately not reducible to, the images that appear on-screen (and vice versa.) They assert only that something happened, but not what, why, or even quite how or who. The failures of Bombay horror are all indexical marks, but they do not confess much about their referents to us: whose skin, why bleached, when scratched? An indexical mark is only proof that "something has happened, that something exists or existed," but that thing is of course remote and intangible.[164] The index is an "impression left behind by a historical source we cannot see"; a record of physical contact," it is "the trace of touch, of having been touched" that finally only "reasserts the centrality of its tactile operations."[165] Touch spectrally animates Bombay horror as a different kind of haunted archive in which we graze the past but don't quite grasp it. Its details retain their secrecy, like ghosts who call out but will not give themselves up. The more I asked questions of images, the more haunted the images came to seem, indicating that the past would never pass fully out of view nor come fully into the light.

1 Paper Cuts

INSIDE THE BUREAUCRATIC
ENCOUNTER WITH *DARWAZA*

Nightmares of a faraway mansion enveloped in fog, the distant echo of a wailing woman, the strange claw marks on his skin: the orphan hero of the Ramsay Brothers' *Darwaza* (Door, Shyam and Tulsi Ramsay, 1978) has lived with mysterious traces of the past since he was a child. Now a young man, Suraj Singh (Anil Dhawan) is determined to pierce the "raaz ka purdah" ("veil of secrecy") that has shrouded his family's history. That history is being kept from him by the guardian in whose care he remains. So, late one night, a stealthy search locates the long-desired *kaagaz* (papers): a flashlight search of three-ring folders arrayed on a shelf stops at one labeled "Pratap Singh Haveli: Shimago." After the folder is spirited into his possession, Suraj exults: "This is that very file on the mansion that I was in search of! The very one I would lose my senses just thinking of!" Paper opens a path back into the past: the next morning, Suraj drives out of Bombay and toward Shimago. As he covers the hundreds of kilometers back to where it all began, he trades the flashlight for a flaming torch; eventually, in a lair below the *haveli*, our hero will come face to face with the growling monster that destroyed his family. A three-ring folder can preserve secrets, but its portability can expose those secrets. Paper hides things, but paper is also a thing in hiding.

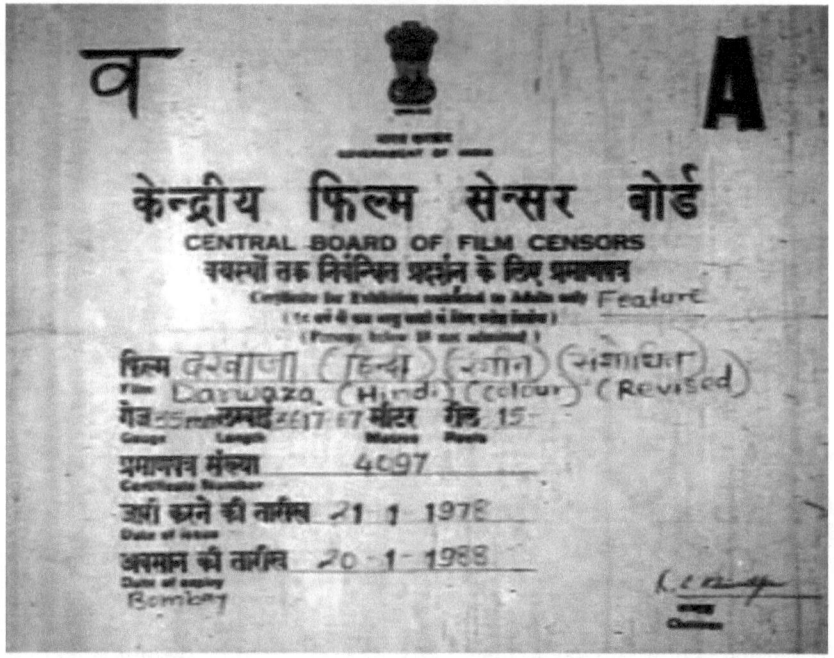

Figure 7. Darwaza's opening shot, its censor certificate (1978). *Source:* Ramsay Pictures.

Darwaza, too, begins with a piece of paper (see figure 7). I do not mean the secret *kaagaz* (documents) our hero Suraj reads. I mean the very first thing I see when I watch the film: its censor certificate. A familiar start to the cinematic experience in India, the censor certificate signals the government's authority over the images to come. Familiar though they are as unmovable symbols of power, these certificates are somewhat forgotten for their materiality. Censor certificates begin as rectangular sheets of white paper that are printed in bulk and transported to the offices of the censor board. Here they are inked in by hand, signed, creased and folded, smudged and scribbled on, photographed so that they can be placed at the head of film prints, saved, and stored for future use. Before and after they surface as images, censor certificates are things that emerge from an underworld of forms, files, and court orders that invisibly control the public life of cinema in India. When the Ramsay Brothers first applied for a certificate for *Darwaza*, the censors reportedly rejected the application.[1]

The film had effectively begun its life with a ban; without a certificate, it could not be shown in theaters. Why was *Darwaza* denied a certificate at first, and how did it receive one under the title *Darwaza (Revised)*?

A paper trail takes us inside the bureaucratic encounter with *Darwaza*, allowing us to discover how "India's First Horror Film" was processed by the censors. Between the initial application for certification and when *Darwaza* was certified, months likely passed in rejection, deferral, revision, and reversal. Throughout, the relationship was mediated by papers that moved between the censor board and the Ramsay Brothers, from letters of application and official notifications to ledgers with scribbled notes and censor scripts with inked deletions. *Darwaza* aimed to induce "a new excitement in motion pictures," and censorship documents help us understand how this new excitement was felt by the film's first audience: the state.[2] Encouraging us to imagine the "moment where the officers of the law are huddled together in a small dark room, notepad and pen in hand, watching a rather bizarre montage of images," Lawrence Liang draws attention to the "affective and libidinal dimension of what happens when censors watch."[3] "Acts of censorship," writes Liang, "expose an underlying secret": that "legal reason has to come down from its elevated position and modes of discourse to enter a murky space."[4] As *Darwaza* verges down toward a cobwebbed cave strewn with corpses, the paper trail of government reports, official digests, and release certificates helps illuminate the journey that censors took as they watched the film. If, as filmmakers felt, the operations of censors "are kept secret, and a film maker is treated like a culprit and his creation is judged in secret by a group of five or ten persons," the documents of censorship enable us to enter that secret room, to witness the making of those judgments *as they were being made*.[5]

Because paper required bureaucrats to take positions on moving images by writing (and writing over) cover letters and censor scripts, the records of censorship are also "evidential structures in the long human history of clues."[6] The documents of censorship allow us to envision how legal reason takes form in the body of the censor. They also encourage us to contemplate how legal reason was transformed by what was seen in that dark room: to catch a new law as it was coming into being. In late 1977 the national film censorship code was amended for the first time in nearly two decades. Among its updated objects of proscription, the revised code listed "scenes of horror." Two weeks later, *Darwaza (Revised)* was certified for release. I propose that "scenes of horror" serves as the discursive codification of the censor's encounter with *Darwaza*. This proposal widens the historiographic value of a regulatory category, serving as an index of the censorial experience *of* a horror film rather than as an item of offense applied *to* horror films. Before it was created by the censor board as a class of proscribed images, "scenes of horror" had to be experienced by the censors. Using the documents surrounding *Darwaza*, we can more closely examine how the meaning of "scenes of horror" may have crystallized.

Darwaza's censorship has left behind fewer public traces than the censorship of other horror films of the period, such as *The Exorcist* (William Friedkin, 1973), *Jadu Tona* (Ravikant Nagaich, 1978), and *Jaani Dushman* (Rajkumar Kohli, 1979). In 1977 the censor board refused to certify *The Exorcist* because it was filled with "revolting obscenities," "lewd and repulsive," and "indecent and offensive to good taste."[7] Having screened *Jadu Tona*, the censor found the film problematic because it "features superstition as a predominant element."[8] And when the censors examined *Jaani Dushman*, they pointed out that it depicted a "number of pointless killings."[9] These were high-profile cases; the films elicited mainstream press coverage (like *The Exorcist*) and underwent courtroom deliberations (like *Jadu Tona* and *Jaani Dushman*) on their way to being released, each after extensive deletions and modifications ordered by the censor board. Similar concerns were likely also operative in the case of *Darwaza* and in the constitution of "scenes of horror." But the censors' qualification of "scenes of horror" as "pointless or avoidable" suggests an aesthetically distinctive experience, an intimate relation between screen and viewer—one that could not be adequately surveilled using existing codes of depicted obscenity, violence, or superstition.

As discussed in the introduction, the fear and fascination provoked by horror is fundamentally dependent on the artful mastery of the cinematic medium. Throughout the twentieth century and well into the present, filmmakers have continuously honed formal conventions by grappling with the inherent capabilities and limitations of film. A camera's orchestrated movements, careful interplays of sound and image, the crafty manipulation of filmstrips: these intricate practices have evolved in response to the creative confinements of filmmaking and profoundly determined the aesthetic experience of the genre (or how we know the world in horror).

Tracking *Darwaza*'s censorship alongside the publication of the new code encourages us to specify how a film's seemingly heterogeneous sights and sounds may have come to be known by the censors as "scenes of horror." Skeletons of the dead, screams of women, the body of the monster: these and other items were the targets of censorship in *Darwaza*, marked for removal or reduction. But what, exactly, was being censored? In its hectic enumeration of "Bad Things," writes William Mazzarella, censorship grasps at specific scenes as "given forms" of a "virtual potential," nasty surprises that "cannot be itemized in advance."[10] Mazzarella provokes us to go beyond the given content of a deletion to ask what "virtual potential" is being policed. Answering this question reveals the complex temporal operations at play in the form and censorship of *Darwaza*. Its paper trail reveals an aspiration to control something beyond the explicit *content* of the film.

Darwaza coordinated choices in storytelling, montage, and mise-en-scène to create a corporeal experience of haunted time. As images and sounds of haunted time, scenes of horror abound in *Darwaza*. These scenes train our attention on the material coordinates of spectral cinema, on the physical practices undergirding images and sounds of haunting. Rendering the spectral presence of the past in visual and sonic forms, *Darwaza*'s dissolves, repetitions, and unsynchronized sounds were themselves the products of tactile manipulation—including stop-motion cinematography, transitional effects, and looped footage. These effects make an intangible dimension of our experience of time palpable. They allowed the film to suspend the separation of past, present, and future, engendering a recursive temporality by which feudal history was relayed to urban modernity and hoary myth filed as paperwork. The recursive temporality of *Darwaza* laced the promise of "India's First Horror Film": a revolving door opened Suraj's present to his family's past, but the film also opened the industrial present of Bombay cinema to the future emergence of a genre.

Darwaza transports Suraj across space back to his family mansion; the hundreds of miles traveled are also coded as a movement in time. The film baits its city-bred hero into a world where a curse sworn decades ago lives on; the monster is the present manifestation of a temporal past. Haunting can "intimate a sense of discrepant temporality," rehabilitating modes of thinking about time in "dis-accustomed terms" otherwise dismissed as primitive, superstitious, or anachronistic.[11] Against the "temporal elitism" of modern rationality or positivist science, films like

Darwaza exhibit what Bliss Cua Lim calls a "propensity towards temporal critique."[12] Because haunting "opens to more than one time," to "plural, enchanted worlds," stories of haunting give popular proof to the belief that the past cohabits with the present.[13] Stories of haunting refuse the universality of linear historical time and incubate experiences of time no less real than the objective measure of duration supplied by a clock in a town square or dates stamped onto documents. While Lim elaborates "the temporal unruliness of haunting" with reference to parallel editing and mise-en-scène in the Filipino film *Itim* (Black, Mike de Leon, 1976), her conceptualization of "immiscible temporalities" bears productively on "India's First Horror Film."[14] The horror film stages the "fantastic as immiscible times—multiple times that never quite dissolve into the code of modern time consciousness, discrete temporalities incapable of attaining homogeneity with or full incorporation into a uniform chronological present."[15] By identifying scenes of horror with material expressions of spectral time, this chapter sets the stage for the spectral materialities that will follow in the coming chapters.

CENSORING TIME

India's Central Board of Film Censors (CBFC) was established in the early 1950s to mediate between the freedom of expression enshrined in the new nation's constitution and equally enshrined restrictions on that freedom. The Cinematograph Act of 1952 first empowered the CBFC to censor a film if "the film or any part of it is against interests of the security of the State, friendly relations with foreign States, public order, decency or morality, or involves defamation or contempt of court or is likely to incite the commission of any offense."[16] No film could be shown without being cleared by the state-run censor board; censor certificates were required to appear before every film screening in a theater or on television as proof and product of a successful certification process. The certificate's flickering appearance on every screen thus accomplished the state's penetration into the private and public spaces of everyday life in India. But the state's power extended as much over the time of cinema. Historically, print laboratories were instructed not to print positives of a film that did not yet have a censor certificate. No film could be preserved at the National Film

Archive without a censor certificate. The continuing mandatory placement of the censor certificate *before* the film is the forced interpolation of a delay, a reminder of the state's power to keep films, as well as their makers and viewers, waiting. A document that delays, the certificate also brings something into view: namely, that film censorship happens *in* time.

I first became attuned to the censor's temporal powers during a research visit. It all began at Ms. Kelkar's desk at the Mumbai office of the censor board, with a letter of introduction in hand and a polite request to see the censor certificate granted to *Darwaza*. I wanted to see the film's censor certificate in print so that I could do to it what I could not do to its image on-screen: flip it over. The reverse of the certificate, I believed, would list the exact length of each part that had been removed from the film.[17] Mrs. Kelkar took the paper I had written my request on and disappeared. Over the sounds of ceiling fans, ringing telephones, and a dripping water cooler, I heard the creaking doors of steel almirahs and the rustling of papers. When Mrs. Kelkar returned, however, she had nothing on *Darwaza*. The National Film Archive, in Pune, she suggested, might have what I was looking for. I had the feeling I was being delayed.

I was not alone. Temporality—or an experience of time—is "central to the experience, navigation, and operation of bureaucracy."[18] During my visit to the censor board office, I saw that it was not easy for filmmakers to track how, where, and for how long paperwork moved in the censor office. Applications moved between folders and officials, floors, and offices, and between Mumbai and Delhi. Some disappeared. Applicants returned to inquire and were sent away. Some were surprised to find their applications had already been processed.[19] Using paperwork, the state can control and capture the time of its citizens—subjecting them to duration with papers that are signed and circulated or misplaced and lost.[20] Beginning with the refusal to certify, the state could force a film into the durational experience of waiting. For film producers, delay could turn financially calamitous as usurious loans compounded and distributors bailed on the film. The longer the film was delayed, the larger the state's authority: films were denied certificates by examining committees, pending revisions; revised films were denied certificates by revising committees, pending further revisions; certified films were referred to the ministry in Delhi, pending further appeal.

The censor certificate is a document of state power, and its status (granted, withheld, delayed, or revoked) signifies the historically antagonistic, envious, cozy, or indifferent decades-long relationship of government administrators and bureaucrats to the producers and consumers of an immensely popular and glamorous industry.[21] From its inception, the postcolonial state recognized India's popular cinemas as having a rival and "tremendous influence over its citizenry."[22] Today, cinema's sensational power continues to be imagined by the state as threatening the hard-won peace, sober progress, and tender stomachs of citizens in a young postcolonial democracy.[23] Film censors are state-appointed guardians of ordinary people, conceived of as young, poor, sweating suspiciously in the cheap seats, and not quite yet ready to speak for themselves. (The use of a two-tier classification system (A/U, or adult/universal) indicates how India's differently educated, located, and classed population is selectively policed.)

The state has historically figured the audience's body exotically: remote and rural, susceptible and in need of protection. "Censorship is entirely done in urban areas," noted Kobita Sarkar, a film critic who served in advisory capacities for the Bombay censor board from 1970 to 1977.[24] Yet "films are seen in rural areas by vast audiences who are known to react differently from urban audiences. And how much contact does the city censor have with this section of the audience?"[25] How much, Sarkar wondered, could the censor really do to "protect" this audience?[26] To protect them, even films certified "A" are continuously purged of "unacceptable words, images, gestures, situations, implications, and procedures."[27] Whether it is the censors holding up a documentary for being seditious or a commercial romance for being obscene, centralized censorship runs on the belief that screen sights and sounds, stories, and subject matter *do* something to malleable viewers, and the belief that what they, the censors, did to the film could reshape viewers to be law-abiding, patriotic, and sober.

To synchronize diverse moviegoers into a homogenous Indian public, censorship has historically coordinated decision-making across a geographically dispersed hierarchy. Like many other large operations that originated in the colonial administrations of the British Raj, it is designed to enable "administration at a distance."[28] These operations in turn elaborated the East India Company's systems for doing business in the colony, systems that ranked paper—receipts and bills—above people, anticipating the form of rationality known as bureaucracy, or rule by desk.[29] In Max Weber's influential description of the modern office, we see the strong correlation between a managerial form and written documents: a bureau is made up of the "body of officials," their "staff of subaltern officials and scribes of all sorts," and the "respective apparatus of material implements and the files."[30] When used in the dispensation of state power, government "by paper" is designed to protect citizens from changes in political regimes by prioritizing predictability, procedure, and paperwork.[31] Knowledge (by) rules: the bureaucracy ensures that the thousands of films submitted for clearance every year to the censor board are processed equally. As a film's file moves between committees, offices, and cities, paper's mobility ensures that the film is insulated from the whims of any one official, politician, or agenda.

Headquartered in Bombay, the CBFC was housed under the Ministry of Information and Broadcasting in New Delhi, and every member of the board and advisory panels served at "the pleasure of the Central Government."[32] Authority flowed from the ministry in Delhi to the minister's secretaries; to the chairman of the board in Bombay; to the board's regional officers in Bangalore, Calcutta, Hyderabad, Madras, and Trivandrum; and from there on to the members of committees and clerks who gathered to examine each film. This sprawling apparatus—popularly rereferred to as "the censors"—was made up of hundreds of salaried government employees and per diem honorees exchanging letters and phone calls, film prints and scripts, arguments and ideas, all converging on the surface of the finished film.

That surface was minutely surveilled through the censorship code, an elaborate, three-page guide announced by the Ministry of Information and Broadcasting.[33] With the publication of the code in 1960, the censors' objects were itemized; any decision—revision or refusal—had to find backing in a clause of the existing code. "In a vast and culturally stratified country like India," the trade journal *Screen* editorialized, "it is impossible for any one film (indeed, any one work of art) to find approval in all quarters."[34] The code aimed to satisfy the interests of producers, distributors, and exhibitors of hundreds of Indian and imported films every year; their audiences—spanning enormous diversities in age, gender, class, language, literacy, religion, and region—and local pressure groups whose members might protest, riot, or petition against a film's exhibition in the name of "ordinary" viewers or "injured" communities.[35] By following a published code and exercising available options of certification, cutting, modification, and classification, state censorship sought to standardize the experience of the filmic text for hundreds of millions of moviegoers across the country.[36]

The code began by declaring: "No picture shall be certified for public exhibition which will lower the moral standards of those who see it; Hence the sympathy of the audience shall not be thrown on the side of crime, wrong-doing, evil or sin."[37] Accordingly, at the end of the code there appeared a list of twenty-six "subjects" that "may be objectionable in a context in which either they amount to indecency, immorality, illegality, or incitement to commit a breach of the law."[38] Referring filmmakers to the code, for example, state censorship regularly intervened to redirect the audience's sympathy (e.g., a point-of-view shot was removed) or reanchor meaning (e.g., a disclaimer was added). In effect, bureaucracy depersonalized—and therefore democratized—censorship: all films were subject to the same code, and all censor certificates signed by the same person, the chairman of the censor board.

Darwaza's censor certificate was signed by the then chairman of the board, K. L. Khandpur, at the headquarters of the CBFC in Bombay in February 1978. Khandpur's tenure as chairman (1976–81) overlapped with the governmental transition out of the Emergency. "The period of the Emergency from June 1975 to March 1977," lamented Aruna Vasudev, "interrupted an otherwise continuous pursuit of democratic freedoms since Independence in 1947."[39] The editor of a popular film magazine, *Film World*, noted that the film censors too were "operating from Delhi, not Bombay": scores of films submitted for clearance to the Bombay office of the censor board were instead sent over for political approval to Delhi.[40] Some delays became permanent when approval was withheld; periodic film bans were self-seriously decreed by an official notification.

After the Emergency ended, voters swept Prime Minister Indira Gandhi out of office. "For the film industry," *Film World* now opined, "the election of the new Government, committed to the freedom of the media, signals the end of a 20-month-long horror drama."[41] The "objectives of film censorship," the freshly elected Janata Party (People's Party) announced in June 1977, "will be to ensure that artistic expression and creative freedom are not unduly curbed."[42] In December 1977 a question came up in the upper house of Parliament. The new minister of information and broadcasting,

L. K. Advani of the Janata Party, was asked "whether there is any proposal under Government's consideration to lay down fresh guidelines for the censorship of films."[43] Advani replied that "the guidelines for censorship are under revision; these have not yet been finalized."[44] Published in January 1978, the new code was shorter, meant to signal the start of a more liberal era in film censorship after the end of the Emergency.

Yet in the decade that followed the Emergency, state bureaucracy grew into "a highly centralized outfit, a sort of "super secretariat," an "interceptor of files and a law unto itself": a super-bureaucracy.[45] The documents through which films were managed also proliferated, one among the numerous paper trails through which a postcolonial regime seemed to be reincarnating the "Kaghazi Raj" (paper empire), or the British colonial administration of South Asia as a "graphic regime of surveillance."[46] The return to transparency, accountability, and rule of law was manifested in an obvious—and in many cases an oppressive—reliance on paperwork.[47] Through the "ceaseless circulation" of paperwork, including memos, letters, and petitions, bureaucrats entered into institutional relationships with one another and those outside the bureaucracy.[48] Proceduralism triggered the proliferation of paperwork in bureaucracies: papers that were written, mailed, copied, shared, and shredded, but papers that may not, necessarily, ever have been fully read. Soon a freshly politicized middle class began driving a larger print boom in investigative journalism and exposé reportage with a focus on unraveling the "paper truths" of the bureaucracy: things that were true only (because they were) on paper.[49]

Every photograph, as Roland Barthes once wrote, "is a certificate of presence."[50] The censor certificate at the start of *Darwaza* is both a visual symbol and a material product of its censorship, but its placement at the head of the film print gives *delay* an authenticating force as strong as a close reading of the certificate's numbers and letters. As an inscription of force, the power to keep films waiting extended to the screen: the certificate's placement at the head of the film print indicates how the nominally invisible bureaucracy of censorship is made present. The collective act of gazing at the certificate would thus constitute an imagined national public at the movies. The photographed certificate affixed to the print was to be displayed for "a minimum duration of 10 seconds" and was stipulated at five meters of footage for a 35mm film of *Darwaza*'s length.[51]

The experience of bureaucratic time in the materiality of cinematic form has a corollary: the experience of cinematic time in the materiality of bureaucratic form. While the state may have used paperwork to control *Darwaza*—to subject the film to an experience of bureaucratic time via files, notifications, scripts, and certificates—the same paperwork can now be used to rematerialize another experience of time sedimented in bureaucratic ephemera around the film. This is the time in which *Darwaza* was seen by the censors, in which feelings were felt and decisions were made. A sensitivity to how duration is inscribed on the page slows down the study of *Darwaza*'s censorship to the time in which state power operated. Paper preserves the official minutiae of *Darwaza*'s regulation— of censors declaring the film's "fearful screams" and "frightening skeletons" deleted—but paper also summons the mood of the regulatory encounter with a horror film, of censors "off balance" and arrested in states of unease while watching *Darwaza*, trapping the uncertainty wrought by cinematic horror in the grain of paper.[52]

That fluctuating mood is also captured by changes in the code. On the last page of the 1960 code, after such proscribed items as "gruesome murders" and "excessive bleeding or mutilation," horror appeared for the first time: "(xvii) accentuations of class distinctions or stimulating class hatred; (xviii) realistic *horrors* of warfare; (xix) *horror* as a predominant element; (xx) scenes and incidents likely to afford information to the enemy in time of war."[53] Horror in the 1960 code is possessed of a stable referentiality outside film (*realistic* horrors *of* warfare) and of relative insignificance as an object of oversight. As it rotated from the end of the old code to the fore of the new one, horror's meaning shifted. The code of 1978 began: "The Board of Film Censors shall ensure that—(i) anti-social activities such as violence are not glorified or justified; (ii) the modus operandi of criminals or other visuals or words of any offence, are not depicted."[54] While the first two lines of the code preserved an interest in policing images of criminal violence from the 1960 code, its third line urged censors to ensure that "(iii) pointless or avoidable scenes of violence, cruelty and horror are not shown."[55] What are "pointless or avoidable scenes . . . of . . . horror," and where did this category come from?

"Scenes of horror" records a time of generic emergence, from the way *Darwaza* imagines hapless victims stumbling on the monster to the censor imagining audiences happening upon *Darwaza*. Newness is never given in advance; it can only be known by inhabiting the time of emergence. "Scenes of horror" was not only a predictive form of sanitization—of what would not happen to viewers—it was also an indent created by an experience—it is what had happened to some viewers. The phrase may be an apt description of the censors' encounter with the film: scenes distributed across seconds, hours, days, weeks, and months, wherein the film was seen by the censors, its excitement was felt, and its fate was decided. Their written words serve as a "residue or deposit" of exposure to the haunted temporality of the horror film, all that remains of the durational experience of *Darwaza*.[56]

Taking seriously the claim that *Darwaza* offered a "new excitement in motion pictures" requires attending closely to how "new excitement" is forged in the relation of viewer to film, a relationship gestured to by "scenes of horror." As the censor watches, writes, underlines, and strikes through images and sounds, scenes of horror "assume concrete shape" in ink, paper, and files.[57] In the documents around *Darwaza*, then, what we find is not some existing rule of the censor being applied to a "new excitement in motion pictures" but a rule gathering into place. In other words, *Darwaza*'s paper trail also brings censorship into view as a practice of bodies in time.

MAKING "INDIA'S FIRST HORROR FILM"

As he turns into a monster, the old man's body is racked by unsightly changes. Blood rises out of bone, and skin recedes to reveal sinewy mass. On-screen, the metamorphosis lasts only a few seconds, but the successive shots of this stop-motion sequence required an actor to lie in position under a bright lamp for eight hours a day, ten days in a row, as more prosthetic flesh was stuck to his skin and synthetic blood was dripped over it. The labor and resources congealed between the frames indicate how seriously the Ramsay Brothers were taking their latest project—and how haunting would be summoned for "India's First Horror Film."

For years, the seven sons of a small-time film producer had been trying to score a hit in the family name, something that had eluded their father through the 1960s. When his 1970 thriller *Ek Nanhi Munhi Ladki Thi* (There once was a little girl, Vishram Bedekar) too failed to make its money back, Fatehchand Uttamchand Ramsay was at a desperate pass. His sons had watched the film in Bombay theaters, and what they saw gave them an idea. "We saw the movie ten times with the public," recalled Tulsi Ramsay, sitting in his Mumbai apartment.[58] There was one sequence that had viewers rapt: the film's opening, in which a gnarly creature prowls a museum after dark and steals a jeweled dagger. When the police arrive and begin shooting, the thief hides amid the museum's paintings, artifacts, statuary, and taxidermy. After killing a constable, the leathery fiend escapes in a getaway car. A woman in a passing car sees its blood-soaked visage, cries out in terror, and drives into a ditch.

In the theater too, the "public was screaming . . . everyone was clapping," Tulsi reminisced, until the spell was broken on-screen. The monster, it is revealed, is a thief, his face and claws a disguise. When he discards the rubbery mask and drives off, the mood in the theater was deflated. "Throughout, the audience was distracted during the fights, walked out during the songs." From this heist film, though, the Ramsays spirited something else. Forging imaginative links that seem obvious now but might easily have been missed then, the Ramsay sons sensed that a commercial future was possible in the film genre best suited to sounding out what they had heard in those screams. Following a pair of crime thrillers in the 1970s, *Do Gaz Zameen Ke Neeche* (Two yards under, 1972) and *Andhera* (Darkness, 1975), Tulsi shared: "I told my father. . . . Why not make a full-fledged horror film?"[59]

Darwaza would not be the first horror film seen in India. Bombay's Capitol Theater had a hit with *Son of Frankenstein* (Rowland Lee, 1939) and the Opera House with *The Walking Dead* (Michael Curtiz, 1936). The Ramsays themselves had grown up attending matinee screenings of American classics such as *Dracula* (James Whale, 1931) and *Frankenstein* (Tod Browning, 1934) in 1950s Bombay. In the 1960s, exhibitors were promoting Eastmancolor imports from Britain, including *Curse of Frankenstein* (Terence Fisher, 1957) and *Horror of Dracula* (Terence Fisher, 1958). In late 1977, South Bombay's poshest theaters were also announcing upgrades to air-conditioning and sound systems for the local releases of international blockbusters *The Exorcist* and *The Omen* (Richard Donner,

1976). Globally, *The Exorcist*'s success set off a new series of American, Japanese, Canadian, Italian, and Mexican productions enabled by permissive censorship codes, cheaper effects materials, and transnational film circulation. Around the world, some of the most celebrated films of the horror canon date to this time. They also forcefully established the names of their directors as "masters" of horror: *House* (Nobuhiko Obayashi, 1977), *Alucarda* (Juan Lopez Moctezuma, 1977), *Suspiria* (Dario Argento, 1977), *Rabid* (David Cronenberg, 1977), *The Hills Have Eyes* (Wes Craven, 1977), *Halloween* (John Carpenter, 1978), *I Spit on Your Grave* (Meir Zarchi, 1978), *Alien* (Ridley Scott, 1979), *Cannibal Holocaust* (Ruggero Deodato, 1980), and *The Shining* (Stanley Kubrick, 1980). Joining the global wave of horror movies that were electrifying audiences around the world at the end of the 1970s, *Darwaza* promised Indian moviegoers a "new excitement in motion pictures."

From what they saw in foreign horror films, the Ramsays would have discerned some of the storytelling and stylistic trend lines redefining horror cinema: elaborate prosthetic effects, expressionistic uses of color film stock, and narratives of demonic possession. From where they saw these films, the Ramsays would have spotted a business opportunity. English- and foreign-language horror films remained confined, by and large, to theaters in cities such as Bombay and Delhi, leaving the country's vast Hindi belt across western and northern India ripe for exploitation. Their somewhat exotic family name—they used to be the Ramsinghanias before they became the Ramsay Brothers—would also help endorse their credentials in a seemingly foreign genre.[60] If they could manage to strike even a dozen prints of their film, a paltry but prohibitive number for such an unproven commodity, the Ramsay Brothers would have to find a path to profitability beyond the established monopolies over city theaters and in the more diffuse networks of screens in suburbs and small towns. Here, their closest competition might be from junk prints of films such as *Mahal* (Palace, Kamal Amrohi, 1949) or *Madhumati* (Bimal Roy, 1958), decades-old black-and-white thrillers steeped in gothic décor but ultimately committed to de-spelling the spectral. If the Ramsays were right, their audience was demanding a show of faith in another world: not only a masked man rifling through primitive artifacts in a city museum, but a prehistoric monster haunting a faraway haveli. It also demanded a show of feeling:

dumbstruck cops and shrieking passersby marked the first rending of the ordinary world that elicited viewers' own claps and screams. *Darwaza* is an instance of how genre cycles originate by "trapping" the "uncanny reception energies" of past films inside new formal strategies.[61] Taken together, they allow us to deduce an emerging family definition of the "horror film" from *Darwaza*, one that would prove enormously influential in the decade to come.

Darwaza opens with a curse: after cruel Thakur Pratap Singh murders her son, a village woman swears her execrations upon him. Grisly death visits the thakur's family; only a young son sent away from the rural haveli to Bombay city survives. The curse acquires a somatic form in the caves under the haveli, from where something emerges to stalk and kill in the foggy hills of Shimago. Villagers live in terror. The haveli pulsates in their imagination as a "veerana kabrastan" (desolate graveyard) that has spawned a bloodthirsty "shaitaan" (demon). Meanwhile, in faraway Bombay, Pratap Singh's only son and heir, Suraj, comes of age to nightmares that beckon him back to the long-lost haveli of his long-dead father. Suraj and his wife Rachna race out of the city in the direction of desolation, driving past hills and rivers toward Shimago. Eventually, Suraj locates the mansion and the "khaufnaak darwaza" (frightening door) inside it, stepping into the caves underneath to lift the "raaz ka purdah" (the shroud of secrecy) on his family's past. With the village watching, our "sheheri babu" (city boy) plunges a holy *trishul* (trident) into the monster's back and ends the reign of terror. The beast folds feebly in Suraj's lap: it is the thakur himself! As he dies in his son's arms, his body is racked by gross changes. "My low and dirty thoughts," the thakur penitently moans, "took form in my face and skin." With its revelation of a monster in the flesh—and not just a man in a "bhayanak naqab" (fearsome mask)—*Darwaza* brilliantly fulfills the promise that had wilted years before when that rubbery mask was thrown out of a car window.

Darwaza's traveled imagination—from how it sweeps us out of Bombay, out across highways, hills, rivers, and lakes toward Shimago—suggests an expansive ambition that becomes explicit in how the film was sold to moviegoers. That February, listeners tuned into their radios at night might have been startled to hear the sounds of doors creaking open, chandeliers swaying in the wind, and a hooting owl just before the end of the day's programming: *Darwaza* was being hyped on All India Radio.[62] For weeks leading up to the film's premiere, "in the evenings," Tulsi recalled, "we could hear the radios being turned up in all the houses in the neighborhood."[63] In a newspaper advertisement in the *Times of India* during the week of the film's release, moviegoers were invited to "open the door to new excitement in motion pictures."[64] If they glanced up above bus stops and buildings, onlookers found themselves under the unblinking eyes of a monster staring down at them from posters designed by D. R. Bhosle. The monster's face took up as much space as Amitabh Bachchan's did on billboards for the gangster action film *Don* (Chandra Barot, 1978). Making way for a new kind of film in the churn of sensational genres characterizing Bombay cinema, "India's First Horror Film" declared a ribbon cutting across the poster.

Darwaza is more appropriately understood as a transitional film. Like the late 1950s British horror films *The Curse of Frankenstein* and *Horror of Dracula*, it was conceived of as "bridging two eras—or, rather, justifying entry into a new era by anchoring itself in the fondly remembered, comparatively distant past."[65] *Darwaza*'s themes of ancestral sins, family property, and generational reckoning link its status as a fictional narrative to its status as a commodity mediating continuity and change. Haunting always "begins by coming back," and the film is thick with the presence of fictional, biographical, and historical pasts.[66] The "khaufnaak yaadein" (terrifying memories) that haunt Suraj are generational: passed from his father to him, inherited by the Ramsay Brothers from their father's filmography, and encrypting the legacies of *Darwaza*'s generic antecedents—of Bombay's gothic thrillers of the 1950s and 1960s such as *Mahal, Madhumati, Kohraa* (Fog, Biren Nag, 1964), and *Woh Kaun Thi?* (Who was she?, Raj Khosla, 1964). The "ruined" mansion of these films, writes Vijay Mishra, enacts a form of mnemonic "recall" in the "space of the gothic."[67] Like these films, *Darwaza* uses architectural forms and natural landscapes as spatializations of clotted time: ruins, environments, and obsolete spaces that allow the "modern" viewer to visually perceive returning historical time in the architectural gothic.

The architectural gothic is also a structure of concealment by which modern transformations are screened (consider the Victoria Terminus in Bombay, behind the façade of which the country's largest and newest railway station was erected in the nineteenth century.) *Darwaza*'s "new excitement" does not then lie in opening the door to the haveli. There is another door, hidden in the walls of the haveli. The "last, forbidden door" is, as Andrew Britton notes in his commentary on Alfred Hitchcock's *Psycho* (1960), a hallmark of fictional treatments of the architectural gothic that enact myths of descent.[68] Built features with a darkly perceived design, these doors are analogous to the gothic stories in which they appear as tools for "exciting surprise."[69] Leading underground, *Darwaza*'s revolving door rotates the film's characters and its viewers into a lair littered with skulls, cobwebs, and a looming, lethal fiend. The film shocks visual space by having the monster's claw suddenly jut into the empty frame: the intrusion, intensified by a stinger on the score, is a felt rending of space and time and a graphic instantiation of a "new excitement."

But the claw has also burst into view before: it swipes on to the screen from bottom left in *Bees Saal Baad* (Twenty years later, Biren Nag, 1962). The claw is an enduring convention, and conventions convene the past of cinema: the passions of bygone audiences are selectively transformed by filmmakers into formal investments; those formal investments trigger, however fleetingly, an imagined encounter with a collective memory of moviegoing. What in *Bees Saal Baad* was thought to be supernatural terror is revealed as actors, plots, and illusions staged to avenge crimes of violence and greed committed in the haveli long ago. In *Darwaza*, instead, such misdeeds have unleashed a very real monster from under the haveli who sets out to kill. Alongside the monster, *Darwaza* cast familiar faces such as Lalitha Pawar, faded stars symbolizing a generational past with sins to atone for. Having appeared in *Kohraa* as a murderess governess, Pawar had participated in the preceding cycle of gothic thrillers to which *Darwaza* pays homage. Pawar's casting—and clearing away by this monster's claw—is indicative of *Darwaza*'s "transitional" status.

Darwaza renders these pasts perceptible in elements of its visual world: in skeletons of the dead and the body of the monster. On the cover of *Darwaza*'s song booklet, cobwebs spread over corpses, while off to the side is a column, its dimensions mimicking a filmstrip, flashing an invitation the color of blood: "Open the door..." (see figure 8). This column was a flap folded over the front of the booklet, a design detail that activates the propulsive lure of the film. Moved by the injunction, viewers may have felt themselves drawn to a door opening not only to a where and a what, but

Figure 8. Darwaza's song booklet, inviting moviegoers to "open the door" (1978).
Source: Author's collection.

to a *when*. The hands of moviegoers may have run over the surfaces inside, where a monster, a red moon, and a cadaver with outstretched arm reached out to them from under the printed text. These are the "semantic" elements of horror, the building blocks of its iconography, but they are also the visualizations of a durational experience that would soon be censored. As a seemingly generic element of the booklet design, the appearance of the filmstrip as a flap is telling, for it makes plain the malleability of film. Individual frames could be detached from inside a sequence, or a series of frames could be looped in a pattern to kindle the uncanny experiences of time favored by horror films. But frames could also be removed to interrupt the temporality of horror. I turn next to the *Gazette of India*, an official digest that carried information about *Darwaza*'s displaced frames to readers across the country.

ROTATING SKELETONS IN THE *GAZETTE OF INDIA*

The discovery of the concealed door in *Darwaza* and the subterranean world of the monster behind it mark the onset of danger. A village woman, Reshma, discovers the revolving door in the thakur's haveli, through which she descends into a cobwebbed cave. A passageway lit by flaming torches pulls her past a slithering lizard, a hanging bat, and a hooting owl, until she happens upon someone seated in a chair, long white hair overflowing, their back to her. When Reshma reaches out, the chair swivels around. To sounds of thunder and under bolts of lightning, a skeleton rotates into view! Screaming, Reshma backs away. Her retreat ends when she backs into the monster, who closes in on her. He passes his claws over her eyes, and Reshma dies without ever seeing his gross visage. Selected by the Ramsay Brothers to serve as the film's trailer, this sequence previews some of the stylish production design and camerawork, surreal special effects, and sound track that marked the film as both familiar and not. The prize was, as Tulsi Ramsay told me, total corporealization: to make "the public scream" (again), as he once had seen and heard them do in a movie theater. It was this very affective temporality of *Darwaza* that would become the focus of bureaucratic control.

"Delete the close-ups of front and back views of the Monster. Also delete the views of the frightening skeleton.... Delete sound of fearful screams of the characters."[70] These were the deletions the censor board mandated before certifying the trailer for theatrical release, publishing its decision in the *Gazette of India*. If censorship's standardized code and top-down operations were fantasies of centralized control, then the *Gazette of India* was the paper technology by which that control was executed.[71]

While it "appears to offer a centralized mode of power" by standardizing every film before it is released, censorship must be performed in person and on site.[72] For example, if an uncensored film was discovered playing in a theater, the Code of Criminal Procedure granted the state the "power of seizure," but that seizure had to be executed in person: "Any police officer may enter any place in which he has reason to believe that the film has been or is being or is likely to be exhibited, search it and seize the film."[73] Therefore, if the censor board was, as a 1979 Supreme Court judge described it, "a statutory gendarme policing films," it required actual policemen to visit theaters and ensure compliance with the law.[74] But how was a police officer to know if the trailer for *Darwaza* playing in a nearby theater was identical to the version approved by the Bombay office of the censor board? The Cinematograph Act specified that all decisions of the censors "shall be published in the *Gazette of India*."[75] Therefore, in addition to carrying notices for government tenders, bids, closures, and job openings, the *Gazette* also printed weekly reports of decisions made by the film censors, along with notices, job openings, policy modifications, and other announcements from the board. These appeared under "Miscellaneous Notifications including Notifications, Orders, Advertisements and Notices Issued by Statutory Bodies," or section 4 of part III of "Ordinary" (that is, weekly) issues of the *Gazette*. Printed in runs approaching five thousand copies, bound copies of each issue would be carried out of the Faridabad compound by mailmen working for the Department of Post. Fanned across India by road, rail, and air, the *Gazette of India* or "Bharat Ka Rajpatra" (paper of India) eventually reached readers in cities and large towns.

A 1978 issue of the *Gazette* carried the censors' decision about the trailer for *Darwaza* among hundreds of decisions made by the censor board during the same period. *Gazette of India* (no. 37) carried the "particulars" of the *Darwaza* trailer across the country, landing on the desks of police officers and theater owners long after its sights and sounds were first marked up by the Bombay censors. In this fifty-page issue of the *Gazette*, censorship's particulars begin on page 5 and run for the next forty-five (censorship's particulars were almost always the longest section in *Gazette* issues in which they appeared). The *Gazette*'s typographic presentation registers the bureaucratic attempt to surveil the dispersive drives of the world's largest film culture. On the first of the *Gazette*'s pages, the centripetal trails of censorship—from India's port cities to its landlocked administrative center in the north—are inverted by the visual declension from the "Ministry of Information and Broadcasting" to the "Central Board of Film Censors." From here, inscriptions flow outward on and as paper, radiated in a centrifugal pattern that disperses a state-approved filmography across India. By consulting the *Gazette*, theatrical exhibitors and police officers far removed from film producers and state regulators could check for itemized deletions, or what were called "particulars," and verify the legal status of what was being screened.

But the *Gazette of India* (no. 37) was issued and printed in September 1978, nearly six months after the trailer for *Darwaza*—and the film—last played in Bombay theaters. In fact, films certified in Bombay in January 1978 were listed in September 1978 issues of the *Gazette*; films certified in September 1978 were listed in June 1979. Films certified in late 1979 did not appear at all in 1980 issues of the *Gazette*, nor in 1981, nor even in the first months of the following year. In the summer of 1982, the Cinematographer Exhibitors Association of India put out a plea to the central government to "keep the public (and in particular) exhibitors informed about the films certified by the CBFC by publishing the relevant information in the *Gazette of India*."[76] Exhibitors, a news story reported, were "particularly worried about this lapse on the part of the Government because, under Section 7 of the Cinematograph Act, 1952, an exhibitor is held responsible for the unauthorized exhibition of uncensored films and can be punished with imprisonment up to two years. While it is true that the exhibitor must get the censor certificate from the distributor whenever he takes up a film for exhibition, the CEAI says that he has no way of verifying the certificate's authenticity."[77] As anxiously felt duration, the delay in printing could well serve as another inscription of state power over popular cinema. (This delay may also have been synchronized to the industry's staggered distribution of film prints, a prior logic of physical delay. The *Gazette* could entirely miss the window of *Darwaza*'s run in Bombay but arrive ahead of it in Rajasthan and Uttar Pradesh.)

Paperwork was the "preparatory phase" of the *Gazette*.[78] The *Gazette's* delay may have indexed the material reality of how decentralized censorship was: an unavoidable result of all the typing, collating, retyping, mailing, collating, retyping, printing, and mailing scattered across a geographically sprawling operational chain. Bureaucracies may be "machines for the production of inscriptions," as Akhil Gupta has put it, but presses are machines for the production of printed paper.[79] Because it unfolds over physical space and in durational time, the very paper chain devised to realize synchronic surveillance also introduces a materiality not fully synchronized with the fantasy of centralized censorship. But the greater the delay, the more this asynchrony in the operation clarifies censorship as a time-based practice. Delay enables us to feel the "work done by censorship" for its temporality: not only the work of being offended but of being offended *in time*.[80]

A "repetitive, monotonous and stressful task that requires constant vigilance," film censorship is a form of what Arlie Hochschild has called "emotional labor."[81] Requiring "one to induce or suppress feeling" so that it "produces the proper state of mind in others," emotional labor constitutes the everyday of censorship.[82] Minute by minute, hour by hour, week by week, censoring films was intense, continuous, and ultimately invisible labor by the censor. The *Gazette* serves as a public receipt for the work performed in exchange for the considerable government-paid perks for being a censor: fees for attending film previews, verifying censored films, daily allowances and travel honoraria, and free admissions to movie theaters. That censorship's particulars converted everything into English also indicates that the *Gazette* was a medium of communication between elites. The government had placed censorial power "into the hands of a select caste," and censorship's particulars frequently read like an inscriptive performance whose anticipated audience was the state itself.[83] In *Gazette No. 37*, alongside the deletions from *Darwaza*'s trailer is a veritable catalog of perceived slights to state authority: "Delete the entire episode showing Sanjay Rao, bearing striking resemblance to Sanjay Gandhi"; "Reduce the comical behavior of three police constables in the Police outpost"; and "Delete the word "bloody" addressed to the Judge in the court."

Because the *Gazette* was perceived as providing a "peep" at "chair-bound bureaucrats" and what they removed from films, it could be read as a public archive of the emotional labor of censoring films.[84] More precisely, it reveals a work cycle in which the censors translated into print what they saw, felt, and did. The offensive image was the evidentiary object of this work, and its textual representation (the "particular") was the medium through which the work was expressed. The act of disappearing the offensive image makes the invisible work of the censor visible—provided it takes up space on paper. The offensive image has to be conjured via descriptive language that recodes moving images through words that move: adjectives, verbs, and other modifiers that lace feelings into the images seen. Such itemized "particulars" of every week in the *Gazette* are representations of a work cycle in which the censor saw and felt, then responded and removed, and finally wrote and published. There were no other images or sounds described in the *Gazette* that year as "frightening" or "fearful" besides those in *Darwaza*. Every new film supplies a new opportunity to make this regularized work visible by adding more print to the page. But if we take seriously the censor's delayed deletions as small sensory charges of feeling, we can feel the "microlabors of censorship" as they devolved on *Darwaza*'s expression of haunted time.[85]

As Reshma rotates into the world behind the door, the sequence chains the film's title to narrative and visual suspense that pulls viewers into the tempo of anticipation, uncertainty, and imminent revelation. Like all trailers, the trailer for *Darwaza* inhabits an "anticipatory, yet present, mode of temporality."[86] The present-continuous intensity of the sequence builds to its climactic revelations. The skeleton and the monster come into view over sixteen shots, most of them under a second long. The skeleton is first revealed in medium close-up as it almost completely rotates into view. Reshma backs away, and her screaming retreat is intercut with five close-ups of the skeleton along different, but not sequential, points along the arc of rotation. Once Reshma brushes up against its back, the monster begins turning around. The sequence intercuts this movement with views of the skeleton—somehow still rotating!—impossibly repeating positions along the arc.

As a formal property of the sequence, *rotation* links the revolving *darwaza* to monstrous bodies, to the time of ancestral sin coming full circle, to viewers returning to the gothic in Eastmancolor. It also instantiates the continuous present of the story as the continuous reanimation of the dead past. To "ex-cite" is to "set into motion": the sixteen shots are segments of single takes, manipulated such that the skeleton and monster emerge quite suddenly and yet very slowly.[87] They are the products of looped bits of film, which enable the skeleton and the monster to remain in perpetual revolution—a duration of emergence in which the viewer is suspended, always in the thick of a "new excitement in motion pictures." The rotating views of the skeleton dramatize Lim's claim that in films about haunting, "time does not merely move forward; it is subject to repetition and return," depicted as "both a return and a permeating presence that was never really put aside in the first place."[88] Along with blocking, makeup, and the musical score, the decoupage too privileges viewers, who experience *more time* than Reshma does: not only to witness the monster's gross visage behind her, but to continue to see the rotating skeleton even after Reshma has slipped out of frame and to hear her scream after she has stopped screaming. Horror time is the time of fantastic recursions, of a present continuously, and literally, made up of images of the past.

We know what was marked for deletion in this sequence: views of a skeleton and a monster, as well as the sounds of screaming. But to understand what was being censored we need to move beyond the itemization of deletions (see figure 9). The censors' ostensible focus was on the "frightening skeletons" and "fearful screams" of the trailer, but closer attention to the described deletions reveals the durational dimension of scenes of horror. By censoring the rotating sequence of skeleton and monster, the censors were recasting the very temporality that intensified the present: the long moment between the aftershock of discovery and before the onrush of death.

Fixing on the multiplication of instants—"views," "front and back views"—the censors were effectively censoring an experience of haunted time. For example, the censors did not target merely the monster, but "3.66 meters" of repeating "views of the Monster." *Darwaza*'s monsters, skeletons, and screams too are ultimately scratched down to their thingness as bits of celluloid: "3.66m," "2.44m," "6.10m." If we think of film as footage—6 meters, or 20 feet, or approximately 320 frames, or 13.3 seconds, of footage—it becomes apparent that depicted iconography or

					U				
B/83854/ 55	"Soviet (Colour) (USSR)	Railways"	English, Tam.,	212·00 (2)	86771 ———— 16-2-78 P.E.	USSR Consulate General.	Kiev Popular Science Film Studios.		
B/83443	'Dhyanu (Colour) (India)	Bhagat" (35 mm)	Punjabi	3901·67 (15)	U 86772 ———— 16-2-78	Dara Productions, 308, Daravilla, Juhu, Bombay-54.	Dara Productions, 308, Daravilla, Juhu, Bombay-54.	With mark.	triangle

Endorsement
B/83443
Film "Dhyanu Bhagat" (Punjabi) (Colour) (35 mm)
Original Length 3940·09 m.
U-cert. No. 86772 dated 16-2-1978.

Cut No.	Reel No.			Mtrs.
1.	XIV	: Delete the mockery by Akthar's men in the temple		38·42
		Actual length of the film after the aforesaid deletions will be :	3901·67 m. in 15 reels.	

					U				
B/84083	"Trailer of "Darwaza" (Colour) (India)	(35 mm)	Hindi	99·36 (1)	86773 ———— 16-2-78	Kiran Bombay.	Ramsay,	Kiran Bombay.	Ramsay, With mark.	triangle

Endorsement
B/84083
Original Length 105·46 m.

Cut No.			Mtrs.
1.	: Delete close-ups of front and back views of the Monster. Also delete the views of the frightening skeleton		3·66

Figure 9. Deleted "particulars" from the trailer for *Darwaza* (1978). *Source: Gazette of India*, 16 September 1978.

action within the frame does not fully explain what a "scene of horror" might have been. In going after skeletons and screams, the censor sought to put off the experience of horror—a kind of temporal jamming denoted by the delayed operations of film censorship.

The frightening skeleton of *Darwaza* is, in fact, described as the "frightening *skeletion* [*sic*]." Breaks in the fantasy of centralized censorship—which extend from the months of delayed print runs to the instants in which typographical errors were made on the page by a distracted stenographer—attune us to the institutional scale of censorship: thousands of films screened, feelings felt and then written up. On paper, this scale can distance the reader from the "particulars" of any one film; the eyes move off toward the surface of the page scored with print, where signifiers are driven to semiotic extreme and broken down to their material substrates.

"The Government *Gazette* is not a popular reading. It is not meant to be," observed one commentator in 1973.[89] "Its literary and production values," he continued, "seem deliberately to be devised to repel rather than attract readers. Even those who are forced to read some part of it by professional or business exigencies do not look at the rest."[90] Perhaps the *Gazette* was designed to be read, just not *too closely*. If you were to keep reading *Gazette* no. 37, as I did, you would see that the censors' decision about the film proper, *Darwaza*, also appears in this issue. Yet nothing was listed under it: its particulars were empty; nothing was removed by the censors from the film. The week of the film's release, the trade journal *Film Information* informed its readers that the film had been certified "without any cuts."[91] I had suspected as much. After all, *Darwaza*'s certificate did not bear the "triangle" mark, the sign that deletions were made before the film was certified. This triangle is clearly visible, by contrast, on the certificate for *Jaani Dushman* (discussed in the next chapter). But if there were no cuts made before *Darwaza* was certified, why had the film been refused a certificate to begin with?

There are papers beneath papers in the scriptural underworld of film censorship. A few months later, following Ms. Kelkar's advice, I visited the National Film Archive, with another letter of introduction in hand. Here I found a ledger of censorship decisions from 1978. The list was nearly identical to the one printed in the *Gazette of India*, except for one detail: the particulars of *Darwaza*'s censorship were not printed on the page. Instead, they had been written on the page by hand. The inked scrawl looked casual, even indifferent—no cuts, it too declared—but the entry's belated addition to the page suggested to me that some difficulty may have attended *Darwaza*'s certification, some more meaningful delay. Not everything the censor did is recorded in the *Gazette*. Sometimes it is in other places, such as in the censor script. In the next section I examine the film's censor script, the inked lines and flagged sections of which allow us to inhabit the bureaucratic encounter with "India's First Horror Film" as it unfolded in real time.

DISSOLVING IMAGES IN *DARWAZA*'S CENSOR SCRIPT

Darwaza's censor script is *not* the film's shooting script; it is not evidence of how the film's production was planned. In other contexts, such scripts have been used by censors to regulate films before they are made.[92] Following the unsealing of the Production Code of America (PCA) files, Stephen Prince has demonstrated how the PCA worked with American film studios in the 1930s to manage the incipient cycle of Hollywood horror films.

The typewritten letters, memos, and files moving speedily between studio bosses and administrators reveal a fascinating institutional arrangement in which censorship safeguarded the commercial interests of movie producers and the moral reputation of an industry of which the PCA itself was a part. The goal of "script approval," or "front-loaded" evaluation and recommendation was for films to circulate freely as soon as they were completed, with few or no "cuts" to the finished film required by the censor.[93] The purpose of *Darwaza*'s censor script was different.

The censor script is a bureaucratic genre: it is a "graphic artefact" through which filmmakers enter into a relationship with the censors.[94] The censor script is not a copy of the film's original screenplay or its shooting script. Instead, it is prepared by filmmakers for the censors and submitted along with the film at the time of application for certification. The censor script allows censors to mark shots for removal or modification. Shared with filmmakers after the screening, the script allows filmmakers to track what changes the censors want to see and provides the censors with a record of what was ordered deleted from the film so that the film could be certified.

Unlike the deletions and decisions printed in the *Gazette of India*, the censor script of *Darwaza* did not have an intended public function. Rather, the script moved along the back channels of censorship, allowing decisions made during a private screening to be relayed back to the film's producer. The operations of censorship separated the Ramsay Brothers from *Darwaza*, because they were not allowed into the preview theater. "All previews of films for the purpose of examination," the state deemed, "and the reports and records relating thereto shall be treated as confidential."[95] Often, members of examining committees would not know what movie they would be watching till they had arrived at the preview theater. Producers were informed of decisions only via registered post. Confidential records from the screening included individual reports, or "verdicts," written by each member of the examining committee, as well as the annotated censor script. As an instrument and record of the censorship process, *Darwaza*'s censor script traces the censors' and filmmakers' private negotiations over what "India's First Horror Film" would be.

Darwaza's censor script is substantial.[96] It consists of 122 foolscap pages, with three holes running along the left edge that were threaded through into a cloth-bound folder in a red hard cover. Foliation is by reel. For example, the nine pages detailing the first reel are numbered 1.1–1.9; the five pages detailing the second reel are numbered 2.1–2.5. Each page of the script breaks moving images down into columns of information. Page 1.1 of the script, for example, scripts the first 167 feet of the film. Beginning with the appearance of the Ramsay Brothers' family monogram to medium close-up shots of the thakur laying prone in his bed, the script transcribes approximately one minute and fifty-one seconds of running time (at twenty-four frames per second). Reading from left to right, the transcript notes the location of footage being described, then the observed camera position or movement, followed by a description of what is seen and, finally, a description of what is heard on the sound track. For example: "54, Medium Shot, The Thakur's Portrait, Voice: This is my curse, Thakur." Reading from top to bottom, the script lists shots in the order in which they appear, noting the elapsed length of footage. For example, immediately following the medium shot of the portrait, the next line of the script reads: "56, Medium Shot, A Woman's Portrait, Voice: Your family too shall." The script rationalizes cinematic time into segments made for easy identification and removal; such segmentation allowed the flagging of specific lengths of footage, along with shots and lines of dialogue or sound effects on paper.

The censor script helps us track the extent of "voluntary deletions" made by the Ramsay Brothers, giving the lie to reports that the film had been cleared for release "without any cuts." On page 2.1, a shot of "Lightning" has been struck through; it is missing from the second reel of the film. On 7.5, a shot of "Ghost" has been struck through and is not found in the seventh reel. And on 13.2 and 13.3, multiple shots of the skeleton, monster, owl, and Reshma screaming have been marked up; they are also absconding from the film (more on this owl later). Next to struck-through lines, "Deleted" appears, an indication of a directive followed through on. Like all producers, the Ramsay Brothers would have been required to deposit a print of the censored film with the board for a year following the release of *Darwaza*. This print—which the state did not pay for the printing of—was naturally of interest to the film's producers, who could recoup its value by circulating it as a projection print. In order to have the print returned to them, the Ramsay Brothers would have had to submit "to the

Board the full shooting script of the film together with dialogues" in exchange for a "release order."[97] This function was served by the film's censor script: returning now as a post facto "shooting script," held by the censor board and eventually the National Film Archive (where I read it).

On the signed cover letter that accompanies this archival copy of the script, the Ramsay Brothers "certify" that the script that follows is "an exact copy of the film as certified by the board with complete dialogue song, sound effects and picturization."[98] But it is, of course, not an "exact copy": for one thing, it is the film in another medium, paper. For another, its pages record not only what is in the film but what was removed from the film before it was certified. Finally, it is not an exact copy of the film because, though it is a genre devised by the state for surveillance over cinema, the script's status—as a paper proxy for film—transforms it into a screening device.

Because the script represents a finished film and determines how it will be read by the censors, it does more than describe some prior action on film: "itself a form of action," it remakes the film and directs the censor.[99] The censor script was a genre for which specialized writers existed, and the best-compensated scriptwriters to this day are those who ensure that the film most easily passes the censors, not the ones who most faithfully reproduce what is onscreen. While there could be "no obvious discrepancies between the script prepared and the film screened," one such scriptwriter detailed how "careful omissions, glossed-over segments, unnecessary detail, emphases on portions that are likely to go down well with the Committee, are staples of [the] censor script."[100] This presentational awareness persists in perceptible divergences between how moments in the film play out on-screen and how they are described on the page—a cannier deflection of the censor's attention through aspects of the page. In *Darwaza*'s censor script, while every line of expository dialogue is transcribed correctly, "script time" appeared to shrink the cinematic duration of other elements of the film: the graphic space of the page disavowed what was spectacularly *there* on-screen. I focus on one such area of the script next.

Early in *Darwaza*, one villager reports: "No one has seen its face till today, and they who have, have been struck blind, crazy, and dumb, so they could never tell anyone what it was they saw." The thakur's metamorphosis is therefore the climax of the film and of the Ramsay Brothers' years-long dream of making a full-fledged horror film: not a mask that

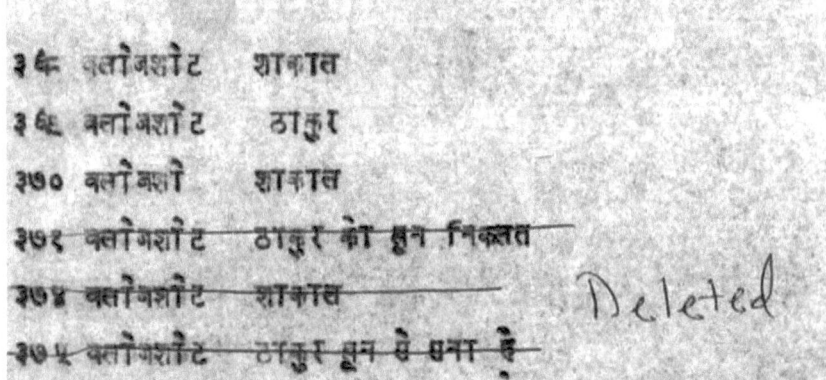

Figure 10. Removals indicated in *Darwaza*'s censor script (1978). *Source:* National Film Archive of India, Pune, file no. 10872/1.

comes off, but a face that bleeds into another. *Darwaza* suspends the fullest visible evidence of the monster's existence until the final reel of the film, when we see the thakur transform into the gnarly beast before a villager's eyes (and behind a closed door). This transformation is transcribed on pages 15.4 and 15.5 of the censor script. A vertical stack forms on these pages: nearly two dozen lines that describe what we see in these shots as "Close shot: Thakur." The script reflects and intensifies the "uncountability" of horror on the page, such that the scattering of a single take into multiple shots could be read as evading the censor's fetishistic fixation on any one shot as offensive.[101] By describing the climactic sequence as a series of shots of "Thakur," the script clears this space in the script of graphic variety and interest—even presence. Slimly, the vertical stack cascades down the page and guides the reader to turn to the next one. Graphic detail focuses the censor's attention on what needs deleting and away from what appears unremarkable. Put another way: the censor script is not a script that merely describes what is being seen; sometimes, it scripts what is seen (or not seen) in the film (see figure 10).[102]

In the censor script, the transformation terminates with two lines that read "Close shot: Thakur bleeds" and "Close shot: Thakur saturated with blood." As the transcription of what is on-screen, the script falls short: the thakur isn't only covered in blood; his face bleeds into flesh. The scripted lie might have snapped the censor to attention, corporealizing them as a body confronted with surprise on-screen. Surprise generates the historical stain of the encounter: ink, which cuts across these two shots. These two shots, which have been struck through with what appears to have been a fine-tipped blue ballpoint pen, instantiate the real time of the act of censorship. When censors struck through lines of dialogue or shots in the script, they seem to have been striking back into the past as if to re-script the film before them for a future audience watching the film. Yet the pages also record a core of something like a real time: when a pen made contact with a page, a particular instant was registered, "call[ing] attention to specific moments of difficulty or stress" for the censor.[103] In these moments, we can discern the gothic temporality of opening doors and surfacing secrets in *Darwaza*—the art of surprise via thunder and lightning, screams, and slow reveals—assuming shape in handmade annotations.

In becoming suddenly visible, the hand of the censor draws attention to another invisible hand. If the censor script is haunted by the hidden hand of the censor who drew across the page in ink, then on-screen animation is haunted by tactile contact as well.[104] The Ramsays had produced the terrifying transformation in detail as the thakur's face appeared to rapidly bleed *into* the face of the monster. "It was only a 30 second scene," recalled Keshu Ramsay. "But we had to shoot for 10 days to get the right effect." As he explained in an interview with *Bombay* magazine: "The transformation was shot frame by frame on a special camera that clicks one print per second. The actor, Trilok Kapoor, had to remain lying down for eight hours, surviving on juices. We would apply some make-up, shoot a little, add to the make-up, shoot again."[105] The transformation unfolds over fifteen discrete shots, which editor Bal Korde intercut with reaction shots of Shakaal (Imtiaz Khan) looking on. The thakur's hair and beard grow long and gray; his skin turns black and leathery; his eyes cry fine rivulets of blood, which stream down his face; and finally, the mark of a shining *trishul* (holy trident) arises out of his forehead to the sound of a temple bell, a reminder that the curse that is surfacing now was placed by a distressed devotee. Human touch transformed the visage of the thakur: a touch that is visually effaced but remains perceptible in the sequence, in the intervals of which was the corporeal effort of adding makeup between the printing of shots ("add the makeup, shoot again").

In *Darwaza*, the transformation between human and monster is made possible by a series of dissolves that bridge the gaps between the hundreds of stills made during the shoot. The decision to stage the transformation on-screen, in a close-cropped composition using interval photography (thereby converting eighty hours' worth of stills into thirty seconds of footage, in turn divided into fifteen shots) had consequences for the way the transformation appears to happen. As the frames accrete, incremental visual changes congeal in stop-start fashion and fill the screen. So closely cropped to the face, the frame disorients spatially and temporally. Halfway through the sequence, the shot flips laterally, creating strange microtemporalities and spatial geometries as the viewer attempts and sometimes fails to make sense of the stuff on-screen: skin, paint, blood, light, and shadow. Playing the film back slowly, trying to break the sequence back down to its constituent stills, I would find myself asking: What am I looking at? Recall that those who saw the monster "could never tell anyone what it was they saw"; this very postponement is spurred by the dissolving images of *Darwaza*.

If horror succeeds by pushing past the proper use of the cinematic medium, *Darwaza*'s evasions suggest that the art of horror is an art of failing in time—of stymieing the "ongoing work of interpretation we pursue as film viewers."[106] What, where, and when are scenes of horror? In the updated code, the only occasion on which the word *scene* appears is also the only time the word *horror* appears. Are they scenes that depict acts one might call horrific? Are they scenes that perceptually produce horror? There is a difficulty here that the phrase is unable to outpace: horror is being produced as something that is both on-screen and off, visual and experiential, outstripping definitional capture, a particular place where visibility and legibility collapse onto one another. "Scenes of horror" articulates the difficulty of articulation, postponing the discursive capture of a genre that thrives when "speaking the unspeakable, showing the unwatchable."[107]

The horizontal line that bisects the word *blood* (blood) becomes an incisive instruction to manage the dissolves, leading to the recutting of *Darwaza*'s climactic transformation. The Ramsay Brothers modified the fifteen-shot transformation following the censor's deletions on the script; there are now thirteen surviving shots in the sequence. Yet it is possible that footage of the bleeding man was not so much deleted as redivided and sped up: we still see the thakur bleed, but in the shots prior to the ones deleted. The "voluntarily" deleted images have been deleted, but perhaps they have only been moved from the position they occupied in the filmstrip (and on the page)—slipped in with the images described as "Thakur." Nothing may eventually have been *removed* from this sequence in *Darwaza* but the medium's powers of delay.

What matters, then, is not what the censors did to *Darwaza*, but what the film did to censorship: that before the code revised *Darwaza*, *Darwaza* revised the code. By 1979, when the board was faced with a new wave of horror films in the wake of *Darwaza*'s success, it was "reiterat[ing] that government's guidelines in the matter of horror films were specific: 'Pointless or avoidable scenes of violence, cruelty and horror should not be shown.'"[108] The guideline pertaining to "scenes of horror" was used to delay, censor, and ban horror films throughout the 1980s. Yet even after the code was published, a minister in Parliament would be heard remarking on "the undesirability of screening horror films," urging the censor board to frame "an official policy on screening (or not screening) films in this genre."[109] No official policy, or list of unacceptable images, was ever created; this aporia is what allowed the censors to remain arbitrarily effective. In the months and years that followed, horror films would run into trouble because they "hurt the sentiment and susceptibility of human beings" and were "more than what people could stomach."[110] The recourse to stomachs hurt by scenes of horror—alongside itemized objections to superstition and violence—kept censorship flexible.

The code also sparked the improvisatory forms of Bombay horror over the years to come: it allowed filmmakers to experiment and the censors to police experimentation. Though scenes like the ones in *Darwaza* would not again appear too frequently in Bombay horror oeuvre, censorship never managed to fully extinguish the affective appeals of "scenes of horror." As we will see in chapters 3 and 4, censorship shifted the stylistic preferences of filmmakers away from the durational expanse of editing and optical effects toward displays of profilmic bodies and spaces.

PAPER BECOMES CINEMA

Darwaza's certificate was photographed and placed at the head of the film print, and running it through the projector turned (state) paperwork into (popular) cinema. Censorship is expressed as, and becomes apprehensible in, the time of cinema. When the bureaucracy was joined, quite literally, to the body of *Darwaza*, the certificate switched material registers: from immovable type into moving images, from paper to photographic frames. As an emblem of state power, the certificate goes wherever the film goes. As a moving image, the certificate has a different life from that of its paper original: it will circulate widely, it will exist past the "expiry date" on the certificate, and it may persist even if the original paper document is lost or destroyed. It will age as film, not as paper. The film remains the only place I have found *Darwaza*'s censor certificate. Censorship, then, is archived by cinema.

Let me explain by drawing attention to an observant owl that witnesses Reshma's demise in the film's trailer. The owl evokes *Bride of Frankenstein* (James Whale, 1935). In that film, an owl watches as Frankenstein's monster kills an aging man and his wife in a flooded cave under a windmill. Tulsi Ramsay recounted watching *Bride of Frankenstein* in a Bombay theater as a young man and has cited it as a family favorite. Reshma too dies underground when the monster passes a claw over her eyes, as though inducing a fatal trance under which she slips out of frame. This gesture, in which a blocked line of vision substitutes for physical violence, is a token of how filmmakers devise conventions through a continuous negotiation with the codes of censorship.[111] The contactless claw tacitly acknowledges the gaze of the censor; like the watchful owl that stares at Reshma's killing, the censor is *inside* the scene of horror in its iconography and part of the durational experience of *Darwaza*.

Indeed, as I have suggested, the proliferation of views and dilations of time in *Darwaza* must be understood also as a practice of creative fragmentation undertaken to evade the censor's fixation on any one shot as offensive. Likewise, it was during negotiations over the violence in *Bride of Frankenstein* that the owl emerged prominently in the finished film. Before that film's release in 1935, several shots in the windmill sequence were removed on instructions from the Production Code Administration, "covered" over with repeated images of an owl looking on.[112] In effect, the looped shots of the owl mark the temporality of censorship as it manifests within the film. Paying homage to the film via its winged watcher, *Darwaza* spectrally inscribes this history of censorship inside the scene of horror. Therefore, when the censor's pen makes contact with a page in the censor script to strike through a shot—"Owl"—the script registers a moment in which the experience of cinematic horror contains within it an experience of censorship.

Cinema circulates censorship—its ideologies, practices, politics, and paperwork—as abrupt cuts and colorful damage within the circuits of the popular. Chapter 2 reads cinema as an archive of censorship's practices, its anxieties and beliefs. Rather than examining paperwork as the site for the storage and retrieval of images that were taken out of circulation, I explore the censored film as a visual record of censorship. The chapter examines the spectral materiality of celluloid censorship by looking at noise generated in the physical regulation of the master negative of *Jaani Dushman*.

2 Celluloid Splatter

THE GRAPHIC VIOLENCE OF *JAANI DUSHMAN*

In Rajkumar Kohli's 1979 horror film *Jaani Dushman* (Mortal enemy), a monster hunts young brides in the valley, abducting them from wedding processions wending their way across the countryside. Every bride—dressed in bright red finery, crying as she departs in a palanquin, carried by her pall-bearing family to her new home—is suddenly snatched into the beast's cave. When the corpse of yet another bride is discovered in the underbrush, a policeman tells another: "Whenever a palanquin passes through this area, the bride is killed suddenly." But how are the brides killed? Horror films, as discussed in the previous chapter, estrange us from a habitual experience of time. They can also make it difficult for viewers to assume a stable orientation in space. Space warps as the women die in the cave. One bride hears the beast snarl from far away; the next moment, she has been viciously mauled. Another bride crumples against the rocky walls of the cave, while the beast lurches distantly. But it isn't only the occlusive design of the warrens, the moves of a supernatural predator, or the stylized shocks of montage. *Jaani Dushman*'s images of screaming women, outstretched claws, and sprays of red on wedding finery seem to split under pressure, like they are being forced off the screen against their will. As they depart, the images leave strange spectra in their wake:

Figure 11. Celluloid damage redividing the frame in *Jaani Dushman* (1979). *Source:* Shankar Movies, frame grab from Time DVD.

flashing white lines can be seen redividing the pillared cave, while welters of gray spread in cobwebbed corners and neon splotches break out over bridal reds (see figure 11).

My bewilderment at *Jaani Dushman*'s visual incoherence first led me on the trail of censorship documents to understand what, if anything, was removed from the film by the state-run censor board. As we saw in the previous chapter, such documents can reveal the back channels of film censorship, in which filmmakers and censors mutually prepare a film for release. The censorship of *Jaani Dushman*, I discovered, was no polite negotiation or creative détente. The "film has a terrifying sensation," the chairman of the censor board declared, pinning his complaint on the fact that *Jaani Dushman* "contains a number of pointless killings."[1] Accordingly, hundreds of feet of footage depicting the monster's attacks on terrified brides were deemed unsuitable for audiences and removed from the film. "A [censor] certificate has been issued to Raj Kumar Kohli's *Jaani*

Dushman," reported *Cine Blitz* in 1979, adding that "this controversial film suffered much at the hands of the censors, resulting in great loss."[2]

In censoring horror films, the censor board would gain infamy as the "slaughterhouse where films were butchered."[3] That phrase was used by the journalist Khalid Mohamed in the pages of the daily national newspaper *Times of India*. Before he became a film journalist for the newspaper, Mohamed cut his teeth on the Bombay crime beat. He wrote of trailing "forensic experts zigzag[ging] past bodies on cold stone slabs," and of police officers "smelling the smell of blood."[4] As though still reporting from a crime scene, Mohamed now informed his readers that the censors were "killing" and "castrating" films.[5] Since he believed that the ordinary viewer "of course is absolutely unaware of what goes on behind the scenes," Mohamed dutifully revealed that while many films were "get[ting] the knife," the "axe has fallen hard, particularly on horror films."[6]

When the axe of censorship falls too hard, viewers do not remain oblivious. One viewer in Calcutta who watched the American serial killer film *The Eyes of Laura Mars* (Irvin Kershner, 1978) in the theater wrote in to *Film World*, "appalled to find the pace getting too fast as considerable portions of the film had apparently found their way to the collections of our 'moral uplifters!'"[7] When the satanic horror film *The Exorcist* was released in 1978, a fan found the film so "ruthlessly censored" that it prompted him to wonder aloud in *Filmfare* if soon "instead of showing the film they will merely show the title and then draw the curtain!"[8] "I wonder," he mused, "what made the censors hack the film like this."[9] Likewise, when thousands of frames disappeared from *Jaani Dushman*, their disappearance recast what remained. Absence riddles the film's story world: scenes of horror are spatially and temporally discontinuous, incomplete both visually and narratively. At the same time, censorship contaminates the scene of horror with a surplus of presence, leaving behind lines and shapes of varying hues and textures. The perceptibility of censorship during my viewing of *Jaani Dushman* is a reminder that censorship, rather than always operating "behind the scenes," is sometimes in the scene.

The first time a monster strangles a bride to death in *Jaani Dushman*, a close-up of the bride's face as she dies fighting for air cuts quickly to a wide shot of a train whistle blowing steam—a literal smoke screen! Such imagistic strategies of self-censoring euphemism and displacement are widespread in films that feature extreme acts. Demonstrating that the "craft of screen violence" is responsive to "regulatory constraint," Stephen Prince has outlined some conventions that filmmakers have devised to bypass scrutiny.[10] For example, Prince notes, a film could convey violence to the human body by showing "environmental damage" to surrounding spaces and objects; he calls this "substitutional emblematics."[11] Writing about rape-revenge films of the 1980s, Ranjani Mazumdar illustrates how the films deliberately withhold direct visual evidence of rape and instead resort to its dispersal through other registers such as the sound track, which give "evidence" to the "unspeakable."[12] Therefore, filmmakers make films with knowledge of what is unshowable, so that all films made to receive censor certificates may be considered censored films.[13] Lalitha Gopalan analyzes editing conventions developed by Bombay filmmakers to preempt the censor's cut, such as the withdrawal of the camera from a scene of amorous passion.[14] The censor's oversight is thus incorporated *into* the conventions of filmic expression. But such conventions have evolved as responses to the use of force, such as when censors roughly remake films.[15] From the same sequence in *Jaani Dushman*, the censors required that a shot of the monster "strangulating [the bride] with his hand" be removed.[16] Thus, the final assembly of images records a specific instance of regulation as well as regulation's generative effects on film conventions. It is as though, in the movement from gasping bride to blowing whistle, the film could be felt thinking about censorship as both already done and yet to come. In the same sequence, from frame to frame, a blueish-green tint rises and falls over the images. In proscribing the graphic violence of the film—what were termed its "lingering details"—censorship produced widespread environmental damage that lingers.

Filmmakers are censors, but censors are filmmakers too: deleting the "pointless violence" of *Jaani Dushman*, censorship left aesthetic traces of its own destructive path through the film.[17] During my viewing of Bombay horror films, such traces continuously deformed distinctions between representation and record, signal and noise, film style and film stock. In *Cheekh*, a serial killer's knife contends with black frames that drop in and out of view. In *Veerana*, the descent of a sawmill blade on a man's head brings on white streaks that dance and dissipate. When Vinod Talwar submitted his first horror film, *Raat Ke Andhere Mein*, to the censors, he was asked to submit in writing a promise that "whatever we will cut you will accept."[18] He agreed, but "they cut my film very badly," causing what he called "jumping cuts" on-screen.[19] Such "jagged visual edges" of a film can surface a "possible submerged history" of cinema.[20] Similar "jumping cuts" in *Jaani Dushman* had made me ask: What happened to the brides? Soon that gave way to another question: What happened to the film?

Damaged images inscribe the deep time of their physical lives as phenomenal data we might dismiss as failures within the representation. Instead, as Susan Schuppli proposes, a forensic excavation can "radicalize what matters as evidence"; it can "explore the ways in which matter archives and refracts complex histories" to yield "significant information in defiance or excess of that which appears self-evident within the representational field of the image."[21] Beyond the representational field of *Jaani Dushman*, beyond fantastical injuries done by a monster to human bodies, there lies aesthetic evidence of another history. What happened to the women in *Jaani Dushman*, where did they disappear to, who killed them, and how—these riddles take on forensic resonance in the regulation of the film by the censor board. Because *Jaani Dushman*'s sequences of "pointless violence" were the only sequences in the film to be regulated by the state, these sequences are also archives of state violence. Like a dead body on cold stone or blood at the scene of a crime, *Jaani Dushman* now confronts its viewers as what remains. What we do with such remains determines what institutional histories can be recalled and what will be "allowed to be forgotten."[22]

THE FRAME OF HORROR

The resonance between the violence of *Jaani Dushman* and its censorship is not mere parallelism. Instead, it reveals the the centrality of the filmic frame to our experience of horror film space. The frame is the first and fundamental means by which visual anxiety is generated, as the play of light, color, and sound dissolves the bounds of spatial certainty. By creating relations between foreground and background elements of the frame, as well as between what is inside the frame and what is outside of it, the frame determines the experience of cinematic space. This space may have no referent outside or inside the film; instead, its reality is of the frame and our viewing of it. More than a slowly opening window, creaking trapdoor, or translucent shower curtain in the story world, the frame is our portal: our spatial perception is tied to the frame, its deep recesses, and its edges. The film makes human bodies vulnerable; the frame makes our vision vulnerable.

For viewers of horror films, "nothing is quite as unsettling as the task of spectating a character who realizes she is lost within and beyond the cinematic frame."[23] Rather than allowing us to master a "defined, verifiable" space, the frame of horror opens out to the infinite open beyond; it generates a "topography" of uncertainty, one that "implicitly resists any attempts to be readily understood and interpreted and instead invites us to interrogate the implied space that lies outside it."[24] This vulnerability is one I contended with throughout my engagement with *Jaani Dushman*. The monster might lunge into the frame or a bride fall out of it. I squint uneasily.

Horror films teach the viewer to see in(to) the dark: to understand that what is in the frame may be in excess of what is patently, or instantly, visible within it. To arrive at empty spaces, open vistas, and mere nothingness on-screen is to feel that someone or something is very much there without being visible. A bride's disorientation in the darkness, therefore, is scary not only because she is in a dark cave but because looking for her in the dark frame foments an experience of "spatial otherness," "a mise-en-scene in which the scene is . . . beyond what can be seen."[25] Look longer and your eyes adjust to the darkness. Something comes into view.

This chapter divides its focus between two kinds of splatter: the blood that stains the walls of the cave in *Jaani Dushman* and the damaged surface of the film, a colorfully mottled canvas on which bursts of blue, yellow, white and green, lines, circles, and misshapen specimens scatter over the film. The "contingent marks that gather on the surface of any one film," Katherine Groo has demonstrated, should not be dismissed as "impediments to film history—the very obstacles that film historians and archivists would need to remove in order to grasp at this thing called 'history'—or extraneous to any understanding of it."[26] While young women are carried in palanquins to their awful deaths in the underground cave, the "violated frames" of *Jaani Dushman* can lead us elsewhere—back inside the slaughterhouse of censorship, where the hands and instruments of the state are seen and felt on the body of the film.[27]

By digging down into *Jaani Dushman*, reconstructing its shattered images, and zooming into the edges, we see how the embodied process of cutting operates on and in fictional sequences of abduction, murder, and violation. These intensely felt incisions temper ethnographies of censorship that have discovered how much boredom, inattention, and casual viewing are involved in censorship.[28] They challenge us to see on-screen a simple verification of what we have "already learned by other means."[29] The "materiality of representation," writes Christopher Pinney, "creates its own force field," so that the image is both a reflection of "struggles elsewhere" and a "site of struggle itself."[30] Reading surfaces draws us into the "corporeality of the image," a "zone in which new narratives are established that may be quite disjunct from the familiar stories of a nonvisual history."[31]

Jaani Dushman prompts recognition of how the typically invisible practices of bureaucratic surveillance operate in, and become sensible through, the aesthetic effects of their technological operations. When film censors experience "an affective intensity" in the act of examining moving images, they seek to excise those images so that the affective intensity "is not even allowed to register on the body of the public at-large."[32] Censorship is a practice of semiotic and sensory control, but this practice is stubbornly material. In order to cut *out* offending scenes of horror from *Jaani Dushman*, censorship had to cut *into* the film. Whatever reasons the censors gave for censoring *Jaani Dushman*—and there were many, ranging from the film's "terrifying sensation" to its "pointless violence" to "ladies . . . being killed" to its "superstition"—the form those reasons took was the same: interventions into the film print. But these interventions set in motion an unpredictable physical process, one that interrupted the integrity of the filmstrip and the visible world of the film. As it revised the perceptible surface of *Jaani Dushman*, its signifying and sensory capacities, the censor's attention was forcefully inscribed onto the body of the film. As a result, it is censorship's affective intensity that registers on my viewing body during the scene of horror.

It initially seemed to me that the point of the censors cutting into *Jaani Dushman* was not to make something invisible by cutting it out, but simply to make cutting visible. The goal may not have been to produce a properly purged or purified text acceptable for viewing, but rather to interpolate a visible hesitation, resistance, or interference into the moment of reception. When watching a damaged film, you may feel that "there were so many scratches, jumps, gaps, and tears that it felt like gazing at, not through, a curtain behind which—far away—the actual story was taking place."[33] I came to realize, however, that damage to the frame doesn't so much draw a veil over the "actual story" of the film as help tell it by other means, inverting relations between surface and depth, figure and ground.

Cinema is the creative "art of destroying images," Paolo Cherchi Usai writes, drawing attention to the destructive nature of creative acts.[34] Censorship used *Jaani Dushman* as its medium of expression; its traces also coauthor the scene of horror in *Jaani Dushman (Revised)* (as the film is titled on its censor certificate). Staring at the damaged frames of *Jaani Dushman*, I sense another stare, someone or something watching and waiting. *Jaani Dushman*'s frayed visual world is thus an embodiment of threateningly tactile vision. As monster and victim, censor and viewer circle one another, the film attunes us to the horror of being observed from the shadows by a covert entity that can reach out and grab the body of a bride or a frame of the film at any second. The state has effectively created a different kind of horror film, wherein a material history of governmental oversight may be experienced no less sensationally or superstitiously than the representations that were removed from the film.

UNLAYERING *JAANI DUSHMAN*

"India's First Multi-Starrer Horror Film," *Jaani Dushman* featured some of the biggest stars of the 1970s—among them Jeetendra, Reena Roy, Yogeeta Bali, Shatrugan Sinha, and Sunil Dutt—as friends and lovers frolicking in a village nestled in a mountain valley. The plot is baroque in the way masala movies are and is presented through an alternation of action sequences, romantic duets, and comic pratfalls. In its review of the film, the *Times of India* was dismissive. "It's meant to be a horror film, but instead of chills and goose flesh, all you get is a cheap display of actresses wearing tight costumes and actors wearing tight faces."[35] (The film, the paper opined, "was banned by the censor board and ought to have remained so.")[36] The sense of disappointment would be shared decades later by horror aficionado Pete Tombs. In his cult cinema magnum opus *Mondo Macabro*, Tombs describes *Jaani Dushman* as a film in which "brief scenes of horror" are "scattered through a multi-layered plot."[37] But the film is more "multilayered" than Tombs may have realized. For one thing, it places a monster's cave under a pastoral idyll. For another, *Jaani Dushman* carefully insinuates a horror film into position beneath melodramatic terrain.

As *Jaani Dushman* begins, many young women, including Champa (Rekha), Gauri (Neetu Singh), and Bindiya (Sarika), are coming of age and will soon be wed. Sending them into marriage brings the village together as a family, singing and dancing in ecstatic celebration with the blessings of the towering thakur (Sanjeev Kumar).[38] But someone haunts this pastoral idyll: the ghost of a man who was poisoned on his wedding night and now haunts the living world, seeking revenge. Looking to avenge himself on any bride, the ghost enters the bodies of living men and turns them into the bridicidal monster. The monster lives in the caves under the village, from where he emerges to interrupt weddings, to abduct brides and kill them. The repeated killings prompt panic, and the village responds with a militarization of the processional routes; gunmen begin to accompany the bridal palanquins. The film concludes with the local police joining hands (literally) with the villagers to rein in the monster and destroy him by exposing him to sunlight. *Jaani Dushman* ends when those who have survived the monster's bloodlust are happily paired with the ones they love; the film concludes with young lovers singing to one another on their *suhaag raat* (wedding night).

As a melodrama, *Jaani Dushman* ably dramatizes the various kinds of psychological violence and physical intimidation women suffer in a feudal patriarchy, ranging from forced marriage to daily harassment. The women speak persuasively about their narrow lives in the feudal family; in near-direct-address declamatory speeches accompanied by mournful music, framed in medium close-up and voiced by appealingly familiar stars, they describe what it means to be property, to be promised to old men in childhood. The melodramatic mode expresses the torment of these women who are daily harassed, objectified, and bartered. As the film's heroines seek receptive audiences in the men around them—the fathers, brothers, and lovers who embody the village's oppressive religious orthodoxy and feudal patriarchy—*Jaani Dushman* addresses its historical moment.

In 1972, a young girl was raped by two constables in a police station a few hours from Bombay. In 1976 the Bombay High Court sentenced the men to prison, but when their appeal reached the Supreme Court in Delhi in 1978, the convictions were overturned. The Supreme Court ruled that absent evidence of a direct physical threat to her life, the girl's submission to sexual intercourse could not be construed as rape—that she had, in fact, given consent. The justices concluded that the girl, named Mathura in proceedings to protect her identity, gave consent because she did not scream and there were no apparent marks or bruises on her body. Sparking outrage with its narrow interpretations of consent, evidence, and force, the Mathura rape case, as it came to be known, unfolded alongside a rapidly changing women's movement focused on broader questions of autonomy, marriage, reproduction, and work.[39] By "exposing the fallacy underlying what was overwhelmingly assumed to the private affair of the family," activists "pointed out that these issues were public and social."[40]

Thus, when one bride in *Jaani Dushman* vows to kill herself rather than be married against her will, while another bride laments hopelessly, "This has been happening for a thousand years," we see how popular cinema articulates a historical crisis in the affective forum of melodrama.[41] Via the aural and visual mise-en-scène, melodrama expresses what realist genres of reportage may not be able to. "Like neurotic symptoms," writes Ben Singer, what is beyond capture "finds an outlet through other channels of expression."[42] *Jaani Dushman*'s most emphatically melodramatic channel is the *bidaii* (farewell) song "Chalo Re Doli" ("Come Let Us Carry the Bridal Palanquin"), which is heard when every wedding ceremony is at its climax at dusk, accompanied by close-ups of the distraught bride in tears over a marriage she hasn't consented to, being carried away into the sunset by the men of the village. Yet, *Jaani Dushman* insists, the expressive powers of melodrama aren't quite enough. The teary farewell song, instead of adequately ventilating the trauma of the unfolding event, turns out to be a threshold to a different expressive mode. The monster lurks in a forgotten cave system that undergirds the village center and drags his victims down with him.

While melodrama expressed the torment of women who are daily harassed, objectified, and bartered in a feudal village, horror throws those same women to their deaths in an airless cave. In terminal moments, the film compresses the women's situations of entrapment into truly exit-free nightmares. Sad songs and teary close-ups give way to the screams, blood, and angled perspectives; as the men of the village literally carry the women to certain death, *Jaani Dushman* returns social and psychic violence as physical, deadly, and bloody violence. The climactic stroke of death that often concludes melodrama—by a long illness or sudden accident—is here supplied by something underneath the melodrama. The stratification of village and cave is therefore also a relation between genres: when the melodrama of film's heroines cannot be resolved aboveground, the space of horror opens up to swallow them.

Horror is therefore carefully tipped out of melodrama rather than meaninglessly "scattered" alongside song-and-dance celebrations of family, romance, and marriage. The film, it seems, endlessly allegorizes: the social and political are transformed into "private affairs" of marriage, consent, autonomy, and social death, which are in turn transformed into cave-dwelling monsters and murderous dismemberment. Supreme Court judgments and government reports about dowry killings and marital rape, songs and sermons about child marriage and family honor; these are laminated within the fantastical. "Multilayered," indeed—scratch through the fantastical laminations of horror, and you may encounter historical reality.

Eventually, history and fantasy end the same way. As the bride is hunted down, her body outstrips generic, fantastical, even cinematic coding; she returns the screams and bruises that Supreme Court justices thought missing. This moment very nearly collapses the distance between the layers that separate fantasy and history, surface and depth. The drive to produce horror has also supplied imagistic evidence and so has short-circuited the allegorical laminations of genre. And so, the image must be displaced again. Controlling what of the bride's body could be seen and heard, censorship interrupted the "multilayered" displacements of *Jaani Dushman* as both representational fiction and material artifact.

THE CLUTCHES OF THE CENSOR

In 1979, when explaining its decision not to certify *Jaani Dushman*, the Ministry of Information and Broadcasting reminded filmmakers "that government's guidelines in the matter of horror films were specific: 'Pointless or avoidable scenes of violence, cruelty and horror should not be shown.'"[43] What is pointless violence, and why must it not be shown? Violence was only entertainment—this, at least, was the line taken by Bombay film producers in the late 1970s. To hear them tell it, according to Aruna Vasudev, commercial cinema violence was to be understood as unrealistic, harmless, meaningless, "a form of adventure."[44] By comparison, "small-budget noncommercial films" were thought to do "greater damage because the violence they show is real": "The suicide in *Garam Hawa* [A hot wind, M. S. Sathyu, 1973], the beating of the poor laborer in *Ankur* [The seedling, Shyam Benegal, 1974], the clash of caste in *Kaadu* [The jungle, Girish Karnad, 1973], the rape of the school-teacher's wife by the landowners in *Nishant* [Night's end, Shyam Benegal, 1975], this, they claim, is the kind of violence which is dangerous."[45] The censor board was unmoved by this argument and warned that "not more than six minutes of violence" were allowed in any film.[46] (Perhaps it shared the concerns of one Bombay psychiatrist who mused that if screen violence "is qualitatively and quantitatively overloaded, morbidly emphasized and of longer durations, the viewer may retain images and develop harmful memories."[47])

Attuned to the "quantitative overloading" of violence in films, censors eventually developed a language for the management of offending footage. "Wherever a scene or sequence is to be reduced," the Cinematograph Act specified, the "extent of reduction should be indicated in one of the following terms": to "reduce to a flash" meant that "only half to one meter to be kept in the film"; a sequence that was "reduced" was reduced by "30% to 40%"; one "reduced considerably" was reduced by "50% to 60%"; one "reduced drastically" was reduced by "80% to 90%."[48] Accordingly, in censor notifications printed in the *Gazette of India* during this time, we see directions to "[r]educe suitably the close shot of Tony's blood smeared face" from the thriller *Besharam* (Shameless, Deven Verma, 1978); "[d]elete the shots of blood dripping from the knife" from the action film *Bhola Bhala* (Innocent, Satpal, 1978); and "[s]ubstantially reduce the shots of the man killed with glass and blood spluttered" from the melodrama *Jhoota Kahin Ka* (The liar, Ravi Tandon, 1979). In a similar vein, a film critic who served on censor board advisory panels in Bombay and Calcutta in the 1970s kept "a list of 'deaths' and methods of liquidation in each film."[49] The "only form of violence to be allowed on the screen," the censor announced, "will be in mythological films and war films."⁵⁰ By sanctioning violence in some genres while regulating it in others, the censors effectively unmarked certain forms of violence as violence.

Yet to truly do violence to something, Raymond Williams writes, is to "wrench" it "from its meaning or significance," advising us to move up the "moving staircase" of the meanings of violence.⁵¹ During the Emergency from 1975 to 1977, when the All India Film Producers Council complained of censorship, the minister of information and broadcasting was said to be "furious" and "ordered the Censor Board not to pass films, to make more and more cuts, and generally to harass the producers."⁵² In the months following the Emergency, witnesses called by the Shah Commission in Delhi recalled how police constables confiscated film reels from theaters, while film cans were burned by politicians, seized from warehouses, or banned from movement.⁵³ Celluloid's persecuted materiality is congealed in sensational stories of impounded prints, raided labs, and burning reels, but the "vulnerability of the image" is also discernible in the general regulation of films by graphic inscription.⁵⁴

Jaani Dushman was submitted to the Bombay office of the censor board in September 1978. The chairman of the censor board, K. L. Khandpur, explained that *Jaani Dushman* was denied clearance because it "contains a number of pointless killings and not merely because the film has a terrifying sensation."⁵⁵ An examining committee recommended cuts to the film before it could be certified. Director Rajkumar Kohli refused, and the film was referred to a revising committee, which refused to clear the film for release with even the most restrictive rating of "A" or "Adults Only." Kohli appealed to the Ministry of Information and Broadcasting in Delhi. "I was advised to go to the center," Kohli recalled, adding, "I wish I hadn't because I just wasted my time there."⁵⁶ In November 1978, the ministry rejected his appeal, its decision reading that "this film contains countless scenes of violence, cruelty and horror which would offend the sensibilities of an average citizen by the extreme wickedness or depravity of its central character depicted in lingering detail, thereby violating items 2(iv) and 2(iii) of the guidelines."⁵⁷ (The referenced guidelines were "(iii) pointless or avoidable scenes of violence, cruelty, and horror are not shown," and "(iv) human sensibilities are not offended by vulgarity, obscenity, and depravity.")

Kohli then filed suit in the Bombay High Court against the censor board and the ministry.[58] The suit challenged the decision to refuse *Jaani Dushman* a certificate "on the ground that it is a horror film."[59] The censors still refused to grant *Jaani Dushman* a certificate, affirming that "refusal was based on the ground that the film in its treatment and handling is replete with sadism, depravity, perversity, morbidity, horror."[60] "I later discovered," Kohli recalled, "that they were biding time." This was, he surmised, in part because "they knew that another judge would be taking up the case after a few weeks—the new judge was a woman."[61] "They probably thought," Kohli guessed, "that since ladies were being killed in my film a lady judge wouldn't pass it."[62] On the day of the special screening in late 1978, Kohli was "shocked" to see Khandpur "sitting with the judge and passing his comments."[63] Even while he perspired, Kohli "found the strength to protest and ask Mr Khandpur to either sit separately or to refrain from making any comments."[64] The lights went down, and *Jaani Dushman* began to play. What did our judge see?

I do not know. The courtroom screening, like the name of the judge, is a mystery to me. Despite repeated attempts to get my hands on it, including during visits to the Bombay High Court and by payment to helpful clerks and intermediaries, the court file has remained out of my reach for almost a decade. What I know is this: after the screening, the judge ordered the censor board to certify *Jaani Dushman* for release. Khandpur signed the film's censor certificate. Kohli, it seems, had won. "I was amused to read the following advertisement on the eve of the release of a film," wrote one moviegoer to *Film World*: "Banned by the Central Board of Film Censors. Certified by the orders of the Court."[65] *Jaani Dushman* was "released from the clutches of the censors" and cleared for release.[66] But something was left behind in those clutches: three hundred feet of the film, "which the censors considered objectionable."[67]

Before *Jaani Dushman* was released, deletions were made from each of the sequences in which the monster kills a bride. These are described extensively in the film's itemized particulars in the *Gazette of India* as images of the monster who "pulls," "pushes," and "catches," who "throws," "strangulates," and "hits with hand's nail." Taken out of the film, these images were added to the stockpile of images removed by the censor board from hundreds of films every year. I have never seen these images. None of the film producers or distributors I talked to had access to an original negative or positive print of *Jaani Dushman*. Though the Cinematograph Act stipulated that deleted portions of films be handed over to the National Film Archive, the redactions of *Jaani Dushman* were not there either. Most of the footage so deleted from films has been dumped, destroyed, or lost. Forced to turn away from bureaucratic documents as the storehouse of state secrets and giving up my pursuit of images that were disappeared, I came back to the film.

Instead of finding in the archive whatever graphic violence was censored from *Jaani Dushman*, I returned to *Jaani Dushman* as my archive of how the film was censored with graphic violence. The marks of film censorship are the results of digging *into* densely layered film: into emulsion, color dye, silver halides, and plastic base. They are graphic marks. "Graphic," Vilém Flusser reminds us, has its root in the Greek *graphein*, which means "to dig."[68] Digging into the bottom layer of filmic fantasy— the cave of horror—cutting displaced something and forced it to the surface: celluloid's internal composition. Exploring *Jaani Dushman* in the light of its regulatory history shows how state control devolved onto the physicality of films *as* celluloid film stock.

COLOR AND THE BOMBAY FILM INDUSTRY

As each bride cries for help in *Jaani Dushman*, the hairy beast occupies center stage through a series of startling optical effects: slow motion, reverse motion, superimpositions, double exposures, and traveling matte compositions. These effects were achieved by tactile manipulations of the film's base and the film business's prize commodity. Stars may have ruled 1970s Bombay, but "the biggest hero," as one actor recalled, "was the stock."[69]

As the industry transitioned to color during the 1960s and 1970s, indigenously produced color film stock was expensive and of poor quality. Raw stock was issued in batches by government committees to producers, and only after they proved that they had not been "wasteful."[70] In September 1976 the president of the Film Federation of India telegraphed V. C. Shukla, the minister of information and broadcasting, with a plea for more raw film, and to import the stock by air immediately to "prevent most costly and disastrous disruptions in shooting schedules and theatre releases, causing financial burden to the industry."[71] Every month, dozens of films were abandoned because producers could not procure more raw stock.[72] Stock's scarcity made filmmaking such an unpredictable proposition that newspapers reported on it (e.g., "Shortage of color film hits 24 movies!").[73] By the time *Jaani Dushman* began filming, a "black market" for Eastman color stock was said to be thriving in Bombay, with film stock going for as much as 6,000 rupees per roll.[74] Eastmancolor films may have been completed using different batches of the stock, sourced months or years apart; they may also have been completed using Orwo or Gevacolor (two color film stocks imported by the state-run Hindustan Photo Films corporation).[75] The length of a completed film therefore also signified its access to capital (for comparison, *Jaani Dushman* is nearly fifteen hundred feet longer than *Darwaza*). Advertisements for new releases regularly carried the name of the printing laboratory next to the names of the stars—"Processed at Filmcenter!" "Processed at Famous Mahalaxmi!"—as a final guarantee that the film being advertised was physically complete. "Brand New Print" were words often printed along with showtimes for films in newspapers, while "Negative Cutting Ceremonies" became as popular as inaugural *mahurats*, the ceremonies that announced the start of work on new films.

The arrival of color film stocks, particularly Eastmancolor, revitalized the on-screen geography and sensational address of Bombay cinema starting in the 1960s.[76] Because of its lower cost relative to Technicolor filming and processing, Eastmancolor had allowed color to spread to low-budget filmmaking around the world. For a period in the 1960s and 1970s, Eastmancolor had heightened associations in Europe and the United States with lower genres.[77] Horror films capitalized on this association with Eastmancolor in their titling and marketing; witness *Horror of Dracula* (Terence Fisher, 1958), *Masque of the Red Death* (Roger Corman, 1966), and *Profondo Rosso* (Deep red, Dario Argento, 1975). That association was somewhat lost in the stock's global diffusion. In India, Eastmancolor (and not Technicolor) *was* color cinema.[78]

At least one moviegoer recalls *Jaani Dushman*'s distinctive use of color to render the natural skin tones of its many stars, the spectacular vistas of a mountain valley, and brightly pictured song-and-dance sequences.[79]

On one such occasion, Bindiya's wedding, arrays of reveling women twirl in pink, yellow, and green skirts, while multicolored streamers festoon the village square. The swirling patterns of primary colors are one approach to color exhibited by Bombay films of this period, evoking the ornamentalism of hand-painted film. Such images perform color as multilayered, superimposed, or additive, bringing what Joshua Yumibe terms "the palimpsestic nature of the chromatic image" to the fore.[80]

But as the sun sets on wedding festivities, the palimpsestic and prismatic palette of *Jaani Dushman* narrows. A storm stalls the bridal procession, and Bindiya is snatched from the daylit displays of music, dance, and family. The familiar presence of kin, song, and ritual is gone; the hairy beast prowls, stalks, and pounces. Her wordless screams ring out but are drowned by growls of an unhuman frequency. Bindiya stumbles through the ancient, seemingly unmappable shafts of the cave, only to land in a suddenly outstretched claw. Wide, static shots of gathered groups, flatly illuminated against strong key lights, give way to distorted, roving close-ups of faces, and we enter the round rather than behold from afar. Bindiya finds herself in a paranoiac elsewhere that is depopulated, dark, and drained—to the inky blackness of night, the impassively gray rock walls of the cave, the aged whites of cobwebs, and the matted brown fur of the monster.

Even as *Jaani Dushman* sheds its colors to enter the cave, one color remains. Red is the chromatic major of the film, one that activates cultural associations and accrues formal significance. The reds of wedding ritual are (in costumes designed by the famous Bhanu Athaiya) staged as *like* the red that splashes on the walls of the cave (with makeup effects designed by Sarosh Modi); both are nearly the same red that colors the film's title. As she lies dying in the dark cave, Bindiya bleeds brightly; her bridal *chunari* (scarf) and *sindoor* (vermillion) are matched by her blood as it runs down the rocks of the cave. As the village seeks to unmask the "doliyon ka lootera," the "dulhanon ka khooni" (the looter of palanquins, the murderer of brides), clues abound: footprints, bones, an earring in the underbrush, and "khoon ke cheetein" ("the splatter of blood"). Red functions as both a sensory clue within the fiction and as a mnemonic trigger for its audience. The monster hunts only women dressed in the color of his treacherous beloved. When he spies a bride dressed in red finery, her feet and hands painted red, wearing vermillion and *bindi* to match, the monster's senses are deranged: rapid zooms and filters cause the frame to fill with red, a signal for the onset of danger. Whenever red spikes, we prepare for the serialized succession of bridal celebration by bestial violence, a recoding of red within the film.[81] The brilliantly expressive publicity for the film primed viewers to read the film this way. On the cover of the song booklet, a stream of red flows from the jaws of the predator into the parted hair of a bride, linking bloody violence to sacred vermillion (see the book's cover and figure 12).

Color film stock charged the imaginations of filmmakers. It also inflected the censor's imagination and may have been at play in the regulation of *Jaani Dushman*. Striking color prints was time consuming and, at three times the cost of a black-and-white print, an expensive process. For this reason, many film producers elected to print a black-and-white print of their film for the censor screening, preferring to wait for censor deletions before color processing. "Regretfully," wrote longtime censor board advisory member Kobita Sarkar, "black-and-white does not always—specially with scenes of violence and a lot of blood—have the same impact as color film, and this in a sense is a form of cheating."[82] In a different passage in her memoir, Sarkar observed that "the screens of miniature theaters and the standard-sized ones also make a difference. For instance, a scene of violence in black-and-white, on a small screen, with a select audience, appears far less violent than the same scene on a standard-sized screen. With the electric reaction of a full house, with a wide screen in the normal auditorium showing the film in color, the same Censor will, I know, react quite differently, for the impact is much stronger and even disturbing."[83]

Yet Sarkar neglects to note that in the smallest towns that so exercised the censor's imagination, films such as *Jaani Dushman* played in cheaper, black-and-white prints. "Even now," noted *Screen* in 1980, "distributors were not giving color prints to cinemas in small towns."[84] But because the censor sensed that what they were seeing was less than what the viewers might see—scenes "with all the gory details and in color and in close-up to boot," which "were much more vivid"—they censored for an excess that was imagined more than seen, an excess connected to the size and color of the film print.[85] Color film stock's scarcity and cost rippled into the imaginations and realities of censorship, which in turn regulated the length of finished film and controlled how much of it was in circulation. While raw

Figure 12. Color design of *Jaani Dushman* (1979). *Source:* National Film Archive of India, Pune, file no. 1979/7242.

stock rationing and regulatory cutting have each been understood as techniques of ideological control, it is important to remember that they were equally premised on the physicality of celluloid. For decades, the Indian state had regulated filmmaking by rationing raw stock on which a film could be shot, as well as by censoring the same film after it was completed. The state's procedural language around censorship also endowed celluloid with the taint of criminality on the loose, and its forceful pursuit of the master negative carried a whiff of material persecution. The offending frames were "surrendered" to the censor board, and the new master negative was then "inspected" by the regional officer or someone delegated by them to "verify" that the film was appropriately modified before the film could be "released."[86]

Only when these requirements were fulfilled to the satisfaction of the chairman of the board would a certificate be issued for release. That certificate would list "the exact length of each part or parts removed and in the case of reduction of scene or sequences, it shall mention the length of the portion reduced and the length of the portion retained and shall bear a clearly visible triangle drawn at the left-hand bottom corner of the certificate."[87]

In an industry where access to raw stock was tightly regulated, tactile manipulations of film to produce optical effects as in *Jaani Dushman* expose an aspirational and imaginative limit militating against the control over stock.[88] In the previous chapter I examined the paper chains of the post-Emergency bureaucracy as technologies that captured time and subjected citizens to waiting. The censor certificate is one instance of this, and the triangle stamped on the bottom left corner of *Jaani Dushman*'s censor certificate is a mark of how certain images from the film have been entirely put off. When the state censors, it removes a selection of frames from a series, but it also intervenes where the financial and imaginative gamble with film stock is most palpable.

THE FORENSIC REMAINS OF BINDIYA'S DEATH

Watching the brides stumble and struggle in the darkness of the cave, unable to escape the omniveillant gaze of the deadly beast, I too struggled to gain a foothold within the world of *Jaani Dushman*. The view was unstable and momentary, rapidly reeling from helpless distance to encroaching over-closeness. At any moment the silence might be broken by a growl, or the tightly composed emptiness be filled with something awful. Down in the cave, *Jaani Dushman* crystallizes as something like a slasher film, comparable to *Tower of Evil* (Jim O' Connolly, 1972, Britain), *The Texas Chainsaw Massacre* (Tobe Hooper, 1974, USA), *Black Christmas* (Bob Clark, 1974, Canada), and *Halloween* (John Carpenter, 1978, USA). The film's plot resembles in significant ways "the immensely generative story of a psychokiller who slashes to death a string of mostly female victims, one by one, until he is himself subdued or killed."[89] *Jaani Dushman* shares something else with slasher films: their interest in exploiting the "off-frame" or the "off-screen," a phenomenal space from which something emerges to do violence to bodies. Vision in the horror film, writes Carol Clover, "calls attention to what it cannot see."[90] "Insofar as its scary project is to tease, confuse, block, and threaten the spectator's own vision," she argues, the horror film "gives rise to the sense ... of vulnerability."[91] The experience of watching horror films is an experience of being "physically assaulted by the projected image—by sudden flashes of light, violent movement (of images plunging outward, for example), or fast-cut or exploded images."[92] Horror films collapse "editorial" and "diegetic" violence; using the shower sequence in *Psycho* (Alfred Hitchcock, 1960) as her example, Clover writes that it is "no surprise that the narrative flow of images should burst into fragments at the most gruesome or shocking moments."[93] "We take it in the eye," she concludes.[94] Horror primes viewers to inhabit a mode of spatial awareness in which what is on-screen remains viscerally open to what is *off* it. The unsettling, assaultive feeling may dissipate with the death of the bride on-screen at the hands of the monster, for it also relieves the imperiled frame of further violations.[95]

But even after its monstrous bodies and places recede from view, the frame of *Jaani Dushman* remains haunted. It is never fully cleared of threats from inside and outside the frame. Moments after the beast pounces on a bride and dispatches her, white lines flash laterally and vertically down the image, intersecting to form a boxy corner in a cave that is already filled with pillars, stones, and bones. The box invites a possible taxonomy of the shapes taken by censorship damage within the film, brethren to the triangle stamped on the face of the film's certificate, the void into which the film's images have disappeared.

Visible damage to the film breeds an awareness of some presence that is there without being there; the vulnerability of the view attunes us, via formal inscriptions of line and color, not only to the slain bride but to injuries suffered by the filmic body, or celluloid. The killings of the brides Aruna, Bindiya, Champa, Reshma, Gauri, Shanti, and Geeta form a "series of bride-snatchings," as one critic noted in the *Hindustan Times*, "that occur with metronomic regularity."[96] With that same regularity, I feel something quicken each time a bride is about to be killed. In terminal moments, the "dead" matter of celluloid suddenly comes alive; the frame of horror is animated by its destruction.

Analog film editing creates relations between frames by a destructive process. It cuts through the filmstrip and splices pieces together. Most assembly carried out by a film's editor is done inside the frameline, the black edges between frames. The progressively fine edges of film blades and the precision with which they can cut inside the frameline help to maintain the invisibility of the cut. Conversely, splices visible within the frame can evidence the reality of a film's (dis)assembly, ushering what is thought of as "beyond" the frame onstage. At the same time, the destructive process by which the joint is created—by the scraping of emulsion—also beckons us to see "into" the frame, awakening us to the filmstrip as horizontal length and vertical depth.

Censorship regulated the master negative of the film, from which frames were removed and remaining frames spliced together. The edges of two filmstrips—the strips immediately preceding and succeeding the bit of film to be removed—would be cut and pasted together to form the approved sequence. If the negative were conformed using masking tape, an editor would have cut within the frameline and taped over the joint. But *Jaani Dushman* was likely reassembled with cement splices, by far the more common practice for conforming prints. In cement splices, frames from the surviving filmstrip are used in the joining. A splicing blade scratches emulsion off the frame or frames, leaving only the base of the film. Film cement is then applied to this film, over which the adjoining filmstrip is pasted. This action would have to be repeated at every point in *Jaani Dushman* that was censored, till nearly three hundred feet of film were removed.

Perhaps it was because it was the most graphically violent, or the third in an unrelenting chain of killings, or perhaps because she was played by the film's youngest star, Sarika, but Bindiya's slaying was the most censored sequence in *Jaani Dushman*. As described in the *Gazette of India*, the deleted images were the following: "Bindiya (Sarika) Close to Zoom open of devil, she goes to wall, close up of Devil, she goes out, she goes to skeleton and goes out, close up on Devil, She in his hand. (Balance of the same is in the pictures of the same portion). Coming down on wall. Devil goes to her then he strangulates her till she dies (Dead shot remains in the pictures)."[97] From Bindiya's killing, almost fifty-one feet (eight hundred frames, or thirty-four seconds' worth of footage) were deleted. The deletions close off the scene of horror from view, presenting the problem of an unwitnessed crime.

When Bindiya first lands in the monster's clutches, an extreme close-up of her face shows her terror. The extreme close-up also causes the frame to fill with the left side of Bindiya's face, her cheek marked by blood-red gashes. Yet a puzzling question emerges: How did these ominous wounds manifest, given that we had not seen the monster touch her till this very instant? An earlier moment holds a clue. As Bindiya cautiously navigates the dim expanse of the cavern, a palpable sense of unease emanates from her. A well-executed point-of-view shot draws us nearer to her visage. In this pivotal moment, a shadow of a hand materializes in the corner, as though poised for an impending strike. However, the scene's composition deftly shifts, cutting to a wide view of the cave as Bindiya retreats to the safety of a far corner. So that the monster was no longer seen scratching Bindiya's face, the instant of the swipe was cut out, thereby amplifying the intrigue surrounding the genesis of Bindiya's malevolent wounds. Repeatedly, we find ourselves asking: How does Bindiya die? Does he strangle her? Does he bite her? Does he hit her? The methods of the monster's attacks are gone—mostly, we see him lurching toward Bindiya as she shrieks and stumbles in terror; we arrive at the "dead shot" when it is too late.

Film printing duplicated the deletions on every print struck, including the internegative, interpositive, and masterpositive; centralized film regulation operates on this indexical guarantee. Each print also carries forward the jagged imperfections that originally scarred the filmstrip. The removal of images is an intervention that can disturb the stratified and secured "integrity" of the filmstrip, loosening the emulsion and other elements from their fixed places. Just as the monster's claw rises to strike and before the view dissolves, a series of scratches form over Bindiya's left cheek in greenish blue. Eastmancolor is a single-strip, multilayered film stock, and damage can cause different layers to become exposed or leak color. Because the emulsion layer that holds the image is only "several tenths of a thousandth of an inch thick," a scratch in the layer may produce visible disturbance, depending on the depth of the scratch.[98] When Eastmancolor film stock is scratched, the scratch can cut unevenly through the emulsion: on a negative print, stripping off the green emulsion can expose the red layer beneath; a positive made from this print reverses the color values, generating cyan, or greenish blue, marks on the image. If the scratch were made into the emulsion of a positive print, it would have to scrape off the magenta layer in order to expose the cyan dye of the layer beneath. In either case, the act of disappearing the monster's scratchy violence induces new scratches on the filmstrip; these scratches pass quickly out of view, only to be replaced by the red scars on Bindiya's face. Thus, even as the field of intelligibility narrows, our field of perception expands.

Bindiya falls into the monster's clutches, but she does not stay there long. Instead, she is next seen in a medium shot slumped against a wall of the cave, the monster conspicuously absent. She slips down the wall, bleeding and breathing heavily. The transition from her initial entrapment to this somber tableau raises a myriad of questions: How did she get here, and what happened to make her bleed so? The "particulars" described by the censor suggest she was strangled to death, but what remains on film shows her bleeding to death, untouched by the monster. Evidently, an unspoken narrative unfolds in the lacuna between Bindiya's captivity and her desolate slouch against the cave's cold embrace, an unfolding enigma concealed within the depths of a dissolve. For, it is a dissolve that transitions between the extreme close-up of Bindiya's face in the monster's clutches and the shot that follows: a wide shot of the cave, with the monster looking off to the side. What is he looking at? As Bindiya's face fades into the wide shot and the second image appears under the first, a white line forms across the image, a visual demarcation hinting at a profound narrative shift lying beneath the surface.

White lines such as these are the "mark of an absence: we see the removal of all layers of dye." As Philippe Theophanidis puts it, "The bright, white scratches themselves are not something we see. It is not a presence on the celluloid film."[99] White lines may form when the negative is damaged—in this case, when all the layers of the emulsion have been scratched through.[100] Light is now able to pass through what has become transparent. What appears in a positive print as a white line is in fact nothing on the negative. But white lines could also indicate a splice: if frames of the film were cut within the picture area (and not in the edge or frameline) and then spliced together using tape, the edge of the tape would appear as a white line. The white line redivides the space of the cave, rendering its geography strange and dislocating—a surrealist logic that could have landed Bindiya on the wall of the cave to die.

THE COLORS OF CENSORSHIP

As brides flee and fall, blue specks, white lines, and yellow splotches gather around them. Censorship creates forms of color divorced from the representation: neon green pools, maroon tears, blue lines, and black marks that lick Bindiya's body. Censorship in color awakens us to color's palimpsestic status because it delayers the film. As one bride struggles to breathe, her feet kick in distress from under her red *lehenga* (skirt). Deletions were made from this sequence, approximately six hundred frames of the monster as he "throws her," then "goes towards her till he kills her." On-screen, something unusual happens as the bride's feet continue to kick: drops of bright green, almost the same color as the *lehenga*'s border, pulsate beneath her feet—as though the film were bleeding. It appears as though parts of the film had been stripped off, causing a color dye to leak.

Jaani Dushman's color design was realized by the photochemical registration of color in the film; the interaction of color dyes in the emulsion in turn produces the carefully orchestrated colors of village life. The monster too brings with him silver bolts of lightning and orange fires as he gets to work capturing and dismembering bodies. The censor's chromatically determined censorial imagination, in turn, has colorful effects. As the occluded substructure of celluloid is intently aspirated onto the filmstrip, it has effects that cannot be easily predicted or controlled.

Figure 13. Eastmancolor bleeds: detail from *Jaani Dushman* (1979). *Source:* Shankar Movies, frame grab from Time DVD.

Eastmancolor, which so far was being used as a medium to capture color, itself seems to scatter color in nonrepresentational excess (see figure 13). Color film stock produces colorful splatter, stretching the affordances of Eastmancolor beyond its much-lauded representation range and loosening the single-strip color film stock back into a multilayered artifact that spills emulsive colors across layers. It induces hallucinogenic yellows that branch out like hand-painted tints and blueish mists, pitching film form into a formlessness that denies color's schematic delivery of the "moral dimension of narrative."[101] These formless inscriptions can create spectatorial experiences of color film as opening out occult, even visionary meaning.[102]

To watch *Jaani Dushman* today is to watch under the commanding shadow of the censor, from whose interventions the original film may never be recovered. The perforated frames of *Jaani Dushman*, the ones physically proximate to the frames that were removed, log something of the reason for, and record of, this censorship process. The very last time we see Bindiya, a shadow seems to pass over and retreat from her. It may be the beast's, but all I know is I am watching someone else watching her die. The "spectral afterlife" of the censor not only jams the film narratively and stylistically but casts a shadow *over* the film.[103] Across times, places, and a chain of felt affect, discursive prohibition, and material mediation, the spectral censor registers as a trace, as an absent body made phenomenally present via lines of damage and clouds of disturbance—the forensic remains of film censorship.

The chromatically diverse slashes, wounds, and incisions that scar the filmstrip are blots in the field of vision. Peering into these gashes in the film's surface, I sensed myself watching someone else watching the film, waiting for the invisible censor to burst into view. Exploring the links between moments of bodily violence in film and the editing practices through which they are created, Genevieve Yue asks us to rethink editing as a practice that "hides as much as it reveals," to "consider cinema as a system of exclusion, of hidings and things that are hidden. We might then ask: What bodies lie behind its trapdoors?"[104] *Jaani Dushman*'s images peel and crack, falter and fade, suggesting yet another world beneath the subterranean cave of the beast. Soon after the brides of *Jaani Dushman* fall to the monster's underground cave, they seem to fall further through the layers of the filmstrip, through its emulsion and scratched surface into other places that register faintly in the violations of the frame, from a censor's examining room to chambers in the Bombay High Court. As the brides fall, they take us with them past the point where the film's paper trail goes cold. Inviting a way of looking "into" the film, the damaged frame of horror indexes the history of what happened. The images that survived, rather than those that were deleted, illustrate that censorship doesn't only work by deleting images but by adding to them, or by adding while deleting images.

But the invisibility of the censor takes on a certain visible form in *Jaani Dushman*: a history registered if not properly represented in the slivered edge of visibility. In the trapdoors that seem suddenly to open up and swallow bits of *Jaani Dushman*, I sensed the reciprocal gaze of censors and judges who had seen the film before me, given it as much attention as I was giving it now. At the very points that visibility collapses into the "avisual," then, are inscribed histories of spectatorial excitement.[105] Someone came before me: someone was here, someone who saw something, did something, took something, felt something. Some other force is at work here, reframing the horror of *Jaani Dushman*.

THE HAND OF THE CENSOR

When *Jaani Dushman* was released, the many excisions from the film were preceded by one forced insertion, a title card added to the film: "*Jaani Dushman* is a work of fiction about spirits. There is no message in the film for those who believe in ghosts and spirits. For those who do not believe, there is no attempt to convince them otherwise." Photographed dimly, this piece of paper enters circulation as popular cinema, going wherever *Jaani Dushman* goes. Its calligraphic imprint also reminds us that film censorship is a form of *inscription*, not only in the addition of an inked disclaimer but also in the removal of images. To inscribe is to "scratch" (*scribere*), applying force to a recording surface in order to generate the inscription.[106] Scrubbing the film of specific images required splicing the filmstrip, scratching off emulsion, and cementing frames over one another. Pushing the invisible inside of *Jaani Dushman*'s filmic fiction—namely, film stock—outward as obliterated grain and emulsion, censorship's visible effects are generated out of the very inscriptive medium that is censored.

The results on display often reminded me of filmmaking practices that actively deform the cellular base of the filmstrip, "drawing, scratching, painting, or bleaching images directly in or on the filmstrip."[107] Developed without access to large capital, this kind of cameraless filmmaking aggressively carves into the filmstrip, enacting thematic explorations of death, decay, and obsolescence.[108] This practice of "plastic detournement" can "suspend the distinction between intact visual space and damaged surface, between figure and ground."[109] In the handmade film *Bite Me Once Already* (Davorin Marc, 1978–80), filmmaker Davorin Maric bit onto film, creating impressions of his teeth as the visible imprint.[110] "Biting and chewing his way through an entire reel of an exposed and developed Super 8mm film," Maric—or specifically, his teeth—"left behind a complex pattern of marks, while his saliva that filled the scratches immediately started fermenting the emulsion around their edges."[111] Such marks, writes Jurij Meden, "profoundly affected the film base, creating deep scratches, dents, and even an occasional hole that transformed the seemingly flat film into a three-dimensional object."[112] By exploiting film's capacity "for indexical inscriptions" and its ability to sustain irreversible violence without entirely disintegrating, filmmakers have sought to bring film closer to "hand writing or drawing."[113]

The striations, spots, and other spectra left by censorship in *Jaani Dushman* are like marks on paper or canvas created by writing, drawing, or painting with a pencil, pen, stylus, or other implement. Consequently, the filmic surface may be thought of as an inscribed artifact, "wherein the traces of an artist's physicality are imprinted on the celluloid, thereby providing a guarantee of bodily presence in both space and time."[114] To behold its traces is to know, in Gregory Zinman's words, that "an individual laid her hands on this material. We can see evidence of this process when we look at the filmstrip with the naked eye as well as when it is projected in front of us on a screen or surface."[115] Where handwork in abstract film draws attention to the corporeality of the artist—"always deictically pointing back to the hand that made it"—the censored film draws attention to the materiality of the film being worked over by a different hand.[116] Indexical marks on film prints can incite a nostalgia for the tactile touch of filmmakers, projectionists, and archivists, but the touched body of *Jaani Dushman* ties the flesh of the film to a different agent of violence, a kind of "historical source that we cannot see" but only feel.[117] In removing the lethal claw of the monster, the hand of the state becomes palpable all over *Jaani Dushman*.

But whose hand is it exactly that we perceive on the film? Is celluloid splatter a performance of power or of protest? Whose hand cut the film, and with what feeling? Though ordered by the state, the cuts may have been carried out by the film's editor: the same person once again opened the film tins, sorted the footage, used a razor blade to scratch off the top layers of the emulsion, and glued strips back together. The inscription of censorship—already a mediated chain of discourse, anxiety, and policy—is never legible just as itself, but carries forward an undecidability about its status that circulates along with the film, opening up the image as one written and written over by multiple signatories, authors, and editors imprinting on certificates, disclaimers, and the master negative. It was not always easy for me to discern whether the damage I observed in *Jaani Dushman* was from its forceful regulation or arose at the time of filming, printing, editing, or circulation. The film appears variously discolored, nicked, scratched, and taped, marks that may derive from water damage, poor handling, or obstructions during projection. As Bindiya's mouth gasps in ecstatic death, a series of blinking white spots constellate and seem to be headed for her open mouth. Meanwhile a moss of yellow grows on the wall. Eastmancolor was cheaper and easier to shoot and process than Technicolor and was "assumed for years by motion picture engineers to be free of the shrinkage, warpage and final deterioration that had plagued nitrate stock."[118] By the end of the 1970s, however, preservationists noticed that this so-called safety film had many of the same deteriorating capacities as the nitrate stock it replaced and was just as prone to perforation damage and the dreaded "vinegar syndrome" (hydrolysis) that could infect adjacent prints in storage.[119] Some of what I encountered while watching *Jaani Dushman* may have to do with other films that it was stored with, in which hydrolysis manifests as a synesthetic constellation of symptomatic smell, sight, and touch. Moreover, abrasions—or disturbances in the picture area—appear to my eye not as material marks on celluloid but as moving images. Barbara Flueckiger writes that "as soon as a film is presented in the exhibition hall, it starts to wear down with scratches and tears, curling, and color fading, not to mention the human intervention by directors, producers, and distributors who often alter the film in destructive ways if it is deemed to be mandated by external forces (such as audience reactions)."[120] The versions of *Jaani Dushman* I watched have been transferred from theatrical release prints, precensorship prints, VHS transfers, and international export prints. (Prints for the film traveled far. In addition to playing widely across India, *Jaani Dushman* traveled internationally; in New York City, for example, the film played at the downtown Bombay theater, at the same time that Satyajit Ray's *Apu* trilogy was playing at the Museum of Modern Art.)

Jaani Dushman has also become redder in the decades since its release, so that it is possible that the film's deranged color design is more obvious to me than it would have been to the film's first audiences. Film is not impervious to the passage of time, and Eastmancolor film is afflicted by color fading, seen in films gradually acquiring "a pinkish or salmon tint."[121] Over time, two of the three layers in the film stock—cyan and yellow—fade, exposing the magenta layer. More precisely, two of the three dyes turn colorless, rendering the third more vivid. The film's own "memory"—or storage of color—is degraded, reshaping our "present visual experience" of the film as our memory of what its color design once was.[122] Further, transfers between the original negative and the final print (across internegatives and interpositives) can also lead to "interimage contamination," or "crosstalk," between the various layers of color."[123] I remain unsure about the history undergirding visual splatter in *Jaani Dushman*. The trace marks the limit of recuperative recall—the past is past and can only be an object of speculation now.

To be more sure, I have sought out as many versions of the film as possible, closely examining a legitimate VCD release, a legitimate DVD release, versions of the film uploaded to amateur streaming sites, and scholarly platforms. I have sought to control for variations that may be connected to the longer life of specific release prints and compared the frame with what is described in censorship documents. The abrasions I focus on may be reasonably related to damage at the internegative stage, when censorship cuts would have been made to the film before release prints were conformed and struck, rather than to other points in the life cycle of the film, given the multiple lines of provenance, circulation, and travel traced by the film's version history.

Always on the lookout for another version with which to compare my notes, I happened upon a copy of the film uploaded to YouTube in 2015. This version is noteworthy for being unmasked: where projection or cropping would have hidden edges of the frame, they are now visible and reveal boom mics, lightboys, wiring, and the plush mattresses on which characters fall inside the monster's cave. In this version of the film, Bindiya dies a bit differently. Till now, I had been very familiar with Bindiya's final moments. It felt incontrovertible: the wedding, the procession, the death. But that incontrovertible record expanded for a brief flash of something more. After she lands in his clutches, the monster lifts Bindiya and throws her against the rock walls of the cave. I didn't know to expect this: the censor's deletions never describe Bindiya as being thrown, yet it explained finally the blood, the pain, and the death. The way the "cut piece" turned up in my reviewing of *Jaani Dushman* fulfilled the nightmare of censorship, but it also fulfilled the virtual promise of cinephilia: the delayed illumination of the cinematic image. Named "Goldmine" and "Time," the variously circulating prints of *Jaani Dushman* are reminders that censored images are never really gone; just looking longer can bring them to the surface.[124] But even as they help remember the scene of horror, these images cause the film (and its viewer) to forget what once happened here.

CENSORSHIP MAKES HORROR

The cuts to *Jaani Dushman* were so extensive and so significant in each of the "pointless killings" that even today viewers describe the film as "disjointed," "confusing," and "one of the most frantically, manically edited films I've ever seen."[125] By visibly modifying and marking the film's blood splatter, reverberating screams, and sharp claws, censorship shaped the stylistic trajectory of horror both in and after *Jaani Dushman*. The film's censorship had come to be "looked upon as something of a test case."[126] *Film Information* observed that producers in Bombay had "become cautious and picky": "Producers, whose films are to go on the floors, are seen meeting the censor officials to get briefed about what is permissible and what is objectionable. Better late than never, the producers have at last realized that prevention is better than excision!"[127]

The censors' regulation of Bombay horror in its originary moment explains the path that filmmakers would take over the next decade. Following the censorship of *Jaani Dushman*, it was understood that "all that a film has to do is to go slow on the actual splash of blood to vault across the censor code."[128] Finding graphic violence under constant surveillance from the state, filmmakers would shift production energy and screen time to prosthetic makeup and special effects, away from scenes of graphic violence to sights of metamorphosing monsters. Censorship transformed the aesthetic experience of Bombay's horror films and eventually the stylistic preferences and production practices of those making the films, which I take up in the two chapters that follow.

3 Unsettling Design

BUILT ATMOSPHERE IN *PURANA MANDIR*

While Bharti gives birth inside an emergency ward in 1984's *Purana Mandir* (Old temple, Shyam Ramsay and Tulsi Ramsay), her husband, Thakur Ranvir Singh, worriedly paces the hall outside. Bharti pleads in agony: "Something is happening to me. . . . I don't want to die! Save me!" Her voice subsides as a newborn's cries reach Ranvir Singh's ears. His relief is short-lived. Nurses and doctors come running out of the emergency ward, telling him to "go and look for yourself" at what has become of Bharti. Ranvir Singh enters the room and approaches his wife's bed (see figure 14). She lies motionless, her face turned away. When Ranvir Singh reaches out to touch her, Bharti whips around. Thunder crashes as a horribly transformed mother leaps forward, bulbous lesions having overtaken her face. Bharti's husband screams and backs away. His wife collapses on the hospital floor. As she lays dying, we see large medical posters on the wall behind her, depicting the insides of the human body: skeleton, bone, mass. The invitation to "go and look for yourself" also lands me on a corner of the frame. Hanging on a wall of the hospital room is a calendar. In the next shot of the same wall, the calendar is gone. The calendar reappears in the next shot, but on a different wall. Something strange is truly afoot, shuffling the calendar across the walls of the emergency ward (see figure 15).

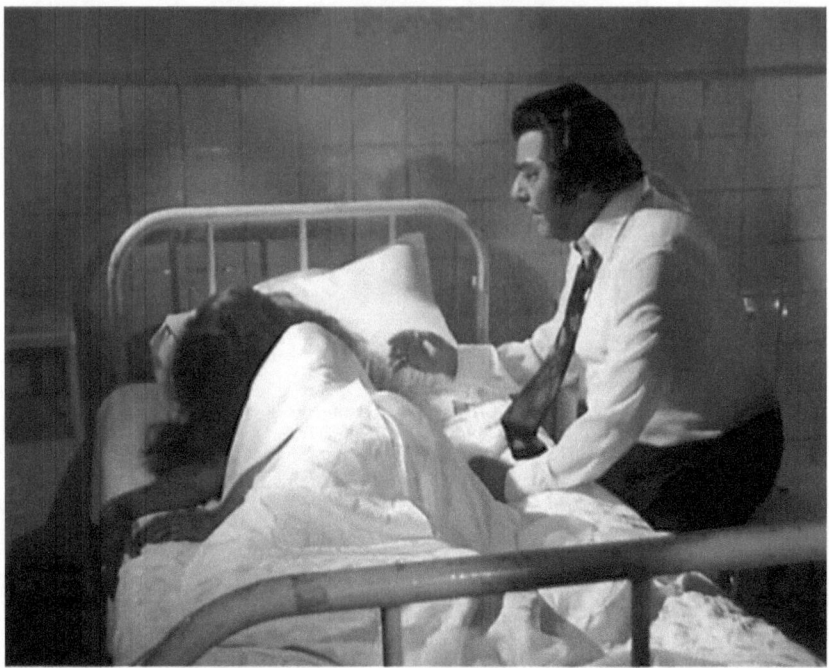

Figure 14. Emergency ward in *Purana Mandir* (1984). *Source:* Ramsay Pictures, frame grab from Mondo Macabro DVD.

Purana Mandir is an atmospheric film, exemplary of how Bombay's horror films delivered their sensational impact through the 1980s. Because censorship had targeted optical effects and graphic violence since the cycle's inception in the late 1970s (see chapters 1 and 2), filmmakers began exploring other ways to summon the genre's appeals. The term *atmosphere* captures how they did this. In the sequence just described, atmospheric elements include the shadows of the window grates that darken the white tiles of the room, the billowing curtains, the lightning that strikes to illuminate the grisly mother, and the clap of thunder that follows. Atmosphere is thus produced by activating spaces, textures, and things within the story world, and privileging them over typically foregrounded elements of character, plot, and dialogue.[1] The focus of cult affection and scholarship, many atmospheric details are iconic of horror films: they serve as icons of the genre in popular culture and serve within films as shorthand for the otherworldly, strange, or surreal.

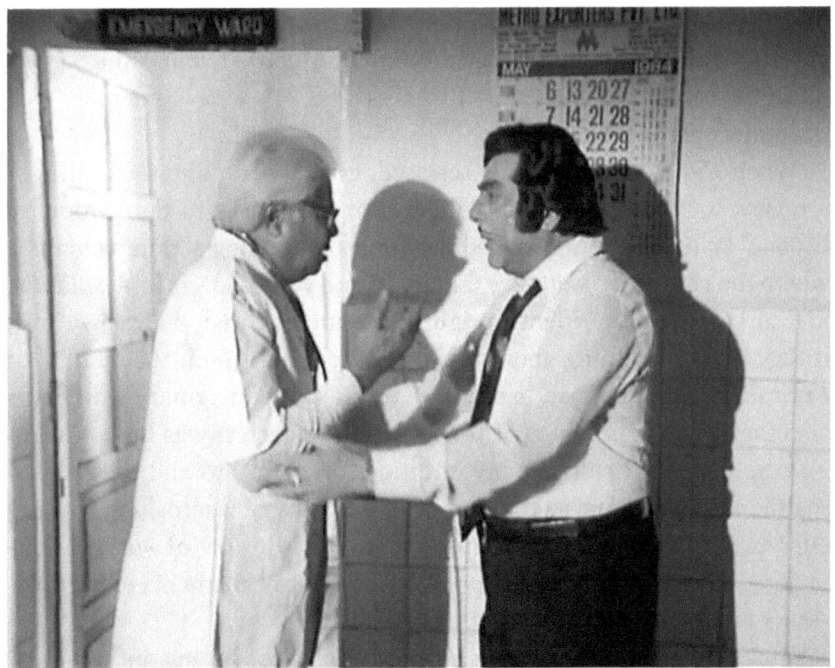

Figure 15. Calendar in *Purana Mandir* (1984). *Source:* Ramsay Pictures, frame grab from Mondo Macabro DVD.

It should be apparent that much of what we call atmospheric in Bombay horror is an effect of its mise-en-scène. The arrangement of elements within the frame, mise-en-scène is the sum of visual choices through which a film speaks when its characters are silent: performative gestures and bodily movement; props, sets, costumes, and color; foreground and background; and center and periphery. Our experience of Bombay horror's mise-en-scène—or how we feel when we see snakes slithering over old ruins, overhanging vines swaying in the moonlight, or a palace door creaking open behind a heroine—determines what meaning we make of the films. Few words are spoken during *Purana Mandir*'s hospital scene. The nameless doctors and nurses have no wisdom, except to "go and look for yourself." When he does, Ranvir Singh *experiences* what he only knew as a whispered legend till then: that his family is cursed, that every woman in it will die painfully after giving birth to her first child. Will his daughter, Suman, suffer the same fate? As audiences found out, *Purana Mandir* became one of the most popular films of 1984, a feat in a year in which 85 percent of all Indian films flopped.[2] *Purana Mandir* remains the biggest hit in the career of the Ramsay Brothers, and fans today remember well the atmosphere of the film.

When *Purana Mandir* was released, critics were unenthusiastic. In a review for *Filmfare*, titled "Indiana Jones Returns to the Temple of Gloom," Pritish Nandy described the film as containing a "purana mandir where the cardboard walls are falling off and you need yards of cellotape just to keep Shiva's trident upright."[3] Caustic as Nandy's criticism was, it registered something about my experience of the film: the tactility of *Purana Mandir*, how an experience of the film's imaginary world was also for me an experience of the stuff from which it was built. Unlike Nandy, however, I cultivate my intuitions of cardboard and cellotape to see the mise-en-scène as the output of a history of filmmaking. I sense encrypted in the film's surreal mise-en-scène the historical world of filmmaking, whether in stabilized practices of reuse or moments of improvisatory failure onscreen.

I take my lead from Suman, *Purana Mandir*'s heroine and amateur photographer. When Suman trains her camera lens on the paintings, walls, and objects of her ancestral haveli, she is startled by what she sees. The viewfinder shows a corpse buried inside the palace wall, while the painted eyes of a royal portrait follow Suman around. Stunned, she attacks the painting with a knife. The canvas begins to bleed, and a gash reveals a false wall beneath. Beyond the wall lies a cobwebbed crypt, which in turn holds a dismembered body. *Purana Mandir* is my viewfinder, permitting me glimpses of something other than what is ostensibly shown. The atmosphere of *Purana Mandir* is thick with the presence of the past: spaces, bodies, and things hide or hold other spaces, bodies, and things. In the elements of visual space—places, bodies, and objects—I see sets, locations, actors, and props, the raw resources of production design. Cinema's technological manipulation of space produces real, discursive, and imaginary "terra-forming" effects. Jennifer Fay draws attention to mise-en-scène as the site where this practice is inscribed, as a "matter of design" that allows us to "focus on the historical materiality of film production and the environmental design of on-location shooting."[4] This chapter explores the film's atmospheric mise-en-scène as effect and evidence of production design.

Mise-en-scène is the result of production design, but it could also serve as affective documentation of the practice: of how shooting locations, props, and actors became cinematic spaces, objects, and bodies. The tactility of cinema, Giuliana Bruno argues, is such that it forms relations between the film viewer and the spaces on-screen through which a film moves. Bruno elaborates a psychogeography of cinema in which there is "reciprocal contact between us and the environment," mirrored in our grasp of objects and places on-screen.[5] As a method, psychogeography extends my reach into a film's production history, allowing me to access sites of filmmaking that may have been long demolished, been cut off from public access, or otherwise been difficult to enter. By stilling the moving images of Bombay horror, we can better flesh out the textured lifeworld out of which the atmospheres of the films were made, better see its locations, props, and actors, as well as imagine what decisions were made, resources were used, and energies were expended to summon the atmospheric surface of horror. In other words, the mise-en-scène of horror can be read for the historical materiality of its production behind the scenes.

If mise-en-scène is about how things appear arranged on-screen, production design shifts attention to the work of arrangement. Despite its centrality to realizing the vision of a film—evident in the fact that Tulsi Ramsay, one of the directors of *Purana Mandir*, was also the film's production designer—production design remains a "poorly recognized and undervalued component of film production."[6] Production design is responsible for the spectacular mise-en-scène of many beloved Bombay films and particularly evident in period spectacles such as *Mughal E Azam* (The great mughal, K. Asif, 1960) or *Bajirao Mastani* (Sanjay Leela Bhansali, 2015). The pleasing density of visual space in such a film encourages an industrial understanding of production design: the rationalized, streamlined, and collaborative process through which a film's director and production designer—working with its cinematographer, editor, set decorators, costumers, and prop makers—produce the perceptible world of the film. In contemporary Bollywood, production design extends across the stages of preproduction, scripting, location scouting, filming, and postproduction, and may involve the film's visual effects supervisor as much as other department heads. The affluent settings and "panoramic interiors" of big-budget Hindi cinema in the 2000s, Ranjani Mazumdar has shown, were given visual form by art-school-trained art directors.[7] How does our understanding of production design change if our focus moves away from the extravagant architectural spaces of golden age Bombay cinema or contemporary Bollywood to the crisis-driven practices of Bombay horror in the post-studio era?

Whether in Bombay or Madras, Hong Kong or Paris, film studios emerged in the twentieth century to rationalize filmmaking and protect it from the contingencies of the environment.[8] Bombay horror became financially, materially, and aesthetically possible in the "post-studio" era, the very moment that the Hindi film industry entered a period of prolonged, multiple, and seemingly unprecedented crises brought on by the end of its studio system. But if we accept what Nitin Govil has described as the permanence of crisis—the axiom that difficulty will attend the production of films—periodization has less explanatory power than we may at first assume: Bombay cinema has been racked by crises throughout its history.[9] Instead, we can examine how a crisis was managed at a given point in film history, or how a rationalist drive toward organization, predictability, and the containment of contingency cohabited with an irrational drive to speculate, take risks, and fail, whether in the studio or post-studio era. This chapter reads Bombay horror for traces of those crises as well as for how they were creatively transformed into atmosphere. Taking *Purana Mandir* as its case study of filmmaking in one genre in the 1980s, it brings into view the pragmatic realities that inform horror film conventions.

WHAT'S IN A CONVENTION?

No other form, posits Eve Sedgwick of the Gothic, has been "as pervasively conventional": "You know the important features of its *mise en scene*: an oppressive ruin, a wild landscape . . . a feudal society."[10] But what is convention? Accruing meaning and feeling over time, the conventional is at once textual, visual, and formal, as well as extratextual, social, and experiential. With each successive use, what is "in" the film—a deliberate formal choice—and what we bring "to" it— memories of similar choices in other films—are mutually coded into the convention. Therefore, conventions also convene the social past of cinema: the passions and preferences of bygone audiences are selectively transformed by filmmakers into formal investments; those formal investments trigger, however fleetingly, an imagined encounter with a collective memory of moviegoing.

In the Ramsay films, the use of the same things to different ends gives a kind of physical expression to the persistence of the past: recycled from *Darwaza* to *Dahshat* to *Tahkhana*, a deathbed accretes the weight of many curses, while a red convertible is worn down by many treacherous sojourns through the woods. Such reuse points to the material intertextuality—or intermateriality—out of which the Ramsays secured their fictional universe. For devoted fans of their films, familiar objects and spaces become weighted with a very cinematic form of historical time, accreting palimpsestic intensity as the same house is cursed over and over, various patriarchs die in the same bed, or the same car breaks down in different films. As the Ramsays reused props and footage, filmed and re-filmed places, the fictional universe was imbued with layered traces of the past, the historicity of a "house style" imprinting onto film at a frequency below that picked up by studies of style in any individual film. As audiences return for film after film in a horror film cycle, the haunted temporality within the film is overlaid with the sedimented memories of having seen something like this unfold before. This repetition endows visual spaces and what they contain with indexical traces of the cinematic past.

Horror films frequently are about returning, an act that in turn threatens to trigger a repetition of the past; ghost, monster, and curse are all figures for repetition. Return, repetition, reuse—the recursive principles of convention—receive heightened expression in the narrative and visual worlds of Bombay horror. As a result of perennial pilgrimages to the same Gothic palace outside Bombay, the Ramsay Brothers' films look uniformly conventional. As Meheli Sen notes, the horror films of the Ramsay Brothers were being made at a time when the "very notions of feudal power and privilege had come to be vilified in the larger, discursive terrain."[11] Films like *Purani Haveli*, *Sannata*, *Saamri*, and *Tahkhana* all stage disputes over *jaidad* (property) that devolve into murder, deceit, and haunting; that property is typically a haveli. Priya Jaikumar writes that such films are also "anti-heritage" films, because they lace iconic architectural sites such as the feudal palace with guilt, danger, and death—linking a "crisis of property" with that of "propriety."[12] Yet the very historical decline of feudal authority that attended the haveli would also ultimately enable filmmakers to access these buildings for film shoots and place the "spectacle of property" on-screen.[13] The haveli shows us how repeated use of one filming location in film after film, a form of intertextual continuity, endows spaces with haunting power. The haveli also allows us to understand how a recursive fictional time of irrational repetitions could be produced through the rationality of production practices. The repeated use of the palace as a filming location, after all, was a strategy to neutralize the contingency of time, economize production, and maintain audience interest.

A different set of practices comes into view if we move our gaze from *Purana Mandir*'s haveli to its hospital. When the young Suman dismisses the curse as mere "superstition," her father replies, "Look, I don't believe in things I've only heard about. I actually saw this with my own eyes." This motivates the film's crucial flashback sequence in which we revisit the night, almost eighteen years before, when his wife went into labor as she delivered Suman. Against the densely detailed haveli and our repeated encounter with it, the emergency ward in *Purana Mandir* is notable for its terrifying bareness and fleeting presence. The wordlessness of hospital staff establishes the abject terror of what transpires; we hear but do not see the newborn, as though all signs of life were being snuffed out of the scene. The emergency ward is also woefully short staffed: one doctor and two nurses, with nary a hint of the buzzing hospital of which the ward must be a part. The nurses who attend to the scene aren't much help either; they offer no words of explanation or comfort, and they choose to flee rather than assist the dying mother. Yet the less they care, the more the nurses also puncture the fiction of *Purana Mandir* with their indifference. The ward reveals how one-off transactions—with "bad" performances, "poor" production values, and continuity "errors" in makeshift settings—can populate a scene and thus induce a horrific experience of something being "amiss or off."[14] The atmosphere of Bombay horror may be conventional, but close attention to how that atmosphere is built draws attention to the constituent parts of conventions.

Single-take filming, small crews, ad hoc use of found and foraged objects, and location-determined shooting all pressure normative understandings of how, when, and where production design happens. They allow us a different way to understand what makes a film studio. As we will see, the Ramsays' was a studio practice in a post-studio era, one in which the opportunistic use of props, speedy filming of sequences, and daily rentals of bungalows took precedence over script breakdown, preproduction, and set building in physical studios, the time-consuming, labor-intensive, and expensive steps typically associated with production design. Warning against a "stagist" history of Bombay cinema, Debashree Mukherjee has demonstrated that "the history of the Bombay film industry cannot be told as a linear journey from the studio period to a poststudio era."[15] Mukherjee instead advises using "materially grounded histories" that can illuminate and adjust the "parameters we adopt to label a film production concern a studio."[16] Though lacking a fixed corporate identity or physical site for filmmaking, the Ramsay Brothers was a studio because it was a repeated imprint that translated various economic and infrastructural crises into horror film style.

"SOMEHOW": FILM PRODUCTION IN THE POST-STUDIO ERA

A film studio can be a place, a corporation, or a style. In Bombay cinema's golden age, the studio was all three. Raj Kapoor Studios, for example, was constructed in the late 1940s in what were then the suburbs of Bombay. Sets were erected inside the studio by Raj Kapoor Films, the production company for which the studio served as headquarters and sometime shooting location. Cast and crew would travel from across the city to the studio, which expanded in acreage to include more shooting floors, offices, makeup rooms, and equipment storage. *Barsaat* (Rain, Raj Kapoor, 1949), partly filmed inside the studio, also supplied what would become the corporation's logo during the studio era of the 1930s to the 1950s. The end of the studio era did not end film production in Raj Kapoor Studios. Hundreds of films would be shot there over the next several decades, most of them not produced by Raj Kapoor Films. The house styles associated with the city's famed studios faded from view as a diversity of genres arose in the 1960s and 1970s; among these were the horror films of the Ramsay Brothers.

Tracking the emergence of the Ramsay Brothers alongside the "industry's relation to the wider economy," Valentina Vitali argues that horror films were made possible by "one single factor": speculative capital, till then "contained by the government's economic policies . . . was allowed to make its entry into the Indian economy."[17] In this period, the film industry cemented its status as "a parallel, non-integrated network for the circulation of a type of capital" that was difficult to track, tax, or regulate.[18] Many films were funded by independent financiers and "fly by night" businessmen. (One actor told me that the financiers who signed him to his first horror film were "what we called Bhendi Bazaar producers.") With little to no interest in filmmaking per se except as a means to circulate capital, they rented shooting floors and equipment from week to week and film to film. At the start of *Purana Mandir*, a title card thanks a prominent Bombay business family for "their invaluable assistance in completing this project." Ramanand Agicha and Ramesh Agicha are credited as "Controller of Production," while the film is "Presented" by Manohar Agicha. In a sign of how far the locus of control had migrated out of the studio, the title "Controller of Production" given to the Agichas was the same one that producer and actress Devika Rani held as studio head at Bombay Talkies in the 1950s. As in other parts of the world, the end of the studio era in Bombay had lowered the barriers of capital, skill, and networked "contacts" required for entry into filmmaking. The result, it seemed, was chaos.

In 1980, *Screen* decried the way in which film production was proceeding in Bombay. "*Somehow*," the journal noted, "has become the watchword of the industry. The producer wants to complete the film 'somehow.' The director wants to direct the film 'somehow.' And the artists want to complete their assignments 'somehow.' Everybody concerned with the completion of the film is concerned with the completion of the film and not with the film itself."[19] Reports of runaway productions blowing past budgets and schedules became a staple of trade reportage. Financiers defaulted and disappeared too, leaving projects incomplete. Most filmmaking resources were in chronically short supply or likely to malfunction. 35mm cameras, of which it was estimated there were only thirty in working condition at the end of the decade, had to be located and borrowed on credit. Harder to find were portable sound equipment and working light bulbs, which had to be imported and were onerously taxed by the government. These resources were not necessarily available all at once, and even the biggest films could only be completed over several "schedules" that were set weeks, months, or years apart as film stock was procured. (During our conversation, one actor suggested that 1980s superstar Mithun Chakraborty preferred to wear the same pants for every shot, no matter what film or scene he was shooting. This minimized the time spent changing between shoots as well as the risk of continuity issues. Over time, Chakraborty's white pants became iconic of the decade.)[20] In 1981, one film producer decided to make a film by compiling many previously incomplete films. This stunt, titled *Film hi Film* (Film and more film, Hiren Nag), was itself repeatedly delayed, abandoned, and resumed over several years leading up to its release in 1983.[21] Some horror films were delayed (*Saat Saal Baad*, *Veerana*, and *Khooni Mahal* were released many years after they were begun) or abandoned. Promotional stills from *Maut* (Death, Shyam and Tulsi Ramsay, 1981), for example, showcase an aquatic fiend, gills and all, carrying his latest prey underwater. *Maut* was indefinitely shelved, as was the Ramsays' remake of *The Omen* (titled *Om*).

The consequences for the film industry's workforce were stark. By the mid-1980s, film production was said to employ 500,000 workers a day. The slow collapse of Bombay's textile industries had sent tens of thousands of skilled and unskilled workers into a film industry where production was booming. These (mostly) men worked as electricians, carpenters, set helpers, deliverymen, and launderers; they freelanced during production season on multiple units and powered the cinematic boom of the period by building, hammering, sawing, wiring, assembling, and dismantling sets. These forms of employment were among the most physically intensive yet poorly compensated in the industry.[22] "For every 100 films started, 70 per cent fall on the way," noted India's minister of information and broadcasting in 1973, adding, "the result is that not only is the money wasted, but those people, who may work for six or seven or eight months, generally remain unpaid because the producer generally vanishes from the scene."[23] Though the minister indicated an interest in legislation to "provide a certain amount of financial security to film workers," insecurity intensified.

At Filmalaya Studio, where the Ramsays would shoot parts of *Purana Mandir*, a series of strikes protesting working conditions stalled multiple film shoots in the early 1980s. In 1978, Filmalaya closed its production business and ended the permanent employment of dozens of employees, some of whom had worked there since the studio's founding in 1958.

Though some workers were rehired as temporary employees, these employees alleged they had been forced to sign documents acquiescing to a change in their employment status from "permanent" to "temporary" so that they could be fired more easily; they called a lightning strike. Producers who rented shooting floors at Filmalaya had to contend with tactics used by striking workers, including preventing staff from entering the studio; squatting around the studio entrance and exit; and damaging and destroying "furniture, fixture, fittings, properties and assets." Demonstrating workers were also "shouting slogans" filled with "abusive language" around the studio. Indexing the moment in which physical ownership of studio space no longer equaled a stable corporate identity, the Filmalaya strike added to the woes of filmmakers squeezed out of studio spaces.[24]

The four-hundred-acre Film City (Chitra Nagari) had been established in Bombay's verdant north in the mid-1970s so that "artists and technicians would not have to commute through the length and breadth of Greater Bombay." But its costly construction was paid for by rising rental rates: within two years, the rate of 500 rupees a day for an outdoor location in Film City became 2,000 rupees a day.[25] By the early 1980s, film producers were calling for a boycott of Film City.[26] Meanwhile, other studio spaces were becoming expensive to rent and even more expensive to maintain or improve, a remarkable decline for spaces such as Mohan Studios, once at the cutting edge of film production and the physical base for Hindi cinema's golden age; it was where *Mughal E Azam* was filmed. For a decade, hundreds of craftsmen including carpenters, sculptors, inlayers, and mirror workers labored under art director M. K. Syed to build the film's sets at full scale and for deep-focus, Technicolor capture.[27] When it wrapped, it was rumored to be the most expensive film produced in India, and when released, it was the most widely seen. In effect, the sets erected at Mohan Studios in Bombay entered the popular imagination not only as lush reconstructions of a Mughal past but also as metonymies of the monumental opulence commanded by film production. By the 1970s, real estate developers prowled the steadily deteriorating studio, signifying the end of the studio era.

Ramsay Brothers, then, was not a studio in the way Raj Kapoor Studios or Bombay Talkies or Mohan Studios was a studio. One may even be forgiven for thinking that the family's films were made by different studios.

The logo that opens *Darwaza* declares it a "Ramsay Brothers" film; *Purana Mandir*, a "Kanta Ramsay Enterprises" film; *Tahkhana*, a "Ramsay International" film; and *Bandh Darwaza*, a "Ramsay Films Combine" film. In communiqués sent to the censor board, the letterhead changes every year: shifts in graphic design, font, and name suggest a family struggling to stabilize a corporate identity. The return address on each of those letters remains the same: "168, Lamington Cross Road, Opposite Apsara Cinema." By the time I visited this address, the shutters were down on the narrow shop face that read "Ramsay Films." Yet what if the Ramsay Brothers' slippery corporate identity from film to film was not so much a struggle to stabilize as a way to evade—a way, for example, to declare bankruptcy on one production studio and open another?

The history of the 1980s Bombay film industry requires thinking not only about the proliferation of crises but also about their productivity. Take the case of film labor. Though film labor had been politically active for decades, the extreme precarity of film work in the 1980s spurred campaigns for better pay and protections. The clamor for representative unions intensified after the Filmalaya strike. In 1983 nearly forty thousand workers—including light-boys, electricians, carpenters, and painters—came together to form the single largest film union in India, the Film Studio Setting and Allied Mazdoor Union (FSS&AMU). Following the formation of the FSS, workers in India's film industries demonstrated for "cine work" to be formally recognized by the state; the Cine Workers Act was signed into law in 1984. For the first time, there was a definition, backed by the force of law, of what constituted a cine worker. The FSS&AMU is today Asia's largest trade union, counting some 500,000 members.

Film producers, in turn, responded to labor's growing negotiating power in the late 1970s and early 1980s. At a time when shooting inside studios was becoming costly and difficult, striking workers were making filming inside studios more expensive and unpredictable. Spurred by budgetary considerations as much as aesthetic trends, many film productions in Bombay were eschewing shooting on set; filming moved far away from the city and beyond the oversight of workers' unions. A discernible trend of shooting in "real buildings" was driving lower-budget film production units to fan out across Bombay city and outside it, thereby "liberating the movie camera from the studio."[28] Heeding the generativity of crisis allows us to see the ways in which risk, danger, and scarcity were not only managed but motivated formal innovations throughout the 1980s, thereby linking transformations in screen imaginaries with histories of labor, technology, and global trends. This generativity enables a "materialist study of creativity" in the lower reaches of the Bombay film industry, where art directors, production designers, and their crew realized visual worlds at breakneck speed.[29] The Ramsay Brothers made films in a context of multiple crises. A closer look at their production design practices illuminates how they did so: how they found repeatable ways to stabilize contingency, generate profit, and maintain a visual style via a studio practice and aesthetic of forbidden places.

THE RAMSAY BROTHERS TAKE YOU TO FORBIDDEN PLACES

"People are tired of seeing posh drawing rooms and restaurants in every second movie," Tulsi Ramsay declared in a 1980 interview, "so we take them to forbidden places."[30] Horror films were named after them: not only the Ramsay Brothers' *Purana Mandir*, *Purani Haveli* (Old house, Shyam and Tulsi Ramsay, 1989), *Tahkhana* (Dungeon, 1986), and *Veerana*, but also Mohan Bhakri's *Kabrastan* and *Khooni Mahal*. Dungeons, mansions, and other forbidden places were widely displayed on film posters, in song booklets, and in trailers. Within the films, characters intoned fearfully about these places while warning against visiting the "kaali pahadi" (black mountains) in *Bandh Darwaza*, the "bhootiya khandar" (haunted ruins) in *Khooni Mahal*, and the "maut ka ghar" (house of death) in *Purani Haveli*. Such places might be out of view because of their cultural liminality, historical obsolescence, or geographic remoteness; they became central to the narrative and visual lure of Bombay horror. In *Tahkhana*, for example, a small-town girl comes to Bombay. We see Sapna walking around the Gateway of India at dusk and then look up at the ultra-luxe Taj Mahal Palace and Tower. But the film quickly abandons the hotel for another kind of place: after all, a visit to that eponymous underground dungeon is what audiences have paid for. Forbidden places typify the iconography of the Ramsay Brothers films, and investigating the production of the films allows us to appreciate the low-budget practices by which ordinary places became forbidden.

"Low-budget" is probably the most common epithet used to describe the films of the Ramsay Brothers. Of course their films were relatively cheap to make. *Sholay*'s budget was once estimated to have been approximately 300 lakhs, while the average budget for a Hindi film in the 1980s was said to be approximately 60 lakh rupees. By comparison, Tulsi Ramsay estimated the cost of making a film like *Purana Mandir* at 6 lakhs. It is important to understand where this money came from. Like most Hindi films at this time, the Ramsay films were distributed on a minimum guarantee model.[31] In this model, a distributor paid a film's producer for the right to distribute a film (in a specific territory) while the film was in production. The distributor disbursed the amount in portions as shooting proceeded, thus contributing to the film's budget. When the film was completed and released, the distributor would claim all revenue from the box office till costs and commission were recovered. Any revenue beyond that was called the "overflow" and would be divided between the producer and the distributor. For a number of reasons, a film's overflow could fail to come through, meaning no money was returned to the producer.

A consequence of the minimum guarantee system for producers with little access to other kinds of money, whether family wealth or business partners, was that the upfront payment from the distributor would not only be the primary budget, it would also be the only payment they might see for the film. In other words, the money disbursed during filming would be used to pay for the film's day-to-day "below-the-line" production costs, of course, but it also paid the salaries of the film's director and compensated its producer. A consequence of a similar model of minimum guarantee in postwar Italy was that as a rule, "the producer actually made the movie using about half of the original estimated budget, keeping the rest as his wages; the distributor was left to face the uncertainties of the market."[32] Likewise, a filmmaking studio like the Ramsay Brothers might "generate profits not by investing money, but by subtracting it from the film's budget."[33]

Once we understand this, other aspects of the business model make more sense. The Ramsays' search for "forbidden places" carried production away from the city's expensive studios; locations were instead scouted for in medieval forts and palaces on the coast, as well as inside Bombay's temples, hospitals, bungalows, and factories. Tulsi Ramsay once explained that a large van or bus would transport the entire cast and crew, along with their equipment, to "outdoor" locations such as a guest house in Mahabaleshwar, a hill station a few hours south of Bombay, which they had rented for 500 rupees a day. The brothers would split responsibilities: Shyam and Tulsi Ramsay would dispatch directorial duties, Kumar would write the scenes, Keshu would light them while Gangu would lens them, Kiran was usually in charge of sound, and Arjun was in charge of postproduction and editing. Their mother, Kanta Ramsay, would cook for everyone. He recalled a crew of thirty-two shooting *Purana Mandir* for six weeks, and members of the cast had stories of how they chipped in as well. "Things today are so professional, there are prop shops," *Purana Mandir*'s star, Arti Gupta, reminded me. "Those days, we had to beg, borrow, do anything," she recalls of working with the Ramsay Brothers: "Even if you needed a sofa—everything would be in-house, we would all go around collecting stuff."[34]

The decision to film a song sequence inside the tony (now demolished) Searock Hotel in Bandra might have had something to do with the fact that Arti Gupta's father was then the security officer of the hotel and may have facilitated a discount and access for the film.[35] Indeed, the map of forbidden places we get from *Purana Mandir* indexes the priority of location filming for low-budget filmmakers. *Purana Mandir*'s titular temple—the old temple of Shiva—is the Babulnath Temple in South Bombay; the Mahakali Caves in Andheri are where the monster is beheaded; Bandra Fort supplies a rocky beach for romantic song and fisticuffs. Early in *Purana Mandir*, Thakur Ranvir Singh asks his secretary if he has sent the payment over for a deal to Jawahar Saw Mill. The mention of Jawahar Saw Mill suggests a different kind of wealth that props up the film's visual world. The mill was one of many firms in the timber and plywood industry owned by the Agicha family—whose "invaluable assistance" to the film, then, may have been not in any budgetary contribution but in supplying timber for the construction of film sets. The film therefore serves as an appendix to a film's credits, inscribing its production itinerary in the visual world while also indicating how production staged, manipulated, and dressed real locations.

In 1980, film critic and journalist Khalid Mohamed chanced upon a film shoot in a bungalow in south Bombay, thirty kilometers away from Film City. Given his eye for detail, Mohamed's report is worth spending some time with, for it helps us understand how the practice of location shooting shaped the iconography of Bombay horror. "A monster more terrifying than Frankenstein is on the loose in the corridors of the Maharashtra state guest-house in Bombay," the story begins. A "majestic, wooden-beamed bungalow" typically used to host visiting ministers and political meetings was, "for the last 20 days," "being shared by some unusual visitors": the "cast and technicians of a film unit making a blood-chilling horror movie." The film shoot in question was *Sannata* (Silence, 1981), and the filmmakers were the Ramsay Brothers. Reportedly the "first ones to be allowed to shoot on the premises," the Ramsays had transformed the interior of the guesthouse. Mohamed noted the use of "thick plastic cobwebs," "sinister statues of goblins and fairies," "antique clocks," and "gadgets to create an artificial fog." When Mohamed inquired about how the brothers had secured the use of the guesthouse, Tulsi said they had hired it at 500 rupees a day "through a contact."[36] At 500 rupees a day, the government guesthouse would have been less than a quarter the rate of shooting inside a film studio. Additionally, the bungalow "fitted perfectly into the eerie atmosphere required for the film," Tulsi told Mohamed: "All the rooms, the garden and even the bath-tubs are being used by us," he added. The film crew worked between 2 and 10 pm every day, because the "ministers and VIPs staying here go to sleep early and want a bit of quiet . . . so we have to pack up. Otherwise we could shoot even as late as 2 am."[37] Under art director Anjani Tiwari, the bungalow was transformed by a number of strategies, such as filming at night, using colored filters on lights, and set dressing with cobwebs, as well as through sound effects and optical manipulations in postproduction.

Tiwari's credits include the Ramsays' *Sannata, Guest House* (1980), *Dahshat* (Terror, 1981), *Tahkhana*, and *Purani Haveli*. Like makeup artist Srinivas Roy (discussed in the next chapter), Tiwari was a trusted and frequent collaborator of the Ramsay Brothers. Such collaboration is "in and of itself an aesthetic choice," making it possible for us to understand how the auteurist signature of the Ramsay Brothers is the collective output of authors inside and outside the family.[38] "Jaldi, Jaldi, Jaldi" (Fast, fast, fast) was always the battle cry on the sets of Ramsay films, Tiwari told me.[39] An issue of the industry periodical *Trade Guide* from the summer of 1985 features a poster for *Tahkhana*, announced as "shooting nonstop" since "10th July at Janjira Palace and Murud Island," a form of promotion that also intimates the rate at which films were being turned over.[40] For the haveli of the film, the Ramsays had secured a nineteenth-century palace a few hours outside Bombay in Murud-Janjira (more on this later). The dungeon that underlies the palace, however, was erected inside a studio in Bombay. To illustrate how he would originate design choices with the Ramsays, Tiwari began drawing on a sheet of paper. He drew curve after curve, creating a crenellated surface. Looking up at me, he said, "goofah" (cave). I realized then that Tiwari was possibly retracing a moment from decades ago, when he first sketched the underground caves for what would become the dungeons of *Tahkhana*. "They didn't give me much time," Tiwari said, "and I suffered budgetary restrictions. Still, I did the best I could."[41] But as Tiwari sketched—on the reverse of one of the seven pages of his CV, a copy of which he had printed for me—I realized how poorly archived the history of this design practice was. In the absence of shooting stills or behind-the-scenes footage, where do we look if we want to understand the mechanical craft of atmosphere?

Perhaps on-screen? On film, many of the materials and strategies of production design present *as* mise-en-scène. The mise-en-scène contains indexical imprints of profilmic space—showing us things as they were once before the camera—but it cannot tell us who put those things there, where they got them from, or how. To speculate about production practices requires deplaning the image, isolating and following bodies, objects, and sites as they appear, disappear, and reappear—from shot to shot, scene to scene, and film to film. To see things in film, as Stanley Cavell wrote, is a "phenomenon in which a particular mode of sight or awareness is brought into play," a capacity for "sensuous awareness" that "objects on film are always already displaced," and that "we as viewers are always already displaced before them."[42] Consider, for example, the lore that the Ramsay Brothers had "amassed a large selection of props and décors"; the family, it was reported, "guards these treasures jealously and stores them in a secure warehouse in Andheri, from where they are brought out to grace film after film."[43] I have never visited this warehouse, but a tracking shot in *Sannata* shows us—under a hellish red glare—a haveli floor filled with stuffed animals, large clocks, and wrought iron statues I have since seen in many other Ramsay films.

While tracking different elements this way, we will notice when the same house appears in different Ramsay films, but we will also notice when a hero's shoes change color from one moment to the next. Disclosing gestures that may be repeated or one-off, such attention has a generative consequence for our understanding of Bombay horror. It awakens us to how practices of reuse generate horror by accreting palimpsestic intensity to specific things and places, as well as to how singular acts of improvisation can trigger an affective experience of the threadbare basis of film production.

RETURNING TO THE HAVELI

Purana Mandir begins by returning to the past. Two hundred years ago, the demon Samri terrorized the kingdom of Bijapur. When King Hariman Singh's carriage breaks down in the forest, his daughter, Princess Rupali, is killed by Samri. Before he is punished by royal decree, Samri swears: "Hariman Singh, I curse you and your house! Till my head and body remain apart, every woman in your family will die as soon as she gives birth to her first child. And the day my head and body are reunited will be the last day of your dynasty!" After Samri is decapitated, his headless corpse is placed in a coffin and buried unmarked in the grounds behind the Shiva temple. On the temple priest's suggestion, Samri's head is locked up in a box with Shiva's *trishul* keeping vigil over it, then walled in behind a portrait in the royal haveli. Time passes, sweeping us across hundreds of years and kilometers—out of Bijapur and the time of monsters and kings and to Bombay, circa the 1980s. Long after Samri cursed the king, his latest descendants are Thakur Ranvir Singh and his daughter Suman, who happily inhabits a modern time in which myth is forgotten, curses are superstition, and the family haveli is a faraway place—to which, of course, return must be made, inevitably.

Once Thakur Ranvir Singh reveals the curse that haunts his family, Suman and her boyfriend, Sanjay (Mohnish Behl), leave Bombay and head down the coast to the haveli in order to defeat Samri's evil power. The most spectacular and narratively significant location in *Purana Mandir* is the "purani haveli," the ancestral mansion where a majority of the action will take place.[44] The first time we see the haveli in *Purana Mandir*, it is as a painting that hangs in the Bombay bungalow. Thakur Ranvir Singh points at it to say: "That *haveli* is such a cursed stain on our family, that we could not wash it away, even with our own blood." The painting is oddly small, but its visual inadequacy paves the way for audiences to thrill in anticipation of the actual haveli.

For the haveli, the Ramsays chose a nineteenth-century palace located south of the city, 165 kilometers down the Konkan coast from Bombay in Murud. Sitting in a taxi speeding down the recently repaved highway, I imagined what their journeys might have been like. Traveling from Bombay to Murud took six hours, and the going was not always smooth, featuring hairpin turns and monkeys scampering across the highway into the lush surroundings, while waterfalls gurgled distantly. As the palace came into view, my delight was instantaneous and uncanny; what I saw out of the car window brought to mind a shot in *Purani Haveli* in which a busload from Bombay first glimpses the palace.

Ahmedganj was built in the 1860s in the Gothic revival/neo-Gothic style that was transforming the Bombay city skyline between the 1840s and the 1870s. Thus, while the haveli is a precolonial architectural form associated with north India and since circulated by Gothic, romance, and other films as the spatialization of an "asynchronous temporality," Ahmedganj is a distinct variant of the Bombay Gothic style.[45] Driven by the architectural reforms of Governor Frere and financed by the trade boom of a major port city, the Gothic revival led to such buildings as the High Court, David Sassoon Library, and JJ School of Art. Deploying pointed rib vaults, carved teakwood balconies, Kurla and Porbandar stone, and Ratnagiri granite, the Bombay Gothic found a way to participate in the "eclecticism" that architectural historians have noted was part of a new sensibility in the nineteenth century. Gothic architecture could look, as Christopher London suggests, like a variant of subcontinental palace architecture, since both featured elaborate slabs of pierced stone (or jalis) as well as rose windows, stone foliage and bestiary, lancet lights, tracery, crocketing on the edges, and foil work, with slender columns along with terracotta roof tiles, bays filled with windows, gargoyles, and a distinctive

Figure 16. Arriving at the haveli in *Purana Mandir* (1984). *Source:* Ramsay Pictures, frame grab from Mondo Macabro DVD.

porte cochere, the patio for carriages to park and deposit visitors.[46] As their red convertible pulls into the porte cochere at Ahmedganj, Sanjay and Suman initiate a series of arrivals in the films of the Ramsay Brothers. The family would return to Ahmedganj almost every year till the early 1990s for films like *Veerana, Tahkhana,* and *Purani Haveli.*

Ahmedganj Palace was a triumphal seat of the nawabs of the Sidi dynasty, descendants of formerly enslaved peoples from the horn of Africa who had ruled parts of the Konkan coast since the sixteenth century. But the palace had fallen on hard times since the 1970s, when it was put up for sale. Nothing came of the attempted sale, and the palace remained open to tourists, like the travelers of *Purana Mandir* and *Purani Haveli,* to marvel at upon arrival (see figure 16). By the time I made it to Ahmedganj, the palace's fortunes had somewhat reversed. The family of the nawab had managed to hold onto the family house—and I was not let in to visit.

But *Purana Mandir* takes me inside this forbidden place. The production enhanced and manipulated profilmic space to produce the sense that characters had left Bombay and entered a dangerous and "sunsaan ilaka" ("abandoned area"), the eponymous "maut ka ghar" (house of death), the "khaufnaak haveli" ("terrifying mansion"). By hanging the insignia of the thakur's family on the palace's gates, I could see how *Purana Mandir* remapped the palace and fort as being inside Bijapur, a Hindu kingdom that worships Shiva at the "nearby" temple. The facade of the palace features ornate woodwork, marbled surfaces, and inlaid stone work—all helpfully indexing the store of heavy, historical time alluded to by *Purana Mandir*'s curse of "two hundred years." By placing the palace further back in time by a century at least, the film had abducted an architectural style out of its place in history, attesting to the creative ways that narrative and visual design can re(ad)dress a location. Fog machines were stationed inside the palace and in the grounds around it, producing milky clouds. Dutch angles on staircases produced filigreed frames, in which banisters and statuary created grid-like effects. Shadows were passed over rose windows, so that this distinctively gothic feature of stained glass appeared suddenly shrouded in darkness. Actors activated the interiors of the palace by touch, sliding their hands along the banisters, caressing stuffed animals, and dragging a coffin across the palace floors and down its magnificent staircase. Wind fans blew leaves across the frame at opportune moments. (When I inquired how they staged their films' climactic leaves-and-dust windstorms, Tulsi smiled: "We used the discarded propellers of airplanes.") Foreshortening made objects loom menacingly; red light falls on the palace's impressive catalog of taxidermied animal heads. Extensive use of rapid zooms into those animal heads transforms aristocratic heritage into an uncanny reminder of a bestial, avenging force—a "shaitaan ki kahar" (the rage of a monster)—on the loose. The architectural features of the palace were restaged as sites of horror, such as when Suman's best friend Sapna (Preeti Sapru) is seen walking the narrow turret walls of the palace and eventually falling to her death.

In *Purana Mandir*, the atmospheric presence of the past is summoned not only through the indexical traces of historical time—a palace facade lashed by a hundred monsoons, its outer walls covered in green moss—but also through the indexical traces of cinematic time congealed in reused locations, props, and footage. The Ramsay Brothers repeatedly placed the same wigs and masks, candelabra and coffins, and haveli and cave before the camera to summon scenes of horror for new films, but gave them different names, histories, and magic powers. Suman's bed in the palace, with its polka-dotted, gold-bordered headboard, is the bed we see the thakur dying on in *Darwaza* and in the background of *Sannata* and *Bandh Darwaza*. The same teakwood mill that had served as the site for murder in *Andhera* serves as one for business in *Purana Mandir* and later becomes the location for monstrous killing in *Veerana*. The thakur's city mansion in *Purana Mandir* is also the city mansion of the family in *Sannata*, one distinguished by its indoor wallpapers depicting waterfalls and forests. The same sunken "khandraat" (ruins) that appear in *Tahkhana* reappear in *Purani Haveli* and *Bandh Darwaza*. The subterranean altar of the vampire in *Bandh Darwaza* is where the condemned demon child lives in *Purani Haveli*. Ahmedganj is the ancestral haveli in *Purana Mandir*. It is the lair of the monstrous chudail in *Veerana* and is the eponymous old palace of *Purani Haveli*.

Production of any one Ramsay film was also preproduction on future films. *Andhera* appropriated significant footage of a nighttime heist from the Ramsays' previous film *Ek Nanhi Munhi Ladki Thi*, allowing the Ramsays to have a car explode on-screen without having to explode yet another car, or allowing them to show a monster stalking the city at night without having to film it again. The "old temple" we first saw in *Purana Mandir* is also seen in *Tahkhana*, but the way it appears as rear-projected image suggests the creative reuse of footage first filmed for *Purana Mandir*. And a series of notes, first heard as the chudail is on the loose in *Veerana*, can be heard again in *Tahkhana* when a clock strikes the witching hour. Indeed, the shot of the car pulling into the haveli grounds in *Purana Mandir* is the very same shot used to bring the hero to the chudail's abode in *Veerana*. The repeated panning movement that brings the car into the porte cochere—and the looping of film footage—reinscribes a past moment of cinematic encounter.

The Ramsay Brothers' frequent return to the Ahmedganj Palace was a kind of "fan service" to be recognized by devoted audiences of their films. While credits for *Purana Mandir* listed city studios as production locations, the opening credits of *Purani Haveli* list Ahmedganj first among its filming locations. When the film's gaggle of teenagers arrive at the palace for a weekend picnic, one of them declares: "The Ramsay Brothers should buy this haveli to make another horror film in." In Mohan Bhakri's *Khooni Mahal*, one character says to another: "This palace is completely desolate, like in the film *Purana Mandir*." Bhakri did not film at Ahmedganj, though *Khooni Murdaa* lists "Film City, Essel & Bunglows" as its filming locations. It suggests how atmospheric elements such as a distinctive location were becoming central to maintaining the lure of the films. The practice of forbidden places took shape, I have suggested, because of striking transformations within the labor history and urban geography of filmmaking in 1980s Bombay. Shifting our focus from the haveli to the hospital flashback in *Purana Mandir* unveils a different set of practices. In contrast to the intricately depicted haveli that we frequently revisit, the emergency ward stands out for its unnerving starkness and transient existence. Here, unsettling performances, modest production standards, and disruptions in makeshift arrangements converge to populate the scene, evoking a chilling sense of disquiet.

NURSING INDIFFERENCE

While Ranvir Singh and his wife struggle with the hand fate has dealt them, two nurses attend to the mother in the throes of labor. She thrashes in agony, screaming, "I do not want to die," but the nurses say nothing. They might be young, inexperienced nurses stunned into immobile surprise, or they might be nurses professionalized into impassivity; they are not perturbed by the pleas, nor do they exhibit any intuition that something is wrong. If anything, they look tired or bored. One nurse stares stonily at the mother, and even steals a glance at her watch. A few moments later, we see the nurses scramble out of the maternity ward, callously avoiding all eye contact with the thakur on their way. Where are they even going?

Perhaps to another filming assignment. After mutely waiting for the mother to die, it was time for these "junior artists"—or extras—to speed to their next filming job. Nurses in Bombay cinema presided regularly over mothers dying, fainting, losing their memory, and regaining it. Or their next job might have involved waiting on a friend as she is wed, or dancing at a festival, or observing a funeral. Our nameless nurses—I do not know the names of the characters or the performers—might also be two working women who every day commuted between distant suburbs and city centers by rail for gigs, only some of which may have been in front of the camera. Overrepresented in urban informal economies as a "surplus" labor force, women workers in 1980s Bombay were much more likely than men to hold multiple short-term jobs that moved them across the city's geography and between ranks of the paid, underpaid, and unpaid.[47] Indeed, women workers raised methodological problems for the very definition of work, of how, where, and when it was happening.[48] Many women found jobs in industries with low levels of formalization and unionization such as "construction, porterage, stone-breaking, rice and oil mills, tanneries, potteries, small factories making plastic and rubber objects, and bidis" or as "film extras."[49] The 1948 Indian Minimum Wages Act had been designed for many such jobs, to establish a fair wage for forms of "sweated labor" where "there is a big chance of exploitation of labor."[50]

Because a casting bureau was never established, women extras remained exposed to predations of casting suppliers, who picked them up from outside the gates of R. K. Studios or Natraj Studios and transported them to film shoots far away in Panvel or Lonavla.[51] In 1956, one thousand regular film extras collectivized, naming their organization the Junior Artists Association (affiliated with the Federation of Western India Cine Employees, or FWICE). In 1972 a "sister union" named the Mahila Kalakar Sangh (MKS; Women Artists Union) was formed for women extras. By the late 1970s, as the ranks of the MKS swelled and film shoots spread out beyond city centers and studios, union membership became harder to control for and extras harder to protect. Wages plummeted as job opportunities grew; the filmmaking economy offered jobs in a city where formal employment was increasingly hard to come by. In the mid-1980s, an extra could expect to make between 31 and 62 rupees per eight-hour shift (depending on whether they were "ordinary" or "decent").[52] In a good month, the luckiest junior artist might make 1,500 rupees.[53] In a letter to *Screen* in May 1984 that was printed under the title "The Sorry Plight of Extras," Dinesh Ranjan wrote that the "film industry plays a villain's role in the sad saga of the extras."[54] Ranjan noted the disparity between the "stars" and "superstars" who were paid lakhs of rupees and extras, while "the backbone of the industry" was left "unfed, or at best half-fed." "Apart from physical and economic exploitation, sexual exploitation is also rampant in the world of extras," Ranjan reminded readers, lamenting that extras are "not included in the film's cast" or given attention by film magazines.[55] Giving his letter "time and space," *Screen* awarded Ranjan a prize for the "best letter" (and 50 rupees) and thus distinguished itself from "film magazines." But the letter was printed next to a headshot of superstar Reena Roy, who had recently announced her retirement. Helping to draw attention to the extra's "sorry plight," while also markedly different from her, Roy's retirement at twenty-seven enacted the gendered passage of the productive bodies of "pretty junior artistes" and female superstars between realms of visibility and invisibility.

A strategic affect of invisibility was, after all, the productive capacity for which extras were compensated. The inculcated blankness of many extras reminds us that the "art" of the background artist was to "make no impression" at all, even if the "camera happens to capture their closeup": to give their faces to the camera while remaining somehow faceless.[56] This was as true of category "Super and A Class" members of the MKS appearing in professional, middle-class, and upper-class backgrounds, as of "B Class" members, also known as the "Chawl (Slum) Class," and consisted of "junior artists who form part of crowds, mobs, groups, slum dwellers, dead bodies or part of the ambience in a college campus."[57] There was no "extra charge" paid to an extra for "clapping, for carrying small luggage, and for standing below thigh-deep water" or for "speaking up to five words."[58] On the other hand, extras who spoke dialogue of "two or three sentences" or whose faces "prominently registered" would be paid wages for an extra shift (so, one extra extra shift); those who carried "heavy luggage, doli, stretcher, an arthi or any heavy weight" or waded into water "above thigh-deep" would be paid half a shift extra. The same went for extras marked by scenes of violence or celebration—if they got *holi* colors on their faces or blood smeared on them—as for those who were willing to "cycle with song" (not so for "normal cycling").[59]

While extras supplied the necessary corporeal base for convincing, realist representation or spectacular form, their persistent figuration as supplements (to stars, to foreground space) was as much a financial calculation as it was an aesthetic decision, and had consequences for their work environments. Film producers and production discourses regularly figured extras as warm bodies that were required to people a party, wedding, or college campus—and therefore to look alive—but this required them to be

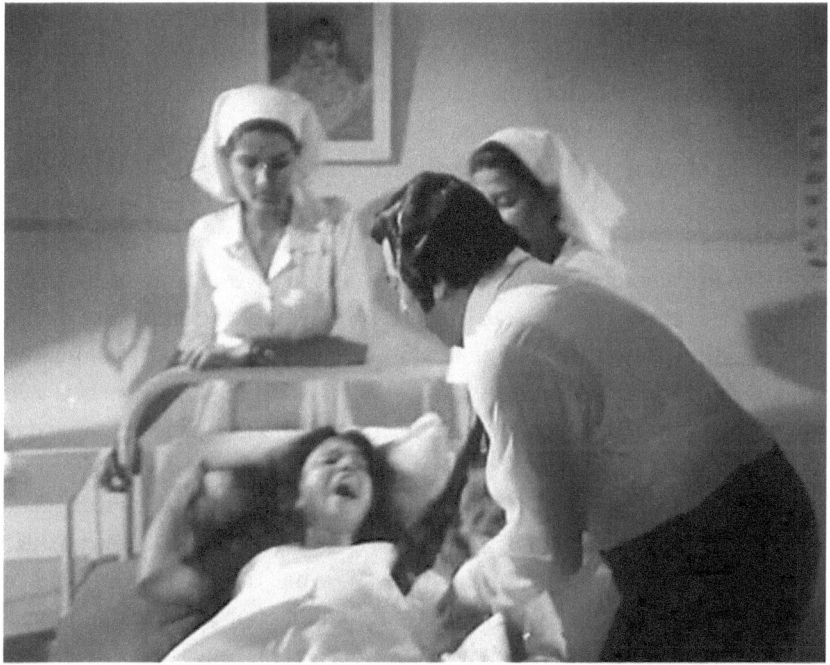

Figure 17. Nurses waiting for the end in *Purana Mandir* (1984). *Source:* Ramsay Pictures, frame grab from Mondo Macabro DVD.

fed, their clothes to be laundered and ironed, and transporting them back and forth. Producers argued that the extras' wages paid for them to feed themselves, but the MKS was adamant that it was the producer who must arrange for breakfast, lunch, or dinner as appropriate. "In outstation shootings where overnight stay is involved," an agreement specified, "if the producers cannot arrange to provide breakfast to the artistes before picking them up from their place of stay, then breakfast will be given to them on the way while traveling or after reaching the location."[60] If it were impossible for a meal to be arranged, then the extra was compensated at the rate of 10 rupees for breakfast and 15 for lunch. The fine gradations of payment—over whether someone spoke fewer or more than five words, whether they clapped or not, whether they waded into water up to their waist or lower, whether their face prominently registered or not—suggest that background artists were engaged in a form of corporeal labor that transformed their persons into mere bodies. The blankness of the nurses (see figure 17), even the wordlessness of the dying mother, in *Purana Mandir* is thus a kind of professional perfectionism, but it is also an imperfection arising from that very compulsion to be invisible yet visible.

Their listless gestures suggest people stuck in a loop, waiting *on* the mother as much as waiting *for* her to be done with: to dissipate into death, to complete a take. While stars languish as they wait between films and takes—experiencing "durational depletion" between jobs—it is the job of extras to appear to wait on.[61] Excised from the mythic time of the foreground, the extras are instead ruled by the watch, the hour, the day: a never-ending presentism that builds the exhaustion of the past but hurtles toward an uncertain future. As "workers constantly shift gears between multiple jobs that they perform for shorter durations during the same day or night," "work time," writes Paul Apostolidis, "becomes disjointed in an everyday sense."[62] Such workers are always "out of time": they inhabit the present moment (of this job) while always being on the lookout for their next job. The cruel silence of the nurses is what they have been paid to perform, but the blank face is as much a product of practice as it is a mask behind which extras are able to dream, worry, and strategize.

Indifferent to the demands of generic affect or performance—and to the pivotal scene of horror unfolding right before them—the nurses look to the terror as though it were nothing. With little patience for the curse, the nurses are out of time: they are not locked into the saga of a centuries-spanning curse or a story of generational trauma. Indeed, they have no backstory or goals in the film, no past and no future. Background extras, as Charles Leary writes, are those "who people the space to achieve a semblance of realism," but they may undercut the sense of liveliness if they "undermine this depiction with their immobility."[63] Nurses may save lives in hospitals, but extras depleted by their practice also prepare the mise-en-scène for horror. Even as the moving images of *Purana Mandir* move the mother closer to death, the nurses remain nearly still; they are drained of, and in turn drain the image of, vitality.

SOMETHING'S WRONG

The flashback codes the past as nested enigmas into which the audience is drawn through suspenseful subjective narration of a decades-ago event and the deployment of off-screen space. The dislocating effect is of course in its narrative function—it moves us from the present to the past and back—but it is also in the spatial disorientation caused by surreal and slight displacements of elements within the space, with the endlessly panning camera evoking the circularity of a nightmare that ever so subtly recodes reality. While production design can be "an additive process"—as it "fills the image with redundant reinforcements of the basic space"—a careful scene analysis of the flashback sequence reveals a single room was used to film the sequence: both the inside and the outside of the emergency ward.[64] Limitations of the space are masked through camera positioning, performance, editing, and the dynamic use of sound to generate horror; a green curtain and an "Emergency Ward" sign were arranged and rearranged between camera setups.

Even as the flashback shows what transpired in the deadly delivery room decades before, the invitation to "go and look for yourself" has landed me on a corner of the frame: the calendar. This in itself is unremarkable. Baldly presented to audiences, the calendar is no more than a charmless thing in the familiar web of social exchange; in India, they are on the walls of shops, schools, living rooms, and offices. The kitsch calendars adorning public and private spaces matter less for what they are—slightly ornamental ways to tell us what day of the week it is—and more, Kajri Jain has argued, for the social relations they enable as they are distributed and received in chains of financial debt, obligation, and gift.[65] The calendar may represent a modern order about to be swamped by an old curse, but the calendar is a slippery symbol. The force of the past is enough to reorder the present, it seems, for the calendar reappears in the next shot, but on a different wall. It appears and disappears and moves from wall to wall without explanation, in displacements that spatially enact time falling out of joint (compare figure 15 with figure 18). Going from outside a maternity ward to inside it within seconds, the calendar instantiates a mundane form of time about to be displaced by some more mythic kind. "Nobody" moved the calendar, but it moved all the same.

Given the Ramsays' reflexive filmmaking, one very much aware of fan attention to atmospheric elements, the itinerant calendar of *Purana Mandir* can have been intentional. Never in my conversations with Tulsi Ramsay did I ask him about the calendar. I didn't ask him because I hadn't yet seen the calendar. I do not know if he has ever seen it either. The calendar is

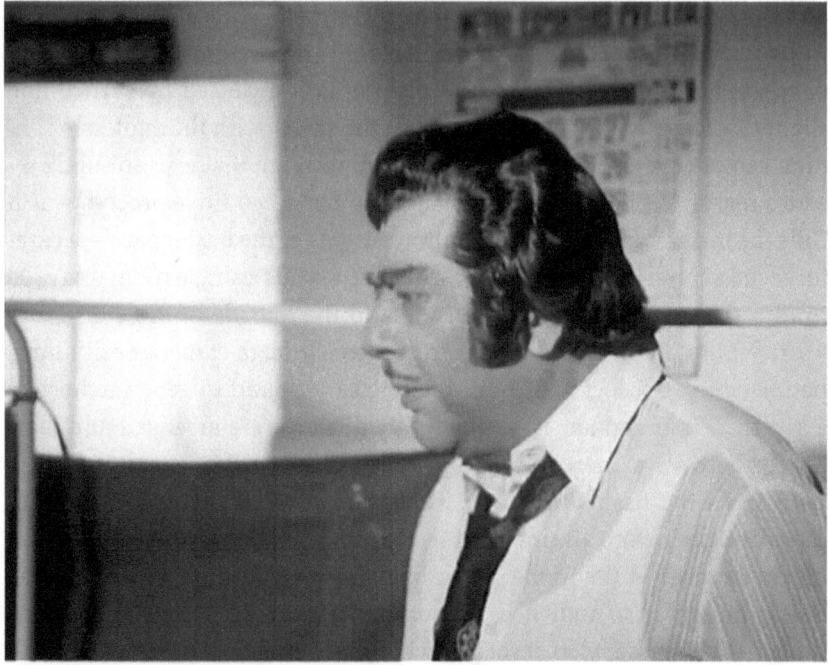

Figure 18. The calendar returns in *Purana Mandir* (1984). *Source:* Ramsay Pictures, frame grab from Mondo Macabro DVD.

seemingly of the unconscious, in the gap between what has been "put into" the scene and what is there despite no one having put it there, in felicity with what Chris Dumas calls the "non-authored aspect" of film. "If no one authored it," Dumas asks of such aspects of a film, "where does it come from?"[66] Asking this question helps us understand another way that budget horror films accrue sensory power. Attention to background details by which atmosphere is piped into the scene, such as attention to background actors or objects, can reveal how forms of a failure to perform as expected can deepen the atmosphere of horror. Made up of "individual elements failing to convince and failing to support one another," the flashback scene exemplifies how failure works to fulfill horror's promise: how "bad" extras or objects together conspire to rescript the scene of horror.[67]

Continuity errors, bloopers, and gaffes are of course ubiquitous in the products of any industrial filmmaking culture. In a letter to *Film World* in

1980, a moviegoer noted that while "the presence of a 'continuity person' in any Hollywood or foreign film production unit, is a must... in India, not even the most well-to-do and organized production concern has such an individual on its pay roll, with the inevitable result that the dresses, settings and compositions frequently keep changing in our films."[68] His shoes are black when Sanjay roams the insides of the temple and white in the next shot as he steps beyond the temple into the wilderness. There are two chandeliers hanging overhead in the bathroom when Suman prepares for her shower. There is only one chandelier hanging on the wall when she is rescued from the bloodbath. One moment, the thakur paces the hall outside the emergency ward; the next moment, he goes inside, but the "Emergency Ward" sign hanging above the door suggests he is once again on the outside. These chandeliers, calendars, shoes, and signs all thrum with what D. A. Miller has termed an "understyle," one that shadows the stylistic program of the Ramsay Brothers. While understyles can be redeemed as ironic, Miller ultimately concludes that they disturb presentation ("I am still certain of what I have seen, but I am unsure whether it is meant to be observed") and point to the contingency of filmmaking.[69] The changing colors of the hero's shoes can indicate different shooting schedules and how an on-screen geography of proximate spaces was put together from disparate places: how a temple located in south Bombay was made to neighbor the wilderness on the coast a few hours away. The Ramsays may not have had continuous access to the room they were using to film the hospital scene, needing to film over multiple days between other shoots. Appreciation of continuity errors and mis-takes can "bolster the fantasy of connecting with the 'original' production and producers, cast and crew."[70] A fan may play the film back slowly, freeze the frame, and zoom into it, "scouring the visual plane"; repeated viewings unleash what Tamao Nakahara calls a melancholic "fascination with the totemic potential of props and costumes."[71] Even as minor details connect me to the production of *Purana Mandir*, they demand a critical account of the film's production as one marked equally by collaboration and contestation between the film's producers, directors, and daily wage extras and laborers. In the flashback scene, for example, we may feel the presence of set dressers moving the calendar on and off the walls and by extension of the performers playing nurses in front of them. The calendar redistributes attention away from the film's credits, its foregrounded narrative, and visual world—and in so doing, also redistributes authorship of that world.

Like curses sworn by monsters, continuity errors too are *made by someone*. The calendar is not only a "non-authored," "unintentional" error that "no one" made; it is, of course, quite literally the result of intentional work by *someone*: someone put it there. They may have done it carefully or carelessly, purposefully or mistakenly, but they did it. All artworks are "created intentionally by humans, for humans": "Any artwork," James MacDowell and James Zborowski remind us, "is the product of both an overall design and a countless series of local decisions, often made by a large number of contributors and with varying degrees of conscious awareness—a fact particularly relevant, of course, for film."[72] Intention, in the last instance, is a substrate of labor past the limits of creativity, authorship, and design. While intention may be understood as volition in conscious, goal-oriented acts (such as the decision to include the calendar in the scene), intention is also operative as a directional force subtending nonconscious or unconscious acts undertaken in states of distraction, exhaustion, or indifference. Given the collective and industrial nature of filmmaking, intention is scalar and multidirectional, inhering in the intention to realize a vision as much as in every physical move on set. Nobody moved the calendar, but somebody moved it for sure—an author who shall remain forever veiled.

No one may have put the calendar in the scene with what we might call intention, yet it is there all the same. Speculating about who might have touched the calendar, and when and why they might have done it, also transforms the calendar into a prop of sorts. Props are traditionally defined as objects that principal actors touch during their performance before the camera or onstage. The prop, as Andrew Sofer notes, is "triggered" into significance by human contact.[73] The prop also has alchemical effects as it "elicits gestural attention" in a "moment of touch," inaugurating a chain of contact between bodies, spaces, and things that generates affective force in the mise-en-scène.[74] The touch of an actor animates the stage object as a prop; touch draws attention to the object and endows it with lively meaning. The prop then is a kind of potential latent in objects, "something an object becomes, rather than something an object is."[75] Objects "shifted by stagehands between scenes do not qualify" as props, Sofer posits.[76] Yet thinking propologically with the calendar in *Purana Mandir* allows me to see in the fictional flashback another film "between scenes": the documentary record of a film set being worked over by those workers most proximate to the background object world of the film such as set assistants, carpenters, electricians, and extras. Speculating about the calendar and how it appears on-screen has the power to illuminate the off-screen spaces beyond the edges of the frame, the historical sites that surrounded profilmic space.[77] Could this "invisible" workforce—one that had just taken to upsetting film shoots and destroying props on set as a form of protest—be enunciated in the mise-en-scène?[78] The repeated failure of the film industry to execute a signed contract for workers and the persistent difficulty of recognizing film's full workforce in the law meant that an invisible workforce resided past the inscriptive capture of discourses of state legislation, trade activism, legal judgments, and press reportage. For that workforce, the prop becomes a portal into the scene of representation.

While *Purana Mandir*'s opening titles make much of those who paid for the film, we know little about those who were paid to make it by expending their physical energy on the film behind the scenes. Credit sequences, Monika Mehta notes, "show that filmmaking is a collaborative effort and not the product of a single person's vision. If films often conceal the labor involved in their production, the credit sequences reveal this labor."[79] Even though they seem to make visible those who perform the hidden labor of filmmaking, the declamatory force of credit sequences is also obfuscatory. As the Hindi magazine *Madhuri* noted in 1985, the graphic size and speed with which a name flashed by on-screen—sometimes "fifteen or twenty names in small letters" that "speed by so fast, you can't read them"—diminished their value through visual scale; "Whose names are these?" the magazine pondered.[80] After we see the names of the film and its cast (but not its extras), we learn of *Purana Mandir*'s makeup and dressmen, controller of production, and the studios at which it was filmed; we also learn who the assistant editors, director, sound, and cinematographers are. Yet there were others still who worked on the film. We do not learn who assisted on the physical actualization of the film's spaces, bodies, and objects, who are the many who executed the film's production design as mise-en-scène. Such workers, *Madhuri* asserted, were "the film's backbone. . . . It is no exaggeration to say that film is impossible without them. They are the bricks on which the foundation for film's vast, glittering world is erected."⁸¹ "It feels like just as the glamorous world of film shines on-screen," the article concluded with a hint of warning, "behind the screen is darkness."⁸²

How do we illuminate this darkness? If we consider that Hindi cinema's backgrounds are places where histories of industrial transformation "reside," we may conclude that the errant calendar remains animated by Bombay cinema's "invisible" workforce of set dressers, light-boys, electricians, carpenters, and extras—those men and women who filled the frame between takes or moved to its edges when the camera was rolling.⁸³ When it enters the field of my perception, the calendar does so as an "irrelevant detail" that pricks open the allegorical power and mythical time of *Purana Mandir*.⁸⁴ Look closer at the calendar, and you will see that it is a calendar for the month of May 1984. Why?

An anachronistic omen, the calendar points to the future from the past: it connects the moment our heroine was born to when she might be struck down by the curse. But there is a simpler explanation. May 1984 likely marks the month and year that *Purana Mandir*'s flashback was being filmed in Bombay. Someone was moving the calendar between takes, and it was always the wrong calendar. Therefore, we can posit that the calendar is itself and many other things, all at once a creeping premonition, a continuity error, and a production gaffe within the scene of horror. A spectral touch enhances the atmosphere of Bombay horror: even as living things within the frame are touched by a lethal curse, inanimate things are given life by bodies out of frame.

Though they may have been taking down and hanging up the calendar with seeming indifference, someone's unrecorded gestures were as meaningful as the thakur puffing his cigarette in close-up in the hospital. Through them, the calendar registers the untimely appearance of film labor within the fictional scene of labor. With the calendar on the wall and the watch on a nurse's wrist, "the film's original moment of registration" has "suddenly burst through" *Purana Mandir*'s "narrative time"; the meaning of the film changes, so that "the fascination of time fossilized overwhelms the fascination of narrative progression," as "the set, the stars, the extras take on the immediacy and presence of a document."⁸⁵ The lights come back on at a film set in 1984 Bombay, but they also cast the set in a particular light.

What kind of film set was this? When it rotates into view as a film set, the flashback brings into view "bad" performances not occluded by editing, framing, makeup, or glamor lighting. Slowly I begin to notice the intentional energy—low voltage though it is—of the extras: not indifferent nurses but background artists playing nurses, a bit directionlessly; not clueless doctors but actors playing doctors, a bit cluelessly; not a dimly lit and sparse emergency ward but perhaps a film set dressed sparsely and lit poorly. Because those extras don't seem to be expending effort, because the props don't seem to have been created with care, what they actually evidence is some stratum of the kind of labor required to "pull off" the scene. In its very untimeliness, the calendar allows a kind of delayed illumination, a "remarkably intense allegory" of the arrangements from which a film emerged.[86]

THE POST-EMERGENCY WARD

The vision of childbirth in *Purana Mandir* is different from that offered by other film genres of the period. In popular melodramas, for example, scenes of childbirth mimic the point of view of doctors, nurses, and expectant families waiting outside the delivery room. When, in the melodrama *Pyaar Jhukta Nahin* (Love doesn't bow down, Vijay Sadanah, 1985), Preeti gives birth to her child with Ajay, we are positioned on this side of a screen beyond which the painless birth takes place, visible in silhouette. Meanwhile, in exploitation films like *Pregnancy and Childbirth* (Ayappan, 1985) and *Sex Vigyaan* (Sex education, Adarsh, 1983), documentary footage fulfilled the pornographic impulse to "show all." The films unveiled the anatomical secrets of childbirth but arrayed this disclosure within a series of views that promised titillation at close-ups of sexual "perversion"; it cathected the putative "education" of viewers to the visceral thrill of seeing bodies at large (and enlarged on-screen). At first, *Purana Mandir* too screens the site of birth, but then tears it open. When the heroine's father is told to "go and look for yourself" at his wife, we move to the other side of the screen and discover a pustulating body dying from a curse—a horrific recall of the fertility panics of the period.

While the forced sterilizations of men during the Emergency (1975–77) may be well known, what followed from them is less so. Among the many social engineering programs unveiled during the late 1970s in India were "family planning camps."[87] Here, citizens (mostly poor, mostly male) were encouraged, pressured, and often forced to undergo vasectomies. This coercion—the preferred term was *motivation*—occurred in more than one way.[88] Sometimes men were rounded up and hauled to these camps; at other times, men were offered "gifts" in exchange for being sterilized. By the early 1980s, however, family planning shifted its focus from the infamous male vasectomy camps of the Emergency era to interventions in women, thus turning fertility—particularly the fertility of young women—into a managerial object. In a 1983 state-issued newsreel by Films Division, reports on the 7th Non-Alignment Summit in Delhi, football matches, and spiritual conventions are juxtaposed with a story on laparoscopic tubectomies: "Because women are by nature shy," intones the narrator of *Indian News Review 1795*, this minimally invasive technique takes only a few seconds and can be performed through the woman's stomach. We see shots of doctors in a clinic in rural Punjab performing the procedure on a smiling woman and of women being helped out of the clinic and being transported in vans. Women, planners noted, could be targeted "on delivery tables immediately following childbirth or abortions, within the confines of public maternity wards."[89] "Even while the discourse spoke of reform," writes Kalpana Ram, the introduction of "less invasive" female sterilization technologies simply made sterilization "less visible" than it was during the Emergency.[90]

With the alignment between obstetric science (care of the patient) and state objectives (care of the body politic), the maternity ward was transformed into a kind of black box into which women could go healthy, fertile, and alive and come out stricken, sterilized, or dead. In April 1984 *Manushi* magazine sent a reporter to a local health center, where one hundred women were in line at a "mass sterilization camp." The women had been waiting "hours with empty stomachs, and minds probably full of the fear of the unknown"; they were led into an operating room that was "very primitive" with "nothing sterile in sight": "a production line—three tables in rotation, women upside down at a 45 degrees angle, abdomens exposed, cut at the navel, something inserted, abdomens blown up with air, various instruments inserted to the fallopian tubes, deflated, stitched up, moved out—all in the space of a few minutes." The reporter noted that "the smell of fear was tangible outside, where they were lined up on the floor. Obviously, such violence on a woman's body must have complications—physical or psychological or both."[91]

Family planning, which envisioned itself as ushering a population out of the darkness of folk medicine into the light of allopathic medicine and obstetric science, produced subjects suspended somewhere in between.[92] Instead of empowering women to make choices, the agents and instruments of science remystified fertility by withholding information and choices from women they conceived of as incapable of making their own choices. This in turn led to reasonable suspicions from women that they were irreversibly sterilized unaware. Unaddressed by the state, the aftershocks of the Emergency had "descended into the everyday" and fed a popular culture of superstition, anecdotes, and black humor that flourished far away from the orbit of governmental "family planning" campaigns.[93] These genres intimated the violence of biopolitical rationality by conjuring rumors of castration, fertility disorders, and monstrous offspring. In *Purana Mandir*, the site of care is unveiled to reveal a mise-en-scène of abjection, torture, and certain death that splits open the maternal body, splayed on a hospital bed and held down by nurses and doctors.

"What does cinematic horror have to tell us about the horrors of history?" asks Adam Lowenstein.[94] Lowenstein argues that the horror film produces unlikely "forms of bodily knowledge" that engage unresolved historical trauma not through realist representation or high-modernist aesthetics but through an unexpected "allegorical moment"; in such a moment, fragments of the traumatic past create a "shocking collision of film, spectator, and history where registers of bodily space and historical time are disrupted, confronted, and intertwined."[95] The allegorical moment of horror viscerally collapses past and present in a "momentary flash," an instant "in which an image of the past sparks a flash of unexpected recognition in the present."[96] A "fragmentary allegory" of the fertility panics of the 1980s, *Purana Mandir* speaks to such horrors of scientific rationality run amok.

Instead of the uncountable agglomeration of things through which atmosphere is made elsewhere, this hospital offers a finite list: one bed; one side table, with a lamp and a jug of water on it; one green partitioning screen; and one calendar. The room is sparse not only by the film's own designs but by comparison to contemporary hospital rooms in other films. In *Pyaar Jhukta Nahin*, for example, the delivery room is a deluxe suite, with a seating area and bed, several sofas, bouquets of flowers, and paintings. Because *Purana Mandir* only fitfully recreates the popular iconography of the hospital—with the slightest accoutrements of white coats, medical trays, and a stethoscope—the bareness of the emergency ward feels distressingly apt. The "go and look" moment in *Purana Mandir* reveals the abdication and failure of family planning as a scientific managerial project, leaving the citizen-subject free to (mis)read the symptoms of reproductive ill health as the doings of ancient monsters and curses.

While an aristocratic family is being violently expunged in the foreground—and an allegory of fertility reaches its punitive climax—the typically occluded work of other bodies comes into view in the listless gestures and small gaffes of the background. The emergency ward is a scene of labor, both fictional and real, and for that reason it is doubly atmospheric. It puts on view objects that are animated by bodies laboring beyond the frame, as well as bodies laboring into inanimacy within the frame. In the next chapter I explore the laboring bodies of Bombay horror in greater detail, focusing on the use of prosthetic makeup effects to generate the genre's grotesque monsters.

4 Making Monsters

VEERANA AND THE CRAFT OF EXCESS

As the bloodthirsty *chudail* prowls the woods, a young man named Raghu seeks safety inside a warehouse. But night has fallen, and the warehouse—by day a sawmill crowded with laboring bodies and buzzing machines—is desolate. In the cavernous darkness, Raghu's flashlight is a feeble beam. A howl sounds out in the silence. Fog rolls over the warehouse floor and its store of felled tree trunks. Stray dogs bare their fangs and bark, as if in warning. Some dread magic is infusing this once familiar world. A subhuman snarl, a flash of talons: the chudail is here (see figure 19). Her ancient body is sheathed in tattered robes, but her face is visible. Craggy skin, fetid teeth, red eyes. With her sorcery, the chudail begins to coil rope around Raghu's body and brings the jagged saw of the mill back to life. He screams as his body barrels into the blade. A final cry is cut off, and the saw comes to a halt. Blood dripping before her, the chudail beholds what she has wrought and lets out a low groan. Whenever this monster rises into view in *Veerana*, her victims flinch at the sight of a body transformed and moving ever closer with the threat of death. I shudder, too, though for another reason. I feel a different fleshly encounter is already underway: an encounter between the actor and prosthetic supplements, between skin and mask, hair and wig, eyes

Figure 19. Chudail in *Veerana* (1988). *Source:* Ramsay Pictures, frame grab from Mondo Macabro DVD.

and lenses, teeth and dentures—a grotesque creation heaving across the nighttime set of *Veerana*.

This chapter is about what passed under the label "special makeup" in Bombay horror. A class of prosthetic effects, special makeup refers to the apparent extension, amputation, or replacement of the human body by the application of latex, plastic, gels, and wigs to face, hair, limbs, and skin. Unlike "straight" makeup, which films use to invisibly enhance or clarify the appearance of an actor, Bombay horror used special makeup to visibly deform the body—to simulate torn flesh, open wounds, and supernatural beings. While horror films also used extensive optical effects (stop-motion animation, dissolves, and superimpositions) and mechanical effects to conjure explosions, hangings, and levitations, makeup effects are the beating heart of every Bombay horror film. Filmmakers used prosthetics to visualize demonic possession or monstrous unbecoming: a cursed mother in *Purana Mandir*, a rubbery evisceration in *Kabrastan*, a grisly crone in *Hatyarin*. "For some time now," *Filmfare* observed with something other than love, "the Ramsays and others have made convulsive attempts at making horror movies," adding that "they have spawned some truly grotesque creations, and all have consistently failed to click."[1] The "goo and monsters of such films," opined another critic, were "disgusting and shoddy."[2] The dismissal of the genre's varied bestiary as "goo and monsters" was widespread; censorship documents too indifferently name them "Ghost," "Devil," or "Spirit."

As censorship targeted scenes of graphic bodily violence, Bombay horror recentered on sights and sequences of the grotesque body, "a body of excess, oozing over and violating the most sacred of borders."[3] *Veerana* was released to theaters nearly three years after the film's production had begun.[4] Repeatedly denied a censor certificate for its graphic violence, the film underwent multiple revisions to become the most censored Indian horror film of the 1980s.[5] What survived was the necrotic, reptilian body of the chudail, displayed in close-ups and medium shots, stalking the woods and abandoned timber mills around the village. "These are the things that people appreciate the most," said Tulsi Ramsay, and "why people love our films."[6] Though these creatures have ensured Bombay horror's hold on audiences as the gory underbelly of Indian cinema, they have not received serious consideration from most contemporary scholars, who are likely to describe them only as "woefully inadequate," "basic," "bad," and "rudimentary."[7] Yet as Meheli Sen notes, the supernatural genres of Bombay cinema "invoke the materiality of the body in a foundational manner": "Supernatural entities in this setting remain stubbornly corporeal, often eliciting correspondingly visceral responses in the audiences as well."[8] This "stubborn corporeality" reminds us that Bombay horror's special effects may be shoddy or bad, but they are also things: objects that were created and shown, images that were seen and felt. How the objects were made and how the images move audiences are questions I answer in tandem in this chapter—via the twin poles of the "disgusting and shoddy."

"Studying disgust," Carolyn Korsmeyer writes, "reveals a physical, visceral aversion that becomes a culturally powerful—and manipulable—aesthetic response."[9] Disgust is an understudied path to the realization of cinematic horror. Artistic forms that seek to inspire horror, writes Noël

Carroll, require "evaluation both in terms of threat and disgust."[10] While threat has been analyzed in relation to visual space in horror films (see chapter 2), disgust remains undertheorized. Critics and scholars have typically not named disgust as a response that "special makeup" *expects* to create in its audience. In failing to recognize that, film critics have set themselves up to feel disgust *at* the film; witness one critic who described Bombay horror as "frequently more hideous than frightening."[11] In its review of *Jaani Dushman*—titled "*Jaani Dushman* Repels"—the *Times of India* wrote: "It's meant to be a horror movie," but the movie is only "extremely repulsive."[12] While repulsion is very much an experience horror films seek to create, it is both underenunciated in popular and scholarly accounts of what Bombay's horror films are thought to aim for (or how they aim for it) and overenunciated in appraisals of how they have failed to do it.

"Once we start to investigate the repeatable formulas of mainstream cinema more closely," Julian Hanich advises, "the more intricate they will turn out to be."[13] As Hanich asserts, the careful choreography of disgust on-screen—via point of view, suspense, and other strategies—eventually collapses the distance between the "distance senses" and the "intimate senses": "The disgusting object's gustatory, olfactory, and haptic qualities 'permeate' the screen."[14] We can better understand the place of *disgust* within the horror film experience by reading the "shoddy" effects of the films in relation to the "repulsive" affects they provoke. For Hanich, "the inconspicuousness of the special effects" is paramount, for they can otherwise "draw our attention toward the artifact and away from the scary object."[15] Yet it is difficult with makeup effects to separate scary objects from their conspicuously artifactual status. Prosthetic special effects are a form of the "disturbing, rough parts" of film denoted by the term "excess."[16] The role of "shoddy" special makeup effects—as a class of "disturbing, rough parts"—is to elicit the experience of horror, to make viewers' bodies do "too much" at the movies: breathe heavier, lean in, or turn away. The disgusting, as Julia Kristeva has described it, is "a vortex of summons and repulsion," "as tempting as it is condemned."[17] Summoning us to look at Bombay horror's "goo and monsters," disgust also sparks the method by which we can feel for condemned histories of craft by which disgust was created. In fact, thinking with the convulsive physicality of grotesque creations allows us to understand what it is that cinema idealizes, allowing us to see anew the transnational "prosthetic frenzy" of the 1980s.

FACING DISGUST

In *Veerana*, the chudail, Nakita, haunts the forests surrounding a village. Every night she awakens to seduce men from the village to her lair, kills them, and drinks their blood. Beseeched by terrified villagers, Sameer, the young son of an aristocratic family, takes it upon himself to intervene in the plight of the village. One evening he drives into the forest and encounters the deadly seductress. Led by Sameer, the villagers bind her writhing body in black sheets and ropes; that night, a black cloth is placed over her face, and she is hung by the neck in the village square. However, Nakita's dead body is salvaged by her zombie acolytes, who place her corpse in a sarcophagus. Even though her body may have been "destroyed," her followers set out to find her a "new body." By their occult magic, Nakita's evil spirit is transferred into the innocent young Jasmine, the daughter of Thakur Pratap Singh. Through the young girl, Nakita's spirit lives on. Misfortunes multiply: Sameer disappears; Jasmine's aunt hangs herself. Years pass. As she grows, so does Jasmine's thirst for human blood. Exorcisms and therapy sessions fail. Night after night, we see Jasmine punishingly possessed by Nakita's desire, leaving the comforts of her aristocratic haveli to venture into the woods, seeking the bodies and blood of men as her body is taken over by the chudail. The thakur's family traces Jasmine's nightly sojourns to a forgotten lair in the woods. The film ends with Nakita's spell breaking, her corpse being destroyed, and the innocent Jasmine being rescued.

Notionally, the terror in *Veerana* is an intersubjective *rooh* (spirit), the ghost of an ancient witch named Nakita who takes seat inside the body of the young Jasmine (played by the actress Jasmin). *Veerana* certainly "fetishizes her body"; the film occupies a special place among enthusiasts of global cult cinemas who are steeped in the memory of the young actress.[18] She is shown off in close-ups as she sings, strips, bathes, and dances; we are beckoned to enjoy the voyeuristic display of her young body amid feudal, ornate interiors and the gauzy decadence of her boudoir. But another body is on the loose and frequently on display in *Veerana*, one that demands and deserves our attention as a possible, and co-constitutive, source of the film's continuing cult appeal: not that of the smooth-skinned Jasmine, but of the chudail, with her bulging eyes, scaly skin, and decayed teeth. Every night, Jasmine lures men to a lair where she is revealed as the ragged chudail, a revenant demon who has possessed the woman's waifish body. Clouds pass over the moon, and her young skin is suddenly covered in aged scales, her hair is tangled and wild, her blue eyes turn bulging and bloodshot, and rotten fangs curdle her siren song into a guttural growl.

Horror films are one of Linda Williams's "body genres," which are organized around the "excess" and "gross display of the human body."[19] Williams's conceptualization of body genres, in the essay "Film Bodies" in 1991, capped a decade in which prosthetic special effects became central to the production and experience of horror films in many parts of the world, leading Richard Hand to label the 1980s the era of "prosthetic frenzy."[20] In North America, "body horror" films like *The Thing* (John Carpenter, 1982), *Reanimator* (Stuart Gordon, 1985), and *The Fly* (David Cronenberg, 1986) evinced a new preference for "showing over telling": a preference for ever more graphic displays of bodily mutation and violence and of the power of special effects technologies themselves.[21] "Special FX makeup" became the site for virtuosic, standout displays of skill within films, and FX artists were identified with their own "shops" that employed dozens of technicians in departmentalized roles.[22] For example, makeup artist Christopher Tucker became famous with his work on *The Elephant Man* (David Lynch, 1980), for which he used foam and silicone rubber in a dozen sections that took eight hours to apply every day. Many of Tucker's contemporaries also established themselves as above-the-line brand names.[23] Tom Savini, Rick Baker, Dick Smith, and Chris Walas came to be known to a wider public more than any previous generation of effects artists, while also refining their reputations as both artisans and auteurs; the first Academy Award for Best Makeup was awarded in 1981. After endowing films with marquee value exploited in posters and trailers, they were profiled in publications such as *Fangoria* and *Cinefantastique*.[24] Here, effects technicians disclosed their DIY (do-it-yourself) tricks and genius obsessions to foster a "cult reputation, an aura of cultural relevance."[25]

In a *Fangoria* cover story, special effects designer Rob Bottin shares that practical effects seen in *The Thing* "originated" in his dreams.[26] He describes how he supervised the execution of his "skull-full of ideas" by thirty-five artists and technicians, an experience the designer likens to "being a director."[27] In addition, Bottin details the processes and resources deployed in his effects shop, including mechanical effects, mold making, and makeup work, as well as large volumes of foam latex generated by three Hobart mixers running around the clock.[28] *Fangoria*'s story on *The Thing* builds to Bottin's punch line, at once authoritative and self-effacing: "In broad daylight," he says, "monsters are just so much foam latex."[29] By making the complex technique of special effects public, *Fangoria* offered a corrective to derisory critical and journalistic dismissals and constituted a significant discursive support for the films.[30]

One of the consequences of this textually, discursively, and industrially visible type of special effects work during the 1980s was a transformed relationship to the image. An emphasis on the mechanics of illusion allowed horror fans to "appreciate gore technologically"; moments of bodily horror could become in their eyes "moments of technological triumph, as they often find pleasure in looking beyond the torn flesh and splattering blood on-screen and imagining the invisible inner workings designed by a makeup effects artist."[31] The despelling rhetoric of technique also informed film scholarship, which cast the decade's "gross-out" horror films as inappropriate to measure by the standards of photographic realism.[32] "Indeed," writes Steven Shaviro, "these films go out of their way to call attention to their own irreality, the hilarious and ostentatious artificiality of their spectacular, outrageous special effects."[33] These "cinematic fabrications," writes Steve Neale of *The Thing*, demand "an awareness on the part of the spectator (an awareness often marked at this point by laughter): the spectator knows that the Thing is a fiction, a collocation of special effects; and the spectator now knows that the film knows too."[34] The knowing artifice of such effects, Shaviro and Neale suggest, makes for a paracinematic attack on the normative practices and tastes of classical cinema.[35]

While both the cult discourse of craft generated by film connoisseurship and the discourse of campy awareness offered by film scholarship break the moralistic and aesthetic discourse around special effects, neither acknowledges nor accounts for the displeasure that special effects in body horror provoke. Such discourses are appreciative but do not exhaust the possible appeals of and audiences for prosthetic special effects. In advancing intellectual pleasure or self-conscious laughter as the primary response, these positions suggest that most viewers either don't see the special effects on-screen because they "look beyond" them or that the "irreal" special effects themselves don't want to be seen. If one insists on the image's right to be seen without irony, they may discover another power that an effect possesses: to intensify, in ways previously unstudied, the meaning and feeling of the film in which it appears. Writing about *The Thing*, Neale goes on to argue that the "spectator . . . like the fictional character" is "astonished and horrified" at what they see, "despite the awareness" of the fabrication.[36] What if the spectator were, in a manner *unlike* the fictional character, horrified *because* of (not despite) their awareness that they are beholding a fabrication? And how do spectators respond to a special effect that announces itself as fabrication per se while saying little about what the fabrication is, how it was achieved, or where it begins and ends?

Physical special effects, as Steffen Hantke reminds us, "place a concrete object in front of the camera."[37] They are, simply put, *there*. Like all physical effects, special makeup effects too are simply there: applied to actors, then filmed by cameras. (Perhaps for this reason, they have not captured the fascination of film scholars the way optical effects in early cinema or virtual effects in digital cinema have: because they are not considered specific to cinema. To wit, one famous and pithy appraisal of such effects is as "ruses essentially analogous to those of conjurers" in which the "specific codes of cinema play a minor role.")[38] Physical effects may simply "place a concrete object in front of the camera," but on film, they are framed images of things that were once (other) things placed in front of the camera.[39] Horror films "remind us, through relentless and aggressive visualization, of the "thereness" of the body."[40] The "thereness" of makeup effects—their depth, dimensionality, and density—therefore sparks a decidedly cinematic experience, one connected not only to what the story tells us we are looking at but connected as well to the vividly displayed yet indeterminate "stuff" we behold in close-ups and slow motion.

The strange bodies of Bombay horror captivate me. I feel the flux of corporeal cognition, as though screen metamorphoses were triggering the slightest physical disturbances in my sensorium. No matter how "irreal" they are designed to be, physical makeup and allied prosthetic effects do not necessarily make me laugh. I know I am looking at *something* that was placed before the camera; I am sure that what I am looking at is not what the fiction says it is; I am unsure of what it is, instead, leaving me looking at an unqualified *thingness*. Such cinematic bodies horrify partly because they are unaligned narratively and perceptually. It is hard, in this moment, to do much with the fatherly reminder that a monster is only "just so much foam latex." And unlike the extensive coverage accorded the production of films like *The Thing* in *Fangoria* or *Cinefantasque*, comparatively little documentation exists of creative craft in the Bombay film industry. The demystifying discourse of craft connoisseurship insists on authority over the material world, but when I look on-screen, I feel exposed to an unqualified, interstitial thingness that is neither monster nor foam latex. Less hilarious than troublesome, it disturbs with a mysterious physicality of uncertain origins, constitution, and limits. My goal is to understand the felt presence of prosthetic effects in Bombay horror: how they get their perceptible "thereness" as fleshy things inscribed in fleeting images and the consequences of that inscription for our experience of Bombay horror.

THE CRAFT OF "TOO MUCH" MAKEUP

When I asked special makeup artist Aloke Dutt (*Hatyarin, Khooni Mahal*) about his work on Bombay horror, he was clear about the nature of his assignment: "Darr lagna chahiye" ("You should feel scared").[41] Dutt confessed the excitement and "mazaa" (fun) he had in transfixing target audiences, a clear sense of his own disposition to the work as well as of the emotional measure of its success.[42] Yet a more precisely imprecise definition of Dutt's work came by way of his one-time colleague, Arun Patil. Patil was an optical effects artist and had worked on the science fiction hit *Mr. India* (Shekhar Kapur, 1987). In *Mr. India*, the acquisition of a wristband gives the film's protagonist the power to vanish at will. Patil's optical effects helped realize this invisible patriot, a performance of the technological sublime that helped turn *Mr. India* into a family blockbuster and one of the best-remembered Bombay films of the 1980s. But a different imagination of the human body was flourishing in the horror films of the period. When Patil worked on *Khooni Murdaa* (Killer corpse, Mohan Bhakri, 1989), he felt that his optical effects—such as those enabling a gigantic ghost to tower over a house—had been eclipsed by prosthetic effects provided by another artist, special makeup artist Aloke Dutt. Dutt gave body to the ghost in *Khooni Murdaa*: a rotting red carcass that lumbers across the screen. According to Patil, such images were instances in which "too much makeup" was used, ruining the atmosphere of Bombay's horror films.[43] In Patil's words are two conflicting yet mutually illuminating ways to understand Bombay horror's prosthetic effects: as a material craft of excess and as a materiality that may have sometimes exceeded craft.

Dutt and his contemporaries defined the craft of bodies that looked and felt like "too much," the bodies of excess that rule each Bombay horror film. Theirs was a craft of achieving the *right* amount of "too much makeup." Bombay horror's bodies of excess were the products of a practice involving the skillful manipulation of resources at small scales.[44] The trained and true craftsman was one who was able to order and remake the material world by working on it and through it with an "intelligent hand."[45] From imagining the makeup effects for a filmic body to applying the makeup in layers to doing this over again on the next film, the intimate and creative labor of the makeup artist is both repetitive and evolving, as new images, things, and performance conditions enter the production matrix. This craft emerged slowly and in the thick of collaboration, competition, and inspiration in the ranks of makeup artists of the Bombay film industry during the 1980s. It is a history we can see play out on the monstrous bodies of horror, which register fluctuations in the creative labor economy as it transitioned from the studio era to the freelance era. On-screen, grotesque bodies seen changing in dissolves, slow motion, and close-cropped compositions register the temporality of this practice that unfolded between shots and developed over the years.

In *Chehre Pe Chehra* (Faces behind faces, Raj Tilak, 1981), a new potion concocted by Dr. Wilson (Sanjeev Kumar) has unexpected consequences when the doctor imbibes it. The makeup effects for the film were devised by Sarosh Modi. Modi had risen to prominence during the golden age of Hindi cinema, when each studio had its own designated makeup department.[46] By the early 1980s he was an industry legend whose expertise was sought under contract per film and was often seen applied to the faces of superstars such as Raj Kapoor and Kumar (whom he also transformed into a monster for *Jaani Dushman*). In preparation for *Chehre Pe Chehra*, Kumar and Modi traveled to Los Angeles for a month, where Hollywood makeup man Michael Westmore devised a number of latex prosthetic layers for Kumar's face and taught Modi how to design more layers when needed.[47] These layers, applied in stages, gave expression to the bestial body of Dr. Wilson: underneath a mop of unkempt head hair, his face swells and bulges irregularly. "After a month of sculpting, molding, and painting," Modi returned to Bombay with "numerous transitional latex prosthetics" as well as specialist knowledge in the art of prosthetic effects.[48] Modi's work on *Jaani Dushman* and *Chehra Pe Chehra* made him attractive to other producers of horror. Back in Bombay and speaking to *Star & Style*, Modi added that he was approached by other filmmakers who "asked me for such results" and "several special effects." But "then they hear my budget and do not come back." This happened, Modi revealed, "with the Ramsay Brothers."[49]

At the start of the 1980s, the Ramsay Brothers placed orders directly with Christopher Tucker, the artist behind *The Elephant Man*. Via phone, one of the Ramsays would call Tucker and request him to make a mask like the one seen in a prominent horror film such as *Dracula*. "The telephone lines were very bad indeed," Tucker recalled, but "somehow we always managed to get the requirements sorted out."[50] An agent of the family in London would drive up to Tucker's craft shop, pick up the mask, and mail it over to India.[51] As the horror boom intensified and films needed to be finished on tighter timelines and lower budgets, producers came to rely on a new generation of makeup artists in Bombay who were experimenting with latex casts and rubber molds at lower costs. This generation included Pradeep Pemgirikar and Ganesh Shelar, but the "latex man" of this era would be Srinivas Roy.[52] Roy rose to the position of special makeup artist after the studio era had ended in Bombay. He became famous in trade circles as the "latex man" of the Ramsay Brothers; his success encouraged others to move to Bombay in search of work. Roy helped some of them secure a place to live and find work in the film industry.[53] Roy was a close friend of Aloke Dutt's father and had helped the family move to Bombay and gain a foothold in the film industry. Now, as the special effects technician for Mohan Bhakri, the younger Dutt would help Bhakri compete with the Ramsay Brothers.

The work of these men (and they were all men) exemplifies how creativity might be "best understood as a way of working resourcefully with the world."[54] Despite budgetary constraints, "kabhi kis cheez ke liye mana nahi kiya" ("He never said no to a thing"), Dutt recalled of working with Bhakri.[55] Not the goat's hide, which Dutt procured from a butchery; not the dentures Dutt obtained from a dentist; not the layers of prosthetics applied to actors as they sat in Yaari Road Cemetery past sundown; not the blood-filled condoms that Dutt rigged to actors' bodies. Dutt furnished *Cheekh* with bodies that dripped, pooled, and splashed blood on-screen, drawing on a supply he maintained on set by the liter.

The Ramsay Brothers may have found Modi "far too expensive"—perhaps a reference to Modi's rate.[56] Along with the creative competition and budgetary difficulty, however, are notes of proximity, cooperation, and family feeling. When the Ramsays couldn't afford Modi, they hired Govind, who had assisted Modi on makeup during the production of the big-budget *Mera Naam Joker* (My name is Joker, Raj Kapoor, 1970) to do the effects for their own Jekyll-and-Hyde film, *Dahshat* (Terror, 1981).

Showcasing the special makeup of the film, a promotional still from *Dahshat* was published in *Filmfare* in 1981. While the Ramsays had supplied the still to advance publicity for the film, magazine editors dismissively captioned the image "The make-up ran out" (see figure 20).[57] When I look at that still, however, I see how artfully it composes key lights and mannered blocking to produce ingénue and beast in a nightmare tableau and how well the makeup artist brings the monster's itchy, purulent dermis to rise against the woman's unblemished skin. Instead of the makeup, it is *Filmfare*'s judgment that comes off as incomplete. As an aesthetic evaluation, the caption's "intersubjective demand" fails, unable to force one to feel what the critic feels and thus to undermine the promotional still or frame my experience of *Dahshat*'s special effects in advance.[58]

Dahshat begins with a mystery: someone has been robbing the crypts of Chandan Nagar's graveyard, befuddling the town's priests and policemen. The stolen corpses end up in an underground laboratory where the reclusive and monomaniacal Doctor Vishal (Om Shivpuri) conducts secret experiments on caged animals. One night the doctor is injected with

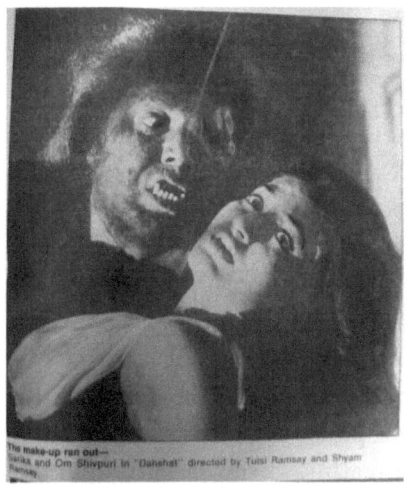

Figure 20. "The make-up ran out": *Filmfare* on *Dahshat* (1981). *Source: Filmfare*, 16–31 July 1981.

the potent serum he has been developing, triggering a transformation: he grows hair like a monkey's, a forked tongue like a snake's, and skin like a bat's. This beastly mongrel is finally shot down in the very hospital where the doctor once worked. The film, like *Chehre Pe Chehra*, is for Meraj Mubarki a "metaphorical" tale about an overreaching "scientific order" that "can no longer be defended."[59] The two films may be unified by their thematic exploration but diverge in the treatment of the crazy scientist. Unlike *Chehre Pe Chehra*, which retains a clear facial outline and articulated teeth for Dr. Wilson, Doctor Vishal in *Dahshat* grows scales, his jaw unhinges, and his tongue grows longer and droops out of his mouth.

When *Dahshat* was released, a reviewer for the newspaper *Times of India* was unable to take the scientist's metamorphosis seriously: "He develops mumps, turns into a gorilla and finally into a monster resembling an outer-space creature from *Alien*."[60] But the paper admitted offhandedly that the film does "succeed in making our skin crawl."[61] Likewise, a reviewer for *Filmfare* complained that the "camera never lingers for too long on the Beast's face" and that the final revelation of the monster "is messed up."[62] Still, he confessed feeling a "general eeriness" while watching the film.[63] Does the skin crawl because of the "messed up" transformation, does its "eeriness" come from its creaturely transformation? While the film's fans may not have left behind notes of appreciation, it is possible to glean from negative reviews some sense of what might have made the film successful.

Let us return to the *Filmfare* caption that accompanied the image from *Dahshat*: "The Make-Up Ran Out." All makeup effects cease somewhere; put differently, they do "run out," preferably out of the frame. An exposed seam can expose the literal limit of a makeup effect. Therefore, a skill required in such makeup work is correctly "masking" or "blending" the edges of the latex with the skin so as to ensure there is no perceptible difference in height between the cosmetic surface of the actor's skin (the "foundation level") and the latex layer. To properly blend the edge, makeup artists use foundation, greasepaint, and acrylic paint, as well as powder in skin tones applied delicately with a brush; matting agents were used to prevent acrylic paints shining under bright lights. In *Dahshat*, we see leathery scabs erupt all over the monster's skin except his chin. The lesions on Doctor Vishal's face grow from shot to shot, then stall awkwardly around his nose and lips. This "second skin" seems to have stopped, its edge visible in the frame. This edge becomes an unnecessary but inescapable *detail*, a kind of supplement central in evaluations of disgust. By pausing and poring over a body that is shown in flashes and sometimes at the speed of a scare, I am indeed subjecting it to a duration for which it was not designed. Yet it is this makeup "running out" within the frame that makes my skin crawl; I am aware that a body lurks under the mask, a thickness, volume, and presence onto which the mask was glued and photographed so it could be shown onscreen.

Though only momentarily glimpsed, the seam collapses the distance between diegetic and profilmic becoming. Even as *Dahshat* pretends that the monstrous skin belongs to the human body, the excessive qualities and inadequate quantities of skin on display divorce it from that body. As the seams of fabrication begin to show, the body in *Dahshat* is shot through with unresolved questions: whether it is a rigged puppet or actor in a bodysuit and whether the things we see are organic or inorganic chemical substances, solids or liquids, or something in between. This irresolution is cognitive, sensory, and doomed to fail. Even misfiring guesses about the ontology of the image have effects, deepening the experience of horror, the genre of category errors. Writing about rear projection's ability to decomposite the image into discrete planes of live actors and artificial background, Laura Mulvey calls the effect it creates a "clumsy cinematic sublime," a dream state achieved by film technology's heightened and "clumsy visibility."[64] Conversely, *Dahshat* achieves an effect akin to a clumsy cinematic grotesque, by sticking live bodies to a prosthetic thingness that pulls away from them.

The impossible bodies of horror create trouble at the join of the indexical chain. The effect is a visual and existential fact for all to see and know, an indexical sign "embodying within its form the existential traces of its referent."[65] Its facticity, however, is undercut by the uncertain origins and essence of its referent, which we cannot necessarily see or know, ascertain, or fix, from the moving image. We are looking at an object, substance, or texture we know had to have existed in order to be filmed, but we do not quite know what that object, substance, or texture was. An index, writes Webb Keane, "affirms the actual existence of its object, but not what, exactly, that object is." Therefore, he continues, "making sense of indexicality . . . commonly involves *ad hoc* hypotheses."[66]

Without fully absorbing makeup effects and actors' bodies into the diegetic fiction, *Dahshat* instead radiates their residual materiality as affective unease and horror. Special effects, though a consequence of low-budget filmmaking practices—such as inadequate resources, inadequate skills, or inadequate idealization—maximize Bombay horror's affective power as a body genre. In the process, they give new meaning and feeling to *Dahshat*, a "cautionary tale" about the corruption of the "sacrosanct" human body and an arrogant technoscientific order that seeks to transcend "*kudrat aur ishwar*" (nature and God).[67] If the narrative and imagery of Bombay horror resurface the body as grotesque excess, the films' special effects concentrate that excess in a craft of makeup that is at once "too much" and yet can "run out."

Practical and profilmic effects in horror films provoke confusion and revulsion at their excessive "thingness"; we are sure that what we are looking at is not what the fiction says it is, but we are not sure what it is instead. That experience intensifies when one looks at prosthetic makeup effects. With prosthetic makeup effects, a gruesome bonus is added to fictional stories and images of ugly mutations and open wounds: the palpable presence of live bodies under the skin of nonhuman thingness.

THE DISGUSTING IS BEAUTY PLUS TIME

Though *Veerana*'s very status as a horror film depends on the "special makeup" of the chudail, her bodily presence and performance have not figured adequately in existing assessments of the film. By sidelining the chudail from her own show, we risk repeating the narrative's compulsive expulsions of the chudail's body, for the film begins with her hanging and ends with her immolation. But before she spectacularly combusts, the chudail is everywhere: she makes a dozen discrete appearances over the film's 140-minute running time, here seen wielding a knife, there seen rocking in a chair. *Veerana* is a horror film on the strength of its atmosphere—a moody, synthesizer-score-assisted assemblage of flaring colors, thunder and lightning, blooming clouds of moonlit fog—and "special makeup."

By combining the wretched and the beautiful in the body of the same character and actress, *Veerana* pays homage to *La Maschera Del Demonio* (*The Mask of Satan*, Mario Bava, 1960), in which Barbara Steele played both the devil-worshipping Asa and the virginal Katia. Though it begins with a gruesome act—the "mask of Satan" is pounded into Asa's face— Bava's film largely eschews transforming its heroine into a monstrous body. By contrast, *Veerana* follows the ruse of *The Exorcist*: the possession of the body is staged through symptoms *on* the body. *Veerana* features priests fighting over Jasmine's soul and a psychiatrist analyzing her mind, but the film is utterly taken with her body. Extended exorcism rituals and psychotherapy sessions ask all of us to believe in another world beyond the body, even as they insistently train our attention on the body. Jasmine's body betrays new wounds, speaks guttural voices, and ages impossibly. The viewer's desire to hear and see the chudail—a desire incited always by having her face rise into the frame first in silence, her hair draped over her visage—is a desire to hear and see the mutilated version of the "pure and innocent" Jasmine, her body overtaken by "a serpent's skin."

Before he dies in the sawmill, before he screams and shivers—before he experiences horror—Raghu too experiences and expresses something else. He sees something, though we are not yet shown what it is. His lips curl, and he spits out the cigarette he's been smoking. The face Raghu makes is a face of disgust. The "fundamental schema of disgust," Winfried Menninghaus suggests, "is the experience of a nearness that is not wanted."[68]

Because the disgusting can seem too close, too near, it can also overwhelm the analytic separation on which aesthetic judgment has traditionally relied. Disgust appears as an irredeemably animal response—to find one's lips curling involuntarily—and yet it is highly refined in the making of aesthetic (and therefore moral) judgments.[69] The disgusting is held at bay by the vocally or visibly—that is performative and publicly—disgusted, from an elevated rank of "caste status and cultural difference."[70] To feel disgust is to be in the grip of a regulatory affect. Disgust somehow draws us toward the object while we struggle to separate ourselves from it. No wonder then that Raghu spits the cigarette out of his mouth. As he becomes conscious of feeling disgust—"part of disgust is the very awareness of being disgusted, the consciousness of itself"—aversion enacts the very separation he finds lacking in the object of his disgust.[71]

Spitting the cigarette out also seems to allow Raghu to keep looking at what it is that caused him disgust. "Even as the disgusting repels," William Ian Miller writes, "it rarely does so without also capturing our attention. It imposes itself upon us. We find it hard not to sneak a second look or, less voluntarily, we find our eyes doing "double takes" at the very things that disgust us."[72] An aversive fascination characterizes our encounter with what we find disgusting, a pulling away from that also pushes in closer. Unlike anxiety, which can seem objectless and so free ranging, or fear, which can cause protective flight away from the object, the experience of disgust is "inseparable from an intrinsic interest in the object."[73] Disgust triggers, in other words, an analytic instinct to sort through what at first glance appears only as so much "goo." The need to unveil and strip down the disgusting—to put it back in its place—engenders an encounter during which indeterminacy reigns, as the disgusting foils available categories and the disgusted are reduced to wordless exclamations. Disgust is the sensory evidence that our rational capacities are in operation as a result of "a sudden estrangement from habitual perception" caused by the grotesque, because "the object disturbs the sense of rational, natural categorization."[74]

"Gothic monsters," writes Steffen Hantke, "reveal more about the interpreter than about themselves. They expose the "stitches," the artifice, the seams of what our culture wants us to perceive as whole, organic, and seamless."[75] Hantke writes that the monster's skin—its "color, its pallor, its shape"—is a double articulation: on the one hand, it is cast by the film as monstrous; on the other, the monster becomes a site where we might be able to observe ideology in a spotlight, so to speak, calling on us to think with what it is that is so terrifying.[76] Disgusting things, Aurel Kolnai argues in gendered terms, are disgusting because they present as something lively but "out of place," something "conspicuous and veiled, like a poisonous red berry or a gaudy cosmetic."[77] As a variant of the "monstrous feminine," the chudail simultaneously channels and revivifies historical hierarchies of gendered, sexualized, racialized, and caste bodies that are "simply understood as deformed" within "normative aesthetic frames."[78]

The latency of the chudail within the young heroine reinforces the claim that "the beautiful is in danger—from the first and by its very nature—of turning out to be in *itself* something disgusting."[79] The chudail comes out of hiding from inside the beautiful body whenever the pendant around her neck is removed. For viewers of the film, this ritual is also a signal that the work of special makeup is beginning. Srinivas Roy made the chudail's mask for *Veerana*, using a process called slush casting or slush molding. The actor's face is first carved on a clay mold, a process of trial and error that could take months. Once it is ready, liquid latex is poured into the clay mold. The latex is brushed over the inside details and surfaces of the mold and allowed to dry. This process is repeated until the desired form and shape are achieved, possibly involving up to twenty coats of latex. As a result, slush casting produces masks that look dense, feel heavy, and have internal variations of texture and concentration across the different coats of latex.[80] The finished mask was cut into three pieces, which could be applied separately or all together to produce different looks. Using three separate pieces enabled the actor wearing them to retain "the most expressive and have lip and eye movement."[81] Fitting the mask could take up to eight hours. The mask was worn on facial skin, teeth were glued onto gums, and paint was applied to the body.

Makeup's additive function is vividly, viscerally on display in *Veerana*. The first time we see Nakita, she emerges out of the form of a beautiful woman (Kamal Roy) and transforms into the haggard chudail. Rather than staging this monstrous becoming through dissolves (as in the censored transformation in *Darwaza*), *Veerana* cuts away and back to her body in different stages of transformation; in successive shots lit by lightning, we behold Nakita beholding herself transform. Each shot is an over-the-shoulder composition of her looking at her face in a mirror before turning to face the camera as it pulls back to capture Nakita's increasingly horrifying (and horrified) face. In each of the three shots, the chudail's face is in different stages of affliction; with each successive shot, the skin on her face appears to grow lesions, scars, and scales before the mirror.

As the chudail metamorphoses on-screen, the actress's body is worked on in the interim between shots (see figure 21). One Bombay horror veteran recalled wearily the time spent waiting for the actor as they were made up further, sometimes up to "seven to eight hours."[82] This process is compressed into a matter of seconds in the fiction; the visible progress of Nakita's facial deterioration thus becomes a fleeting allegory of metamorphosis shuffled behind the lightning-speed cuts between shots of the chudail's face. These successive shots add surfaces to surfaces, body to body, volume to volume, and weight to weight; between each shot, another of the three latex pieces devised by Roy is pasted onto the face. The disgusting is, quite literally, a function of time. The filmed image emits an indexical trace of a performed real: both that it was once placed before the camera and that it was once photographed. By the end of her transformation, all the pieces of Roy's latex mask are visible on the chudail's face (see figure 22).

Served up to us in close-ups isolated from diegetic space and time, Nakita's latex visage beholds us directly and pulls us into the scene to feel the surface of her skin as it mutates, ages, and accretes scabs and scars. Nakita's habitat is an abandoned, decrepit manor in the woods. In this "veerana," the chudail is truly abandoned. Here, she is cut off from the world, but she is also cut out from the rest of the film: in almost every given instance that Nakita's face is in the frame, nothing and no one else is, even in scenes in which she is closing in for the kill. In these compositions, her isolation is social, spatial, total: she is truly abject. For filmmakers, the close-up allows phantasmatic creatures to exist without requiring the execution of a full-body prosthetic. For viewers, such compositions offer the chance to roam inside another order of images, to explore surfaces that aren't flattened out by cinematic idealization into two dimensions, surfaces that stick on top of and up out of other surfaces. In one particularly grisly shot, her nose seems to cleave open. In another, her lips move over her teeth repeatedly, shaping her mouth into a hole gasping for air. In yet

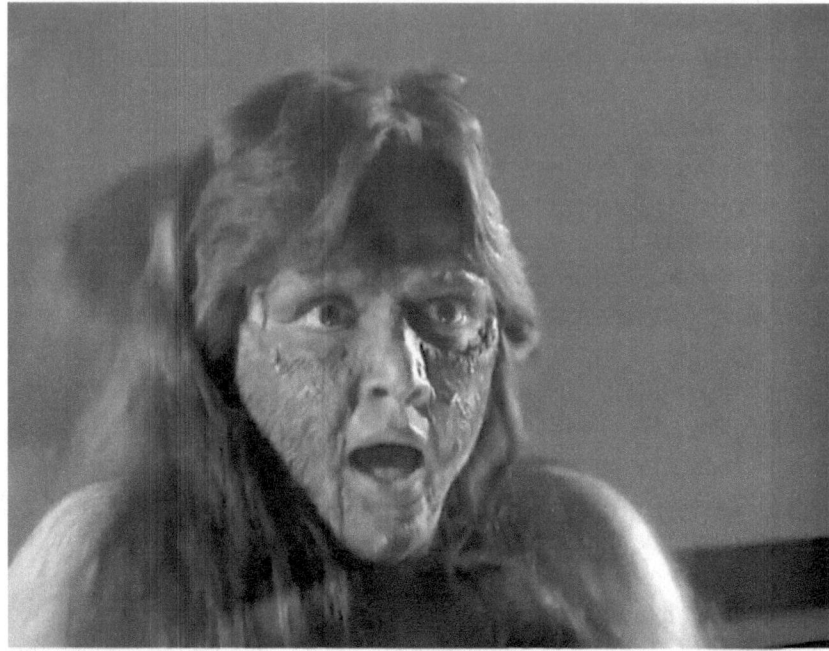

Figure 21. Making up in *Veerana* (1988). *Source:* Ramsay Pictures, frame grab from Mondo Macabro DVD.

another, her mouth doesn't move at all, yet we hear deep groans. In these close-ups, we survey the face like a terrain made up of many layers: some parts are mobile and therefore seemingly alive, but others are immobile and seemingly "dead" skin.

The flinch I feel looking at the chudail's face—complete with that cleaved nose—may be a flinch at this grotesque physical body on-screen, a touched body that I now feel I can *almost* touch, though I literally cannot. Perhaps it is the tactility of light, which once traveled from inside the split to touch photographic film on the set; that touch was then transferred in a chain from the emulsion to film print, then to projected image, then to my viewing eye in the now. The makeup is utterly effective in that it suggests that the possessed body is not just itself but some*thing* more. The doctor warns Jasmine's father: "It seems someone else is speaking from inside her. . . . Behind her innocent face hides a terrifying witch."

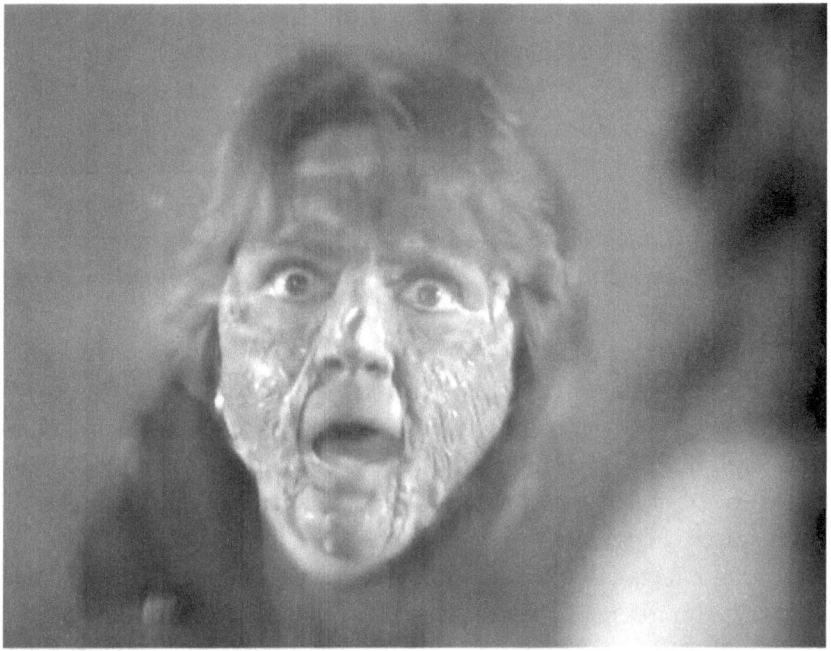

Figure 22. Made up in *Veerana* (1988). *Source:* Ramsay Pictures, frame grab from Mondo Macabro DVD.

Prosthesis, though it is meant to dramatize a haunting from within, works by adding from without so that the prosthetic body is always a body *plus something*. Prosthetic effects intend to appear as grotesque versions of human skin, which they achieve by supplementing that skin. They are additive layers pasted, painted, or glued onto the human body and then photographed to produce two-dimensional images of the grotesque body on-screen, disrupting the idealized view of the human body. The purpose and power of prosthetic effects in horror films is their ability to open or explode the body, to suggest depth, dimension, ruptures, and tears. These additions modify the boundaries of the body: they add grotesque mysteries, surfaces, spaces between surfaces, gaps, holes, protrusions, and extrusions; they add dimension; they add physical weight; and they raise the skin literally, so that the external edge of the human body extends beyond its ordinary threshold.

By co-constituting the beautiful and the disgusting in the woman's body, *Veerana* indicates that the disgusting may be nothing more than the beautiful plus time: her eyes look like hard, red shells that bulge out of her face; there are putrescent boils on her neck and chest; her fingers have become thick, misshapen talons the color of parched skin; and she now has decaying, fetid teeth. *Veerana* betokens the centrality of the "disgusting old woman" to repertoires of the disgusting, for she is the "embodiment of everything tabooed: repugnant defects of skin and form, loathsome discharges and even repellent sexual practices—an obscene, decaying corpse in her own lifetime." The prescribed forms of the beautiful woman, Menninghaus writes, are also "prescriptions for the avoidance of disgust." Every positive description of silhouette and shape, age and weight, manicure and pluck holds within it a tacit description of what it should not be—if, for example, "unbroken skin without fold or openings" should suddenly sprout "folds, wrinkles, warts" to become "disgusting zones."[83]

Special effects fabricate the fictive monster, the performatively deformed body on-screen. If, in the "aesthetics of the grotesque," the "insides of the body and its functioning—all that proper decorum dictates remain hidden—are laid bare," prosthetic effects in Bombay horror seemed to be doubly grotesque, breaking both eugenic and cinematic taboos of the visual order.[84] The disgust you may feel looking at them is an affective index of cinematic idealization failing and of horror movies clicking into place. While special effects in a different genre such as science fiction or fantasy can generate sublime mystery, here they pulsate with off-putting indeterminacy. The categorical transgressions visualized and embodied by horror film monsters—such as human/nonhuman, dead/alive, animal/plant, and earthling/alien—stir up first our disgust at the classification error and then our curiosity as the film's protagonists seek to understand and fix the error.[85] Categorical uncertainties are also operative in the experience of disgust prompted by makeup effects.

When the trade journal *Screen* reviewed *Veerana*, its critic complained that "the makeup . . . could have been less hideous."[86] For critics, "good" prosthetic effects are correctly calibrated along the line that divides "less" from "too much"; "bad" ones slip uncontrollably along it. The craft of Bombay horror's makeup artists is remarkable for being so accomplished in industrial conditions historically marked by scarcity and precarity. As effectively repellent as they could be, prosthetic makeup effects also exposed Bombay horror's technicians to the properties of materials such as latex. There is pleasure in the application of the intelligent hand to a craft, but also risk. Makeup effects that "ran out" and yet were "too much," Bombay horror's prosthetics were summoned using labor- and skill-intensive yet unstable materials that exerted considerable influence over the final look achieved on-screen. The tight schedules and budgets of Bombay horror also meant not having much time or money for second attempts at most effects. The makeup might run out, or it might outrun. That the craft sometimes failed means also that it could have left on-screen an affecting assemblage of "vibrant matter" that exceeds any assigned semiotic function and troublingly cannot be "localized" in human intention.[87] Bombay horror's prosthetic special effects sometimes fell short of or exceeded the craft of practitioners, producing an uncrafted excess on-screen.

Grotesque creatures on-screen court the corporeality of filmmaking, surfacing something of the human body and craft of filmmaking in heightened ways; in doing so, they also risk doing "too much" of "too much." Yet insofar as it is calibrated to spectacles of "too much," disgust is a slippery sensation. When the craft of "too much" gives way to *much* too much, our disgust might index the recalcitrance of production labor—unmasked, and grimacing directly at us in the form of a chudail's botched visage. What comes into view at the scene of horror is a mise-en-scène charged with traces of forgotten human bodies who inhere in this body genre par excellence.

IT GOT STUCK!

Masks are uncanny things in horror films. In films as varied as *Onibaba* (Kanedo Shindo, 1964) and *Demons* (Lamberto Bava, 1985), masks are able to induce psychosis and terror and estrange people from themselves. While the narrative may at first attribute to the mask a power to transform the wearer, the mask is found to have been activated "by the actions of the whole body of its wearer."[88] A latex mask was botched on the sets of *Veerana*, filmed as it had become painfully fused with the skin of an actress.

While this seems at first like a horrific accident, how it happened in fact discloses the activations, not only of its wearer but of the "whole body" of the filmmaking apparatus.

To create his masks, Roy used Max Factor latex, imported from Belgium at 900 rupees for a two-hundred-milliliter bottle; masks would typically consume three or four bottles.[89] The latex mask in *Veerana* appears a dozen times in the film as the chudail moves from her crypt and lair into other spaces: into a bedroom in the haveli and into the woods, into a sawmill and a temple. It is possible that some of these appearances were inserts created using the same footage, but it is reasonable to speculate that the mask was worn at least ten times by one or more actors. (It is also possible the mask was used for *Tahkhana*, which was filmed at the same time as *Veerana*.)

Though I never spoke to Roy—who rated *Veerana* his "best film," the one in which his "experiments with latex, wax, cotton, and spirit gum" all paid off—I did speak to Sheila Kapoor, a hairdresser on the film.[90] Kapoor started out as a junior artist in the Bombay film industry in the 1970s, worked briefly as a background dancer under famed choreographer Saroj Khan, and then became a hairstylist. In 1985 Kapoor was hired to work as hairdresser for *Veerana*'s lead actress, Jasmin. Kapoor recalled, "Kya height thi, kya personality, Mala Sinha se bhi zyada sundar" ("She was tall, impressive, more beautiful than Mala Sinha [a Bombay film star of the 1950s and 1960s]"). Though Kapoor did not remember working closely with Srinivas Roy ("some Bengali," she vaguely recalled), she did remember one evening during the shoot. On the final night of shooting, something went wrong with the mask of the chudail. After shooting wrapped and the makeup was being removed, the mask wouldn't detach from Jasmin's face. Kapoor described the moment: "Esel Studios [a studio in Bombay] is a deserted type of place, right? There, they'd built an underground dungeon type set. It was the last day of shooting, and the mask got stuck. It wouldn't come off! Everyone got really scared. We had to inform [director] Tulsi Ramsay. Then, somehow, just by pressing and peeling, we got it off hours later, around two am. I stayed with her. She [Jasmin] was crying through the whole thing."[91]

What happened that night in Bombay? Let us stick with the moment of the accident as it may have unfolded—and was filmed. As Jasmin growled and lurched, the mask made for her was perhaps adhering to her face, latex seeping into the pores in her skin. Latex reacts unpredictably with the heat of arc lamps, the humidity in the air, and the exertions of its wearer—with the whole "cine ecology" into which it is insinuated.[92] Foam latex is meant to be flexible, filled with pockets of air that allow for stretch. But over time the bubbles can collapse and the air can escape; the spirit gum itself hardens and makes it easier for the layers of application to crack as the mark hardens onto the face of the performer. If a producer uses hobby latex instead of cosmetic latex, if a makeup artist uses the same latex mask repeatedly without cleaning it, if the latex contains excess ammonia, or if an excess of adhesive glue is used: these decisions can burn the skin of the wearer, cause the latex to tear or a mask to stick to the skin.

Do we know *when* the latex mask got stuck to Jasmin's skin? Moving us away from assumptions of solidity toward energy, flux, and flow, what we call "things" may be momentary stabilizations in which virtual potentials actualize as arrangements—invisible elements that suddenly stick together in a formation that temporarily is visible, perceptible, or felt as "matter" under arrest. What we see in the chudail is an alchemical mix of sweat, latex, and skin, deepening our experience of the cinematic grotesque as it lurches toward us. (To quote Kolnai once again: disgust is about this adjacency, this "adhesive contact" with otherness, of "vitality" that is "out of place.")[93] In the duration of this corporeal encounter, what should be only an actress playing a part is being returned to embodiment as skin, sweat, and stickiness. Here, materiality pulls a surprise, staging the revenge of the profilmic abject on the filmic ideal. The catalytic force of latex stuns: the body emerges as a lively protagonist on the film set and with it brings a phenomenology of filmmaking into view. Seen this way, makeup and cosmetic work continues during filming as things seep, swell, and stick while the camera rolls.

Anecdotes of accidents trail the history of cinematic masks: actresses are burned (*Wizard of Oz*, Victor Fleming, 1939), their eyes are glued shut (*The Beyond*, Lucio Fulci, 1981), or contact lenses freeze their retinas in subzero temperatures (*The Exorcist*). When such accidents happen, they apparently fulfill some other, minatory potential that is always in the materials of film craft, something beyond engineering. When latex sticks to skin (and refuses to come off), prosthetic effects' otherness comes to the fore: not simply a thingness that we will never know, but a thingness that was never fully known. "Too much makeup" implies something unmastered swamping craft in an accident.

The horror film has long retailed stories of unbirthed life and killer objects. But the botched formations of bodies and things we find in 1980s horror films were particularly vivid, popular cultural intuitions of contemporary theories of the animist agency of the nonliving. The accident outstrips human agency while making visceral a sense of what lies beyond the limit: processes, objects, and bodies born of human intention and now run amok. These contingencies arise from the "active potential of diverse forces, feelings, beings and things" with which humans work, "which involves far more than an exercise of human agency on an inert and inactive nonhuman world."[94] Prosthetic effects force an encounter with the nonsignifying thingness of bodies, spaces, and accidents recorded in the profilmic event—an excess that gives heft to the story world and continues to haunt contemporary digital visual effects.

But accidents are made by humans, and the accident in *Veerana* uncovers a film set on which a female performer's distress became part of a scene of horror via transactions between men, including the film's directors and producers, the cinematographer, and the makeup artist. The interviews that I have presented in this chapter have given voice to veteran and retired film personnel who have historically not had access to other means of representation. Their narratives may have emerged out of spontaneous embellishment and a nostalgic desire for recognition, but they also allow us to see the gendered terrain on which Bombay horror's images of the monstrous feminine were forged and filmed. The anecdote of the accident, by contrast, was shared by a hairdresser who worked on *Veerana*—a woman who was not (and because she was a woman, was at the time not allowed to be) a makeup artist. Her memory breaks with the romanticization of "behind-the-scenes" handicraft and insider expertise.[95] An oral history that looks at craft sideways and allows us to glimpse its limits, Sheila Kapoor's memory of an accident on set shows how a lack of control tipped the art of "too much makeup" into punishing excess.[96]

BEHIND THE MASK

With the anecdote of the accident, the chudail's skin transformed before my eyes into a tantalizing almost-archive of the work of creating disgust. But as much as Sheila Kapoor's memory revealed to me, it may have been mistaken; after all, this was nearly thirty years after she had worked on the film. In a profile on the Ramsay Brothers published in the early 1990s in *Bombay* magazine, Uma Kheni Prabhu wrote: "When they [the Ramsays] were shooting *Veerana*, Kamal Roy, the girl who played the vampiress, used to weep bitterly as her make-up took almost six hours."[97] Who is the woman behind the mask whose visceral distress I sense on-screen: Kamal Roy, or Jasmin, or someone else?

We may know "from deduction" that there is *someone* "behind those grotesque layers of latex pushing it around," but I do not *who* is behind the mask at any given point.[98] At different points in the film, the chudail is played by Jasmin, Kamal Roy, a puppet, and finally, an unnamed performer. In each of these cases, Nakita is a prosthetic supplement, her on-screen liveness the painstakingly realized work of invisible bodies (makeup artists, effects technicians, and dress wallahs), a cinematic composite that exists only for the film. Lisa Bode writes that prosthetically augmented performance has "presented challenges to ideas of actorly achievement and excellence."[99] Unlike models of interiority ascribed to actorly performance, the explicitly collaborative nature of prosthetics work convenes and collects the traces of multiple other bodies, agencies, and intentions in its realization of the special effect on the external surface of a body. The actor's work (of voice, movement, and passions) is layered with the work of makeup artists and hairdressers. "It is hard," writes Adrienne McLean in her study of studio era makeup in Hollywood, "not to think of the personnel who actually applied the products to a performer's face and body, even if doing so in accordance with someone else's instructions . . . as intimately involved in the construction and meaning of the film image."[100] The disturbing power of prosthetics is that actors, makeup, and their combination into the intended effects are on-screen simultaneously in unknowable, uneven, and sometimes quite unpredictable ratios. "It's not Jasmine, it's someone else," one doctor concludes, following a session in which Jasmine speaks to him in a crone's voice.

The horror film, as Barbara Creed correctly observes, "abounds in images of abjection, foremost of which is the corpse, whole and mutilated, followed by an array of bodily wastes such as blood, vomit, saliva, sweat, tears and putrefying flesh."[101] In helping achieve the cinematic abject, prosthetic effects also perform a different kind of abjection, oozing over and violating the boundaries between filmic-fictional idealization and material base. In her engagement with Creed's reading of theories of abjection, Eugenie Brinkema advises that a narrow focus on images of the abject can foreclose understanding that abjection is a continuous—a necessarily incomplete—process of abjecting. There is another sense in which the horror film is replete with images of abjection: those of prosthetic special effects, which keep crossing a border—between human and nonhuman, live body and dead matter, diegetic and the profilmic—that we erect in our analysis of a film's representations.[102] I sense that Nakita's on-screen body is something more than a chudail's; altogether, it is a lurching animation of latex, skin, and hair, a somewhat anonymous mix deformed to produce a cinematic body that now is creeping across a filmed space.

Prosthetic effects may be a privileged instance of "our common sensuous experience of the movies: the way we are in some carnal modality able to touch and be touched by the substance and textures of images." Writing that she feels film, without a doubt, "in the flesh," Vivian Sobchack then confesses, "Precisely whose flesh I felt was ambiguous and vague." This sensory enigma pushes Sobchack to write through her quest to locate feeling.[103] The mystery thickens when we are moved by prosthetic makeup effects. It is not the case, then, that the accident discloses any one body over others; instead, it discloses the collective corporeality of their efforts. To look directly at the chudail in *Veerana* is to look at the corporeal work and technological base of filmmaking, at human and nonhuman bodies pressing up through the seams of her monstrous body: cinematographers and cameramen, hair and makeup artists, and costume and set designers (and their teams) all converging on a layer of latex glued to skin. Forcing viewers to stare directly at something that is habitually effaced from popular visual culture, makeup effects appear "bad" because they decline to be good, because they embarrass our desire to forget where they came from.

Recall this scene of horror: the chudail is on the loose in the mill. She overpowers Raghu with her supernatural strength and brings the mill's saw back to buzzing life. *Veerana* also shows us the same mill by day, when millworkers labor over tree trunks sourced from the "dark woods" and process it into lumber using large, buzzing blades. By night, however, the chudail is able to run the mill by herself: she ties Raghu down like a log, brings the saw to life, and kills him with it; she is a magic master of the material world. No need for the millworkers; the chudail's "kaala jadu" (black magic") is enough. When Raghu's corpse is discovered in the morning, his death is considered a clumsy accident of his own making. But the real accident in *Veerana* was happening to the chudail, reminding us what is at stake in thinking magically about the dangers inherent in bodily work.

It is within and against Bombay horror's dense and hallucinogenic diegesis that prosthetic effects pop: as thingness exposed, as presence perpetually splitting from referentiality, as labor separating from intention, and as clumsily rendered bodies deepening an experience of the cinematic grotesque. What makes makeup effects "hideous," "repulsive," "shoddy," and "disgusting"? Jean Louis Comolli once noted that cinema "rarely films work," suggesting instead that work appears only in and as "unperceived trace."[104] Even when it does film work, Comolli cautions, the "visible now functions as mask": "that which is shown conceals something else"; what is on-screen—the baldly presentational world of film—dissembles and hides what cannot be shown.[105] By making the "invisible" work and risks of filmmaking particularly vivid, *Veerana*'s prosthetic witch discloses the practices of filmmaking on terms different from those allowed by the discourse of craft, which insists on masculine authority over the material world.[106] The botched mask refuses to save face, instead clinging to its labored origins, even carrying them along into visible thereness.[107] It is perhaps because the prosthetic effect remains perceptibly haunted by the occult and "objectified labor" of those in front of the camera and those behind the scenes that we feel the mask "demonically grimacing" at us.[108]

"Get me out of here," a tortured Jasmine can be heard pleading with her family about the predicament she finds herself in. *Veerana* ends with Nakita's expulsion and the explosion of her underground lair as the pure is separated out from the impure, the ancient evil from the young and the innocent. The last time we see the witch's mask, we see it burn, char, and be destroyed. But the way in which the film ends invites a second look;

after Nakita's wretched body is reduced to skeletal ash and her grand sarcophagus implodes, the film cuts for its final shot to Jasmin, walking along the beach. *Veerana* begins with a disclaimer stating that the film "deals with evil powers, ghosts, spirits, witches, and black magic, none of which have any place in our modern world." If disgust marks the presence of the anomalous—something primitive in modern time, some primal feeling in the civilized body, with "no place in our modern world"—it has been exorcised. Along with ending the run of the chudail and her mythical powers, the film finally breaks the spell of the prosthetic body, eliminating what is "out of place" to leave us with a human body in ostensibly untouched nature.

CLEANING UP

The special makeup artists who worked on Bombay horror look back at their work with a mixture of nostalgia and regret. I met Aloke Dutt in the summer of 2013. By then it had been nearly twenty-five years since Dutt had worked on *Khooni Murdaa* and more than a decade since he had worked on any film at all as a makeup artist. Since the early 2000s, Dutt had moved out of production work; he found it too unpredictable, the pay low, with little compensation by way of respect or union support. The ascendancy of digital effects had endangered his livelihood, and he needed to save money for his daughter's marriage. Dutt changed jobs but didn't leave the industry. He started a costume laundry and cleaning service. He narrated his work to me while seated amid the fresh laundry of his Star Laundry Service in Andheri: "Clothes come at night, washed and ironed overnight, readied in the morning."[109]

Prosthetic effects too have been transformed by the "cleanup" of the digital revolution that arrived soon after *Veerana*. Rubber suits and layers of latex now appear on-screen only after having been passed through a digital intermediate, then filtered and composited by visual effects supervisors.[110] But why use prosthetic effects only to have them be retouched digitally? The stated goal of visual effects supervisors, software, and technicians—in consultation with cinematographers, directors, and production designers—is to make sure that physical objects filmed at different times, places, and frame rates are smoothly composited alongside digital objects into a single *seamless* image. Digital cinema seeks to manage the materiality of prosthetic effects, to channel their comforting thereness while regulating their disturbing otherness. What is described by visual effects shops as "clean-up" and "beauty work" ameliorates a perceptual anxiety: that the felt thingness of the effect, its once having existed in profilmic space and time, may be experienced by viewers as disrupting diegetic space and time by recalling production space and time. Indeed, when the seams show in such images, viewers are able to sense the digital production pipeline of overworked, underpaid VFX artists choking at the labor demanded by big budget films.[111] Even as they smooth the prosthetic effect into the image, the digital augmentation of prosthetic effects subtracts something from them: a transgressive sense of *too much*.[112] If left unchecked, it may even expose that which is usually hidden: the sticky materiality of the thing that is cinema.

Unpleasant ridges within films can plunge us into disgust, but they can also alert us to the warp and woof of the medium itself: lured to look at goo and monsters held in closeup, our vision of film itself might be contaminated by an appetite for uneven texture. Let me explain by returning, one more time, to the scene with which this chapter begins. As the chudail arrives at the derelict sawmill, we see three dogs barking at the approaching danger. Each of the three times the dogs are on-screen, they look faded and far away to me. It is difficult to ascertain exactly where they are in the sawmill, where they came from, or where they vanish to. The dogs, it can be surmised, were meant to suggest a threat in the vicinity; the mode of their presentation, however, makes them obstinately remote. Watching *Veerana* over and over, I have leaned in closer to see them better. But the dogs remain grainy and uncertain, as though they are not quite there. To confront the uneven textures of images is to be "always, immediately, and de facto to be immersed in a field of active narrative hypothesizing, testing, and re-understanding of how physical properties act and are acted upon over time."[113] The sequence from *Veerana* did not seem to matter at all to Gulshan Grover, the actor who played Raghu, the *chudail*'s victim. When we spoke, Grover could not recall filming the sequence, much less how the dogs were added to it.[114]

One day I realized I had seen the dogs many times before I had ever seen *Veerana*: barking in an Antarctic research station. The dogs of

Veerana were interpolated from an American film I was familiar with: John Carpenter's *The Thing*! For a while, *The Thing* had been denied clearance to release in India: the *Times of India* reported it had been officially banned by the censor board.[115] Perhaps the Ramsay Brothers had procured the film print from the Bombay censors or a bootleg copy on videotape; a camera may have dimly recorded *The Thing* as it played, and the footage was spliced into *Veerana* using a blade and some masking tape. In the process of being incorporated into *Veerana*, the hulking huskies of *The Thing* had also become a bit smaller, insubstantial. They were reminders that the representational, formal, historical, and sensual dimensions of spectral images are laced with the materiality of the past. That was a consummate gesture by filmmakers of their fandom, and the enduring visual noise will forever call attention to their act of cinephilia. With its transplanted canines, *Veerana* had also executed an audacious eyeline match across the horizon of horror film culture in the 1980s, thereby turning Hollywood horror into an audience of Bombay horror.[116] As we will see in greater detail in the next chapter, the objects and forces of film circulation continuously shaped the making of horror movies before and after the arrival of videocassettes in 1980s India.

5 Hidden Circuits

KABRASTAN FROM FILM TO VIDEOTAPE

In *Kabrastan* (Graveyard, 1988, Mohan Bhakri), a man is forced to spend a night in the graveyard. When midnight strikes, mummies, witches, zombies, and ghouls begin clambering out of graves and gather around him. As he beseeches the many gods to save him—"Oh God! Ishwar! Allah!"—phone numbers begin to scroll, somewhat unhelpfully, across the bottom of the frame: "Ph Bandra: 6404646/ 6403332," "Ph Fort: 2046233/ 2048625," "Ph Factory: 694654/ 692151/ 690425." Below the telephone numbers, a watery line shines, a thin bar in which the images of *Kabrastan*'s danse macabre are refracted. The digits of the phone numbers are now visual junk, but they were once contact numbers for a videotape business run by Bombino Private Limited, which released *Kabrastan* for sale on videotape in 1988. The line is the distinctive, distorting underscan of videotape that forms in videocassette dubs. Ticking across the screen in perpetuity, *Kabrastan*'s undead corpses, dead phone numbers, and shimmering underscan offer ways for us to turn the dial on film history (see figure 23). Focusing on the horror films of Mohan Bhakri, this chapter tracks the transforming circuits of Bombay horror's distribution, exhibition, and circulation across the arrival of commercial videocassettes in 1980s India.

Figure 23. Kabrastan's (1988) circuits traced on-screen. *Source:* Bhakri Films Combine, frame grab from VCD.

The lusty witches and bloodthirsty vampires of Bombay horror were widely believed to be the kinds of lurid images demanded by their audience: an audience of men, who watched the films in theaters located in working-class neighborhoods in cities and small towns. As competition for this audience intensified during the horror boom of the mid-1980s, a concomitant decline in the "quality" of the films as the decade progressed was also blamed on the audience. This discourse of decline held sway over film censors, critics, distributors, and audiences, as well as filmmakers, shaping the production, regulation, and reception of the films. For example, *Jaani Dushman*'s director Rajkumar Kohli claimed, "It's only the *char anna wallas* [colloquially, penny-paying] who appreciate their [the Ramsay Brothers'] kind of horror. Intellectuals want a clear storyline, cleverer screenplay and a good star cast."[1] The Ramsay Brothers in turn complained, "Horror movies got a bad name because people like Mohan Bhakri and Vinod Talwar have tried to imitate us without ever matching our quality . . . to draw in the *char anna* classes. Their films didn't work and we suffered. Since we're a brand name, every horror movie—good or bad—is identified with us."[2] Rather than reinforcing affective affinity between Bombay horror and its classed and gendered audiences, this chapter explores Bombay horror's path of circulation as determined by the drive to make money in a highly stratified and scarcity-driven exhibition culture. This account shows that distribution, exhibition, and circulation don't just happen to films "after" production. They are world-making forces that produce the film text.[3]

The production of horror films sped up after 1984, as filmmakers enticed by the box office success of *Purana Mandir* entered the fray. But the drive to monetize audience interest in the genre came up against the material realities of film exhibition: there were not nearly enough theaters for every film to play in. Enter video. Around the world, horror has had a particularly productive relationship with the video revolution, benefiting from the liberties it afforded niche audiences, small filmmakers, and alternative tastes. In 1980s India, video would offer many kinds of things to many kinds of audiences, from devotional content to straight and gay pornography. Media historians have chronicled the circulation of documentary films, wedding videos, right-wing propaganda, and news magazines on videotape, revealing the medium as a revolutionary ensemble of epistemic, sensory, and sociocultural practices in 1980s India.[4] Another story of videotape—its imbrication with Bombay cinema in 1980s India—is possible if we plot video's multiple technological, aesthetic, and economic intersections with the life of Bombay horror.

The video revolution, as Caetlin Benson Allott has demonstrated in the North American context, also found its way into horror films, which can be examined to understand how films responded "to their new exhibition platforms both formally and narratively."[5] In India, video was a new form of the experience of Bombay horror, and Bombay horror was a form of the new experience of video. The material impact of video can be gleaned in the style and story worlds of Mohan Bhakri's horror films. Unlike the films of the Ramsay Brothers, many of Bhakri's horror films are less about journeying to a placeless haveli to confront an ancient curse or demon and more about families that stay put to find that horror has come home to them. The home in these films is populated by young, English-speaking men and women, as well as by the Walkman cassette players, television sets, and push-button telephones they own. When they do leave home, heroes and heroines might drive a Maruti 800 to the local video library, movie theater, or discotheque. These nightly sojourns carve out spaces of privacy, consumerism, and sexual intimacy for the young men and women, but they find upon returning that a serial killer has burned the cook to death or cut the electric power supply. It is a consumer world charged with cautionary menace: television screens beam spectral static and headphones emit ghostly garble, while the maid, last seen asking for detergent powder to wash the clothes with, shows up drowned in the bathtub. The brand names of the decade, from Sony to Surf, appear inside Bhakri's films, while other brand names appear over the films. Logos for emerging home video companies—Bombino, Shemaroo, Captain, and Texla—glisten on top left or bottom right, while their phone numbers scroll across the bottom of the screen. Such visual clutter is somewhat at odds with the modernist, clean lines of the film's title sequences, yet it reminds us that the audience for Bombay horror was far from monolithic, internally differentiated by class, gender, and platform.

When he began making horror films, Bhakri's imagined viewers seemed to be those who looked like the consumers in his films, the characters of young men and women who go to the club (*Cheekh*), watch television in their bedrooms (*Khooni Murdaa*), and listen to the latest hits on their portable cassette player (*Kabrastan*). Yet surviving copies of Bhakri's horror films indicate that they may have escaped the designs of the film's producers and video distributors, entering a parallel network of circulation in an "illegal ecology of video": as copies shown in video parlors.[6] Video piracy would dry up a significant financial revenue stream for filmmakers and usher in the end of Bombay horror. The steep drops in image quality, watery underscans that form from copy to copy, and logos printed over other logos in the corners of images—what Lucas Hilderbrand terms "bootleg aesthetics"—indicate a history of value extraction that took films beyond the control of film producers.[7] Both the promise and perils of this moment are archived in Bhakri's films, wherein the boom and bust of Bombay horror are writ large in spectral images.

THE MATERIAL LIMITS OF THEATRICAL EXHIBITION

Bhakri's first horror film, *Cheekh* begins, like *Purana Mandir*, as a tale of feudal violence. A lusty *zamindar* (landlord) rapes and kills a young bride and her husband on their wedding night. Revenge is vowed and comes to haunt the present-day descendants of the *zamindar*'s family. Yet the danger that stalks them is not a curse or monster. Instead, it is a serial killer who picks his victims off one by one, burning, slashing, and shoving them to their deaths. The leather-gloved maniac distinguished Bhakri's horror films from those of the Ramsay Brothers, as much as *Cheekh* represented a break in the filmmaker's career. Before he made Hindi-language horror films, Bhakri made Punjabi actions films. The audience for these films was in "East Punjab," a distribution territory that designated parts of northwestern India. This audience began shrinking in the early 1980s, drying up the market for Bhakri's action films and causing him to pivot to Hindi horror. Bhakri's contemporary, Vinod Talwar, also moved from Punjabi films into Hindi horror around this time. Using a script by Dharamveer Ram (who wrote Bhakri's *Cheekh*), he completed his first horror film, *Raat Ke Andhere Mein/In the Darkness of the Night* (1987), starring Deepika Chikhlia (also from Bhakri's *Cheekh*). When I asked him why the Punjab market shrank in the early 1980s, Talwar said it was "due to the insurgency": threats and bombings were gutting theaters, and moviegoing shriveled in response.[8]

By the 1980s, moviegoing in India was so popular as to reliably attract full-house matinees as much as lethal acts of terrorism, yet it was not a leisure activity that attracted major material investment from cinema owners or the state. In Secunderabad, a ceiling fan fell on a woman in a movie theater, killing her instantly.[9] In Rajasthan, a fire ripped through the only theater in a small town, gutting it.[10] In Ludhiana, a bomb exploded in a theater, and when a curfew was ordered in Gwalior, the lights came on to prematurely end the late night show.[11] In Nagpur, heavy rains flooded cinema halls.[12] In Lucknow, moviegoers found theaters closed in protest against a tax.[13] And in Birpur, a small town on India's border with Nepal, there was simply no theater at all.[14] Bombs, riots, curfews, strikes—in such volatile moments, the airy fantasies of what cinema could be are undone by extreme experiences of danger, risk, or failure that return moviegoers to their bodies.

How films are shown and seen—from the quality of a film print to the screening conditions of a movie theater—are material facts that shape the experience of going to the movies. One moviegoer from Rourkela wrote in about the "awful condition of some of the cinemas" in his hometown, where "the plaster is peeling off the walls, the seats have no padding, the curtains have patchwork on them, vermin chase each other in the auditorium, and the all-pervading stink equals that in the toilets."[15] Another from Karnal noted that "film-viewing is not only an aesthetic or emotional experience but also an endurance test requiring stamina" to navigate "creaky, bug-ridden seats," "defective exhaust fans," a "floor littered with cigarette stubs," and the "stench-ridden air."[16] These details help us understand just how much one receives at the site of film reception: the cinematic text includes the "concrete allegories" of architecture, layout, location, and the built environment of the theater.[17] When plaster peeled or a fan fell from a ceiling, infrastructural failures decades in the making materialized as sudden accidents. Something was concretized in India's movie theaters in the 1980s: as the six hundred chairs in a Bombay theater creaked, they sounded the disdain of state policy and exhibition practices toward audiences of Bombay cinema.

Theater construction had remained marginal to the postindependence Indian government's developmental, nation-building objectives. A moratorium on "non-essential building" since the 1950s restricted the construction of new movie theaters. Theaters needed cement and steel, electricity, and skilled workers: throughout the 1980s, instead, there were acute power shortages, dwindling steel supplies, and an undersupply of skilled labor.[18] Cement—the thing that kept theaters glued together and "the yardstick of a nation's prosperity"—was hard to come by, with mass layoffs at cement plants and a black market causing prices to soar.[19] As a result, while an estimated twelve million people watched films in Indian theaters every day, there were only seven seats for every thousand citizens, one of the lowest averages in Asia.[20] Limited exhibition facilities plagued the Tamil, Telugu, and Malayalam film industries, too, but it was the Hindi film industry that, as the *Hindustan Times* put it, was facing the "problem" of a production boom without exhibition outlets to match.[21] Half of the nearly 6,000 theaters operating in the country in the 1980s were located in southern India (most scholarly studies of theatrical film culture in India are sited in one of four southern states.) In Bombay, Delhi, and across the Hindi-speaking northern belt that represented Bombay cinema's primary markets (and two-thirds of the country's population), cinemas were "even more sparse."[22] Hindi cinema's most lucrative market was Bombay, which had 127 theaters serving nearly eight million residents. By the early 1980s, some of these theaters were being scouted for redevelopment as shopping malls, office blocks, and apartment complexes.[23]

Cinema was a primarily extractive resource for the state from which to generate monies, while high rates of taxation at the site of exhibition also meant little money circulated back to the theater owners to run and maintain their theaters: to keep up projection facilities, have toilets cleaned, preserve appearances. The highest entertainment taxes in India were levied in the Hindi heartland—in Uttar Pradesh, a state that comprised a sixth of the country's population and one-twenty-fourth of its built theaters, and that reported the lowest wages of any working population.[24] While increasing the number of theaters would likely increase revenues, state governments elected instead to raise entertainment taxes on existing theaters or to introduce new taxes on each sale from producer to distributor and on each rental from distributor to exhibitor. Entertainment taxation exploited cinema exhibitors and patrons at exorbitant rates—from 75 to 125 percent tax on the value of the ticket—but the state did not put any of that money back toward theater construction. The result was that "the Government has become a partner without investment."[25]

Despite this crisis, film production in Bombay was not slowing down—overproduction was a strategy to keep capital circulating, even as the production sector remained in the red. "In spite of all odds and oppositions," *Trade Guide* noted in 1985, "film production is at its top quantitatively. In Bombay alone, about 900 films are under production."[26] Scarcity bred fierce competition. Historically, a high degree of influence has been concentrated in Bombay film exhibitors, who communicated their interests to distributors before agreeing to book films in their theaters. Distributors, in turn, were financing films at the production stage (see chapter 3), thereby deciding which kinds of films were (and were not) made. Over time, the "audience" became the discursive mediator between these sectors; appeals to a constructed yet seemingly empirical moviegoing public helped to naturalize and maintain the relationships of power in a vertically unintegrated film business.[27] Films, unless they ran to full houses, were unlikely to run much longer than a week; this of course dictated the kinds of films that were made and booked. For moviegoers, it meant being willing to buy tickets "in black" so as to not miss the film altogether; these were tickets sold by scalpers or by theater exhibitors themselves, with an exorbitant, off-the-books margin. "The root cause," noted *Screen*, "is the excessive demand as against the restrictive supply." "The demand for cinema tickets," the magazine went on to explain, "has perennially exceeded the supply because the number of cinema houses in the cities is hardly sufficient to meet both the output of the motion picture industry and the cinema-goers steadily increasing need to go to the cinema in the absence of any other entertainment in the country."[28] By the summer of 1985, an precedented dozen horror titles were in various stages of completion or release, including the Ramsay Brothers' *Saamri*, Bhakri's *Cheekh*, and Joginder Shelly's *Pyasa Shaitan*. Where would these films circulate?

The years preceding the horror boom had given the Ramsay Brothers time to carve out a share of the theatrical market in which access to "A" center screens in Delhi and Bombay was monopolized by long-standing arrangements between monied producers, their loyal distributors, and exhibitors. The family's strategies included aggressive ballyhoo to ward off competitors. Released in 1985, *Saamri*, the follow-up film to *Purana Mandir*, was sold as a "sequel" despite only superficial continuities. Advertised as coming "from the Only Genuine Makers of Horror Films in India," *Saamri* was reported to be "creating havoc in Bombay suburbs."[29] Yet *Saamri* did not stay in Bombay long. Of the dozen prints of the film, most had left the city's suburbs by the second week and began their journey inland, playing on one screen in Pune one week and another in Ahmedabad a few weeks later. The staggered circulation of a few film prints through a very stratified exhibition sector also made the Ramsays "very dependent" on the industry trade journals, who had to be vigorously persuaded. "We were always after *Film Information*. Report should come good, should come good." Tulsi explained why: "These trade papers [*Film Information*, *Trade Guide*] were enjoying a tyrannical reign, people were scared of them. . . . If the report comes good, if the film is [a] 'hit' in Bombay, then the price for it in Delhi doubles from 4 lakhs to 8 lakhs. But if a bad report comes. . . . Today, because of simultaneous releases, no one even cares about them."[30]

The film market in the 1980s, Rosie Thomas explains, "was divided into seven territories, which more or less corresponded to those established before Independence—and reflected British India's geographical divisions, rather than the linguistic/cultural/state divisions of the post-Independence era."³¹ These seven territories were further "subdivided into 21 main sub-territories and beyond that into A, B, and C circuits, which reflected both the quality of their cinemas and the class backgrounds of their audiences."³² The Ramsay Brothers' films ran in what is often described as the B circuit—that is, the films circulated beyond first-run theaters in metropolitan centers visited by middle-class audiences, instead reaching the urban and rural poor in second-run city theaters as well as smaller cities and towns.³³ The B circuit, per S. V. Srinivas, is the "final frontier" of film distribution: "Beyond this there is no market"; "[f]ilms reach this segment after their run in the more profitable distribution and exhibition circuit is fully, truly, over; after they have been run into the ground." Not only are theaters in this circuit characterized by "low levels of investment," films are also marked "by repeated interventions by both distributors and exhibitors, which results in the de-standardization of a film's status as an industrial product."³⁴ If the Ramsays had established early control over the B circuit, the circulatory history of Mohan Bhakri's horror films demonstrates how the paths that were taken by films to reach their audiences were also the paths *given* to them by a variety of state actors and industry operatives—and how forks in those paths reshaped the films that would travel them.

Horror films, Bhakri said to me, "are like soda water": they fizzle after an initial burst of effervescence.³⁵ In Bombay city, Bhakri's films had to make their money quickly, before they were forced off-screen by newer horror films. From listings in *Film Information*, *Trade Guide*, and *Times of India*, we find that *Cheekh* did not run in the relatively posh Eros and Empire theaters in south Bombay, where *Gremlins* (Joe Dante, 1984) was in its fourth week, and *The NeverEnding Story* (Wolfgang Petersen, 1984) in its seventh. Nor did *Cheekh* play in theaters that hosted the biggest Hindi blockbusters of the year: the melodramatic howler *Teri Meherbaniyan* (Your graces, Vijay Reddy, 1985), the action film *Bepanah* (Endless, Jagdish Sidana, 1985), or the Amitabh Bachchan–starring *Mard* (Man, Manmohan Desai, 1985). While 116 prints of *Mard* were printed for the first week of its Bombay release, only eight prints of *Cheekh* were sent out, all to theaters that lined Lamington Road, the historic nerve center of the film distribution business and home to a number of working-class theaters where *Cheekh* jostled with dacoit thrillers and exploitation

Figure 24. Projection cues in *Cheekh* (1985). *Source:* Bhakri Films Combine, frame grab from VCD.

films. By the end of its first week, *Cheekh* had largely exited Bombay; those eight prints were now circulating in other parts of the western interior and north India. Once that happened, they would move in a pattern away from the city toward smaller markets in the "C circuit" of Bombay cinema's distribution territories.

When *Cheekh* was released, the *Times of India* labeled it "another C-grade horror film."[36] "C" names a circuit—the networked movement by which the film's prints could eventually recoup value—but as a "grade" it was also of course a pejorative evaluation. It collapsed third-run distribution venues, those who patronized them, and the films that played in these venues. For film distributors and producers, the so-called C circuit presented its own difficulties: money would flow back very slowly, if at all, over months and years, as the film's showings went off the books. *Cheekh* disappears from box office reports less than a month after its release, yet the long tail of its circulatory life may be gleaned from surviving copies of the film.

On the run from the masked killer, a hapless victim finds herself out in the woods in the middle of nowhere. Her throat is slashed, and her body is left to rot. But as she dies, several changeover cues marking the end of a reel flash in the upper right corner of the frame (see figure 24). These are multiple marks, as though cues were scratched into a print of the film one on top of the other. Perhaps the print was traveling from one theater to the next and from there to the next, changing hands between projectionists and projectors, each leaving their marks on the film. No wonder then that *Trade Guide* noted the "biggest problem is that most 'C' class centers have such bad projection that cost of print damage is more than the share" made back by the film's distributors.[37] The drive to keep extracting value in C centers from the same print is recorded as and results in visible degradations within the visual field.

A young woman in *Cheekh* pleads, "Don't kill me!" while the leather-gloved maniac plunges a knife into her body. She opens her mouth in agony and a scream erupts, but it is not hers. Instead, it is the scream of *Cheekh*'s heroine, Deepa, who has been watching this horror movie scene unfold in a movie theater. When her boyfriend Sunil asks what is wrong, Deepa replies: "Sunil, take me home, I don't want to see all this, take me home please!" Sunil, Deepa, and their friend Rita get up out of their seats and leave the theater, muttering "Excuse us."

Even as film production boomed, a box office analyst warned that "cinemagoers in India in general and in Bombay in particular seem to be slowly losing the theater-going habit."[38] "All the classic symptoms are here," concurred film critic Iqbal Masood. "Falling audience figures, the bulldozing of theatres, and a series of flops of 'big' movies."[39] A journalist visiting the film distribution offices located on Lamington Road in Bombay found that "an atmosphere of terror, reminiscent of a horror film made by the Ramsay Brothers, prevails in the Naaz building, which houses the offices of most of the leading distributors and exhibitors, and which is the center for big deals for the sale of territories of films and releases in cinemas."[40] "We are jittery in our pants," one distributor said to *Screen*.[41] When a headline asked: "Cinemagoers losing theater-going habit?," these cinemagoers were implicitly marked by coordinates of class, gender, and location.[42] The "crisis" of film exhibition was understood to be happening because middle-class women were retreating from the movie theater and taking their families with them.

The difference between the film Deepa is in and the one she walks out of may be less a matter of what is in the film and more a changing idea of where the film should be seen; she is indeed a "cinemagoer losing the theater-going habit." In order to meet Deepa outside the movie theater, cinema needed a tangible form through which it could escape the limits of theatrical film exhibition. Under these conditions, what would happen if films could bypass the difficulties of celluloid film exhibition and the film culture it had shaped? What happened next can be seen as an attempt to get Bombay horror out of the movie theater—like the moviegoers in *Cheekh*.

VIDEO: "AS BIG AS BOMBAY"

In Bhakri's *Khooni Murdaa*, a young woman lures a psychotic serial killer into a police ambush. The crazed murderer arrives, red rose in hand for his reluctant valentine. Quickly, police sirens sound, and he is surrounded. Shocked at Rekha's betrayal, Ranjit vows never to forgive her and threatens revenge. He is dragged away by the police, but his corpse will soon return as a killer to decimate Rekha's world. Before Ranjit makes his declaration to her, a different kind of promise is made to Rekha when her eyes alight twice on a streetside advertisement: "Texla Color & B.W. TV, VCR, VCP" (see figure 25). This message about television sets and videocassette players may serve as a warning sign or reassuring presence for Rekha, but it also indicates an unmapped historical juncture in the history of Bombay cinema. Instead of reinforcing conventional wisdom about widespread hostility between the Bombay film industry and the nascent video market of the 1980s, the Texla sign traces a moment in which horror filmmakers were exploring the commercial possibilities of a new medium.

During the late 1970s and early 1980s, rumors, hype, images and user manuals for consumer video trickled into India, shoring up a futuristic technological fantasy and fomenting desire for video. "Ironically," noted *Screen* in 1981, "the comparative poverty of the Indian people has proved to be an asset for the filmmaker, since, with the present cost structure in mind, it is impossible to visualize video as a serious threat to cinema."[43] It was at this time that the first video libraries appeared in Bombay. The Maroo family's rental business started in the early 1960s as a book library, Shemaroo, for South Bombay's well-heeled on Warden Road, in the upscale neighborhood of Kemp's Corner. Paper-based renting cards were used to create reading histories and member customization, and a network of delivery boys circulated books around South Bombay. By the 1980s, the Maroos had decided to open out the Shemaroo lending library as a hub for the exchange of videocassettes between users; "we became a central repository,"

Figure 25. Texla advertisement: detail from *Khooni Murdaa* (1989). *Source:* Bhakri Films Combine, frame grab from VCD.

says Gada, transferring their expertise in book lending to imported American videotapes and "facilitating the informal circulation of cassettes." Thus, the first circulation of videocassettes in India occurred among the "crème de la crème of the country, not just the city."[44]

In 1980, the All India Film Producers Council (AIFPC) issued a memo "prohibiting producers from selling the video rights of their films for distribution within India."[45] The AIFPC advised that the sale of video rights might appear attractive but promised only "small, short-term gains": that the amounts offered, such as "Rs 50,000 and Rs 70,000 for a film," were "peanuts compared to its cost of production."[46] Yet divisions within the Bombay film business—between the ranks of film producers, as well as between producers, distributors, and exhibitors—inhibited the enforcement of a collective response to the arrival of videotape. The Bombay film business was not a vertically integrated business but rather one in which "decentered" power centers determined the industrial response to the commercial potential of commercial videocassettes.[47]

Consider, for contrast, Hollywood, for which video would become a gigantically profitable ancillary industry during the 1980s, when nearly sixty-five million VCRs had been sold in the United States alone, suggesting a penetration of two out of every three television households in the country. Once both adversary and alternative to the studios, video became "home video," "remade into a medium for movies" as video rental libraries became part of Hollywood distribution channels.[48] As media historians note, home video also marked the successful capture of a new, possible alternative to broadcast television and Hollywood as corporate and copyright regimes successfully created demand for must-own "original" copies among middle-class individuals and families for private consumption in the "home theater."[49] By the end of the 1980s, the "world's most aggressive film industry" had recognized that "it was actually in the video business," with the greatest share of profits banked from home video sales.[50] These profits prompted a second round of business integration after the initial breakup of studio monopolies in the late 1940s. Now studios merged vertically (across production, distribution, and exhibition), horizontally (across film, music, and television), and transnationally.[51]

Developed over decades, the deeply entrenched and competing sites of power in the Bombay film industry had made producers rely on distributors for film financing, and distributors on exhibitors who controlled India's film theaters—relationships that were as dependent as they were distrustful, frustrating, and antagonistic. Distributors' reliance on theatrical exhibitors made them wary of entering the video distribution business; producers, in turn, were forbidden by distributors from selling rights to independent video companies. Yet for low-budget film producers squeezed out of theatrical exhibition—the majority of filmmakers—the "peanuts" proposed by video rights looked like a potential lifeline, new sources with which to finance film production and new avenues for film circulation. One producer complained, "Today, just a few individuals, so-called industry leaders hold the entire video trade and the industry to ransom. As many as ninety per cent of the producers today are willing to sell domestic video rights but the AIFPC and the IMPPA [Indian Motion Picture Distributors Association] have forbidden them from doing so."[52] A complaint registered by a leading videocassette manufacturing company with the Monopolies and Restrictive Trade Practices Commission (MRTPC) led to a ruling in June 1983 ordering the AIFPC to "cease and desist" from issuing such prohibitions. In September 1983 the MRTPC set aside the AIFPC prohibition and unleashed the market potential of video for film producers.[53] Unlike the top producers of the Bombay film industry, who continued issuing press statements representing the industry's antipathy to video, Bhakri quietly began brokering deals with video companies to distribute his horror films to customers as "day and date" releases, meaning simultaneously with their theatrical releases.

Hence the Texla sign in *Khooni Murdaa*. "Some friends of mine were opening a Texla agency in Bombay," director Mohan Bhakri recalled when I asked him about the two shots, "and they requested free advertising from me, so I said okay."[54] Owned by the South Korean electronics giant Goldstar, Texla aspired to prominence in the television and videocassette player market in India. Texla was the "most popular solid state TV in the country" and the "Last Word in Computerized Televiewing" according to its own advertising, and it was lowering prices on TV sets to make them affordable.[55] Such friendly and seemingly "free" transactions between a low-budget filmmaker and a fledgling video company can be understood within the context of a televisual landscape in which "the state had a virtual monopoly over television programming."[56] By 1984 it was reported that sales of color TV sets had crossed the seven million mark.[57] But the speedy uptake of televisual hardware—Texla's color television sets—was not being accompanied by the creation of content that could feed it; there wasn't much color programming on television. Till the end of the 1980s, there was only one channel, Doordarshan, to watch on Indian television sets, with a second channel, DD2, concluding the day's programming before prime time. Texla was a sponsor for the first sponsored program on the national broadcaster Doordarshan, the morning Sikh-devotional *Sarab Sanjhi Gurbani* (1984), but the absence of color programming for India's first national television generation was notable. What could people watch on their television sets?

In schedules printed daily in the *Times of India*, a random sampling of the last show to run at night at this time included several "B/W" (black and white) shows: *Mohiniattam* at 10:50 .p.m., followed by *Poetic Tributes* to Mrs. Indira Gandhi; *The Great Salt March—a FD Film*; *Nehru Parliamentary Quiz*; *A Programme on the Achievements of the 7th Five Year Plan*; *Flute Recital*; *Pandit Nehru's Multifaceted Personality: A Special Programme*; and sometimes, going out with a bang by playing some *Light Music*. As *TV & Video World* put it, "viewers were once again forced to go back to black and white, except for two hours a day on the national network.... All that this helped do was to let people discover the color of Mrs Gandhi's [the Prime Minister Indira Gandhi's] sarees."[58]

Doordarshan did expand its programming beyond the decidedly respectable, high-minded, and explicitly pedagogic. Instructional lectures about agriculture and family planning were now scheduled next to runs of American comedies, children's shows, and soap operas, while advertisers hawked instant noodles, detergent powders, and bedroom linens. The most popular thing on television was, not surprisingly, color cinema, and the state relied on the Hindi film industry to expand television's audiences. But the film industry balked at the pittance the state paid to broadcast blockbusters (sometimes without the permission of the film's producers). In 1983 the AIFPC "demanded more royalty as color telecasting of films over a wider area would adversely affect the theatrical business," and producers were told to stop supplying films to Doordarshan.[59] In order to grow its audiences, Doordarshan commissioned a mythological soap opera based on the *Ramayana* (Ramanand Sagar, 1987–89), a weekly telecast that allegedly brought life to a standstill across the country whenever it aired. It was said that the serial convened tens of millions of men and women, young and old, in cities and villages; stories multiplied of the devout worshipping the television set as if it were a temple idol, of *darshan* received from the show's special effects, gods, and goddesses.

For viewers unmoved by the state's idea of entertainment, other pleasures awaited. *Ramayana* went into production as Vinod Talwar was completing his maiden horror venture, *Raat Ke Andhere Mein*, about a young woman who gives birth to a demonic child. The film's star was Deepika Chikhlia—Sita in the TV adaptation of the *Ramayana*! On the show, Chikhlia was the very incarnation of feminine modesty, locked under yards of shiny saris. The show's success transformed the actress into a revered icon at whose feet people were known to fall when they spotted her in public (even out of costume and character). Unfortunately for Talwar, his film showcased Chikhlia in a very different light. "I had dances under the rain and she was a modern girl," Talwar told me, "so my film got stucked [*sic*] with the censors and they banned it two-three times and I was very short of money."[60] His film was held up at the censors for nine months, with no end in sight. It was at this point that a videotape distributor reached out to him. "It was a positive for me," he said, allowing him to make money off selling videotape rights so he could repay rapidly growing loans. Talwar's tale of woe (and eventual relief) highlights the avenues of finance opened up to small-time producers of lowbrow genres caught in the snares of the censor. For Bhakri, too, such payments provided a much-needed respite—and revenue stream—when blocked by state censorship. Fed up with the routine harassment and delays courtesy of the censor board, Bhakri had these choice words for the censors: "ek number ke haraami" ("bastards of the first order"), who held up his films until money changed hands in hotel rooms. Bhakri's movies, blocked by the censors for months on end, could be presold to video distributors, enabling the film's producers to pay back rapidly growing loans before the film opened in cinemas.

In 1984 the Ministry of Information and Broadcasting began requiring each video release to obtain a clearance certificate from the censor board, while also having a "Not Valid for Video" be stamped on censor certificates. The government mandated that video screenings of any film were to be permitted only after the producers or distributors of the film had sold such rights to interested parties under the Copyright Amendment Act of 1984. Bhakri's *Cheekh* begins with a view of its censor certificate, but its displayed text—"Not Valid for Video"—is interrupted by a bright green bar that rolls down the certificate, causing a hum on the sound track. As films began to be transferred onto videotape copies, the monochrome authority of state censorship and the legibility of the images they certify was deranged by the psychedelic colors of a new medium. With the arrival of videotape, writes Mayur Suresh, the Indian state "was presented with a crisis of its regulatory authority," having "lost control over the actual space of a media, but also the ability to police the content of the media as well."[61] Starting in 1985, censor certificates on-screen began to crack with lines of noise, traces of the circulatory dynamics of videotape. Alongside the changeover cues for projectionists, *Cheekh*'s bloody corpses, pitch-dark nights, and grisly monsters are pressed by narrower color ranges, lower resolutions, and denser noise: the print was transferred at some point to videotape. One version of *Cheekh*, for example, appears to be an early generation videocassette copy produced by Captain Video, a Delhi-based video distribution and circulation business established in 1985. When *Cheekh*'s title card bursts onto the screen moments later with a human scream on the sound track, what I see and hear are the sensory expressions of the historical circuits in which the film traveled.[62]

Between 1985 and 1988, Bhakri sold all-India rights to video companies including Bombino; these companies in turn sublicensed films for video sales in other territories to companies like Eagle and Captain. The *First Indian Film and Video Guide* lists *Cheekh* as follows: "*Cheekh* (C-1985); Suspense (A), copyright Bombino (N.E. Eagle) (Overseas—Emca)."[63] In an interesting articulation, Bhakri told me that "video was as big as Bombay."[64] In the 1980s, the Bombay territory—which included Bombay city as well as the subterritories of Gujarat, Maharashtra, districts of Karnataka, and Goa—was estimated to be valued at 17 percent of the national total. In other words, "the Bombay territory was considered to have the potential to bring in about 17 percent of the total all-Indian returns, thus Bombay distributors paid 17 per cent of the total 'price' of the film."[65] "I got money on the table" from video, Talwar said of video distribution, adding that "it was a new territory for me."[66]

Prizing open a "new territory," video was a reterritorializing force by which Bombay horror films could reach empty television screens. In *Khooni Murdaa*, the corpse of the serial killer Ranjit refuses to die; reanimated as a ghost, he begins killing the many young men and women who spurned him. Tina Malhotra is alone in her bedroom one night when her television flickers to life with static. Surprised, Tina walks over to the TV to turn it off. Suddenly, the killer corpse bursts out from inside the television set! He lifts the terrified Tina off the ground. He smashes her head into the television set, electrocuting her to death. As a fitful industrial allegory, this death in *Khooni Murda* folds back on its Texla advertising, warning of the dangers of not having anything to watch on your television set. Tina dies because there is simply nothing on television; it is just an empty box for a monster to invade (see figure 26). If television programming, "which is controlled by the Government, is so thin as to be almost transparent," the "current video madness" would bring Bombay's horror films home.[67]

Figure 26. Empty screen: detail from *Khooni Murdaa* (1989). *Source:* Bhakri Films Combine, frame grab from VCD.

"OH, THIS VIDEO CRAZE!"

"I don't see Hindi movies," Bhakri once announced. While mimicking the Ramsay Brothers' investment in gothic horror with films like *Sau Saal Baad* and *Khooni Mahal*—and hiring some of the same actors and technicians as the Ramsay Brothers did—Bhakri appeared dismissive of their films. Instead, he described how he watched videotape copies of foreign horror films. "I never sleep before 4 or 4.30 in the morning. I have to see 2 English movies. . . . If something strikes me, I definitely try to convert it into good scenes for my film." The Bhakri motto was "get 3 or 4 writers, tell them: 'This is the VHS, I want the same.'"[68]

Yet Bhakri's films tell a different story. In addition to plumbing Italian *giallo* as well as American slasher films, Bhakri remade the films of the Ramsay Brothers, an act of imitation that at once branded Bhakri as contemporary and dated his chief competitors. Consider, for example, the sequence from Bhakri's *Kabrastan* with which this chapter began, in which a young man is surrounded by graveyard ghouls. It is possible to see in it an imitation of the music video for the Michael Jackson song "Thriller." *Thriller* (John Landis, 1983), in which the American superstar singer dances with a zombie horde, is one of the most circulated artworks of the twentieth century. Soon after the music video premiered on American television and home video, imitations of the dance also began to appear in Indian films of the 1980s. In the Hindi melodrama *Kasam Paida Karne Wale Ki* (*The Pledge of the One Who Has Borne You*, Babbar Subhash, 1984), "disco dancer" Mithun Chakraborthy dances in a graveyard. In the Telugu action film *Donga* (A. Reddy, 1985), superstar Chiranjeevi is dressed head to toe in red latex, outfitted with fangs and neon eyes. Likewise, then, the danse macabre of *Kabrastan*, featuring the veteran actor Jagdeep.

But this wasn't Jagdeep's first time imitating Jackson's *Thriller* for a Hindi horror film. A few years earlier in the Ramsay Brothers' *Saamri*, Jagdeep is seen wearing a red jacket and wandering into a graveyard at midnight. In the fog, he perceives corpses clambering out of graves: zombies! As bloodstained bodies and bandaged mummies begin marching toward him, a song thumps onto the sound track. Man and zombie dance in choreographed unison, until Jagdeep's character wakes out of his sleep, exclaiming directly to the camera: "Itna bhayanak sapna! Magar kitna sundar roop apna! ... Michael Jackson! Thriller!" ("What a scary dream, but what a beautiful form I took! ... Michael Jackson! Thriller!").

Saamri is a story of wealth usurped. After a wealthy man is murdered, he comes back from the dead to taunt the wily family seeking his estate. His ghost is a telekinetic, taunting presence in their lives, and his magical powers are enlivened by *Saamri*'s fantastical visuality: the film was one of the first films of the period to be processed and screened in 3D at select theaters in Bombay. "Horror comes closer to you than ever before" was the guarantee made in one listing for the film, and it was a promise met by the film.[69] In the graveyard sequence, for example, three rows of "undead" dance behind Jagdeep, each creating visual interest with different costuming and movements. Jagdeep himself moves between foreground and background, and our eyes follow his red jacket into deep space. The depth and dimensionality of 3D also makes for visual gimmicks in which things shoot out from the visible rear of the image to the front, such as a spurt of blood. In doing this, the Ramsay Brothers were binding the affective powers of cinematic horror to the structures of theatrical exhibition. ("The people really enjoyed it," Tulsi said, but admitted that the "difficulty with the Bombay audiences was that they would take the 3D glasses home.")[70] To compete with *Saamri 3D*, Bhakri first announced the launch of his new production *Khooni Mahal 3D* (Bloody palace 3D) in 1985.[71] The film was released two years later and one dimension poorer. No wonder then that in the film, a character played by Jagdeep fondly recalls watching the Ramsays' *Saamri 3D*, specifically his own performance: "Jagdeep ji, film *Saamri* mein, bhayanak sapna dekhe" ("Jagdeep, in *Saamri*, saw a scary dream").

A year later, in Bhakri's *Kabrastan*, Jagdeep is once again cast as the house help. In *Kabrastan*, in order to inherit his father's lands and wealth, Hitler (Jagdeep) must spend a night alone in the graveyard to prove he's no coward. If he cannot, his father's estate will instead be diverted by Hitler's scheming cousins. At his father's wake, an attorney presents Hitler with a videotape:

ATTORNEY: I'm sorry Mr. Hitler.
HITLER: It's alright.
ATTORNEY: Take this (offers a videocassette).
HITLER (STARTLED): Don't you have any shame or sense? My father lies dead before me and you've brought me a blue film. I'd requested it for tomorrow.
ATTORNEY: This is not a blue film, it is your daddy's will.
HITLER: Daddy's will? On videotape? Oh this video craze! Which parlor are you coming from? Whichever parlor you're from, I don't want to see this.
ATTORNEY: It was your father's wish that you see this before he is buried.
HITLER: Is the print original or duplicate?
ATTORNEY: Original.

Video's insertion into the film as material artifact and a message from "beyond the grave" initiates the journey to the graveyard and into the world of video, all layered through questions of morality, authenticity, succession, and death. When the video is played, Hitler's father Napoleon appears on the screen to announce he's leaving his millions to his son, but on the condition that his son spends one night alone in a graveyard. That night, Hitler does indeed attempt a night's stay in the local graveyard. The graveyard sequence begins with Jagdeep sitting on a grave by candlelight, reading a book about how to ward off witches and ghouls. Soon enough, though, all kinds of monsters appear on the scene: women in white, a mummy, dancing skeletons, a menagerie he calls "musical-minded bhoot-chudail/ghosts-and-witches." As the undead clamber out of graves, Jagdeep climbs a tree and sings the song "Oh God, Ishwar, Allah!" Skeletons dance as he invokes "Holy Father," "Allah," and "Kaali Maa." At song's end, however, it is revealed that these scary creatures are only so many actors hired by Hitler's cousins to scare him away from the graveyard.

In *Kabrastan*, the dead ancestor appears not by way of 3D but on video—a format war that allegorizes the drama of succession between the Ramsays' *Saamri* and Bhakri's *Kabrastan*. *Kabrastan* was released with an opening title card thanking "Bombino Video," indexing a transition seen in other aspects of the film. Something changes in the *Thriller* routine from *Saamri 3D* to *Kabrastan*: the three rows of dancers behind Jagdeep now become one that flanks him left and right. (I learned from speaking to Jagdeep's son that the "Thriller" sequences were always very much Jagdeep's idea, but he received little financial or material support to create them, reflected in the narrative insignificance of these sequences.) Instead of the kinetic editing and creation of depth of field via blocking, choreography, and 3D, *Kabrastan* favors movements between wide shots and close-ups predicated on a zooming camera. The changing platform address is therefore seen not only in the phone numbers for Bombino that scroll across the frame, but also in the way the frame sometimes sheds deep space compositions in favor of high-contrast and close cropping: the filmmaker was "shooting for the box" as he imagined a nontheatrical audience, one gathered around a smaller screen.[72] *Thriller* cheapens as the decade declines: *Kabrastan* is a lower-budget film than *Saamri*, with fewer dimensional details. But it is also poorer in the way of its clarity. "Once a film is transferred on to video tape," noted Ajit Duara in 1987, "a lot of intended cinematic effect that the filmmaker thought out is lost."[73] Among the evident losses are bleeding colors (particularly red), cropped frames, and loss of depth and detail. Transferred onto tape, celluloid images and sounds shed detail and fidelity; the medium's features—lack of information, decay, and distortion, its "insufficiently visual" qualities—seem to plunge viewers beyond the limits of perception, due "to its unstable and incoherent characteristics ... anchored in signal processes that differ from the spatial-temporal unity of a 'tableau' or 'frame image.'"[74]

This failure to constitute is textualized in the decomposing colors, noises, and lines of static that overtake the diegetic narrative and image as *Kabrastan* concludes. Audiences may have been accustomed to, and had come to expect, certain kinds of distortion and interference from these films, not as an interruptive layer placed over once-correct images but as part of the aesthetic experience of the genre, what to Brian Larkin is a "hallucinogenic quality": "Detail is destroyed as realist representation fades into pulsating light. Facial features are smoothed away, colors are broken down into constituent tones, and bodies fade into one another. Reproduction takes its toll, degrading the image by injecting dropouts and bursts of fuzzy noise, breaking down dialogue into muddy, often inaudible sound."[75] Bhakri's late-in-the-game horror films stage horror as a crisis of textual (im)possibility, a series of endlessly reconstituting lines on the screen that never stabilize.

THE END OF BOMBAY HORROR

On a winter's day in Rajkot, Gujarat, a theater advertised a matinee show of an expensive period piece, *Raziya Sultan* (Kamal Amrohi, 1983). The film, reported *Trade Guide*, "had the weirdest opposition one could think of": "While the main feature played inside the theatre, the canteen in the theatre had *Coolie* being shown on Video!"[76] At first this seems like a business-wise solution for the hard-pressed exhibitor. "Is exhibition their main business or the canteens or cafeterias that are run in the theaters?" asked *Trade Guide* incredulously.[77] Yet what better emblem could there be of the coming crisis that would split cinema's publics along class lines? *Coolie*'s canteen show was possible because of the decentered and disparate motivations of producers, distributors, and exhibitors. Remaking the literal edge of film exhibition, the canteen show registers the unreachability of the main stage for many audiences, who were paying less to watch a more popular film on video. Having seceded from the screen, though, film would soon split from the showcases to which it was accustomed and continue its journey out of the film theater—away from the grasp of censors, taxes, licenses, film producers, distributors, and theatrical exhibitors.

By the end of the 1980s, only 1 percent of Indian households owned a VCR. But the penetration of video as a new media imaginary and infrastructure was driven by the numbers of videocassettes that were borrowed, resold, and shared. A pirate video culture emerged to fill the gap between those who could afford to purchase their own videocassette players and videocassettes and the rest of India, which could not: this culture comprised hundreds of thousands of videocassettes illegally sold, borrowed, and copied; cassette players owned and lent and "sublent"; and small rooms outfitted with a VCR, a projector, and a screen, with thirty or forty-five seats at two rupees a show, that quickly came to be known as *video parlors*. Video parlors were cheap, tin-roofed or tented spaces in which rows of chairs and floormats were arrayed before a television hooked up to a video player. Video parlors expanded Bombay cinema's audiences, soliciting spectators who were chronically underserved by the hegemonic trade and taste formations of the world's largest film culture. Video parlors abridged the painful, frustrating experience of waiting for things, an experience that is built into the uneven, classed, raced, and geographically spatialized structures of media distribution.[78] In big cities, inflation and price gouging were driving audiences to video parlors; in small towns, video parlors replaced movie theaters, which had been at the bottom of the traditional film distribution pyramid and were often years behind in the fare they screened using run-down prints; in smaller places still, video created audiences where theaters were yet to arrive. Seen from this perspective, the video parlor was the lowest rung on the ladder of aspiration to access, inhabit, and participate in film culture, "serving minority audiences whose needs are seldom met by the existing film distribution and exhibition system oriented to mass audiences."[79] Daniel Herbert reminds us that the term *distribution* in *media distribution* glosses how resources are allocated in unequal societies.[80] Video parlors could bypass some of the costs that came with being theatrical film distributors. "The cost of a print of a Hindi film was assessed at around 30,000 rupees while the cost of a video tape about 300 rupees."[81] If *territory* was the term used by Bombay film distributors to describe how film markets—and implicitly, the audiences in them—were valued, then videotape created a post-territory organized around the cellular site of the video parlor. Shattering the temporalities that have governed film distribution, video broke the monopoly of the state and the film industry, revolutionizing what, when, and how moving images circulated in India.

More Indians experienced new films in the atmosphere of video parlors than as home video. The "video craze," one newspaper reported, "is fast spreading to the city's slums. In Dharavi, Chembur, and other parts of the megapolis, enterprising men hold regular shows ... predictably to packed audiences. The main attraction is, of course, the rate of admission which is a measly two rupees. With ticket prices in cinema houses increasing by leaps and bounds over the years, people prefer to patronize video shows."[82] In 1985 *Film Information* feigned amusement at the fact that while many cinema theaters were named "Cine Palace" and "Film Mandir," a "video parlor has recently opened in Jamnagar has been christened Video Hut."[83] Video parlors did not have the public facades of film theaters; they could emerge and thrive on word of mouth and familiarity, and their "always on" show times well into the night allowed them to serve some of the functions of a shelter for the otherwise unhoused.[84]

The video parlor is an unwritten chapter in the story of film circulation in India outside the "loop of the big institutional history," one that stretches from the traveling shows of the colonial *bioscopewallah* to shared digital memory cards in today's small towns.[85] A site for the "productive decentralization of media life," video parlors were an early example of what Ravi Sundaram has termed the "sensory infrastructures" of postcolonial media publics.[86] Bringing people and technology affectively closer (instead of remaining at a "safe distance"), sensory infrastructure used a combination of "pirate tactics, media forms, and paralegal space" to bring people "together by affective resonances and technocultural circulation practices."[87] In 1983 the *Times of India* complained that "[t]he video shows do not have atmosphere of the theaters"; missing are "the ad films, the trailers, the vast darkness of the hall, the crackling of popcorn packets, and above all the pithy comments from the blocks in the lower stalls."[88] In Bombay the urban working classes gathered here to watch movies, eat, and sleep in. The video parlor was of course not the same as the theaters patronized by the *Times*'s readership, for whom "pithy comments" from the "lower stalls" were assumed to be part of the "atmosphere" of moviegoing.

In 1984 the newly appointed chairman of the censor board noted that "cinema is returning to the cafes and parlors from where it had started about a century ago."[89] In the same way that early cinema audiences were fascinated by the heat and hiss of the oil lamp, the video parlor too made cinema intimate with its audience; this was a place of childlike wonder.[90] One reporter analogized technological excitement as akin to "fiddling with the knobs like a child in a video parlor."[91] Yet, the video parlor was also marked by constant contingency in any given parlor at any given time, there may or not be viewers, chairs, or fans. The power supply might fail; cassettes, players, or projectors might fail; and of course, there was the dreaded police raid.

Almost everything I know about video parlors I learned from those who complained about, raided, and destroyed them. These raids on video parlors were often initiated not by concerned citizens or upright consumers, but by employees of the Indian Federation Against Copyright (INFACT). Formed in 1986, INFACT was modeled after the British Federation Against Copyright Theft (FACT) and cofounded by the National Film Development Corporation, Star Video (the leading body representing Bombay film producers' video rights), the AIFPC, and Shemaroo Home Entertainment.[92] Earlier that year, Shemaroo had been incorporated as a video distribution label and thus became a legitimate (and the country's largest) national video distributor; according to Shemaroo's Hiren Gada, "we became a national player instead of a regional player because our videos went into literally every corner of the country."[93] Shemaroo's self-legitimizing participation in INFACT suggests a classed division of power and pleasure: as it crossed from the home into the street, the changing scales of video threatened the emergent "clean" video business and so attracted surveillance. G. P. Sippy, the producer of *Sholay*, headed both the AIFPC and the newly formed Anti-Video Piracy Organization and lobbied politicians in Delhi to introduce antivideo legislation, to move the Ministry of Broadcasting and Information and the CBFC to censor foreign films on videotape, and to encourage top cops to carry out raids.

In writing the story of the video parlor in 1980s India, my primary sources are the thousands of raid reports printed in trade journals such as *Trade Guide* and *Film Information*, as well as newspapers such as the *Times of India*. A "noble crusade" to control the illegal manufacture and consumption of films on tape, INFACT trained its eye on the video parlor.[94] This parastate, paracorporate federation operated in the interstices of civil and criminal law, sometimes carrying out raids with hired muscle power while at other times tipping off the police about the existence of a video parlor. With branches in all the major metropolitan centers (Bombay, Delhi, Calcutta, and Madras) and retired police officers in charge of operations, INFACT was "optimistic about curbing and ultimately crushing the evil of video piracy."[95] These raids were then reported back to newspapers and industry trade journals such as *Trade Guide* and *Film Information*, which did their part by announcing the gory conquests of each raid and so driving a sensational wave of "news" during the euphoric expansion of print in the decade.

Such reports move between two registers: the long shot, in which cities were described as teeming with parlors numbering in the thousands (fifty thousand in Bombay at their peak, twenty thousand in Delhi in 1985), and the close-up, in which the eye of the state penetrates the shadows of slums and alleys to find the parlor in its operational glory. In raid reports, incriminating details proliferate, and rhetorical declamations of a "shocking discovery" abound: of children watching horror films, of the type of equipment being used, and of the names of the operators and the titles of the films being watched, as well as some characterization of the audience and time of day, followed by the names of the organizations carrying out the raid alongside the police. Bombay police discovered a man "displaying" an "illegal video cassette" copy of *Purana Mandir* to an "audience of about 70 children," "charging one and two rupees per head."[96] In these reports, the operators do not resist. They barely exist. We rarely hear from the owners or audiences; the stories do not show any curiosity about why people came to operate or patronize the video parlor. A raid on a parlor in 1987 yields fourteen video players and 1,379 rupees at Playland Video Parlor in Ghatkopar, where Noor Mohamed and Hussain Khushru Irani were arrested.[97] And when the vigilance branch of the Bombay police raided a video parlor at Love Lane, Byculla, the manager, Ashpak Abdul

Shaikh, twenty-three years old, was also arrested.[98] While *Purana Mandir* was playing in theaters, a videocassette of *Purana Mandir* that was "being shown to about 75 persons was seized from the video parlour.... The police also seized a Nelco VCR, Weston TV, and Rs 105 in cash. Mohd. Rafiq and Mohd. Shafi were arrested."[99]

The moral panic around video parlors allows us to see how the status quo was managed. If we reject the performative trope of "discovery" that attends the parlor raid, we can instead rediscover the long histories of power sharing, cinematographic control, ontological anxiety, and financial insecurity that brought together the agents and interests of the state, exhibitors, distributors, and producers as they converged on the door of the video parlor in a coordinated raid. In the raid, agents of the state and the film industry together resorted to moral panic and physical violence to (not) address the infrastructural failures that had birthed the video parlor.

Despite the threat of the raid, however, the video parlor was here to stay. "The video fever is spreading like malaria," *Screen* reminded readers. "The government is not able to eradicate malaria even after spending millions of rupees every year."[100] In the decade of biological pandemics— and mere months after the first cases of HIV infection were reported in India—filmmaker Manmohan Desai warned that the spread of the video parlor is "not even like cancer, it's like AIDS. It cannot be cured."[101] Viral spreads are often attributed to the opportunistic vitality of the contagion, but the shape, size, speed, and scale of a spread almost always index the material, cultural, and social distribution of infrastructure, access, and political will. Reread today, raid reports constitute a different kind of forensic archive, one of displacement and violence carried out by agents of the state and the film industry against a major site of subaltern media circulation and consumption.

Consider this typographical juxtaposition of two stories from the *Times of India* in 1985. Stories by staff reporters for the paper's Bombay edition are collated in the Metro News section led by a baiting title, "Mystery of Severed Limbs Solved," and a story about a pair of legs found in a suitcase at a railway station; a few hours later, across the city, at a different railway station, the torso was found in a steel trunk; the head had washed up on Juhu Beach behind a hotel. (A postmortem of the parts and examination of teeth and hair revealed that they all belonged to the same victim.)[102]

This story was followed by something less sensational. In the western suburb of Jogeshwari, the Bombay police raided a video parlor and "seized" cassette tapes of the film that were being screened there: the Hindi revenge melodrama *Aandhi-Toofan* (Dust storm, B. Subhash, 1985) and the recently banned American horror film *The Entity* (Sidney Furie, 1983). The raid had been carried out with the "assistance" of the Indian Film Industry Anti-Video Piracy Organization. Because it is legal, the violence of the raid, as opposed to the violence of the grisly murder, vanishes.

Recall that one of the videotapes found during the raid was the banned American horror film *The Entity*. One video patron writing to the *Times of India* in the summer of 1984 confessed (to a national newspaper, no less) to seeing a bootleg copy of *The Entity* at home, having missed it in theaters "before the ban."[103] What made this national admission possible? In 1985 a Supreme Court judgment was announced rendering home video beyond the pale of governmental surveillance and facilitating the historic retreat of middle-class audiences from theaters. Photocopies of this judgment were sent out to video libraries, which "prominently displayed" them to customers while promising that police were instructed not to surveil private homes where videos were being watched; news of the judgment was also carried in magazines such as *TV & Video World*.[104]

Let us return to the scene of technocrime in *Khooni Murdaa*, Tina's death by television. The imagination of privacy proffered by *Khooni Murdaa* is the same one evident in legal judgments and police raids about the "proper," defensible place of the consumer and the image. But in the film, it is domestic media consumption that invites a penalty and that the police are too late to stop: a scrambled record of the raid, it offers a voyeuristic spectacle by "breaking into" that other sheltered site of cinema. Bhakri stages the sequence by first showing us what this horrific violence violates—namely, the notional security of the middle-class home, the seclusion of teenagers in their bedrooms, and the benign presence of the television. Yet Tina's seclusion makes her both desirable and defenseless, beyond the reach and rescue of the police, who arrive at the scene too late: they open her bedroom door and find her head smashed into the television set. Tina's death at the "hands" of the television set undeniably eroticizes middle-class privacy, feminizes domestic consumption, and lethally violates both. It is a violent fantasy of revenge enacted by (and for) a different kind of spectator—constructed through a gaze that is male, public, and collective—watching Tina die at the altar of her own television set, alone in her bedroom, her feet hanging off the ground, her negligee in tatters.

To these multiple historical viewing positions, figured on-screen as fictional images and allegorical impressions, my viewing added another: when I saw my silhouette reflected on my desktop computer screen while this sequence from *Khooni Murdaa* played on YouTube. When the life of a videocassette comes to its technical end—when it falls into disrepair or disuse, fifteen or twenty years after first playback—it is usually disposed of. The slow decomposition and eventual dumping of videotapes erases their moving images from history, rendering them effectively unreadable, unreachable, and unwatchable. Sometimes, though, the images live on and continue to circulate aboveground for decades after the tape is lost. Without ever encountering a videocassette of Bhakri's horror films, I have encountered his horror films on videotape: online. By way of a conclusion, I turn finally to the perpetual, unsteady remediation of Bombay horror from the 1980s to contemporary times. Dumped and dredged up from the margins of visibility, Bombay horror's continued circulation produces mnemonic surplus and unsettles film industries, canons, histories, and filmographies by its illicit futurization.

Epilogue

AN ARCHIVE OF FAILURES

When the sun sets and night falls, a vampire rises from his crypt. Emerging from a cave deep inside the mountains, the *shaitan* is desperate to quench his thirst for human blood. His eyes are red, and his fangs are sharp. As the vampire awakens in the inky twilight, we are shown the territory he will hunt: hills shrouded in what the stentorian voice-over describes as the "darkness of death." The vampire looks out over the Stygian shadows that lie before him and takes flight into the night. So, with this perfectly executed horror film convention, begins the 2023 Blu-ray release of the Ramsay Brothers's *Bandh Darwaza*.

This is not what I was expecting to happen. What happened to the sun I had spotted during this very scene? Left waiting for the failure that had hitherto broken the spell on-screen—the failure with which this book begins—I had to consider the possibility that the daylight that once drenched the hills in *Bandh Darwaza* may not have been an error made during the film's shoot or in the development of its prints before theatrical release. Rather, it may have been introduced when a print of the film was transferred to videotape, DVD, or another format; someone may have neglected to tint the image or mistakenly re-adjusted its exposure, thereby (over)exposing the film's night for what it was (daytime). This version of the film, which I had watched repeatedly on YouTube, turned out to have been the wrong version all along. Here now was Mondo Macabro's new transfer of *Bandh Darwaza* from the original negative. This was a "good" copy of the film, restoring to the film its stylistic integrity. But it was also bad for me. With the night of *Bandh Darwaza* now correctly underexposed, I could see failure's immense illuminating power dimming.

The operations of preservation, transfer, and restoration undertaken by film archives continually fight the ravages of time to bring old films newly into view. The newest version of a film is accordingly advertised as the most revelatory: a clearer, richer, and more detailed image than ever before. The example of *Bandh Darwaza* should remind us that restorations of a film do not only enhance but also delimit the picture.[1] Each version may redefine how much of the frame we can see or what we can see in the frame, in the process eliminating any marks made by filmmakers, regulators, distributors, projectionists, and preservationists considered extraneous to the perfect image. So, while the "perfect image" may be said to "lack a history," it is the imperfect image that carries imprints that invite historical interpretation.[2] This contingent history of practice, from a film's production to its regulation, distribution, and continuing circulation, is cataloged in marks that accrue as failures within the perceptual surface. These were failures made *in* time—their erasure erases the durational history in which the film was made, censored, released, and seen. Without a failure at the scene of horror, there would have been no *Seeing Things*. Corrections can also rob the film of its own mortal glow. The failures explored in this book might one day vanish from the scene of horror, taking with them the spectral histories of Bombay horror's material past.

Seeing Things has chronicled how horror films were made and moved in 1980s India. It has tracked the practices by which filmmakers, editors, censors, art directors, production designers, set dressers, makeup artists, hairdressers, actors, distributors, and projectionists worked to transform celluloid filmstrips, color stock, filming locations, makeup effects, film prints, videocassette copies, movie theaters, and video parlors into aspects of the horror film experience. A materialist historiography and aesthetics of horror, *Seeing Things* reconstructs the practical worlds in which moving images were created and reassesses the viscerality of those movies in the light of their physical history. By revealing the infrastructures undergirding a global genre's beloved conventions, I have sought to expand our sense of the film medium's materiality in the experience of horror.

A survey of contemporary horror film and streaming media suggests that the genre is returning to the medium's materiality as a performative proxy for presence in our digital age. In horror films of the twenty-first century, film stock, Foley sound, profilmic effects, and celluloid film projection frequently serve as important story elements while exuding a sensuous fascination. Repeatedly recreated for nostalgic celebration, they are also cast as dangerous things in a virtual world. Making sense of this contemporary ambivalence requires being alert to the changing dynamics of film's materiality across a "new horror ecology" that includes television, video games, virtual reality (VR), and augmented reality (AR).[3]

Overcoming the material limits that once defined the medium has transformed Indian cinema. Streaming has eliminated the costs of striking film prints and the damage wrought by substandard projection facilities, making it possible for films to reach bigger audiences in better condition. Virtual effects have taken the production of spectacle out of the hands of makeup artists and set dressers, reducing the risks of on-set accidents and delays. Digital editing has altered how and what of a film can be manipulated, so that film images need no longer be mutilated but only morphed. Supporting these transformations are of course new infrastructures; servers, computer banks, and global chains of postproduction and delivery. These are not immaterial infrastructures but differently material, in which digital tools both maintain and overhaul enduring cinematic conventions. If we took full stock of current filmmaking practices, we would discover how human programmers and performers interact with and are embedded in algorithms and imaging software.[4]

Decades after Bombay horror, for example, prosthetic makeup effects have not disappeared or even become a minority practice in filmmaking. Despite triumphal technophilic narratives of the arrival of perfect and total virtual simulation, prosthetics persist, in no small part because of enduring inequities in the distribution of competence and capital. But the spectacular and growing display of prosthetic effects in a diverse range of films made around the world, from low-budget Bangladeshi action films to midbudget independent European extreme cinemas to Hollywood fantasy films, suggests a new role such effects play: they allow filmmakers to exploit a nostalgic and naive ontologic of "thereness" in the age of digital simulation.[5] The resplendent visibility of prosthetic effects across geography and genre, across the film text proper and its promotional paratexts, evokes and commodifies lay notions of old-school authenticity, artisanal craft, and real presence, stalling commonplace criticisms of spectacular images today as lacking in detail, density, or personality. Kristen Whissel has described the ways in which digital characters in recent science fiction and fantasy films are haunted by viewers' suspicions that such on-screen bodies "are often pure code and never existed."[6] As "graphic" images have "become the new index of the real," analog puppets have returned as funds of the immediate real, "haptic entities that abrade the skin of cinema."[7] When cleanup artists scan intermediate images for what seems like "too much," the image's very glossiness serves as a trace of human effort.

At other times, the forces of digitization help to preserve more direct traces of that effort. Digitization may turn everything into a number, but this doesn't always mean that digitization erases everything that distinguished different media. Sometimes digitization archives difference by preserving medium-specific features of images and sounds. Absent print restorations or Blu-ray editions, Mohan Bhakri's fans have ripped and uploaded copies of *Cheekh*, *Kabrastan*, and *Khooni Murda* as low-resolution digital files to YouTube. As their most ubiquitous contemporary copies, low-res online versions of Bhakri's films, which cross lines of legal and nonlegal, ownership and orphanhood, original and dub, mark Bhakri's films as inferior to the big-banner Bombay cinema products (whose pristine prints have been digitally scanned by their proprietors and are available to view through official pay-per-view platforms) and to Ramsay films (whose prints, in somewhat better condition, have been restored by the London-based Mondo Macabro for DVD and Blu-ray re-release starting in the 2000s and also made available illegally by uploaders to streaming sites). Yet it is these illicit intermedia transfers that ensure the survival and international circulation of Bhakri's corpus today, alongside the only legitimate format for the distribution of Bhakri's films today on video compact disc (VCD) format.

YouTube's multiple versions of Bhakri's horror films comprise a particular kind of archive of Bombay horror. Since its inception in 2005, YouTube has become a film archive by default; as users have uploaded personal copies of films across time and space, YouTube has begun to "function as an auxiliary for film history."[8] This is a peculiar historiography of film, full of the stammer we expect of contemporary streaming images, but it had rich implications as I tried to reconstruct the media sensorium of Bombay horror on videotape in 1980s India. Where physical archives must contend with the materiality of different media formats and the special conditions they require to remain accessible, YouTube reduces everything to the same format. Yet between the folds of these Flash-formatted digital glitches and errors, the streams reveal the unmistakable presence—the medium-specific errors and aura—of preceding media platforms that themselves might now be largely obsolete.

The spread of cheap and simple digitization technologies for amateur users has created new modes of cinephiliac film preservation and sites of online storage away from and outside the ambit of the National Film Archive of India (NFAI). Kuhu Tanvir names this the "pirate archive" of Indian cinema.[9] Away from the restrictive, purist project of the NFAI, the theoretically infinite pirate archive of cinema is not guided by the narrow criteria of traditional film selection (merit, censor certification, respectability) or preservation (print quality). Indeed, the "original print," the archive's "monument," the fetishized foundational unit of film preservation, is displaced in the pirate archive by an antimonumental proliferation of copies, versions, dubs, and points of access. As opposed to the traditional film archive, a site such as YouTube operates with less regard for copyright or quality than for access. "Consisting largely of pirated material, often of poor quality and unknown origins, this pirate archive of cinema," writes Tanvir, "occupies an illicit space in the moral economy of the copyright regime": "The cinephile is at the center of this archive, because he is one of several archivists contributing to this global phenomenon in productive or destructive ways. There is then a fundamental change in the constitution of the archivist and the archive, as the fluid, pirate, and networked archive of cinema poses a potent challenge to the contours of control wielded by a state-run archive."[10]

We should consider the pirate archive not only as an archive of particular films, but also as potentially archiving the experience of an obsolete form of 1980s global popular culture. The digital repository of videotape copies offers us something a proper, pedigreed archive cannot: clues about the lost medium of videotape, its technology, its aesthetics, and its experience in 1980s India. What persists into the present is a telecine recording that I can stream or download as a digitally compressed MP4 or MKV file, but that in "live" playback decompresses to a performance of signifying, cinematic memory and "nonsignifying," machinic memory, radiating bloody corpses, pitch-dark nights, and grisly monsters through videotape's narrower, radioactive color ranges, lower resolutions, and denser noise and the absence of a true black. This is an archive in the double sense, preserving both 1980s cinema and the "circulatory dynamics" of its consumption.[11]

The desire at the heart of media archaeology—to redeem and represence forgotten media objects and events—is, as Vivian Sobchack notes, deeply romantic. Sobchack argues that this "desire for presence" invites and incites a host of historiographic strategies: counterhistories of the archive, material histories of the trace, and forensic histories of the fragment.[12] These signs, however, could be fruitfully conceived of as media-archaeological traces. What does it mean to think and write about videotape media archaeologically? A media-archaeological approach to media objects and images recognizes, emphasizes, and reflects on the mediating distance between past and present and "even makes it the basis of its methodology."[13] As Wolfgang Ernst puts it, media archaeology foregrounds the remainder, "what is actually there: what has remained from the past in the present like archaeological layers, operatively embedded in technologies."[14] Of course, what preferably remains in the present, and what media archaeologists usually focus on, is some material artifact that has withstood the ravages of time and indifference; in this case, these artifacts may have been remnants of the material worlds of Bombay horror.[15] But those artifacts are gone; what remains are worlds "actively generating sensual and informational presence."[16]

Film-to-video-to-digital transfers of Bhakri's films trigger a sensuous encounter with the different eras, owners, and circuits across which the film traveled: as celluloid, as videotape, and as contemporary data stream. We can characterize this as a pirate archive of "poor images," which Hito Steyerl describes as "illicit fifth-generation bastard[s] of an original image," "copied and pasted into other channels of distribution." Poor images are the "lumpen proletariat in the class society of appearances, ranked and valued according to its resolution," those that are threatened with invisibility in a corporate-cineaste economy that fetishizes beauty, genealogy, and clarity; as such, the poor image's persistence indicates possible resistance to those hierarchies of value and their implicit politics.[17]

The pirate archive, then, is a continuation of a project that began almost as soon as Bombay's horror films were released: an extension of their virtual life, without value cycling back to the makers of the films. The 1980s were marked by an intensification of piracy as a mass "culture of the copy."[18] Allowing consumers to break the queue and access goods "ahead of time," copy culture emerged to provide a parallel exit to uneven temporalities of supply and demand. "If piracy is ubiquitous in most parts of the world," argues Joe Karaganis, it is because systemic inequity is ubiquitous. "The enormously successful globalization of media culture over the past two decades," he notes, "has not been accompanied by a comparable democratization of media access—at least in its legal forms. The flood of legal media goods available in high-income countries has been a trickle in most parts of the world."[19] A riposte to media empires built on vertical integration, enforced anticipation, copyright, and conglomeration, piracy foments prolific, horizontal markets of its own.

Outside South Asia's elite enclaves, the bootleg, the knock-off, the cheap imitation predominates, central to what Sundaram identifies as the subcontinent's unauthorized, recycled, or "pirate modernity."[20] Rejecting the claims of intellectual property discourse, pirate modernity espouses an ethics "unconcerned with modernity's search for originality."[21] As globalization's terrifying alter ego, this pirate modernity intervenes in the gulf between high prices and low incomes, engaging inexpensive technologies of reproduction to saturate street kiosks and bazaars with "counterfeits, fakes or copies."[22] Piracy, as a mode through which media goods *and* media images circulate, closes the gap between supply and demand, anticipation and arrival, originality and imitation, production and consumption, filmmaker and fan—and pirate and scholar.

The bad copies and "poor images" of Bombay horror are also, for me, good: richly informative and allowing me to do more with the past. Where previously the attention of moviegoers generated money for film producers, now the films generate other values. The unpredictable circulation of uncanonized films and media objects as "poor images" takes us to the edge of value, where, as Kaveh Askari has shown, pressure builds on junk prints and bad copies to be of use to film producers, fans, or critics.[23] The unlicensed, uncontrolled circulation of Bombay horror films on bootleg videotapes eventually died out, but the films' continued circulation online today marks the climax of a trajectory that began almost as soon as the films were first released. From the projection of junk prints in rundown theaters to the moment of my viewing, downloading, and streaming the films, we can trace an ensemble of practices that keep extracting value from the films long after they could accrue value to those that made them. Paying attention to these archival markers allows me to mark my own spectatorial position and point of access in relation to Indian film history as it reincarnates in an emergent intermedia archive. This is my archive of failures, where I have discovered multiple copies of *Bandh Darwaza, Purana Mandir, Jaani Dushman, Kabrastan,* and *Veerana*. Even as I continue to find new versions of these films uploaded by users, I have been surprised occasionally to find other versions taken down.

The pirate archive was originally conceived of in opposition to the NFAI. In the years since the NFAI has suffered a series of destructive fires. This has left in flux the fortunes of many types of materials you have encountered in this book—censor scripts, trade magazines, and print ephemera—to say nothing of the films themselves. But in 2023, the film archive was merged with the National Film Development Corporation (NFDC), and NFAI-NFDC has announced a series of high-profile preservation projects centered on Bombay cinema. What will happen to film history? In the vanishing failures of films you are yet to encounter lie stories of the past yet untold.

Notes

INTRODUCTION

1. Henriques, "Toast to an Indian Ghost."
2. Lim, *Translating Time*, 15. See also Todorov, *Fantastic*, 31.
3. Nemerov, "Seeing Ghosts," 529.
4. Jaikumar, *Where Histories Reside*.
5. *Report of the Working Group on National Film Policy*, iii.
6. *Report of the Working Group on National Film Policy*, 1.
7. Sen, *Haunting Bollywood*, 39.
8. "3-D Creates Havoc in Bombay Suburbs."
9. "Kanta Distributors."
10. *Filmfare*, 16–30 September 1987, 19–21.
11. Klein, *American Film Cycles*, 3–4.
12. "Writ Petition against Ban on Film."
13. Mohammed, "Vampires Don't Live Here Anymore."
14. Mohammed, "Vampires Don't Live Here Anymore."
15. Cho, "Genre, Translation, and Transnational Cinema."
16. Iyer, "Nevla as Dracula."
17. Tulsi Ramsay, interview with the author, 9 February 2010 .
18. For "spurious," see "Tale of 3 Films," 8. For "second-hand," see Henriques, "Toast to an Indian Ghost," 9. For "bad copies," see Dwyer, *Filming the Gods*.
19. *"Purana Mandir."*

20. Thomas, "Indian Cinema," 120.
21. Thomas, "Indian Cinema," 130.
22. Vasudevan, *Melodramatic Public*; Prasad, *Ideology of the Hindi Film*; and Gopalan, *Cinema of Interruptions*.
23. Gopal, *Conjugations*, 100.
24. Gopal, *Conjugations*, 100.
25. Gopal, *Conjugations*, 101.
26. Nair, "Review"; see Sen, "Spectral Pixels"; Sen, *Haunting Bollywood*, 107–131; and Ghosh, "Security Aesthetic in Bollywood's High-Rise Horror."
27. Subba, "Rebels without a Cause," 105.
28. Subba, "Rebels without a Cause," 105. See also "*Shaitani Dracula*: The Worst Movie Ever Made?"
29. Mukherjee, Bhaumik, and Allana, *Filmi Jagat*.
30. Chatterjee, "On Disreputable Genres," 32.
31. Thomas, *Bombay before Bollywood*; Bhaumik, "Emergence of the Bombay Film Industry"; and Vitali, *Hindi Action Cinema*.
32. Mazumdar and Majumdar, "Introduction," 15.
33. Ganti, *Producing Bollywood*, 79–81.
34. Ganti, *Producing Bollywood*, 79–81.
35. See Mazumdar, *Bombay Cinema*; Punathambekar, *From Bombay to Bollywood*; and Rai, *Untimely Bollywood*.
36. Masood, "Not So Popular Cinema."
37. Masood, "Not So Popular Cinema," 25; and Nair, "What Makes Full Houses Full?"
38. For more on the social necessity of traces, see Ferraris, *Documentality*.
39. Tarratt, "Monsters from the Id," 258.
40. Wood, "Introduction to the American Horror Film," 10.
41. Wood, "Introduction to the American Horror Film," 14.
42. Berenstein, *Attack of the Leading Ladies*, 10.
43. Benshoff, "Preface," xiv; and Jameson, "Reification and Utopia in Mass Culture," 34.
44. Dumas, "Horror and Psychoanalysis," 29.
45. Mubarki, *Filming Horror*, 72–143.
46. Dhusiya, *Indian Horror Cinema*. Dhusiya also includes an extensively annotated filmography of Hindi, Tamil, Telugu, Kannada, Bangla, Marathi, and Malayalam horror films (209–269).
47. Sen, *Haunting Bollywood*, 53.
48. Sen, *Haunting Bollywood*, 53–63.
49. See Sen, *Haunting Bollywood*; Mubarki, *Filming Horror*; Dhusiya, *Indian Horror Cinema*; Chaudhury, "Sound of Horror"; Sen, "'I Wasn't Born with Enough Middle Fingers'"; Iyer, "Nevla as Dracula"; Tombs, "Beast from Bollywood," Vitali, "Hindi Horror Film"; Valančiūnas, "Indian Horror"; Goldberg, Sen, and Collins, *Bollywood Horrors*.

50. Crane, "Scraping Bottom," 153.
51. Crane, "Scraping Bottom," 153.
52. Shaviro, *Cinematic Body*, 11.
53. Shaviro, *Cinematic Body*, 11.
54. Brinkema, *Forms of the Affects*, xvi; and Brinkema, *Life-Destroying Diagrams*.
55. Martin, "Standing Up Too Close or Back Too Far?," 512–513.
56. Martin, "Standing Up Too Close or Back Too Far?," 512–513.
57. Martin, "Standing Up Too Close or Back Too Far?," 512–513.
58. Brinkema, "Colors without Bodies," 7.
59. Brinkema, "Colors Without Bodies," 7.
60. See Brown, "Thing Theory."
61. See Roberts, *Transporting Visions*. For some recent examples of the material turn in film studies, see Ezra, *Cinema of Things*; Benson-Allott, *Stuff of Spectatorship*; Askari, *Material Cultures in Transit*; Zhou, *Cinema Off Screen*; and Yue, *Girl Head*. For "new film history" see Chapman, Glancy, and Harper, *New Film History*.
62. Benson-Allott, *"Grindhouse,"* 21.
63. Frank, *Frame by Frame*.
64. Wasserman, *Death of Things*, 7
65. Kraus, "Reinventing the Medium," 289.
66. Doane, "Indexical and the Concept of Medium Specificity," 130–131.
67. Doane, "Indexical and the Concept of Medium Specificity," 130–131.
68. Hart, *Monstrous Forms*, 8.
69. Loew, *Special Effects and German Silent Film*. See also Gunning, "To Scan a Ghost."
70. Abbott, *Celluloid Vampires*, 50.
71. Abbott, *Celluloid Vampires*, 58.
72. Abbott, *Celluloid Vampires*, 58.
73. Abbott, *Celluloid Vampires*, 58.
74. Hesselberth, "From Subject-Effect to Presence-Effect."
75. Spadoni, *Uncanny Bodies*.
76. See Spadoni, *Uncanny Bodies*; Frith, "Curse of the Thing Is Technicolor Blood"; and Prince, *Classical Film Violence*, 30–86.
77. See Clasen, *Why Horror Seduces*.
78. Buscombe, "Idea of Genre," 19.
79. Buscombe, "Idea of Genre," 17.
80. Young, "In Defense of Psychoanalytic Film Theory."
81. Gopal, *Conjugations*, 96.
82. Dwyer, *Filming the Gods*, 48.
83. Sen, *Haunting Bollywood*, 49.
84. Sen, *Haunting Bollywood*, 49.
85. Rhodes, "Belabored," 53.

86. Thompson, "Concept of Cinematic Excess," 134.
87. Sen, *Haunting Bollywood*, 117.
88. McDonagh, *Broken Mirrors/Broken Minds*, 19.
89. Sipos, *Horror Film Aesthetics*, 29.
90. Sipos, *Horror Film Aesthetics*, 29.
91. Gorfinkel, "Body as Apparatus," 158.
92. Pandian, *Reel World*, 9.
93. See Halberstam, *Queer Art of Failure*.
94. Modleski, "Terror of Pleasure," 271. See also Schaefer, *Bold! Daring! Shocking! True!*; and Gorfinkel, *Lewd Looks*.
95. Baudry and Williams, "Ideological Effects of the Basic Cinematographic Apparatus," 42.
96. Farmer, *Spectacular Passions*, 114.
97. Sontag, "Notes on Camp," 276.
98. Sconce, "'Trashing' the Academy," 391.
99. Bartlett, *Badfilm*, 9.
100. Bartlett, *Badfilm*, 40.
101. Sconce, "'Trashing' the Academy," 391.
102. Perez, *Material Ghost*, 38; see also Sconce, *Haunted Media*.
103. Barthes, *Camera Lucida*, 4.
104. Perez, *Material Ghost*.
105. Lippit, *Atomic Light (Shadow Optics)*.
106. For more on the "uncanny role given to [things] and the expressive hyperbole granted objects by horror diegesis," see Karl Schoonover, "Scrap Metal," 111.
107. Keathley, *Cinephilia and History*, 27–51; and Cardinal, "Pausing over Peripheral Detail."
108. Koutsourakis, "Modest Proposal," 23.
109. Richards, *Cinematic Flashes*, 4.
110. Coole and Frost, *New Materialisms*, 9–10.
111. Blanco and Peeren, "Introduction," 6.
112. Weinstock, "Introduction," 63.
113. Blanco and Peeren, *Spectralities Reader*, 94.
114. Kane, *High-Tech Trash*, 3.
115. Nair, "Taste, Taboo, Trash."
116. Chandaver, *Anurag Minus Verma Podcast*.
117. Hoek, *Cut-Pieces*, 9–11.
118. Govil, "Bollywood and the Frictions of Global Mobility," 94.
119. Govil, "Bollywood and the Frictions of Global Mobility," 94.
120. Govil, "Bollywood and the Frictions of Global Mobility," 94.
121. Mukherjee, *Bombay Hustle*, p. 12
122. Mathijs and Sexton, "Introduction," 5.
123. Field, "Acts of Speculation"; Hastie, *Cupboards of Curiosity*; and Siddique, *An Evacuee Cinema*.

124. Sen, *Haunting Bollywood*, 50.
125. Iyer, *Dancing Women*.
126. Mehta, *Censorship and Sexuality in Bombay Cinema*; Jaikumar, *Cinema at the End of Empire*; Gopalan, *Cinema of Interruptions*; Ghosh, *Fire*; and Bhowmik, *Cinema and Censorship*.
127. Ganti, "Limits of Decency," 90.
128. See Prakash, *Emergency Chronicles*; and Tarlo, *Unsettling Memories*.
129. Hafizji, "When the Film Industry Was Sterilized"; and Vasudev, *Liberty and License in the Indian Cinema*, 161.
130. Sen, *Haunting Bollywood*, 48.
131. Kermode, "Horror," 160.
132. Gopalan, *Cinema of Interruptions*; and Mehta, *Censorship and Sexuality in Bombay Cinema*.
133. See Bunn, "Reimagining Repression," 44; Hoek, *Cut-Pieces*; Liang, "Law, Affect and the Media Event"; and Mukherjee, "Specter Haunts Bombay."
134. Brophy, "Horrality."
135. Vitali, *Hindi Action Cinema*, 193.
136. Vitali, "Hindi Horror Films of the Ramsay Brothers," 123.
137. "India Once Again Tops in Film Production."
138. Vitali, "Hindi Horror Films of the Ramsay Brothers," 147.
139. Vitali, "Hindi Horror Films of the Ramsay Brothers," 147.
140. Wilkinson-Weber, *Fashioning Bollywood*; and Sengupta, "Reflected Readings in Available Light."
141. Caldwell, *Production Culture*; and Mayer, *Below the Line*.
142. Pillai, *Madras Studios*; and Jacobson, *In the Studio*.
143. Mukherjee and Mehta, "Introduction," 1.
144. Mukherjee, *Bombay Hustle*.
145. Nair, "What Makes Full Houses Full?," 46.
146. Prabhu, "How to Make a Killing at the Box Office."
147. Mazumdar, "Invisible Work," 26.
148. Mahadevan, *Very Old Machine*, 60.
149. "Film Industry Faces Problem of Boom."
150. Pendakur, "New Cultural Technologies," 69.
151. Brown, "Thing Theory," 4.
152. Galt, *Alluring Monsters*, 24.
153. Bartlett, "It Happens by Accident," 46.
154. Ganti, *Producing Bollywood*, 141.
155. Staiger, *Interpreting Films*, p. 13
156. Stevens, "Introduction," 2.
157. Williams, "Film Bodies."
158. See Marks, *Touch*, 1–22, 91–112; Sobchack, *Carnal Thoughts*, 53–84; Barker, *Tactile Eye*, 23–55; Bruno, *Atlas of Emotion*, 55–71; and Dudenhoeffer, *Embodiment and Horror Cinema*.

159. Ndalianis, *Horror Sensorium*, 16–17.
160. Wood, "Introduction to the American Horror Film," 10.
161. Groo, *Bad Film Histories*, 280.
162. See Bird, "'Dancing, Flying Camera Jockeys'"; Nair, "Towards a Phenomenology of Film Production"; and Hebert, "Experiments in the Cine-Olympic Cycle."
163. Huang, *Urban Horror*, 5–6.
164. Doane, "Indexicality," 135.
165. Groo, *Bad Film Histories*, 280.

CHAPTER 1. PAPER CUTS

1. "Film Import," 1980. Between 1977 and 1980, the story reported, fourteen Hindi films and short features were denied certificates, among them *Darwaza*.
2. "India's First Horror Film," 2.
3. Liang, "Law, Affect and the Media Event," 48, 49.
4. Liang, "Law, Affect and the Media Event," 49.
5. "Keep Us Informed about Certified Films—CEAI."
6. Gitelman, *Paper Knowledge*, 1.
7. Khosla, *Pornography and Censorship in India*, 155.
8. Ramanathan, "Censors without Clout," 11.
9. Rao, "Censor's Scissors," 8.
10. Mazzarella, *Censorium*, 199.
11. Lim, *Translating Time*, 21, 1–41.
12. Lim, *Translating Time*, 12.
13. Lim, *Translating Time*, 25, 12.
14. Lim, *Translating Time*, 8, 12.
15. Lim, *Translating Time*, 12.
16. Cinematograph Act of 1952, sect. 5B.
17. Cinematograph Act of 1983, 63–64.
18. Hoag, "Dereliction at the South African Department of Home Affairs," 415.
19. See Gill, "Censorship and Ethnographic Film."
20. See Carswell, Chambers, and De Neve, "Waiting for the State"; and Stasik, Hänsch, and Mains, "Temporalities of Waiting."
21. See Thomas, *Bombay before Bollywood*.
22. Gopalan, *Cinema of Interruptions*, 36.
23. Mazzarella, *Censorium*, 162.
24. Sarkar, *You Can't Please Everyone!*, 52.
25. Sarkar, *You Can't Please Everyone!*, 52.
26. Sarkar, *You Can't Please Everyone!*, 52.
27. Mazzarella, *Censorium*, 28.

28. Hull, *Government of Paper*, 7. On the colonial origins of film censorship, see Jaikumar, *Cinema at the End of Empire*.
29. Raman, *Document Raj*, 1–19.
30. Weber, "Bureaucracy," 197.
31. Hull, *Government of Paper*, 7.
32. Cinematograph Act of 1952.
33. "Notification from the Ministry of Information and Broadcasting," 280–282.
34. "Of Censors and Super Censors."
35. See Ganti, "Limits of Decency."
36. See Mehta, *Censorship and Sexuality in Bombay Cinema*.
37. "Notification from the Ministry of Information and Broadcasting," 280–282.
38. "Notification from the Ministry of Information and Broadcasting," 280–282.
39. Vasudev, *Liberty and License in the Indian Cinema*, ix.
40. Hafizji, "When the Film Industry Was Sterilized."
41. Ramachandran, "Editorial," 5.
42. "Film Censorship."
43. "Written Answers to Questions" (1977).
44. "Written Answers to Questions" (1977).
45. Jaisingh, *India after Indira*.
46. Hull, *Government of Paper*, 10.
47. Gupta and Sharma, *Anthropology of the State*, 1–41.
48. Hull, *Government of Paper*, p. 4.
49. Tarlo, *Unsettling Memories*. See also Jeffrey, "Monitoring Newspapers."
50. Barthes, *Camera Lucida*, 87.
51. Cinematograph Act of 1983, 33.
52. Stoler, *Along the Archival Grain*, 2.
53. "Notification from the Ministry of Information and Broadcasting," 280–282.
54. "Notification of the Ministry of Information and Broadcasting."
55. "Notification of the Ministry of Information and Broadcasting."
56. Ong, *Orality and Literacy*, 11.
57. Vismann, *Files*, xiii.
58. Tulsi Ramsay, interview with the author, 9 February 2010.
59. Tulsi Ramsay, interview with the author, 9 February 2010.
60. Nair, "Taste, Taboo, Trash."
61. Spadoni, *Uncanny Bodies*, 7.
62. "Tune to Vividh Bharati Today."
63. Tulsi Ramsay, interview with the author, 9 February 2010.
64. "India's First Horror Film," 2.
65. Hart, "Transitional Gothic," 63.

66. Lim, *Translating Time*, 152–153.
67. Mishra, *Bollywood Cinema*, 57. See also Dwyer, "Bombay Gothic."
68. Britton, "Meet Me in St Louis," 173.
69. Walter Scott, as cited in Molesworth, "Gothic Time, Sacred Time," 90.
70. "Particulars of Films," *Gazette of India*, 16 September 1978, 1534–1535.
71. *Report of the Working Group on National Film Policy*, 79.
72. Hughes, "Policing Silent Film Exhibition in Colonial South India," 55.
73. Cinematograph Act of 1952, sect. 5A.
74. *Raj Kapoor v. Laxman*, 14 December 1979, Supreme Court of India.
75. Cinematograph Act of 1952, sect. 5A.
76. "Keep Us Informed about Certified Films—CEAI."
77. "Keep Us Informed about Certified Films—CEAI."
78. Goswami, *Evolution of Gazette of India*, 3.
79. Gupta, *Red Tape*, 141.
80. Abel, *Redacted*, 25.
81. Parks, "Points of Departure," 187. See also Roberts, *Behind the Screen*.
82. Hochschild, *Managed Heart*, 20.
83. Boyer, "Censorship as a Vocation," 515–532.
84. Razdan, "Film Censorship in India," 58.
85. Boyer, "Censorship as a Vocation," 537.
86. Kernan, *Coming Attractions*, 20.
87. "Excite."
88. Lim, *Translating Time*, 156.
89. Razdan, "Film Censorship in India," 58.
90. Razdan, "Film Censorship in India," 58.
91. "Darwaza."
92. See, for example, Frith, "'Curse of the Thing Is Technicolor Blood'"; and Jacobs, *Wages of Sin*.
93. Prince, *Classical Film Violence*, 38. See also Johnson, *Celluloid Paper Trail*.
94. Hull, *Government of Paper*, 14.
95. Cinematograph Act of 1983, 24.
96. *Darwaza*, Censor Script, National Film Archive.
97. Cinematograph Act of 1983, 28–33.
98. *Darwaza*, Censor Script Cover Letter, National Film Archive, 3.
99. Gupta, *Red Tape*, 36.
100. See Khanna, "Censor Script Writer." Censor scripts for Ramsay films varied over the 1970s; unlike the script for *Darwaza*, the 1972 script for *Do Gaz Zameen Ke Neeche* is handwritten.
101. Mathur, *Paper Tiger*, 1–35.
102. As Annelise Riles reminds us, "moments of document creation anticipate future moments in which documents will be received, circulated, instrumentalized, and taken apart again." Riles, *Documents*, 18.

103. Jacobs, *Wages of Sin*, 26.
104. Torre, *Animation*, 58.
105. Prabhu, "How to Make a Killing at the Box Office."
106. Caruthers, *Doing Time*, 13.
107. Kermode, "Horror," 60.
108. "Horror Films," 7.
109. "Tale of 3 Films," 8.
110. Ramanathan, "Censors without Clout"; and "Indian Government Bans *The Exorcist*," 38.
111. Prince, *Classical Film Violence*, 6.
112. Prince, *Classical Film Violence*, 80.

CHAPTER 2. CELLULOID SPLATTER

1. Rao, "Censor's Scissors."
2. "*Jaani Dushman*."
3. "Audiences Need Holiday from Violence."
4. Mohamed, "Crime Beat," 11.
5. Mohamed, "Vampires Don't Live Here Anymore"; and Mohamed, "Film Censorship," 13.
6. "How Films Are Censored"; Mohamed, "'Bepanaah' Revels in Gore & Destruction," 5; and Mohamed, "Vampires Don't Live Here Anymore."
7. "Let's Be Practical."
8. "So What's Left?"
9. "So What's Left?"
10. Prince, *Classical Film Violence*, 9.
11. Prince, *Classical Screen Violence*, 240.
12. Mazumdar, "Legal Unspeakable," 172.
13. Mehta, *Censorship and Sexuality in Bombay Cinema*. See also Butler, "Ruled Out," 248.
14. Gopalan, *Cinema of Interruptions*
15. Gopalan, "Avenging Women in Indian Cinema," 51.
16. "Particulars of Films" (1979), 2563.
17. See Hoek, *Cut-Pieces*.
18. Vinod Talwar, interview with the author, 18 September 2014, Mumbai.
19. Vinod Talwar, interview with the author, 18 September 2014, Mumbai.
20. Hoek, *Cut Pieces*, 212.
21. Schuppli, *Media Forensics*, 20–39.
22. Ernst, *Digital Memory and the Archive*, 139.
23. Pascuzzi and Waters, "Introduction," xv.
24. Pascuzzi and Waters, "Introduction," xv.

25. Schoonover, "What Do We Do with Vacant Space in Horror Films?," 345.
26. Groo, *Bad Film Histories*, 258.
27. See Ruétalo, *Violated Frames*.
28. See Hoek, *Cut-Pieces*; and Mehta, *Censorship and Sexuality in Bombay Cinema*.
29. Pinney, "Things Happen," 261.
30. Pinney, "Things Happen," 261. See also Thielemans, "Beyond Visuality," 2.
31. Pinney, "Things Happen," 261.
32. Mukherjee, "Specter Haunts Bombay," 54.
33. Stiasny and Togler, "Twilight of the Dead," 247.
34. Usai, *The Death of Cinema*, 5.
35. "*Jaani Dushman* Repels."
36. "*Jaani Dushman* Repels."
37. Tombs, *Mondo Macabro*.
38. To use Madhava Prasad's words, films like *Jaani Dushman* interpellate filmgoers as "political subjects" to "witness and legitimize the splendor of the ruling class," to shore up the "unity and jouissance of the feudal family." Prasad, *Ideology of the Hindi Film*, 67.
39. See Menon, *Recovering Subversion*.
40. Phadke, "Thirty Years On," 4568.
41. See Vasudevan, *Melodramatic Public*.
42. Singer, *Melodrama and Modernity*, 35.
43. "Horror Films," 7.
44. Vasudev, *Liberty and License in the Indian Cinema*, 143.
45. Vasudev, *Liberty and License in the Indian Cinema*, 143.
46. "Film."
47. "Sex, Violence."
48. Cinematograph Act 1983, 63, https://www.cbfcindia.gov.in/main/CBFC_English/Attachments/cine_rule1983.pdf.
49. Sarkar, *You Can't Please Everyone!*, 37.
50. Mohamed, "'The Exorcist' Awaiting Only Formal Ban," 5.
51. Williams, "Violence."
52. Vasudev, *Liberty and License*, 161.
53. See Nahata, *Kissaa Kursee Kaa*; Bobb, "Case of a Missing Film"; "Hunt for the Wrong Film"; and "*Bobby* Was Shown at Shukla's Orders."
54. Watkins, "*Don't Look Now*," 449.
55. Rao, "Censor's Scissors."
56. "Raj Kumar Kohli."
57. "Writ Petition against Ban on Film."
58. "Censor Verdict Challenged."
59. "Writ Petition against Ban on Film."
60. Rao, "Censor's Scissors."

61. "Raj Kumar Kohli."
62. "Raj Kumar Kohli."
63. "Raj Kumar Kohli."
64. "Raj Kumar Kohli."
65. Mehta, "Letter 'A' for Adults or for Adolescents?"
66. "Raj Kumar Kohli."
67. "Censors Snip India's Multistar Horror Film."
68. Flusser, *Does Writing Have a Future?*, 11.
69. Gulshan Grover, telephone interview with the author, 23 December 2020. Everything about a film, its labor and effects, its stars and songs, was meaningless without film stock, and all of this labor was colloquially commutable to stock. For example, when in 1976 stuntmen agitated for limits on workdays, they successfully negotiated with producers that no single action sequence would exceed "more than 90 feet." "Concession on Fight Scenes."
70. Priya Jaikumar has shown how stock was issued only after a producer furnished a "consumption certificate" from a printing laboratory; the laboratory attested that the producer had not thus far transgressed the stipulated "waste ratio" of 1:5. With their power to falsify or authenticate consumption certificates, laboratories expanded their power over producers; the sale of stock and trade of consumption certificates quickly became a "big racket" in the Bombay film industry (*Where Histories Reside*, 112). As Rosie Thomas has found, the primacy of celluloid transformed printing laboratories into centers of power: as "keepers of the negative," they could refuse to process or return film negatives or to release prints of the film. Thomas, *Bombay before Bollywood*, 189.
71. "FFI President's SOS to Delhi." Later that year, as Nitin Govil notes, the Indian government responded to the industry's cry for help and "decided to allow the use of imported film stock (including Eastman Color and Fujicolor) for domestic release prints; previously, imported color stock was used only for prints destined for the overseas market." Govil, "Something to Declare," 138.
72. For actors who were afraid producers would not follow through on the final installment of their salary, "the only thing helping was the lab letter": a letter, issued by the laboratory, promising that the film would not be printed or released from the laboratory until the actors were paid. Jaaved Jaaferi, telephone interview with the author, 5 February 2021.
73. "Shortage of Color Film Hits 24 Movies."
74. "FFI President's SOS to Delhi."
75. "HPF May Go in for Colour"; and "Industry Condemns Stock Price Raise."
76. See Mazumdar, "Aviation, Tourism and Dreaming in 1960s Bombay Cinema."
77. Dootson, "Perversion of the System."
78. See Dootson, "'Mapping the Laboratory'" on the role played by Technicolor printing laboratories in facilitating the Eastmancolor revolution in India.

79. Raj Hate, conversation with the author, 6 March 2022.
80. Yumibe, "Colour as Performance," 299.
81. See Berry, "Every Colour Red?"
82. Sarkar, *You Can't Please Everyone!*, 52.
83. Sarkar, *You Can't Please Everyone!*, 28.
84. "Trade Leaders Flay Working Group's Superficial Report."
85. Sarkar, *You Can't Please Everyone!*, 37. In his study of Hammer horror censorship, Paul Frith finds that the BBFC was "making requests to remove shots from [*The Curse of Frankenstein*, 1957] based upon the likelihood that they would eventually become more unsuitable when seen in color." Frith, "'Curse of the Thing Is Technicolor Blood," 239.
86. In 2021, driven by the COVID-19 pandemic, the CBFC announced a new policy whereby it would "accept modifications/cuts in the films on its online e-cinepramaan system itself," and applicants would be allowed to upload video files in mp4 formats showing the sequences before and after modification, which would be screened, verified, and approved by the regional officer or examining officer. "Important Communication No. 2/2021."
87. Cinematograph Act of 1983, 63–64.
88. "Industry Closure," 1.
89. Clover, "Her Body, Himself," 187.
90. Clover, "Eye of Horror," 184, 196.
91. Clover, "Eye of Horror," 196.
92. Clover, "Eye of Horror," 202.
93. Clover, "Eye of Horror," 202.
94. Clover, "Eye of Horror," 202.
95. See Lowenstein, "*Giallo*/Slasher Landscape"; and Kelly, "*It Follows*."
96. "Invasion of Bride-Snatchers."
97. "Particulars of Films" (1979), 2563.
98. "Handling of Processed Film."
99. Theophanidis, "Scratches in Kubrick's *2001*."
100. Theophanidis, "Scratches in Kubrick's *2001*."
101. Price, "Color, the Formless, and Cinematic Eros."
102. Yumibe, "Colour as Performance," 299.
103. Abel, *Redacted*, 14.
104. Yue, *Girl Head*, 78; see also Cazenave, *Archive of the Catastrophe*.
105. Lippit, *Atomic Light*.
106. Flusser, *Does Writing Have a Future?*, 11.
107. Zinman, *Making Images Move*, 4.
108. Tralli, "Layers of Film," 77–78.
109. Tralli, "Layers of Film," 78; and Moskatova, "Unstable Matter Destruction," 102.
110. Meden, *Scratches and Glitches*, 30.

111. Meden, *Scratches and Glitches*, 30.
112. Meden, *Scratches and Glitches*, 30.
113. Moskatova, "Unstable Matter Destruction," 95–96.
114. Zinman, *Making Images Move*, 9.
115. Zinman, *Making Images Move*, 9.
116. Zinman, *Making Images Move*, 14.
117. Groo, *Bad Film Histories*, 280.
118. Hincha, "Crisis in Celluloid," 126. See also Heckman, "We've Got Bigger Problems."
119. Hincha, "Crisis in Celluloid," 131.
120. Flueckiger, "Material Properties of Historical Film."
121. Higgins, *Harnessing the Technicolor Rainbow*, 226.
122. Usai, *Silent Cinema*, 33.
123. Higgins, *Harnessing the Technicolor Rainbow*, 226.
124. Hoek, *Cut Pieces*, 153.
125. Jackson, "Movies and Mania."
126. "Jaani Dushman Cuts."
127. "Jaani Dushman Cuts."
128. Mohamed, "Film Censorship."

CHAPTER 3. UNSETTLING DESIGN

1. Spadoni, "Carl Dreyer's Corpse," 126.
2. Thomas, "Indian Cinema," 120.
3. Nandy, "Indiana Jones Returns to the Temple of Gloom."
4. Fay, *Inhospitable World*, 5.
5. Bruno, *Atlas of Emotion*, 6.
6. Fischer, *Art Direction and Production Design*, 1. See also Barnwell, *Production Design*; and Affron and Affron, *Sets in Motion*.
7. Mazumdar, *Bombay Cinema*, 110–148.
8. See Jacobson, *In the Studio*.
9. Govil, "Bollywood and the Frictions of Global Mobility," 94.
10. Sedgwick, *Coherence of Gothic Conventions*, 9–11.
11. Sen, *Haunting Bollywood*, 59.
12. Jaikumar, "Haveli," 228.
13. Rhodes, *Spectacle of Property*. See also Gorfinkel and Rhodes, *Taking Place*.
14. Risner, *Blood Circuits*, 65.
15. Mukherjee, *Bombay Hustle*, 320–321.
16. Mukherjee, *Bombay Hustle*, 320–321.
17. Vitali, "Hindi Horror Films of the Ramsay Brothers," 123.

18. Vitali, "Hindi Horror Films of the Ramsay Brothers," 123.
19. "Putting the Industry in Order."
20. Gulshan Grover, telephone interview with the author, 23 December 2020.
21. Focusing on the film's fragmented textuality and circulatory afterlife, Sudhir Mahadevan has described *Film Hi Film* as a "popular film historiography" of Hindi cinema. See Mahadevan, *Very Old Machine*, 161–180.
22. One could estimate that in the mid-1980s electricians were paid 65 rupees for an eight-hour shift; light men, 52 rupees; carpenters, 40 rupees; spot-boys, 43 rupees; assistant carpenters, 25 rupees; polish-men, 30 rupees; welders, 44 rupees; casters, 40 rupees; helpers, 25 rupees; head painters, 50 rupees; tapists, 40 rupees; and painters, 40 rupees. I arrived at these figures using terms from a 1987 agreement between the All India Film Producers Council and the FWICE, which carved out a 25 percent increase in wages for extras and other workers ("Details of Agreement").
23. "Written Answers to Questions" (1973).
24. *Federation of Western India Cine Employees v. Filmalaya Pvt. Ltd.*
25. Vohra, "Film City May Remain Only Paper Plan," 3.
26. "Trade Delegation Meets CM."
27. See Lutgendorf, "Notes on Indian Popular Cinema."
28. "Discipline within Three Months"; and "Dabbling with Day-Dreams."
29. Ede, "Art in Context," 73.
30. "House of Horror."
31. See Ganti, *Producing Bollywood*, 189.
32. Baschiera and Di Chiara, "Once upon a Time in Italy," 31.
33. Bizzari, cited in Guarneri, "Gothic bet," 6.
34. Aarti Gupta, interview with the author, 2010.
35. "Shooting."
36. Mohamed, "Government Guest House Turns into Chamber of Horrors."
37. Mohamed, "Government Guest House Turns into Chamber of Horrors."
38. McDonagh, *Broken Minds/Broken Mirrors*, 5.
39. Anjani Tiwari, interview with the author, 29 September 2014.
40. "Kanta Distributors."
41. Anjani Tiwari, interview with the author, 29 September 2014.
42. Cavell, "What Becomes of Things on Film?," 256.
43. Tombs, *Mondo Macabro*, 488–489.
44. In order to put the film's production geography together, I relied extensively on horror film cinephiles of YouTube, such as Manohar Rathore, "Purana Mandir," https://www.youtube.com/watch?v=5YxDgT_wHUw&t=444s.
45. Jaikumar, *Where Histories Reside*, 211. See also Dwyer, "Bombay Gothic"; Sen, "Haunted Havelis"; and Bhaskar and Allen, *Islamicate Cultures*, 65–90.
46. London, *Bombay Gothic*.
47. See also McKenna, "Photoplay or the Pickaxe."

48. Joshi, "Informal Urban Economy."
49. Joshi, "Informal Urban Economy," 641.
50. Joshi, "Informal Urban Economy," 641.
51. Chanana, *Missing 3 in Bollywood*.
52. "Agreement."
53. "Details of Agreement."
54. Ranjan, "Sorry Plight of Extras."
55. Ranjan, "Sorry Plight of Extras."
56. Chanana, *Missing 3 in Bollywood*, 313.
57. "Details of Agreement."
58. "Details of Agreement."
59. "Details of Agreement."
60. "Details of Agreement."
61. Mukherjee, "Somewhere between Human, Nonhuman, and Woman."
62. Apostolidis, *Fight for Time*, 6.
63. Leary, "*Air Hostess* and Atmosphere," 127.
64. Tashiro, *Pretty Pictures*, 46.
65. Jain, *Gods in the Bazaar*, 19.
66. Dumas, "On Film Studies and the Unconscious," 60.
67. Bartlett, *Badfilm*, 17.
68. Jethanand, "Keeping Continuity," 58.
69. Miller, "Hitchcock's Understyle," 5.
70. Nakahara, "Production Play," 356.
71. Nakahara, "Production Play," 356.
72. MacDowell and Zborowski, "Aesthetics of 'So Bad it's Good,'" 6.
73. Sofer, *Stage Life of Props*, 12.
74. Stern, "Paths That Wind through the Thicket of Things," 321.
75. Sofer, *Stage Life of Props*, 12.
76. Sofer, *Stage Life of Props*, 12.
77. Barthes, *Camera Lucida*, 45.
78. Mazumdar, "Invisible Work," 26.
79. Mehta, "Analyzing and Writing about Credit Sequences," 164.
80. Aggarwal, "Assistant Technicians," 28.
81. Aggarwal, "Assistant Technicians," 28.
82. Aggarwal, "Assistant Technicians," 31.
83. Jaikumar, *Where Histories Reside*, 237.
84. Barthes, *Camera Lucida*, 59.
85. Mulvey, *Death 24x a Second*, 31. See also Conley, *Film Hieroglyphs*, on the hieroglyphic power of "graphisms" to rupture the linearity of narrative.
86. Connor, "Like Some Dummy Corporation," 141.
87. See Nair, "Temple of Womb."
88. See Tarlo, *Unsettling Memories*.

89. Van Hollen, *Birth on the Threshold*, 146.
90. Ram, *Fertile Disorder*, 28.
91. Mangala, "Story of a Sterilisation Camp."
92. Van Hollen, *Birth on the Threshold*, 146.
93. Cohen, "Other Kidney."
94. Lowenstein, *Shocking Representation*, 2.
95. Lowenstein, *Shocking Representation*, 2.
96. Lowenstein, *Shocking Representation*, 14.

CHAPTER 4. MAKING MONSTERS

1. Nair, "What Makes Full Houses Full?," 46.
2. Nair, "What Makes Full Houses Full?," 46.
3. Siddique and Raphael, *Transnational Horror Cinema*, 4.
4. *Veerana*, Certificate Number 872.
5. Tombs, *Mondo Macabro*, 478.
6. Prabhu, "How to Make a Killing at the Box Office."
7. For "woefully inadequate," see Tombs, *Mondo Macabro*, 388; for "basic" and "bad," see Dwyer, *Filming the Gods*, 48; and for "rudimentary," "tacky," and "patently fake," see Sen, *Haunting Bollywood*, 49.
8. Sen, *Haunting Bollywood*, 6.
9. Korsmeyer, *Savoring Disgust*, 7.
10. Carroll, *Philosophy of Horror*, 55.
11. Masood, "Not So Popular Cinema."
12. "*Jaani Dushman* Repels," 4.
13. Hanich, "Towards a Poetics of Cinematic Disgust," 13. See also Paul, *Laughing, Screaming*.
14. Hanich, "Towards a Poetics of Cinematic Disgust," 13.
15. Hanich, *Cinematic Emotion*, 82.
16. Thompson, "Cinematic Excess," 133.
17. Kristeva, *Powers of Horror*, 1.
18. Mubarki, *Filming Horror*, 128. See also Vitali, "Hindi Horror Films of the Ramsay Brothers."
19. Williams, "Film Bodies," 3.
20. Hand, "Proliferating Horrors," 132.
21. Brophy, "Horrality," 3.
22. See Timpone, *Men, Makeup, and Monsters*.
23. Turnock, "Auteur Renaissance," 117.
24. See, for example, "How to Make a 'Fly,'" 34–38, which profiles Chris Walas; and "Are These the Scariest Men in America?," which profiles Tom Savini.
25. Mathijs, "They're Here!," 162.

26. Carlomagno, "Rob Bottin and *The Thing*."
27. Carlomagno, "Rob Bottin and *The Thing*," 13.
28. Carlomagno, "Rob Bottin and *The Thing*," 14.
29. Carlomagno, "Rob Bottin and *The Thing*," 16.
30. Kendrick, *Hollywood Bloodshed*, 155.
31. Kendrick, *Hollywood Bloodshed*, 155.
32. Purse, "New Hollywood," 142. See also Prince, "True Lies," 27.
33. Shaviro, *Cinematic Body*, 101.
34. Neale, "'You've Got to Be Fucking Kidding!,'" 161.
35. Sconce, "'Trashing' the Academy," 373.
36. Neale, "'You've Got to Be Fucking Kidding!,'" 161.
37. Hantke, "Spectacular Optics," 48.
38. Metz, "'Trucage' and the Film," 661.
39. Hantke, "Spectacular Optics," 48.
40. Hantke, "Spectacular Optics," 48.
41. Aloke Dutt, interview with the author, 19 August 2013.
42. Aloke Dutt, interview with the author, 19 August 2013.
43. Arun Patil, interview with the author, 20 September 2013.
44. Adamson, *Craft Reader*, 2.
45. Sennett, *Craftsman*.
46. For more on this period, see Mukherjee, "'Material World.'"
47. For more on the Westmore family's work in Hollywood makeup, see McLean, *All for Beauty*.
48. Westmore, *From "Rocky" to "Star Trek"*, 285.
49. Vesuna, "Sarosh Modi."
50. Christopher Tucker, email communication with the author, 18 August 2012.
51. Dasgupta, *Don't Disturb the Dead*.
52. Pradeep Pemgirikar, interview with the author, 21 September 2014, Mumbai.
53. Aloke Dutt, interview with the author, 19 August 2013.
54. Pandian, *Reel World*, 9.
55. Aloke Dutt, interview with the author, 19 August 2013.
56. Prabhu, "How to Make a Killing at the Box Office."
57. Kumar, *"Dahshat,"* 51.
58. Ngai, *Our Aesthetic Categories*, 39.
59. Mubarki, *Filming Horror*, 108.
60. Mohamed, *"Dahshat,"* 4.
61. Mohamed, *"Dahshat,"* 4.
62. Kumar, *"Dahshat,"* 51.
63. Kumar, *"Dahshat,"* 51.
64. Mulvey, "Clumsy Sublime," 3.

65. Doane, *Emergence of Cinematic Time*, 70.
66. Keane, "Signs Are Not the Garb of Meaning," 190.
67. Mubarki, *Filming Horror*, 108.
68. Menninghaus, *Disgust*, 1.
69. Samalin, *Masses Are Revolting*, 17.
70. Samalin, *Masses Are Revolting*, 5.
71. Miller, *Anatomy of Disgust*, 8.
72. Miller, *Anatomy of Disgust*, x.
73. Kolnai, "Standard Modes of Aversion," 586.
74. Csicsery-Ronay, "On the Grotesque in Science Fiction," 71.
75. Hantke, "Review of *Skin Shows*."
76. Hantke, "Review of *Skin Shows*"; see also Halberstam, *Skin Shows*.
77. Kolnai, "Standard Modes of Aversion," 589. See Brinkema for a reading of this essay in *Forms of the Affects*, 152–180.
78. Tompkins, "Crude Matter, Queer Form," 267–268.
79. Menninghaus, *Disgust*, 7.
80. Pradeep Pemgirikar, Roy's onetime contemporary and competitor, walked me through the process Roy used to create his latex masks. Pemgirikar, interview with the author, 21 September 2014, Mumbai.
81. Prabhu, "How to Make a Killing at the Box Office," 29.
82. Mohan Baggad, interview with the author, October 14, 2014. Baggad was a frequent collaborator on action scenes for the Ramsays, and his name appears under the designation Thrills-in-Charge.
83. Menninghaus, *Disgust*, 7.
84. Siddique and Raphael, *Transnational Horror Cinema*, 4; and Smith, *Hideous Progeny*.
85. Carroll, *Philosophy of Horror*, 158–214.
86. "Our Reviewer."
87. Bennett, *Vibrant Matter*, 23.
88. Heller-Nicholas, *Masks in Horror Cinema*, 11.
89. Prabhu, "How to Make a Killing at the Box Office," 29.
90. Quoted in Prabhu, "How to Make a Killing at the Box Office," 29.
91. Sheila Kapoor, telephone conversation with the author, 19 August 2013.
92. Mukherjee, *Bombay Hustle*.
93. Kolnai, "Standard Modes of Aversion," 589.
94. Pandian, *Reel World*, 9.
95. Caldwell, *Production Culture*, 42–51.
96. Sheila Kapoor, telephone conversation with the author, 19 August 2013.
97. Prabhu, "How to Make a Killing at the Box Office," 29.
98. Bode, "Fleshing It Out," 34.
99. Bode, "Fleshing It Out," 33.

100. McLean, *All for Beauty*, 14.
101. Creed, "Horror and the Monstrous-Feminine," 48.
102. Brinkema, *Forms of the Affects*, 152–180. See also Jones, "Processes of Abjection."
103. Sobchack, *Carnal Thoughts*, 65–66.
104. Comolli and Michelson, "Mechanical Bodies."
105. Comolli and Michelson, "Mechanical Bodies."
106. Mayer, *Below the Line*, 1–30.
107. On embarrassment as the affective index of an overclose, other-regarding relationship, in which we "cringe" on another's behalf, see Salvato, *Obstruction*, 33–62.
108. Adorno, "Theses against Occultism," 239.
109. Aloke Dutt, interview with the author, 19 August 2013.
110. See Ayers, "Bleeding Synthetic Blood"; de Seife, "Ectoplasm and Oil"; and Abbott, "Battlefield for the Soul."
111. See Turnock, *Plastic Reality*; Chung, *Media Heterotopias*; and Brown, "Wakaliwood."
112. Lucca, "Cleaning Crew."
113. Sedgwick, *Touching Feeling*, 13, cited in Bradley, "Vicissitudes of Touch."
114. Gulshan Grover, telephone interview with the author, 23 December 2020.
115. "Vampires Don't Live Here Anymore," A2.
116. On Hollywood as a "horizon of technological achievement" for Bombay filmmakers, see Govil, *Orienting Hollywood*, 4.

CHAPTER 5. HIDDEN CIRCUITS

1. Prabhu, "How to Make a Killing at the Box Office."
2. Saxena, "Scareface."
3. See Sunya, *Sirens of Modernity*; Vitali, *Hindi Action Cinema*; Thomas, *Bombay before Bollywood*; and Hughes, "Pride of Place."
4. Sengupta, "Video-Walla's Images of Life"; Tiwary, "Unsettling News"; and Battaglia, "Video Turn."
5. Benson-Allott, *Killer Tapes*, 7.
6. Tiwary, "What Is Video?"
7. Hilderbrand, *Inherent Vice*.
8. Vinod Talwar, interview with the author, 18 September 2014.
9. "Woman Killed."
10. "Theater Gutted."
11. "Bomb"; and "Losing Ground."
12. "Rains."

13. Ghosh, "Entertainment."
14. Ranjan, letter to *Screen*.
15. "Shocking Condition of Theaters."
16. "Shocking Condition of Theaters."
17. Larkin, "Materiality of Cinema Theaters in Northern Nigeria."
18. "Filip to Film-Making." See "International"; and Eswar, "International."
19. Rangan and Pandya, "Cement Muddle," 6; and Rangan, "Concrete Truth."
20. *Report of the Working Group on National Film Policy*, 25.
21. "Film Industry Faces Problem of Boom."
22. "Diminishing Returns."
23. "Hindi Film Industry Faces Its Worst Recession"; "Cinemagoers Losing Theater-Going Habit?"; and Eswar, "9,700 Cinemas in India Inadequate."
24. "Video Will Extinguish Exhibition Trade"; "Cinemas Closed"; and "UP Govt Warned of Closure of Cinemas."
25. "Exhibition Sector in Doldrums."
26. "Against all Odds."
27. See Ganti, *Producing Bollywood*.
28. "Supply and Demand"
29. "3-D Creates Havoc in Bombay Suburbs."
30. Tulsi Ramsay, interview with the author, 9 February 2010.
31. Thomas, *Bombay before Bollywood*, 194.
32. Thomas, *Bombay before Bollywood*, 195.
33. Gopal, *Conjugations*, 100.
34. Srinivas, "Hong Kong Action Film in the Indian B Circuit," 49.
35. Mohan Bhakri, interview with the author, 17 August 2013.
36. *"Cheekh."*
37. "Losing Ground."
38. "Cinemagoers Losing Theater-Going Habit?"
39. Masood, "Not So Popular Cinema," 20–25.
40. "Cinemagoers Losing Theater-Going Habit?"
41. "Cinemagoers Losing Theater-Going Habit?"
42. "Cinemagoers Losing Theater-Going Habit?"
43. "Box Office Collections Up."
44. Hiren Gada, interview with the author, 2013, Mumbai.
45. "AIFPC Notice."
46. "AIFPC Notice."
47. Ganti, "Risky Business."
48. Greenberg, *From Betamax to Blockbuster*, 5. See also Newman, *Video Revolutions*; and Wasser, *Veni, Vidi, Video*.
49. Klinger, *Beyond the Multiplex*.
50. Benson-Allott, *Killer Tapes*, 14.
51. Balio, "Major Presence," 61.

52. "Copyright Bill"; see also "No FFI Directive on Video Rights Sale."
53. Ganti, "Risky Business."
54. Mohan Bhakri, interview with the author, 17 August 2013.
55. Classified Ads, 1983, 10 and 11.
56. Rajagopal, *Politics after Television*, 80.
57. Kagal, "As the Video Virus Spreads."
58. "Colour," 31.
59. AIFPC demanded 3 lakhs for A films, 2 lakhs for B films, and 1 lakh for C films. "AIFPC-TV Dispute over Telecast Payments."
60. Vinod Talwar, interview with the author, 18 September 2014.
61. Suresh, "Policing the Networks and Practices of Video"; and Suresh, "Video Nights and Dispersed Pleasures."
62. Hilderbrand, "Grainy Days and Mondays."
63. *First Indian Film and Video Guide*, 38.
64. Mohan Bhakri, interview with the author, 17 August 2013.
65. Thomas, *Bombay before Bollywood*, 196.
66. Vinod Talwar, interview with the author, 18 September 2014.
67. Stevens, "Bazaars of India Are Now a Toyland of High Tech."
68. Bhakri and Bhakri, "Wild Side of Asian Cinema."
69. Classified Ads, 1985, 2.
70. Tulsi Ramsay, interview with the author, 9 February 2010.
71. "Khooni Mahal."
72. Bordwell, "How to Hypnotize the Viewer."
73. Duara, "Can the Big Screen Strike Back?"
74. Cubitt, "Grayscale Video," 51; and Spielman, "Video," 57.
75. Larkin, *Signal and Noise*, 237.
76. "'Razia' in the House."
77. "'Razia' in the House."
78. Karaganis, "Introduction," i.
79. Pendakur, "New Cultural Technologies," 72.
80. Herbert, *Videoland*.
81. "Videotape."
82. "City Lights."
83. "Now a Video Hut."
84. In Shaunak Sen's documentary *Cities of Sleep* (2015), day laborers in Delhi are seen congregating, chatting, and often sleeping, in the cool, dark, loud space of a video parlor.
85. Vasudevan, "In the Centrifuge of History," 135–140; and Mukherjee and Singh, "MicroSD-ing 'Mewati Videos,'" 153.
86. Sundaram, *Pirate Modernity*, 89.
87. See Chattopadhyay and Sarkar, "Introduction," 357–363; and Warner, "Publics and Counterpublics," 49–90.

88. "City Lights," 3.
89. See Singh, "Impact of Video."
90. Tsivian, *Early Cinema in Russia and Its Cultural Reception*.
91. Chatterjee, "Madhattan Episode."
92. "Star Video."
93. Hiren Gada, interview with the author, 2013, Mumbai.
94. "INFACT to Curb Video Piracy."
95. "INFACT to Curb Video Piracy."
96. "Parkar Arrested."
97. "City News in Brief."
98. "Video Parlors Raided."
99. "Parlor Raided."
100. "Video Fever."
101. Sayani and Ahmed, "Watch Out," 50.
102. "Mystery of Severed Limbs Solved."
103. Wadia, "Video Zombies."
104. Sayani and Ahmed, "Watch Out," 50.

EPILOGUE

1. See also Hediger, "Original Is Always Lost."
2. Flueckiger, "Material Properties of Historical Film." See also Usai, *Death of Cinema*.
3. Hart, *Monstrous Forms*, 3.
4. For fuller versions of this argument, see Nair, "Towards a Phenomenology of Film Production"; and Nair, "Striking Out."
5. Gurevitch, "Special Effects and the Cult Film," 341.
6. Whissel, in conversation with Regina Longo.
7. Constable, "Analogue and the Digital Head-Death," 68.
8. Lundemo, "In the Kingdom of Shadows," 314.
9. Tanvir, "Pirate Histories," 116.
10. Tanvir, "Pirate Histories," 116.
11. Cooper, "Circulatory Dynamics of Pirate Cinema."
12. Sobchack, "Afterword."
13. Elsaesser, "New Film History," 104.
14. Ernst, "Media Archeaography," 241.
15. Ernst, "Media Archeaography," 241.
16. Ernst, "Media Archeaography," 241.
17. Steyerl, "In Defense of the Poor Image."
18. Sundaram, "Other Networks," 67.

19. Karaganis, "Introduction," i.
20. Sundaram, *Pirate Modernity*.
21. Sundaram, *Pirate Modernity*, 112.
22. Sundaram, *Pirate Modernity*, 106.
23. Askari, *Material Cultures in Transit*.

Bibliography

Abbott, Stacey. "The Battlefield for the Soul: Special Effects and the Possessed Body," in *Special Effects: New Histories/Theories/Contexts*, ed. Dan North, Bob Rehak, and Michael S. Duffy, London: BFI Palgrave, 2015, 141–153.
———. *Celluloid Vampires: Life after Death in the Modern World*, Austin: University of Texas Press, 2007.
Abel, Jonathan. *Redacted: The Archives of Censorship in Transwar Japan*, Berkeley: University of California Press, 2012.
Adamson, Glenn. *The Craft Reader*, Oxford, New York: Berg, 2010.
Adorno, Theodor. "Theses against Occultism," in *Minima Moralia: Reflections from Damaged Life* (1974), trans. E. F. N. Jephcott, London: Verso, 2005.
Affron, Charles, and Mirella Jona Affron, *Sets in Motion: Art Direction and Film Narrative*, New Brunswick, NJ: Rutgers University Press, 1995.
"Against All Odds," *Trade Guide*, 32, no. 8, 28 December 1985.
Aggarwal, Subhash. "Assistant Technicians," *Madhuri* 21, no. 527 (4 January 1985), 28–31.
"Agreement," *Trade Guide*, 33, no. 4, 8 August 1987.
"AIFPC Notice," *Screen*, 13 May 1983.
"AIFPC-TV Dispute over Telecast Payments," *Screen*, 1 April 1983.
Aldana Reyes, Xavier. *Horror Film and Affect: Towards a Corporeal Model of Viewership*, London: Taylor and Francis, 2016.
Alilunas, Peter. *Smutty Little Movies: The Creation and Regulation of Adult Video*. Oakland: University of California Press, 2016.

Allen, Richard, *Hitchcock's Romantic Irony*, New York: Columbia University Press, 2007.
Apostolidis, Paul. *The Fight for Time: Migrant Day Laborers and the Politics of Precarity*, New York: Oxford University Press, 2019.
Appadurai, Arjun. "Spectral Housing and Urban Cleansing: Notes on Millennial Mumbai," *Public Culture* 12. no. 3 (2000), 627–651.
"Are These the Scariest Men in America?," *Cinefantastique*, 13, no. 1 (September-October 1982).
"As the Video Virus Spreads," *Times of India*, 22 January 1984, 1.
Ashforth, Adam. *The Politics of Official Discourse in Twentieth-Century South Africa*, Oxford: Clarendon Press, 1990.
Askari, Kaveh. *Material Cultures in Transit: Relaying Cinema in Midcentury Iran*, Oakland: University of California Press, 2022.
Atwood, Blake. *Underground: The Secret Life of Videocassettes in Iran*. Cambridge, MA: MIT Press, 2021.
"Audiences Need Holiday from Violence," *Screen*, 24 August 1984.
Awwal, Arpana. "From Villain to Hero: Masculinity and Political Aesthetics in the Films of Bangladeshi Action Star Joshim," *BioScope: South Asian Screen Studies* 9, no. 1 (June 2018), 24-45.
Ayers, Drew. "Bleeding Synthetic Blood: Flesh and Simulated Space in 300," in *Special Effects: New Histories/Theories/Contexts*, ed. Dan North, Bob Rehak, and Michael S. Duffy, London: BFI Palgrave, 2015, 102–113.
Baer, Nicholas, Maggie Hennefeld, Laura Horak, and Gunnar Iversen, eds. *Unwatchable*, New Brunswick, NJ: Rutgers University Press, 2019.
Bakhtin, Mikhail. *Rabelais and His World* (1941), trans. Hélène Iswolsky, Bloomington: Indiana University Press, 1993.
Balio, Tino. "A Major Presence in All of the World's Most Important Markets: The Globalization of Hollywood in the 1990s," in *Contemporary Hollywood Cinema*. London: Routledge, 1998, 58–73.
Barker, Jennifer M. *The Tactile Eye: Touch and the Cinematic Experience*, Berkeley: University of California Press, 2009.
Barnwell, Jane. *Production Design: Architects of the Screen*, London and New York: Wallflower, 2004.
Barthes, Roland. *Camera Lucida: Reflections on Photography* (1980), New York: Farrar, Straus and Giroux, 2010.
———. "The Third Meaning: Research Notes on Some Eisenstein Stills" (1970), in *Image Music Text*, trans. Stephen Heath, London: Fontana, 1977.
Bartkowski, Lindsay. "Caring for the Internet: Content Moderators and the Maintenance of Empire," *Journal of Working-Class Studies* 4, no. 1 (2019), 66–78.
Bartlett, Becky. *Badfilm: Incompetence, Intention and Failure*, Edinburgh: Edinburgh University Press, 2021.

———. "It Happens by Accident: Failed Intentions, Incompetence, and Sincerity in Badfilm," in *The Routledge Companion to Cult Cinema*, ed. Ernest Mathijs and Jamie Sexton, Oxon: Routledge, 2019, 40–49.
Baschiera, Stefano, and Francesco Di Chiara. "Once Upon a Time in Italy: Transnational Features of Genre Production 1960s–1970s," *Film International* 8, no. 6 (December 2010), 30–39.
Battaglia, Giulia. "The Video Turn: Documentary Film Practices in 1980s India," *Visual Anthropology* 27, nos. 1–2 (2014), 72–90.
Baudry, Jean-Louis, and Alan Williams. "Ideological Effects of the Basic Cinematographic Apparatus," *Film Quarterly* 28, no. 2 (1974), 39–47.
Bellour, Raymond. "The Unattainable Text," *Screen* 16, no. 3 (Autumn 1975), 19–28.
"Benefits Gained from Morning Shows Should Not Be Lost by Fake Jubilees," *Movieland*, 1–15 November 1976, 12.
Bennett, Jane. *Vibrant Matter: A Political Ecology of Things*, Durham, NC: Duke University Press, 2010.
Benshoff, Harry. "Preface," in *A Companion to the Horror Film*, ed. Harry Benshoff, Oxford: Wiley Blackwell, 2014, xiii–xix.
Benson-Allott, Caetlin. "*Grindhouse*: An Experiment in the Death of Cinema," *Film Quarterly* 62, no. 1 (1 September 2008), 20–24.
———. *Killer Tapes and Shattered Screens: Video Spectatorship From VHS to File Sharing*, Berkeley: University of California Press, 2013.
———. *The Stuff of Spectatorship: Material Cultures of Film and Television*, Oakland: University of California Press, 2021.
Berenstein, Rhona. *Attack of the Leading Ladies: Gender, Sexuality and Spectatorship in Classic Horror Cinema*. New York: Columbia University Press, 1996.
Berlant, Lauren. *Cruel Optimism*, Durham, NC: Duke University Press, 2011.
Berry, Chris. "Every Colour Red? Colour in the Films of the Cultural Revolution Model Stage Works," *Journal of Chinese Cinemas* 6, no. 3 (2012), 233–246.
Beugnet, Martine. "Cinema and Sensation: Contemporary French Film and Cinematic Corporeality," *Paragraph* 31, no. 2 (2008), 173–188.
Bhakri, Mohan, and Neeraj Bhakri. "The Wild Side of Asian Cinema," in *The Bollywood Horror Collection*, Vol. 1, *Mondo Mocabro*, London: Boum Productions, 2006.
Bhaskar, Ira, and Richard Allen. *Islamicate Cultures of Bombay Cinema*, Delhi: Tulika Books, 2009.
Bhaumik, Kaushik. "The Emergence of the Bombay Film Industry 1913–1936," PhD diss., University of Oxford, 2001.
Bhowmik, Someshwar. *Cinema and Censorship: The Politics of Control in India*, New Delhi: Orient Blackswan, 2009.

Bird, Katie. "'Dancing, Flying Camera Jockeys': Invisible Labor, Craft Discourse, and Embodied Steadicam and Panaglide Technique from 1972 to 1985," *The Velvet Light Trap*, no. 80 (Fall 2017), 48–65.

Biswas, Moinak. "In the Mirror of an Alternative Globalism: The Neorealist Encounter in India," in *Italian Neorealism and Global Cinema*, ed. Laura E. Ruberto and Kristi M. Wilson, Detroit: Wayne State University Press, 72-91.

Blanco, Maria del Pilar, and Esther Peeren, eds. *The Spectralities Reader: Ghosts and Haunting in Contemporary Cultural Theory*, London: Bloomsbury Publishing, 2013.

Bobb, Dilip. "The Case of a Missing Film," *India Today*, 15 June 1977.

"*Bobby* Was Shown at Shukla's Orders," *Indian Express*, 27 October 1977.

Bode, Lisa. "Fleshing It Out: Prosthetic Make Up Effects, Motion Capture and the Reception of Performance," in *Special Effects: New Histories/Theories/Contexts*, ed. Dan North, Bob Rehak, and Michael S. Duffy, London: BFI Palgrave, 2015, 32–44.

"Bomb," *Trade Guide*, 4 July 1987.

Bordwell, David "How to Hypnotize the Viewer," 2 June 2019, http://www.davidbordwell.net/blog/2019/06/02/how-to-hypnotize-the-viewer-mizoguchis-street-of-shame-on-the-criterion-channel/.

Bose, Nandana. "'We Do Not Certify Backwards': Film Censorship in Postcolonial India," in *Silencing Cinema: Film Censorship Around the World*, ed. Daniel Biltereyst and Roel Vande Winkel, London: Palgrave Macmillan, 2013, 191–206.

"Box Office Collections Up," *Screen*, 22 May 1981.

Boyer, Dominic. "Censorship as a Vocation: The Institutions, Practices, and Cultural Logic of Media Control in the German Democratic Republic," *Comparative Studies in Society and History* 45, no. 3 (2003), 511–45.

Bradley, Rizvana. "The Vicissitudes of Touch: Annotations on the Haptic," *b2o: An Online Journal*, 21 November 2020, https://www.boundary2.org/2020/11/rizvana-bradley-the-vicissitudes-of-touch-annotations-on-the-haptic/.

Brinkema, Eugenie. *The Forms of the Affects*, Durham, NC: Duke University Press, 2014.

———. *Life-Destroying Diagrams*, Durham, NC: Duke University Press, 2022.

Brinkema, Eugenie, in conversation with Ruth Mayer. "Colors without Bodies," *Return of the Aesthetic in American Studies* (December 2018), 7.

Britton, Andrew. "Meet Me in St Louis: Smith, or the Ambiguities" (1994), in *Britton on Film: The Complete Film Criticism of Andrew Britton*, ed. Barry Keith Grant, Detroit, MI: Wayne State University Press, 2009, 157–174.

Brophy, Philip. "Horrality: The Textuality of Contemporary Horror Films," *Screen* 27, no. 1 (1986), 2–13.

Brosius, Christiane, and Melissa Butcher. "Introduction: Image Journeys," in *Image Journeys: Audio-Visual Media and Cultural Change in India*, ed.

Christiane Brosius and Melissa Butcher, New Delhi: Sage Publications, 1999, 11–40.

Brown, Bill "Thing Theory," *Critical Inquiry* 28, no. 1 (2001), 1–22.

Brown, William. "Wakaliwood: Where Supercinema Meets Non-Cinema," *wjrcbrown on film* (blog), 24 March 2017, https://wjrcbrown.wordpress.com/2017/03/14/wakaliwood-where-supercinema-meets-non-cinema.

Bruno, Giuliana. *Atlas of Emotion: Journeys in Art, Architecture, and Film*, London: Verso, 2002.

Bukatman, Scott. *Matters of Gravity: Special Effects and Supermen in the 20th Century*, Durham, NC: Duke University Press, 2003.

Bunn, Matthew. "Reimagining Repression: New Censorship Theory and After," *History and Theory* 54, no.1 (2015), 25–44.

Buscombe, Edward. "The Idea of Genre in the American Cinema," in *Film Genre Reader II*, ed. Barry Keith Grant, Austin: University of Texas Press, 1995, 12–26.

Butler, Judith. "Ruled Out: Vocabularies of the Censor," in *Censorship and Silencing: Practices of Cultural Regulation*, ed. Robert C. Post, Issues & Debates, Los Angeles: Getty Research Institute for the History of Art and the Humanities, 1998, 247–260.

Cahill, James Leo, and Timothy Holland, "Double Exposures: Derrida and Cinema, an Introductory Séance," *Discourse: Journal for Theoretical Studies in Media and Culture* 37, no. 1 (2015), 3–21.

Caldwell, John Thornton. *Production Culture: Industrial Reflexivity and Critical Practice in Film and Television*, Durham, NC: Duke University Press, 2008.

Canby, Vincent. "The Thing," *New York Times*, 25 June 1982.

Cardinal, Roger. "Pausing over Peripheral Detail," *Framework*, nos. 30/31, 1 January 1986.

Carlomagno, Ellen. "Rob Bottin and *The Thing*," Fangoria 21 (August 1982), 13–16.

Carroll, Noel. *Philosophical Problems with Classical Film Theory*, Princeton, NJ: Princeton University Press), 1988.

———. *The Philosophy of Horror, or Paradoxes of the Heart*, New York: Routledge, 1990.

Carswell, Grace, Thomas Chambers, and Geert De Neve. "Waiting for the State: Gender, Citizenship and Everyday Encounters with Bureaucracy in India." *Environment and Planning C: Politics and Space* 37, no. 4 (June 2019), 597–616.

Carruthers, Lee. *Doing Time: Temporality, Hermeneutics and Contemporary Cinema*, Albany: State University of New York Press, 2016.

Castle, Terry. *The Female Thermometer: Eighteenth-century Culture and the Invention of the Uncanny*, New York and London: Oxford University Press, 1995.

Cavell, Stanley. "What Becomes of Things on Film?." *Philosophy and Literature* 2, no. 2 (Fall 1978), 249–257.
Cazenave, Jennifer. *An Archive of the Catastrophe: The Unused Footage of Claude Lanzmann's Shoah*, Albany: State University of New York Press, 2019.
"Censor Verdict Challenged," *Screen*, 29 December 1978, 1.
"Censors Snip India's Multistar Horror Film," *Variety*, 30 May 1979, 41.
Chakravarty, Sumita S. *National Identity in Indian Popular Cinema, 1947–1987*, Austin: University of Texas Press, 2011.
Chanana, Opender. *The Missing 3 in Bollywood: Safety Security Shelter*, Nyon, Switzerland: UNI Global Union, 2011.
Chandaver, Aseem. *Anurag Minus Verma Podcast*, Episode 24, 9 June 2021.
Chapman, James, Mark Glancy, and Sue Harper, eds. *The New Film History: Sources, Methods, Approaches*, Basingstoke and New York: Palgrave Macmillan, 2007.
Chatterjee, Kishore. "The Madhattan Episode," *Times of India*, 31 October 1987, A4.
Chatterjee, Saibal. "Genres: Genres and Narrative Forms," in *Encyclopedia of Hindi Cinema*, ed. Govind Nihalani Gulzar and Saibal Chatterjee, Noida: Thomson Press, 2003, 267–270.
Chatterjee, Subhajit. "On Disreputable Genres: B Movies and Revisionary Histories of Bombay Cinema," *Marg* 64, no. 4 (2013), 32–41.
Chattopadhyay, Swati, and Bhaskar Sarkar. "Introduction: The Subaltern and the Popular," *Postcolonial Studies* 8, no. 4 (2005), 357–363.
Chaudhury, Shubham Roy. "Sound of Horror: Sound and Dread in Hindi Cinema," *Journal of the Moving Image* 6 (December 2007).
"Cheekh," *Times of India*, 18 October 1985, 2.
Cho, Michelle. "Genre, Translation, and Transnational Cinema: Kim Jee-woon's *The Good, the Bad, the Weird*," *Cinema Journal* 54, no. 3 (2015), 44–68.
Chung, Hye Jean. *Media Heterotopias: Digital Effects and Material Labor in Global Film Production*, Durham, NC: Duke University Press, 2018.
Church, David. "One on Top of the Other: Lucio Fulci, Transnational Film Industries, and the Retrospective Construction of the Italian Horror Cinema," *Quarterly Review of Film and Video*, 32 (2014), 1–20.
"Cinemagoers Losing Theater-Going Habit?," *Screen*, 3 December 1982.
"Cinemas Closed," *Pioneer*, 5 April 1978.
Cinematograph Act of 1983, https://www.cbfcindia.gov.in/main/CBFC_English/Attachments/cine_rule1983.pdf.
"City Lights: Plenty of Time," *Times of India*, 4 July 1983, 3.
"City News in Brief," *Times of India*, 5 December 1987, 5.
Clasen, Mathias. *Why Horror Seduces*, New York: Oxford University Press, 2017.
Classified Ads, *Times of India*, 4 August 1983, 10; 11 November 1985, 2; and 7 November 1986, 11.

Clover, Carol. "The Eye of Horror," in *Viewing Positions*, ed. Linda Williams, New Brunswick: Rutgers University Press, 1994, 184–230.
———. "Her Body, Himself: Gender in the Slasher Film," *Representations*, Autumn 1987, 187–228.
———. *Men, Women, and Chainsaws: Gender in the Modern Horror Film*, Princeton, NJ, and Oxford: Princeton University Press, 1992.
Cohen, Lawrence. "The Other Kidney: Biopolitics Beyond Recognition," *Body & Society* 7, nos. 2–3 (September 2001), 9–29.
"Colour," *TV & Video World*, June 1987, 31.
"Commissioner Stays Order Regarding Use of Air Conditioners," *Screen*, 18 September 1981.
Comolli, Jean-Louis, and Annette Michelson, "Mechanical Bodies, Ever More Heavenly," *October* 83 (Winter 1998), 19–24.
"Concession on Fight Scenes," *Movieland*, 1 September 1976.
Conley, Tom. *Film Hieroglyphs: Ruptures in Classical Cinema*, Minneapolis: University of Minnesota Press, 1991.
Connor, J. D. "Like Some Dummy Corporation You Just Move around the Board," in *Reading Capitalist Realism*, ed. Alison Shonkwiler and Leigh Claire La Berge, Iowa City: University of Iowa Press, 2014, 140–176.
Constable, Martin. "The Analogue and the Digital Head-Death," *Visual Studies* 30, no. 1 (2015), 68–78.
Coole, Diana, and Samantha Frost, *New Materialisms: Ontology, Agency, and Politics*, Durham, NC, and London, Duke University Press, 2010.
Cooper, Timothy. "The Circulatory Dynamics of Pirate Cinema," *Rhizome*, 17 March 2016, https://rhizome.org/editorial/2016/mar/17/the-circulatory-dynamics-of-cinema/.
"Copyright Bill," *Screen*, 14 September 1984.
Craig, G. J. "Eastman Colour Films for Professional Motion Picture Work," *British Kinematography* 22, no. 5 (1953), 146–158.
Crane, Jonathan. "Scraping Bottom: Splatter and the Herschell Gordon Lewis Oeuvre," in *The Horror Film*, ed. Stephen Prince, New Brunswick, NJ: Rutgers University Press, 2004.
Creed, Barbara. "Horror and the Monstrous-Feminine: An Imaginary Abjection," *Screen* 27, no. 1 (January 1986), 44–71.
Csicsery-Ronay, Istvan, Jr. "On the Grotesque in Science Fiction." *Science Fiction Studies* 29, no. 1 (2002), 71–99.
Cubitt, Sean. "Grayscale Video and the Shift to Color," *Art Journal* 65, no. 3 (Fall 2006), 40–53.
Cvetkovich, Ann. *An Archive of Feelings: Trauma, Sexuality, and Lesbian Public Cultures*, Durham, NC: Duke University Press, 2003.
"Dabbling with Day-Dreams," *Times of India*, 1 January 1978.
"Danger: Your Secrets Will Leak Out Someday!," *Times of India*, 23 February 1978.

"Darwaza," *Film Information* 5, no. 22, 25 February 1978.
Darwaza, Censor Script, National Film Archive, Pune, File no. 10872/1.
Dasgupta, Shamya. *Don't Disturb the Dead: The Story of the Ramsay Brothers*, Delhi: HarperCollins India, 2017.
Dass, Manishita. *Outside the Lettered City: Cinema, Modernity, and the Public Sphere in Late Colonial India*, New York: Oxford University Press, 2016.
Davis, Colin. "État Présent: Hauntology, Spectres and Phantoms," *French Studies* 59, no. 3 (2005), 373–379.
de Seife, Ethan. "Ectoplasm and Oil: Methocel and the Aesthetics of Special Effects," in *Special Effects: New Histories/Theories/Contexts*, ed. Dan North, Bob Rehak, and Michael S. Duffy, London: BFI Palgrave, 2015, 16–31.
Derrida, Jacques, in conversation with Bernard Stiegler, in *Echographies of Television: Filmed Interviews*, trans. Jennifer Bajorek, Cambridge, UK: Polity Press, 2002.
"Details of Agreement," *Trade Guide*, 33, no. 42, 15 August 1987.
Dhusiya, Mithuraaj. "Bestiality, Compassion and Gender Emancipation: The Snake Woman in Hindi Horror Films," *Cineforum* 15 (2012), 105–134.
———. *Indian Horror Cinema: (En)gendering the Monstrous*, New York and London: Taylor & Francis, 2017.
———. "The Ramsay Chronicles: Non-normative Sexualities in *Purana Mandir* and *Bandh Darwaza*," in *Bollywood and Its Other(s): Towards New Configurations*, ed. V. Kishore, A. Sarwal, and P. Patra, London: Palgrave Macmillan, 2014, 174–185.
Diffrient, David Scott. "Dead, but Still Breathing: The Problem of Postmortem Movement in Horror Films," *New Review of Film and Television Studies* 16, no. 2 (2018), 98–122.
"Diminishing Returns: Exhibition Trade Crisis Infects Whole Industry," *Screen*, 2 May 1980.
Dinshaw, Carolyn. *Medieval Texts, Amateur Readers, and the Queerness of Time*, Durham, NC: Duke University Press, 2012.
"Discipline within Three Months," *Screen*, 7 March 1980.
Doane, Mary Ann. *The Emergence of Cinematic Time: Modernity, Contingency, the Archive*, Cambridge, MA: Harvard University Press, 2002.
———. "The Indexical and the Concept of Medium Specificity," *differences* 18, no. 1 (2007), 128–152.
———. "Indexicality: Trace and Sign: Introduction," *differences* 18, no. 1 (2007), 1–6.
Dootson, Kirsty. "Mapping the Laboratory: Technicolor's Post-War Expansion across Europe and Asia," in *Global Film Color*, ed. Sarah Street and Joshua Yumibe, New Brunswick, NJ: Rutgers University Press, 2024.
———. "The Perversion of the System: *Peeping Tom* (1960) and Eastmancolor," 15 February 2018, https://eastmancolor.info/2018/02/15/the-perversion-of-the-system-peeping-tom-1960-and-eastmancolor/.

———. "Skin, Colour, Sensitivity: The Racial History of Film Stock," paper presented at Screen Studies Conference, Glasgow, 2023.
Duara, Ajit "Can the Big Screen Strike Back?," *Cinema in India*, 1, no. 4 (October–December 1987).
Dudenhoeffer, Larrie. *Embodiment and Horror Cinema*, New York: Palgrave Macmillan, 2014.
Dumas, Chris. "Horror and Psychoanalysis: An Introductory Primer," in *A Companion to the Horror Film*, ed. Harry Benshoff, Oxford: Wiley Blackwell, 2014, 21–37.
———. "On Film Studies and the Unconscious," *Camera Obscura* 27, no. 3, (2012), 39–67.
Dutta, Madhushree, Kaushik Bhaumik, and Rohit Shivkumar, eds. *Project Cinema City*, New York: Columbia University Press, 2013.
Dwyer, Rachel. "Bombay Gothic: On the 60th anniversary of Kamal Amrohi's *Mahal*," in *Beyond the Boundaries of Bollywood*, ed. Rachel Dwyer and Jerry Pinto, New Delhi: Oxford University Press, 2011, 130–155.
———. *Filming the Gods: Religion and Indian Cinema*, London: Routledge, 2006.
Dwyer, Rachel, and Jerry Pinto, eds. *Beyond the Boundaries of Bollywood*, New Delhi: Oxford University Press, 2011.
Dyer, Geoff. "Foreword," in Roland Barthes, *Camera Lucida: Reflections on Photography*, New York: Farrar, Straus and Giroux, 2010.
Ede, Laurie. "Art in Context: British Film Design of the 1940s," in *The New Film History: Sources, Methods, Approaches*, ed. James Chapman, Mark Glancy, and Sue Harper, New York: Palgrave Macmillan, 2007, 73–88.
Egan, Kate. *Trash or Treasure: Censorship and the Changing Meanings of the Video Nasties*, Manchester, UK, and New York: Manchester University Press, 2007.
Elkins, James. "Marks, Traces, 'Traits,' Contours, 'Orli,' and 'Splendores': Nonsemiotic Elements in Pictures," *Critical Inquiry* 21, no. 4 (1995), 822–860.
Elsaesser, Thomas. "The New Film History as Media Archaeology," *Cinemas: Journal of Film Studies* 14, nos. 2–3 (2004), 75–117.
Ernst, Wolfgang. *Digital Memory and the Archive*, Minneapolis: University of Minnesota Press, 2012.
———. "Media Archeaography: Method and Machine versus History and Narrative of Media," in *Media Archaelogy: Approaches, Applications and Implications*, ed. Erkki Huhtamo and Jussi Parikka, Berkeley: University of California Press, 2011, 239–255.
Eswar, N. V. "International: An Overview of India's Pics," *Variety*, 13 January 1982.
———. "9,700 Cinemas in India Inadequate to Cover Nation," *Variety*, 9 May 1979.
"Excite, v." *Oxford English Dictionary Online*, Oxford University Press, December 2022, https://www-oed-com.libproxy.temple.edu/view/Entry/65795.

"Exhibition Sector in Doldrums," *Screen*, 2 May 1980.
Ezra, Elizabeth. *The Cinema of Things: Globalization and the Posthuman Object*, London and New York: Bloomsbury Publishing, 2017.
Ezra, Elizabeth, and Catherine Wheatley, "Introduction to Special Issue: Film Objects," *Film Philosophy* 27, no. 1 (2023), 1–6.
"A Fairytale Fortress: Janjira," *Times of India*, 25 March 1988.
Farmer, Brett. *Spectacular Passions: Cinema, Fantasy, Gay Male Spectatorships*, Durham, NC: Duke University Press, 2000.
Fay, Jennifer. *Inhospitable World: Cinema in the Time of the Anthropocene*, Oxford: Oxford University Press, 2018.
Federation of Western India Cine Employees v. Filmalaya Pvt. Ltd., Bombay High Court, Dharmadhikari, (1981) 83 BOMLR 423, (1981) IILLJ 393 Bom, 20 March 1981.
Fenwick, James. *Unproduction Studies and the American Film Industry*, New York and London: Routledge, 2022.
Ferraris, Maurizio. *Documentality: Why It Is Necessary to Leave Traces*, trans. Richard Davies, New York: Fordham University Press, 2013.
"FFI President's SOS to Delhi," *Movieland*, 1 September 1976, 1.
Field, Allyson Nadia. "Editor's Introduction: Acts of Speculation," *Feminist Media Histories* 8, no. 3 (2022), 1–7.
"Filip to Film-Making," *Amrit Bazaar Patrika*, 3 April 1978.
"Film," *Morning Echo*, New Delhi, 7 July 1977.
"Film Censorship," *Indian Express*, 4 June 1977.
"Film Import," *Times of India*, 9 July 1980.
"Film Industry Faces Problem of Boom," *Hindustan Times*, 22 August 1978.
Filmfare, 16–30 September 1987, 19–21.
First Indian Film and Video Guide, 3rd ed., ed. Ratan Sharda, New Delhi: Update Video Publication Pvt. Ltd., 1991–1992, .
Fischer, Lucy. *Art Direction and Production Design*, New Brunswick, NJ: Rutgers University Press, 2015.
"Five-Fold Increase in Show Tax?," *Screen*, 10 April 1981.
Flueckiger, Barbara. "Material Properties of Historical Film," *Tangibility*, Autumn 2012, https://necsus-ejms.org/material-properties-of-historical-film-in-the-digital-age/.
———. "Timeline of Historical Film Colors," https://filmcolors.org/.
Flusser, Vilém. *Does Writing Have a Future?*, Minneapolis: University of Minnesota Press, 2011.
Frank, Hannah. *Frame by Frame: A Materialist Aesthetics of Animated Cartoons*, ed. Daniel Morgan, Oakland: University of California Press, 2019.
Franklin, Simon. "Mapping the Graphosphere: Cultures of Writing in Early 19th-Century Russia (and Before)," *Kritika: Explorations in Russian and Eurasian History* n.s., 12, no. 3 (Summer 2011), 531–560.

Frith, Paul. "'The Curse of the Thing Is Technicolor Blood: Why Need Vampires Be Messier Feeders Than Anyone Else?'; The BBFC and Hammer's Colour Films, 1957-1962," *Historical Journal of Film, Radio and Television* 39, no. 2 (2019), 233-250.
Fujiwara, Chris. "Boredom, *Spasmo*, and the Italian System," in *Sleaze Artists: Cinema at the Margins of Taste, Style, and Politics* ed. Jeffrey Sconce. Durham, NC, and London: Duke University Press, 2007, 240-258.
Ganti, Tejaswini. "The Limits of Decency and the Decency of Limits: Censorship and the Bombay Film Industry," in *Censorship in South Asia*, ed. William Mazzarella, Indianapolis: Indiana University Press, 2009.
———. *Producing Bollywood: Inside the Contemporary Hindi Film Industry*, Durham, NC, and London: Duke University Press, 2012.
———. "Risky Business: The Structure and Practice of Formal Film Distribution in the Hindi Film Industry," in *A Companion to Indian Cinema*, ed. Ranjani Mazumdar and Neepa Majumdar, London: Wiley Blackwell, 2022, 37-69.
Ghosh, Arup "Entertainment: At What Cost?," *Times of India*, 21 April 1982, 5.
Ghosh, Bishnupriya, "The Security Aesthetic in Bollywood's High-Rise Horror," *Representations* 126, no. 1 (1 May 2014), 58-84.
Ghosh, Shohini. *Fire*, Vancouver, BC: Arsenal Press, 2010.
Gibbs, John. *Mise-en-Scene: Film Style and Interpretation*, New York: Columbia University Press, 2002.
Gill, Harjant. "Censorship and Ethnographic Film: Confronting State Bureaucracies, Cultural Regulation, and Institutionalized Homophobia in India," *Visual Anthropology Review* 33, no. 1 (2017), 62-73.
Ginzburg, Carlo. *Threads and Traces: True False Fictive*, Berkeley: University of California Press, 2012.
Gitelman, Lisa. *Paper Knowledge: Toward a Media History of Documents*, Durham, NC, and London: Duke University Press, 2014.
Goldberg, E., Aditi Sen, and Brian Collins, eds. *Bollywood Horrors*, London: Bloomsbury Publishing, 2020.
Gopal, Sangita. *Conjugations: Marriage and Form in New Bollywood Cinema*, Chicago: University of Chicago Press, 2011.
Gopalan, Lalitha. "Avenging Women in Indian Cinema," *Screen* 38, no. 1 (Spring 1997), 42-59.
———. *Cinema of Interruptions: Action Genre in Contemporary Indian Cinema*, London: BFI, 2002.
Gordon, Avery. "Her Shape and His Hand," in *The Spectralities Reader*, ed. Maria del Pilar Blanco and Esther Peeren, London: Bloomsbury Publishing, 2013.
Gorfinkel, Elena. "The Body as Apparatus: Chesty Morgan Takes on the Academy," in *Unruly Pleasures: The Cult Film and its Critics*, ed. Xavier Mendik and Graeme Harper, Godalming, UK: FAB Press, 2000, 155-170.

———. *Lewd Looks: American Sexploitation Cinema in the 1960s*, Minneapolis: University of Minnesota Press, 2017.
Gorfinkel, Elena, and John David Rhodes, eds. *Taking Place: Location and the Moving Image*, Minneapolis: University of Minnesota Press, 2011.
Goswami, P. R. *The Evolution of Gazette of India: Paperwork, Bureaucracy, and Official Document*, New Delhi: Synergy Books India, 2022.
Govil, Nitin. "Bollywood and the Frictions of Global Mobility," in *Media on the Move: Global Flow and Contra-Flow*, ed. Daya Thussu, New York: Routledge, 2006, 84–98.
———. *Orienting Hollywood: A Century of Film Culture Between Los Angeles and Bombay*. New York: New York University Press, 2015.
———. "Recognizing 'Industry,'" *Cinema Journal* 52, no. 3 (Spring 2013), 172–176.
———. "Something to Declare: Trading Culture, Trafficking Hollywood and Textual Travel," PhD diss., New York University, 2005.
Greenberg, Joshua. *From Betamax to Blockbuster: Video Stores and the Invention of Movies on Video*, Cambridge, MA: MIT Press, 2008.
Greller, Johannes, Agathe Jarczyk, and Joanna Phillips, eds. *Compendium of Image Errors in Analog Video,* Bern: Bern University of the Arts, 2012.
Groo, Katherine. *Bad Film Histories: Ethnography and the Early Archive*, Minneapolis: University of Minnesota Press, 2019.
Guarneri, Michael. "The Gothic Bet: Riccardo Freda's *I vampiri* (1957) and the Birth of Italian Horror Cinema from an Industrial Perspective," *Palgrave Communications* 3, no. 29 (2017), 1–10.
Guild, Hazel. "'Bloody Wave' of U.S. Horror Pix Stirs W. German Censors, Police," *Variety*, 30 May 1979.
Gunning, Tom. "Foreword," in *Early Cinema in Russia and Its Cultural Reception*, trans. Alan Bodger, London and New York: Routledge, 1994.
———. "What's the Point of an Index? or, Faking Photographs," in *Still Moving: Between Cinema and Photography*, ed. Karen Redrobe Beckman and Jean Ma, Durham, NC: Duke University Press, 2008, 23–40.
Gupta, Akhil. *Red Tape: Bureaucracy, Structural Violence and Poverty in India*, Durham, NC, and London: Duke University Press, 2012.
Gupta, Akhil, and Aradhana Sharma. *The Anthropology of the State*, Pondicherry: Blackwell, 2009, 1–41.
Gurevitch, Leon. "Special Effects and the Cult Film," in *The Routledge Companion to Cult Cinema*, eds. Ernest Mathijs and Jamie Sexton, Oxon: Routledge, 2019, 338–348.
Hafizji, Jimi. "When the Film Industry Was Sterilized," *Film World*, June 1977, 26–28.
Halberstam, Jack. *The Queer Art of Failure*, Durham, NC, and London: Duke University Press, 2011.
———. *Skin Shows: Gothic Horror and the Technology of Monsters*, Durham, NC, and London: Duke University Press, 1995.

Hand, Richard. "Proliferating Horrors: Survival Horror and the Resident Evil Franchise," in *Horror Film: Creating and Marketing Fear*, ed. Steffen Hantke, Jackson: University of Mississippi Press, 2004.

"Handling of Processed Film," Kodak, accessed: 21 March 2022, https://www.kodak.com/en/motion/page/handling-of-processed-film.

Hanich, Julian. *Cinematic Emotion in Horror Films and Thrillers: The Aesthetic Paradox of Pleasurable Fear*, New York: Routledge, 2010.

———. "Review of Eugenie Brinkema: *The Forms of the Affects*," *Projections: The Journal for Movies and Mind* 9, no. 1 (2015), 112–117.

———. "Towards a Poetics of Cinematic Disgust," *Film-Philosophy* 15, no. 2 (2011), 11–35.

Hantke, Steffen. "Review of *Skin Shows: Gothic Horror and the Technology of Monsters*," H-PCAACA, *H-Net Reviews*, December 1995, https://networks.h-net.org/node/13784/reviews/13821/hantke-halberstam-skin-shows-gothic-horror-and-technology-monsters.

———. "Spectacular Optics: The Deployment of Special Effects in David Cronenberg's Films," *Film Criticism* 29, no. 2 (2004/2005), 34–52.

Harrington, Erin. *Women, Monstrosity and Horror Film: Gynaehorror*, New York and London: Taylor & Francis, 2017.

Hart, Adam Charles. *Monstrous Forms: Moving Image Horror across Media*, New York: Oxford University Press, 2020.

———. "Transitional Gothic: Hammer's Gothic Revival and New Horror," in *Gothic Film: An Edinburgh Companion*, ed. Richard Hand and Jay McRoy, Edinburgh: Edinburgh University Press, 2022, 58–76.

Hastie, Amelie. *Cupboards of Curiosity: Women, Recollection, and Film History*, Durham, NC, and London: Duke University Press, 2007.

Hebert, Adam. "Experiments in the Cine-Olympic Cycle: Camera Technology and Operation in *The Grand Olympics* (1961) and *White Rock* (1977)," *The Velvet Light Trap*, no. 87 (Spring 2021), 4–21.

Heckman, Heather. "We've Got Bigger Problems: Preservation during Eastman Color's Innovation and Early Diffusion," *The Moving Image* 15, no. 1 (2015), 44–61.

Hediger, Vinzenz. "The Original Is Always Lost: Film History, Copyright Industries and the Problem of Reconstruction," in *Cinephilia. Movies, Love and Memory*, ed. Marijke de Valck and Malte Hagener, Amsterdam: Amsterdam University Press, 2005, 135–149.

Heller-Nicholas, Alexandra. *Masks in Horror Cinema: Eyes without Faces*, Cardiff: University of Wales Press, 2019.

Henriques, Anthony. "Toast to an Indian Ghost," *Filmfare*, 1–15 March 1988.

Herbert, Daniel. *Videoland: Movie Culture at the American Video Store*, Oakland: University of California Press, 2014.

Hesselberth, Pepita. "From Subject-Effect to Presence-Effect: A Deictic Approach to the Cinematic," *Tangibility*, Autumn 2012, https://necsus-ejms.org/from-subject-effect-to-presence-effect-a-deictic-approach-to-the-cinematic/#_edn10.

Higgins Scott. *Harnessing the Technicolor Rainbow: Color Design in the 1930s*, Austin: University of Texas Press, 2009.

Hilderbrand, Lucas. "Grainy Days and Mondays: Superstar and Bootleg Aesthetics," *Camera Obscura* 19, no. 3 (2004), 56–91.

———. *Inherent Vice: Bootleg Histories of Videotape and Copyright*, Durham, NC, and London: Duke University Press, 2009.

Hincha, Richard. "Crisis in Celluloid: Color Fading and Film Base Deterioration," *Archival Issues* 17, no. 2 (1992), 126.

"The Hindi Film Industry Faces Its Worst Recession" *Screen*, 3 June 1983.

Hoag, Colin. "Dereliction at the South African Department of Home Affairs: Time for the Anthropology of Bureaucracy," *Critique of Anthropology* 34, no. 4 (December 2014), 410–428.

Hochschild, Arlie Russell. *The Managed Heart: Commercialization of Human Feeling*, Berkeley: University of California Press, 2012.

Hoek, Lotte. *Cut-Pieces: Celluloid Obscenity and Popular Cinema in Bangladesh*, New York: Columbia University Press, 2013.

Holly, Michael Ann. *The Melancholy Art*, Princeton, NJ, and Oxford: Princeton University Press, 2013.

"Horror Films," *Times of India*, 28 February 1979, 7.

"House of Horror," 13 July 1980, *Time of India*, A2.

"How Films Are Censored," *Times of India*, 11 July 1982, 2.

"How to Make a 'Fly,'" *Fangoria* 58 (October 1986), 34–38.

Hoy, David Couzens. *The Time of Our Lives: A Critical History of Temporality*, Cambridge, MA: MIT Press, 2012.

Hoyos, Héctor. *Things with a History: Transcultural Materialism and the Literatures of Extraction in Contemporary Latin America*, New York: Columbia University Press, 2019.

"HPF May Go in for Colour," *Economic Times*, 7 June 1978.

Huang, Erin. *Urban Horror: Neoliberal Post-Socialism and the Limits of Visibility*, Durham, NC, and London: Duke University Press, 2020.

Hughes, Stephen. "Policing Silent Film Exhibition in Colonial South India," in *Making Meaning in Indian Cinema*, ed. Ravi Vasudevan, New York: Oxford University Press, 2000, 39–64.

———. "Pride of Place," *Seminar*, no. 525 (2003).

Hull, Matthew. *Government of Paper: The Materiality of Bureaucracy in Urban Pakistan*, Berkeley: University of California Press, 2012.

"Hunt for the Wrong Film," *Hindustan Times*, 27 October 1977.

"Increase in Show Tax," *Screen*, 10 April 1981.

"Important Communication No. 2/2021: Subject: Online Submission of Cuts/Modifications," Central Board of Film Certification, 8 July 2021, https://www.cbfcindia.gov.in/main/CBFC_English/Attachments/Notice_09JULY2021.pdf.

"India Once Again Tops in Film Production," *Screen*, 14 January 1982.

"India's First Horror Film," *Times of India*, 23 February 1978, 2.

"Indian Government Bans *The Exorcist*," *The Hartford Courant*, 10 February 1979, 38.
"Industry Closure If HPF Price Hike Is Not Annulled," *Screen*, 18 July 1980, 1.
"Industry Condemns Stock Price Raise," *Screen*, 18 July 1980, 2.
"INFACT to Curb Video Piracy," *Trade Guide*, 29 August 1987.
"International: Shortage of Steel Curbs Construction of India Theatres," *Variety*, 14 August 1974.
"The Invasion of Bride-Snatchers," *Hindustan Times*, 5 June 1979.
Iyer, Usha. *Dancing Women: Choreographing Corporeal Histories of Hindi Cinema*, London and New York: Oxford University Press, 2020.
———. "Nevla as Dracula: Figurations of The Tantric as Monster in the Hindi Horror Film," in *Figurations in Indian Film*, ed. M. Sen and A. Basu, Hampshire, UK: Palgrave Macmillan, 2013, 101–115.
Izquierdo Tobias, Carlos. "Designing the Urban Experience: Art Direction in Contemporary Bombay Cinema," PhD diss., Jawaharlal Nehru University, 2016.
"*Jaani Dushman*," *Cine Blitz* 5, pt. 1 (1979), 17.
"*Jaani Dushman* Cuts," *Film Information*, 7 October 1978.
"*Jaani Dushman* Repels," *Times of India*, 27 May 1979, 4.
Jackson, Dave. "Movies and Mania: *Jaani Dushman*," 8 May 2016, www.moviesandmania.com.
Jacobs, Lea. *The Wages of Sin: Censorship and the Fallen Woman Film, 1928-1942*, Berkeley: University of California Press, 1997.
Jacobson, Brian, ed. *In the Studio: Visual Creation and Its Material Environments*, Oakland: University of California Press, 2020.
Jagannathan, Shakuntala, "It May to Too Late," *The Illustrated Weekly of India*, 10–16 February 1980.
Jaikumar, Priya. *Cinema at the End of Empire: a Politics of Transition in Britain and India*, Durham, NC: Duke University Press, 2006.
———. "*Haveli*: A Cinematic Topos," *Positions* 25, no. 1 (1 February 2017), 223-248.
———. *Where Histories Reside: India as Filmed Space*, Durham, NC, and London: Duke University Press, 2019.
Jain, Girilal. "India's Upward Struggle," *World Press Dialogue, World Press Review*, January 1983, 32–35.
Jain, Kajri. *Gods in the Bazaar: The Economies of Indian Calendar Art*, London and Durham, NC: Duke University Press, 2007.
Jaisingh, Hari. *India after Indira: The Turbulent Years, 1984-89*, Delhi: Allied Publishers, 1989.
Jameson, Fredric. "Reification and Utopia in Mass Culture" (1979), in *Signatures of the Visible*, New York and London: Routledge, 1992, 9–34.
Jeffrey, Robin. "Monitoring Newspapers and Understanding the Indian State," *Asian Survey* 34, no. 8 (1994), 748–763.
Jethanand, Krishin. "Keeping Continuity," *Film World*, August 1980, 58.

Johnson, Kevin. *The Celluloid Paper Trail: Identification and Description of Twentieth Century Film Scripts*. New Castle, DE: Oak Knoll Press, 2019.

Johnston, Keith M., and Carolyn Rickards. "The Colour Fantastic: Fantasy, Horror, and Science Fiction," in *Colour Films in Britain: The Eastmancolor Revolution*, ed. Sarah Street, Keith M. Johnston, Paul Frith, and Carolyn Rickards, London: Bloomsbury Publishing, 2021.

Jones, Rhys Steven. "Processes of Abjection: Toward a Marxist Theory of Horror," *Lit: Literature Interpretation Theory* 33, no. 4 (2023), 277–295.

Joshi, Heather. "The Informal Urban Economy and Its Boundaries," *Economic and Political Weekly* 15, no. 13 (29 March 1980), 638–644.

Joshi, Sarah. "Monsters of Every Stripe: Navigating the Werebeasts of Indian Horror Cinema," in *South Asian Gothic: Haunted Cultures, Histories and Media*, ed. DeimantasValaniūnas and Katarzyna Ancuta, Cardiff: University of Wales Press, 2021, 167–184.

Kafka, Ben. "Paperwork: The State of the Discipline," *Book History* 12 (2009), 340–353.

Kagal, Ayesha "As the Video Virus Spreads," *Times of India*, 22 January 1984.

Kane, Carolyn. *High-Tech Trash: Glitch, Noise, and Aesthetic Failure*, Oakland: University of California Press, 2019.

"Kanta Distributors," *Trade Guide*, 15 June 1985.

Karaganis, Joe. "Introduction," in *Media Piracy in Emerging Economies*, New York: Social Science Research Council, 2011.

Karanjia, B. K. "How Not to Settle Disputes," *Screen* 31, no. 41 (2 July 1982), 1.

Keane, Webb. "Signs Are Not the Garb of Meaning: On the Social Analysis of Material Things," in *Materiality*, ed. Daniel Miller, Durham, NC: Duke University Press, 2005, 182–205.

Keathley, Christian. *Cinephilia and History, or the Wind in the Trees*, Indianapolis: Indiana University Press, 2005.

"Keep Us Informed about Certified Films—CEAI," *Screen*, 9 July 1982.

Kelly, Casey Ryan. "*It Follows*: Precarity, Thanatopolitics, and the Ambient Horror Film," *Critical Studies in Media Communication* 34, no. 3 (2017), 234–249.

Kendrick, James. *Hollywood Bloodshed: Violence in 1980s American Cinema*, Carbondale: Southern Illinois University Press, 2009.

Kermode, Mark. "Horror: On the Edge of Taste," *Index on Censorship* 24, no. 6 (1995), 59–68

Kernan, Lisa. *Coming Attractions: Reading American Movie Trailers*, Austin: University of Texas Press, 2009.

Khanna, Ankur. "The Censor Script Writer," in *Complicating the City*, Sarai Reader 05: Bare Acts, Delhi: Center for the Study of Developing Societies, 2005, 264–268.

Khosla, G. D. *Pornography and Censorship in India*, New Delhi: Indian Book Company, 1976.

"Khooni Mahal," *Trade Guide*, 6 July 1985.
Klein, Amanda Ann. *American Film Cycles: Reframing Genres, Screening Social Problems, and Defining Subcultures*, Austin: University of Texas Press, 2011.
Klinger, Barbara. *Beyond the Multiplex: Cinema, New Technologies, and the Home*, Berkeley: University of California Press, 2006.
Kolnai, Aurel. "The Standard Modes of Aversion: Fear, Disgust and Hatred," *Mind* 107, no. 427 (July 1998), 581–595.
Korsmeyer, Carolyn. *Savoring Disgust: The Foul and the Fair in Aesthetics*, Oxford: Oxford University Press, 2011.
Koutsourakis, Angelos. "A Modest Proposal for Rethinking Cinematic Excess," *Quarterly Review of Film and Video* 38, no. 2 (December 2020), 1–27.
Krauss, Rosalind. "Reinventing the Medium," *Critical Inquiry* 25, no. 2 (1999), 289–305.
Kristeva, Julia. *Powers of Horror: An Essay on Abjection*, trans. Leon S. Roudiez, New York: Columbia University Press, 1982.
Kumar, Arun. "*Dahshat*: Nothing to Scream About," *Filmfare*, 16–31 July 1981.
Kumar, Ramesh. "Alas, Nitrate Didn't Wait, but Does It Really Matter?: Fiery Losses, Bureaucratic Cover-Ups, and the Writing of Indian Film Histories from the Relics of Cinema at the National Film Archive of India," *BioScope: South Asian Screen Studies* 7, no. 1 (2016), 96–115.
Kunze, Peter. "Herding Cats; or, the Possibilities of Unproduction Studies," *The Velvet Light Trap*, no. 80 (Fall 2017), 18–31.
Larkin, Brian. "The Materiality of Cinema Theaters in Northern Nigeria," in *Media Worlds: Anthropology on New Terrain*, ed. Faye Ginsburg, Lila Abu-Lughod, and Brian Larkin, Berkeley: University of California Press, 2002, 319–336.
———. "The Politics and Poetics of Infrastructure," *Annual Review of Anthropology* 42 (2013), 327–328.
———. *Signal and Noise: Media, Infrastructure and Urban Culture in Nigeria*, Durham, NC: Duke University Press, 2008.
Laxman, S. "Must an Infant Have Ticket to Enter Cinema?," *Times of India*, 30 October 1982.
Leary, Charles. "*Air Hostess* and Atmosphere: The Persistence of the Tableau," in *Asian Cinema and the Use of Space: Interdisciplinary Perspectives*, ed. Lilian Chee and Edna Lim, New York: Taylor & Francis, 2015, 126–138.
Leeder, Murray. *The Modern Supernatural and The Beginnings of Cinema*, London: Palgrave Macmillan UK, 2017.
Lethem, Jonathan. "Loving the Ruins; or, Does *The Magnificent Ambersons* Exist?," *Criterion*, 26 November 2018.
"Let's Be Practical," letter from Amit Dutta (Calcutta), in *Film World*, August 1980, 7.
Liang, Lawrence. "Law, Affect and the Media Event," in *No Limits: Media Studies from India*, ed. Ravi Sundaram, Delhi: Oxford University Press, 2013, 47–69.

———. "A *Sholay* We Don't Know," *Indian Express*, 16 February 2015.

Lim, Bliss Cua. *Translating Time: Cinema, the Fantastic, and Temporal Critique*, Durham, NC: Duke University Press, 2009.

Lippit, Akira Mizuta. *Atomic Light (Shadow Optics)*, Minneapolis: University of Minnesota Press, 2005.

Lobato, Ramon, and Mark David Ryan, "Rethinking Genre Studies through Distribution Analysis: Issues in International Horror Movie Circuits," *New Review of Film and Television Studies* 9, no. 2 (2011), 188–203.

Loew, Katharina. *Special Effects and German Silent Film: Techno-Romantic Cinema*, Amsterdam: Amsterdam University Press, 2021.

London, Christopher W. *Bombay Gothic*, Mumbai: India Book House, 2002.

"Losing Ground," *Trade Guide*, 24 January 1987.

Lowenstein, Adam. "The *Giallo*/Slasher Landscape: *Ecologia Del Delitto*, *Friday the 13th* and Subtractive Spectatorship," in *Italian Horror Cinema*, ed. Stefano Baschiera, and Russ Hunter, Edinburgh: Edinburgh University Press, 2016, 127–144.

———. *Horror Film and Otherness*, New York: Columbia University Press, 2022.

———. *Shocking Representation: Historical Trauma, National Cinema, and the Modern Horror Film*, New York: Columbia University Press, 2005.

Lucca, Violet. "The Cleaning Crew," *Film Comment*, November–December 2016, https://www.filmcomment.com/article/the-cleaning-crew-vfx/.

Luckhurst, Roger. "The Contemporary London Gothic and the Limits of the 'Spectral Turn,'" *Textual Practice* 16, no. 3 (2002), 527–546.

Lundemo, Trond. "In the Kingdom of Shadows: Cinematic Movement and its Digital Ghost," in *The Youtube Reader*, ed. Pelle Snickars and Patrick Vonderau, Stockholm: National Library of Sweden, 2009, 314–329.

Lutgendorf, Philip. "Notes on Indian Popular Cinema: Mughal E Azam," accessed: 2 April 2020, https://uiowa.edu/indiancinema/mughal-e-azam.

MacDowell, James, and James Zborowski. "The Aesthetics of 'So Bad it's Good': Value, Intention, and The Room," *Intensities*, Autumn/Winter 2014, 1–30.

Mahadevan, Sudhir. *A Very Old Machine: The Many Origins of the Cinema in India*, Albany: State University of New York Press, 2015.

Mangala, "The Story of a Sterilisation Camp," *Manushi*, no. 21 (March–April 1984), 17–18.

Marks, Laura U. *Touch: Sensuous Theory and Multisensory Media*, Minneapolis: University of Minnesota Press, 2002.

Martin, Adrian. "Standing Up Too Close or Back Too Far? A Slanted History of Close Film Analysis," in *The Oxford Handbook of Film Theory*, ed. Kyle Stevens, New York: Oxford University Press, 2022, 505–525.

Martin, Sylvia. *Haunted: An Ethnography of the Hollywood and Hong Kong Media Industries*, Oxford and London: Oxford University Press, 2017.

Masood, Iqbal. "The Not So Popular Cinema," in *Film Utsav 1985-86*, New Delhi: DIFF, 1985, 20–25.
Mathijs, Ernest, "They're Here! Special Effects in Horror Cinema of the 1970s and 1980s," in *Horror Zone: The Cultural Experience of Contemporary Horror Cinema*, ed. Ian Conrich, London: I. B. Taurus, 2010.
Mathijs, Ernest, and Jamie Sexton. "Introduction: The Cult Cinema Studies Experience," in *The Routledge Companion to Cult Cinema*, ed. Ernest Mathijs and Jamie Sexton, Oxon: Routledge, 2019, 1–6.
Mathur, Nayanika. *Paper Tiger: Law, Bureaucracy and the Developmental State in Himalayan India*, Delhi: Cambridge University Press, 2016.
Mayer, Vicki. *Below the Line: Producers and Production Studies in the New Television Economy*, Durham: Duke University Press, 2011.
Mazumdar, Ranjani. "Aviation, Tourism and Dreaming in 1960s Bombay Cinema," *BioScope: South Asian Screen Studies* 2, no. 2 (July 2011), 129–155.
———. *Bombay Cinema: An Archive of the City*, Minneapolis: University of Minnesota Press, 2007.
———. "'Invisible Work' in the Indian Media Industries," *Media Industries Journal* 1, no. 3 (2015), 26–31.
———. "The Legal Unspeakable: Rape in 1980s Bombay Cinema," in *Gendered Citizenship: Manifestations and Performance*, ed. Bishnupriya Dutt, Janelle Reinelt, and Shrinkhla Sahai, Delhi: Orient Black Swan, 2017, 163–180.
———. "Retro in Contemporary Bombay Cinema," in *The Routledge Companion to Global Popular Culture*, ed. Toby Miller, London: Routledge, 2015, 366–375.
Mazumdar, Ranjani, and Neepa Majumdar. "Introduction," in *A Companion to Indian Cinema*, ed. Neepa Majumdar and Ranjani Mazumdar, London: Wiley Blackwell, 2022, 1–33.
Mazzarella, William. *Censorium: Cinema and the Open Edge of Mass Publicity*, Durham, NC, and London: Duke University Press, 2013.
McDonagh, Maitland. *Broken Mirrors/Broken Minds: The Dark Dreams of Dario Argento*, Minneapolis: University of Minnesota Press, 2010.
McGuirl, Erin. "Printing the Screenplay in Hollywood and Beyond," *Printing History*, n.s., no. 24 (2018), 28–40.
———. "The Screenplay as Material Text," Bibliographical Society of America, 2 October 2020, https://www.youtube.com/watch?v=qQ5toBPb1Mo.
McKenna, Denise. "The Photoplay or the Pickaxe: Extras, Gender, and Labour in Early Hollywood," *Film History* 23, no. 1 (2011): 5–19.
McLean, Adrienne. *All for Beauty: Makeup and Hairdressing in Hollywood's Studio Era*. New Brunswick, NJ: Rutgers University Press, 2022.
Meden, Jurij. *Scratches and Glitches: Observations on Preserving and Exhibiting Cinema in the Early 21st Century*. New York: Columbia University Press, 2021.

Mehta, Monika. "Analyzing and Writing about Credit Sequences," in *Writing about Screen Media*, ed. Lisa Patti, London: Routledge, 2019, 163–168.

———. *Censorship and Sexuality in Bombay Cinema*, Austin: University of Texas Press, 2011.

Mehta, Monika, and Madhuja Mukherjee. "Introduction: Detouring Networks," in *Industrial Networks and Cinemas of India: Shooting Stars, Shifting Geographies and Multiplying Media*, London: Taylor & Francis, 2020, 1–17.

Mehta, S. M. "Letter 'A' for Adults or for Adolescents?," *Film World*, July 1979, 90.

Menninghaus, Winfried. *Disgust: The Theory and History of a Strong Sensation*. Albany: State University of New York Press, 2003.

Menon, Bindu. *Re-Framing Vision: Malayalam Cinema and the Invention of Modern Life in Keralam*, PhD diss., Jawaharlal Nehru University, 2014.

Menon, Nivedita. *Recovering Subversion: Feminist Politics Beyond the Law*, Delhi: Permanent Black, 2004.

Metz, Christian. "'Trucage' and the Film," trans. Francoise Meltzer, *Critical Inquiry* 3, no. 4 (1977), 657–675.

Miller, D. A. "Hitchcock's Understyle: A Too-Close View of *Rope*," *Representations* 121, no. 1 (Winter 2013), 1–30.

Miller, William Ian. *The Anatomy of Disgust*, Cambridge, MA, and London: Harvard University Press, 1998.

Mini, Darshana Sreedhar. "The Rise of Soft Porn in Malayalam Cinema and the Precarious Stardom of Shakeela," *Feminist Media Histories* 5, no. 2 (1 April 2019), 49–82.

Mishra, Vijay. *Bollywood Cinema: Temples of Desire*, New York and London: Routledge, 2013.

Modleski, Tania. "The Terror of Pleasure: The Contemporary Horror Film and Postmodern Theory," in *Studies in Entertainment: Critical Approaches to Mass Culture*, ed. Tania Modleski, Bloomington: Indiana University Press, 1986, 155–166.

Mohamed, Khalid. "'Bepanaah' Revels in Gore & Destruction," *Times of India*, 8 September 1985.

———. "The Crime Beat," *Times of India*, 7 November 1976.

———. "*Dahshat*: Smiling Snakes," *Times of India*, 28 June 1981.

———. "'The Exorcist' Awaiting Only Formal Ban," *Times of India*, 9 June 1976.

———. "Film Censorship: Corrupt, Confused, Castrating; Which Way Permissive?," *Times of India*, 29 October 1978.

———. "Government Guest House Turns into Chamber of Horrors," *Times of India*, 1 May 1980.

———. "Vampires Don't Live Here Anymore," *Times of India*, 21 April 1985.

Molesworth, Jesse. "Gothic Time, Sacred Time," *Modern Language Quarterly* 75, no. 1 (1 March 2014), 29–55.

Moskatova, Olga. "Unstable Matter Destruction, Destructuring, De-Obstruction in Camera-Less Film," in *Art and Destruction*, ed. Jennifer Walden, Newcastle upon Tyne: Cambridge Scholars Publishing, 2013, 95–114.
Mowitt, John. *Text: The Genealogy of an Antidisciplinary Object*, Durham, NC, and London: Duke University Press, 1992.
Mubarki, Meraj Ahmed. *Filming Horror: Hindi Cinema, Ghosts and Ideologies*, Delhi: Sage Publications, 2016.
Mukherjee, Debashree. *Bombay Hustle: Making Movies in a Colonial City*, New York: Columbia University Press, 2020.
———. "'A Material World': Notes on an Interview with Ram Tipnis," *BioScope: South Asian Screen Studies* 1, no. 2 (2010), 199–205.
———. "Somewhere between Human, Nonhuman, and Woman: Shanta Apte's Theory of Exhaustion," *Feminist Media Histories* 6, no. 3 (1 July 2020), 21–51.
———. "A Specter Haunts Bombay: Censored Itineraries of a Lost Communistic Film," *Film History: An International Journal* 31, no. 4 (Winter 2019), 29–59.
Mukherjee, Debashree, Kaushik Bhaumik, and Rahab Allana. *Filmi Jagat: A Scrapbook-Shared Universe of Early Hindi Cinema*, New Delhi: Niyogi Books, 2015.
Mukherjee, Rahul. *Radiant Infrastructures: Media, Environment, and Cultures of Uncertainty*, Durham: Duke University Press, 2020.
Mukherjee, Rahul, and Abhigyan Singh. "MicroSD-ing 'Mewati Videos': Circulation and Regulation of a Subaltern-Popular Media Culture," in *Asian Video Cultures*, ed. Bhaskar Sarkar and Joshua Neves, Durham, NC: Duke University Press, 2017, 133–157.
Mulvey, Laura. "A Clumsy Sublime," *Film Quarterly* 60, no. 3 (2007), 3.
———. *Death 24x a Second: Stillness and the Moving Image*, London: Reaktion Books, 2006.
"Mystery of Severed Limbs Solved," *Times of India*, 29 March 1985, 5.
Nahata, Komal. *Kissaa Kursee Kaa: The Film Which Will Never Be Released*, New Delhi: Young Men Mass Media Publications, 1977.
Nair, Kartik. "Review," *BioScope: South Asian Screen Studies* 8, no. 2(2017), 280–285.
———. "Striking Out: Visual Space, Production Design, and Labor History in *Joker*," *Quarterly Review of Film and Video* 39, no. 8 (2021), 1905–1933.
———. "Taste, Taboo, Trash: The Story of the Ramsay Brothers," *BioScope: South Asian Screen Studies* 3, no. 2 (2012), 123–145.
———. "Temple of Womb," *New Inquiry*, July 2013.
———. "Towards a Phenomenology of Film Production," *Discourse: Journal for Theoretical Studies in Media and Culture* 44, no. 2, (2022), 158–80.
Nair, N. "What Makes Full Houses Full?," *Filmfare*, 16–31 July 1981, 46–47.

Nakahara, Tamao. "Making Up Monsters: Set and Costume Design in Horror Films," in *Horror Zone: The Cultural Experience of Contemporary Horror Cinema*, ed. Ian Conrich, London: I. B. Taurus, 2010.

———. "Production Play: Sets, Props, and Costumes in Cult Films," in *The Routledge Companion to Cult Cinema*, ed. Ernest Mathijs and James Sexton, Oxon: Routledge, 2019.

Nandy, Pritish. "Indiana Jones Returns to the Temple of Gloom," *Filmfare*, 1–15 January 1985, 62–63.

Ndalianis, Angela. *The Horror Sensorium: Media and the Senses*, Jefferson, NC: McFarland, 2012.

Neale, Steve. "'You've Got to Be Fucking Kidding!': Knowledge, Belief and Judgement in Science Fiction," in *Alien Zone: Cultural Theory and Contemporary Science Fiction Cinema*, ed. Annette Kuhn, London: Verso, 1990, 160–168.

"Negative Cutting Ceremony," *Trade Guide*, 8 February 1986.

Nemerov, Alexander. "Seeing Ghosts: *The Turn of the Screw* and Art History," in *The Spectralities Reader: Ghosts and Haunting in Contemporary Cultural Theory*, ed. Maria del Pilar Blanco and Esther Peeren, London and New York: Bloomsbury, 2013, 527–548.

Newman, Michael Z. *Video Revolutions. On the History of a Medium*, New York: Columbia University Press, 2014.

"NFDC Flooded with Loan Applications," *Times of India*, 26 October 1982.

Ngai, Sianne. *Our Aesthetic Categories: Zany, Cute, Interesting*, Cambridge, MA: Harvard University Press, 2012.

"No FFI Directive on Video Rights Sale," *Screen*, 6 September 1985.

"Notification of the Ministry of Information and Broadcasting," 7 January 1978.

"Notification from the Ministry of Information and Broadcasting," *Gazette of India*, 13 February 1960, 280–282.

"Now a Video Hut," *Film Information* 12, no. 19 (1985).

O' Brien, Daniel Paul. "Hap-Tech Narration and the Postphenomenological Film," *Philosophies* 4, no. 3 (2019), 47.

"Of Censors and Super Censors," *Screen*, 31 October 1980.

Olivier, Marc. *Household Horror: Cinematic Fear and the Everyday Life of Objects*, Bloomington: Indiana University Press, 2020.

Olivier, Marc, and David Walter, "Wallpaper+Horror," 20 October 2020, http://www.horrorhomeroom.com/wallpaper-horror/.

Ong, Walter. *Orality and Literacy: The Technologizing of the Word*, London: Methuen, 1982.

"Our Reviewer," *Screen*, 37, no. 35 (13 May 1988).

Pandian, Anand. *Reel World: An Anthropology of Creation*, Durham, NC: Duke University Press, 2015.

Pape, Toni. "Method Unchained: To New Adventures of Ideas," in *NECSUS: European Journal of Media Studies* 9, no. 2 (2020), 77–91.

"Parkar Arrested," *Times of India*, 25 October 1984, 3.

Parks, Lisa. "Points of Departure: The Culture of U.S. Airport Screening," *Journal of Visual Culture* 6, no. 2 (2007), 183–200.
"Parlor Raided," *Film Information*, 27 October 1984.
"Particulars of Films" (1978), *Gazette of India*, 16 September 1978, 1534–1535.
"Particulars of Films" (1979), *Gazette of India*, 3 November 1979, 2562–2563.
Pascuzzi, Francesco, and Sandra Waters. "Introduction," in *The Spaces and Places of Horror*. Wilmington, DE: Vernon Art and Science Incorporated, 2020, xiii–xxviii.
Patrick-Weber, Courtney. *The Rhetoric and Medicalization of Pregnancy and Childbirth in Horror Films*, London: Lexington Books, 2020.
Paul, William. *Laughing, Screaming: Modern Hollywood Horror and Comedy*, New York: Columbia University Press, 1994.
Pendakur, Manjunath, "New Cultural Technologies and the Fading Glitter of Indian Cinema," *Quarterly Review of Film and Video* 11. no. 3 (1989), 69–78.
Perez, Gilberto. *The Material Ghost: Films and Their Medium*, Baltimore, MD: Johns Hopkins University Press, 2000.
Petley, Julian. "Horror Films," in *Censorship: A World Encyclopedia*, ed. Derek Jones, vol. 2. London and Chicago: Fitzroy Dearborn Publishers, 2001.
Phadke, Shilpa. "Thirty Years On: Women's Studies Reflects on the Women's Movement," *Economic and Political Weekly* 38, no. 43 (2003), 4567–4576.
Pillai, Swarnavel Eswaran. *Madras Studios: Narrative, Genre, and Ideology in Tamil Cinema*, Delhi: Sage Publications, 2015.
Pinedo, Isabel Cristina. *Recreational Terror: Women and the Pleasures of Horror Film Viewing*. Albany: State University of New York Press, 1997.
Pinney, Christopher. "Things Happen: Or, from Which Moment Does That Object Come?," in *Materiality*, ed. Daniel Miller, Durham, NC, and London: Duke University Press, 2005.
Pow, Whitney (Whit). "A Trans Historiography of Glitches and Errors," *Feminist Media Histories* 7, no. 1 (1 January 2021), 197–230.
Powell, Anna. *Deleuze and Horror Film*, Edinburgh: Edinburgh University Press, 2005.
Prabhu, Uma Keni. "How to Make a Killing at the Box Office," *Bombay: The City Magazine* 11, nos. 7–18 (1990).
Prakash, Gyan. *Emergency Chronicles: Indira Gandhi and Democracy's Turning Point*, Princeton, NJ, and Oxford: Princeton University Press, 2019.
Prasad, Madhava. *Ideology of the Hindi Film: A Historical Construction*, Delhi: Oxford University Press, 1998.
Price, Brian. "Color, the Formless, and Cinematic Eros," *Framework: The Journal of Cinema and Media* 47, no. 1 (2006), 22–35.
Prince, Stephen. *Classical Film Violence: Designing and Regulating Brutality in Hollywood Cinema, 1930–1968*, New Brunswick, NJ: Rutgers University Press, 2003.

———. "The Horror Film," in *An Introduction to Film Genres*, ed. Friedman et al., New York: Norton, 2014.
———. "True Lies: Perceptual Realism, Digital Images, and Film Theory," *Film Quarterly* 49, no. 3 (1996), 27.
Provencher, Ken, and Mike Dillon, eds. *Exploiting East Asia*, New York: Bloomsbury, 2017.
Punathambekar, Aswin. *From Bombay to Bollywood: The Making of a Global Media Industry*, New York: NYU Press, 2013.
"*Purana Mandir*: More Farcical Than Fearsome," *Screen*, 26 October 1984.
Purse, Lisa. "The New Hollywood, 1981–1999," in *Editing and Special/Visual Effects*, ed. Charlie Keil and Kristen Whissel, New Brunswick, NJ: Rutgers University Press, 2016.
"Putting the Industry in Order," *Screen*, 24 October 1980.
Rahman, Harisur. *Consuming Cultural Hegemony: Bollywood in Bangladesh*, Cham, Switzerland: Palgrave Macmillan, 2019.
Rai, Amit. *Untimely Bollywood: Globalization and India's New Media Assemblage*. Durham, NC: Duke University Press, 2009.
"Railways May Abolish Casual Labour System: Rajya Sabha Questions," *Times of India*, 10 May 1984.
"Rains," *Trade Guide*, 4 July 1987.
Raj Kapoor vs Laxman Supreme Court of India, 14 December 1979.
"Raj Kumar Kohli," *Star & Style*, 30 April–13 May 1982, 16–17.
Rajagopal, Arvind. *Politics after Television: Hindu Nationalism and the Reshaping of the Public in India*, Cambridge: Cambridge University Press, 2001.
Ram, Kalpana. *Fertile Disorder: Spirit Possession and its Provocation of the Modern*, Honolulu: University of Hawaii Press, 2013.
Ramachandran, T. M. "Editorial," *Filmworld*, May 1977.
Raman, Bhavani. *Document Raj: Writing and Scribes in Early Colonial South India*. Chicago: University of Chicago Press, 2012.
Ramanathan, Jaya. "Censors without Clout," *Times of India*, 17 February 1980, 11.
Rangan, R. K., "The Concrete Truth," *Times of India*, 5 October 1980.
Rangan, R. K., and Mukul C. Pandya, "The Cement Muddle," *Times of India*, 1 June 1980, 6.
Ranjan, Dinesh. "The Sorry Plight of Extras," *Screen*, 4 May 1984.
Ranjan, Dinesh. Letter to the editor, *Screen*, 1 June 1984.
Rao, Uday. "The Censor's Scissors," *Times of India*, 23 May 1980, 8.
Razdan, C. K. "Film Censorship in India," *Film World*, August 1973, 58–61.
"'Razia' in the House: 'Coolie' in the Canteen!," *Trade Guide*, 14 January 1984.
Report of the Working Group on National Film Policy, New Delhi: Ministry of Information and Broadcasting, May 1980.
Rhodes, John David. "Belabored: Style as Work," *Framework* 53, no. 1 (2012), 47–64.

———. *Spectacle of Property: The House in American Film*. Minneapolis: University of Minnesota Press, 2017.
Richards, Rashna Wadia. *Cinematic Flashes: Cinephilia and Classical Hollywood*, Bloomington: Indiana University Press, 2012.
Richardson, Judith. "A History of Unrest," in *The Spectralities Reader: Ghosts and Haunting in Contemporary Cultural Theory*, ed. Maria del Pilar Blanco and Esther Peeren, London: Bloomsbury Publishing, 2013.
Rickards, Carolyn, Sarah Street, Paul Frith, and Keith Johnston. *Colour Films in Britain: The Eastmancolor Revolution*, London: Bloomsbury Publishing, 2021.
Riles, Annelise. *Documents: Artifacts of Modern Knowledge*, Ann Arbor: University of Michigan Press, 2008.
Risner, Jonathan. *Blood Circuits: Contemporary Argentine Horror Cinema*, Albany: State University of New York Press, 2018.
Roberts, Jennifer. *Transporting Visions: The Movement of Images in Early America*, Berkeley: University of California Press, 2014.
Roberts, Sarah. *Behind the Screen: Content Moderation in the Shadows of Social Media*, New Haven, CT: Yale University Press, 2019.
Rooney, Ellen. "Foreword," in *Reading in Detail: Aesthetics and the Feminine*, ed. Naomi Schor, London and New York: Taylor & Francis, 2013.
Rosen, Philip. *Change Mummified: Cinema, Historicity, Theory*, Minneapolis: University of Minnesota Press, 2001.
Ruétalo, Victoria. "¡Prohibida! Armando Bó and Isabel Sarli's Struggle with Censorship in Argentina," *Porn Studies* 5, no. 4 (2018), 380–392.
———. *Violated Frames: Armando Bó and Isabel Sarli's Sexploits*, Oakland: University of California Press, 2022.
Salvato, Nick. *Obstruction*, Durham, NC: Duke University Press, 2016.
Samalin, Zachary. *The Masses Are Revolting: Victorian Culture and the Political Aesthetics of Disgust*, Ithaca, NY: Cornell University Press, 2021.
Sarkar, Kobita. *You Can't Please Everyone! Film Censorship: The Inside Story*, Bombay: IBH Publishing Company, 1982.
Saxena, Shraddha Jahagirdar. "Scareface," *Filmfare*, October 1993, 92–94.
Sayani, Sanjay, and Nilofer Ahmed, "Watch Out: We're Being Raided," *TV and Video World*, May 1986, 50.
"SC Stays Order against Ticket Prices," *Screen*, 21 January 1983.
Schaefer, Eric. *Bold! Daring! Shocking! True: A History of Exploitation Films, 1919–1959*, Durham, NC: Duke University Press, 1999.
Schoonover, Karl. "What Do We Do with Vacant Space in Horror Films?," *Discourse* 40, no. 3 (Fall 2018), 342–57.
———. "Scrap Metal, Stains, Clogged Drains: Argento's Refuse and Its Refusals," in *Italian Horror Cinema*, ed. Stefano Baschiera and Russ Hunter, Edinburgh: Edinburgh University Press, 2016, 111–125.

Schor, Naomi. *Reading in Detail: Aesthetics and the Feminine*, New York and London: Routledge, 2007.

Schulze, Joshua. "James Wan's Dead Space: *The Conjuring* Films, Siegfried Kracauer and the Revenge of Physical Reality," in *The Cinema of James Wan: Critical Essays*, ed. Fernando Gabriel Pagnoni Berns and Matthew Edwards, Jefferson, NC: McFarland, 2022, 143–154.

Schuppli, Susan. *Material Witness: Media, Forensics, Evidence*, Cambridge, MA: MIT Press, 2020.

Sconce, Jeffrey. *Haunted Media: Electronic Presence from Telegraphy to Television*, Durham, NC: Duke University Press, 2000.

———. "Introduction," in *Sleaze Artists: Cinema at the Margins of Taste, Style, and Politics*, Durham, NC, and London: Duke University Press, 2007, 1–16.

———. "Movies: A Century of Failure," in *Sleaze Artists: Cinema at the Margins of Taste, Style, and Politics*, ed. Jeffrey Sconce, Durham, NC, and London: Duke University Press, 2007.

———. "'Trashing' the Academy: Taste, Excess, and an Emerging Politics of Cinematic Style," *Screen* 36, no. 4 (1995), 371–393.

Sedgwick, Eve Kosofsky. *The Coherence of Gothic Conventions*, New York: Arno Press, 1980.

———. *Touching Feeling: Affect, Pedagogy, Performativity*, Durham, NC: Duke University Press, 2003.

Sen, Aditi. "'I Wasn't Born with Enough Middle Fingers': How Low-Budget Horror Films Defy Sexual Morality and Heteronormativity in Bollywood." *Acta Orientalia Vilnensia* 12, no. 2 (2011), 75–90.

Sen, Meheli. "Haunted Havelis and Hapless Heroes: Gender, Genre and the Hindi Gothic Film," in *Figurations in Indian Film*, ed. M. Sen and A. Basu, Hampshire, UK: Palgrave Macmillan, 2013, 116–136.

———. *Haunting Bollywood: Gender, Genre and the Supernatural in Hindi Commercial Cinema*, Austin: University of Texas Press, 2017.

———. "Terrifying Tots and Hapless Homes: Undoing Modernity in Recent Bollywood Cinema," *Literature Interpretation Theory* 22 (2011), 197–221.

Sen, Shaunak. "Spectral Pixels: Digital Ghosts in Contemporary Hindi Cinema," *Wide Screen* 5, no. 1 (2013).

Sengupta, Shuddhabrata. "Reflected Readings in Available Light: Cameraperson in the Shadows of Hindi Cinema," in *Bollyworld: Popular Indian Cinema through a Transnational Lens*, ed. Raminder Kaur and Ajay J Sinha, New Delhi and London: Sage, 2005, 118–140.

———. "The Video-Walla's Images of Life," in *Image Journeys: Audio-Visual Media and Cultural Change in India*, ed. Christiane Brosius and Melissa Butcher, New Delhi and London: Sage Publications, 1999, 279–307.

Sennett, Richard *The Craftsman*, New Haven, CT: Yale University Press, 2008.

Sethi, Devika. *War over Words: Censorship in India, 1930–1960*, Cambridge: Cambridge University Press, 2019.

Sevea, Iqbal. "'Kharaak Kita Oi!': Masculinity, Caste, and Gender in Punjabi Films," *BioScope: South Asian Screen Studies* 5, no. 2 (2015), 129–140.
Sevea, Teren. *Miracles and Material Life: Rice, Ore, Traps and Guns in Islamic Malaya*, Cambridge: Cambridge University Press, 2020.
"Sex, Violence: No Effect on Indian Audiences?," *Screen*, 11 July 1980.
"*Shaitani Dracula*: The Worst Movie Ever Made?," *Beth Loves Bollywood*, 23 August 2009, http://www.bethlovesbollywood.com/2009/08/shaitani-dracula-worst-movie-ever-made.html.
Shaviro, Steven. *The Cinematic Body*, Minneapolis: University of Minnesota Press, 1993.
"Shiva Temple Found at Janjira Fort," *Times of India*, 28 October 1985.
"Shocking Condition of Theaters," *Screen*, 2 May 1980.
"Shooting," *Trade Guide*, 8 February 1986.
"Shortage of Color Film Hits 24 Movies," *Morning Echo*, 2 June 1978.
Shukin, Nicole. *Animal Capital: Rendering Life in Biopolitical Times*, Minneapolis: University of Minnesota Press, 2009.
Siddique, Salma. *Evacuee Cinema: Bombay and Lahore in Partition Transit (1940–1960)*, Cambridge and New York: Cambridge University Press, 2022.
Siddique, Sophia, and Raphael Raphael. *Transnational Horror Cinema: Bodies of Excess and the Global Grotesque*, London: Palgrave Macmillan, 2016.
Singer, Ben. *Melodrama and Modernity: Early Sensational Cinema and Its Contexts*, New York: Columbia University Press, 2001.
Singh, Bikram. "Impact of Video," in *Indian Cinema: The Next Decade*, Bombay, Indian Film Directors Association, 1984.
Sipos, Thomas M. *Horror Film Aesthetics: Creating the Visual Language of Fear*, Jefferson, NC: McFarland, 2010.
Smith, Angela. *Hideous Progeny: Disability, Eugenics, and Classic Horror Cinema*, New York: Columbia University Press, 2011.
Smith, Greg M. "'It's Just a Movie': A Teaching Essay for Introductory Media Classes," *Cinema Journal* 41, no. 1 (Fall 2001), 127–134.
Smith, Iain Robert, "'Beam Me up, Ömer': Transnational Media Flow and the Cultural Politics of the Turkish Star Trek Remake," *The Velvet Light Trap* 61 (2008), 3–13.
"So What's Left?," letter from P Janardhanan, in "This Fortnight's Mail," *Filmfare*, 1–15 June 1978.
Sobchack, Vivian. "Afterword: Media Archaeology and Re-presencing the Past," in *Media Archaelogy: Approaches, Applications and Implications*, ed. Huhtamo and Jussi Parikka, Berkeley: University of California Press, 2011, 323–333.
———. *Carnal Thoughts: Embodiment and Moving Image Culture*, Berkeley: University of California Press, 2004.
Sofer, Andrew. *The Stage Life of Props*, Ann Arbor: University of Michigan Press, 2003.

Solomon, Stefan. "'The Cloak of Technicolor': Intermedial Colour in *Antônio das Mortes*," *Screen* 60, no. 1 (Spring 2019), 137–147.
Sontag, Susan. "Notes on Camp" (1964), in *Against Interpretation and Other Essays*, New York: Delta, 1981, 275–292.
Spadoni, Robert. "Carl Dreyer's Corpse: Horror Film Atmosphere and Narrative," in *A Companion to the Horror Film*, ed. Harry Benshoff, West Sussex: John Wiley & Sons, 2014, 151–167.
———. *Uncanny Bodies: The Coming of Sound Film and the Origins of the Horror Genre*, Berkeley: University of California Press, 2007.
Spielmann, Yvonne. "Video: From Technology to Medium," *Art Journal* 65, no. 3 (Fall 2006), 54–69.
"Splatter," *Oxford English Dictionary Online*, Oxford: Oxford University Press, 2021, https://doi.org/10.1093/OED/1377136301.
Srinivas, S. V. "Hong Kong Action Film in the Indian B Circuit," *Inter-Asia Cultural Studies* 4, no. 1 (2003), 40–62.
"Star Video: A Gang of Thirty Five," *Star &Style*, 7–20 November 1986.
Stasik, Michael, Valerie Hänsch, and Daniel Mains. "Temporalities of Waiting in Africa," *Critical African Studies* 12, no. 1 (2020), 1–9.
Steinhart, Daniel. *Runaway Hollywood: Internationalizing Postwar Production and Location Shooting*, Los Angeles: University of California Press, 2019.
Stern, Lesley. "Paths That Wind through the Thicket of Things," *Critical Inquiry* 28, no. 1 (Autumn 2001), 317–354.
Stevens, Kyle. "Introduction: The Very Thought of Theory," in *The Oxford Handbook of Film Theory*, ed. Kyle Stevens, New York: Oxford University Press, 2022, 1–12.
Stevens, William. "Bazaars of India Are Now a Toyland of High Tech," *New York Times*, 2 February 1984.
Steyerl, Hito. "In Defense of the Poor Image," *E-flux Journal*, no. 10 (November 2009), https://www.e-flux.com/journal/10/61362/in-defense-of-the-poor-image/
Stiasny, Philipp, and Bennet Togler. "Twilight of the Dead," in *Unwatchable*, ed. Nicholas Baer, Maggie Hennefeld, Laura Horak, and Gunnar Iversen, New Brunswick, NJ: Rutgers University Press, 2019, 244–248.
Stiegler, Bernard, in conversation with Jacques Derrida, in *Echographies of Television: Filmed Interviews*, trans. Jennifer Bajorek, Cambridge, UK: Polity Press, 2002.
Stoler, Ann Laura. *Along the Archival Grain: Epistemic Anxieties and Colonial Common Sense*, Princeton, NJ: Princeton University Press, 2010.
Subba, Vibhushan. "Rebels without a Cause: The Bombay Cult Film," in *The Routledge Companion to Cult Cinema*, ed. Ernest Mathijs and Jamie Sexton, Oxon: Routledge, 2019, 105–110.

Sundaram, Ravi. "Other Networks: Media Urbanism and the Culture of the Copy in South Asia," in *Structures of Participation in Digital Culture*, ed. Joe Karaganis, New York: Social Science Research Council, 2007.
———. *Pirate Modernity: Delhi's Media Urbanism*, London and New York: Routledge, 2010.
Sunya, Samhita. *Sirens of Modernity: World Cinema via Bombay*, Oakland: University of California Press, 2022.
"Supply and Demand," *Screen*, 30, no. 9, 14 November 1980.
Suresh, Mayur. "Policing the Networks and Practices of Video 2002, http://www.sarai.net/research/media-city/field-notes/film-city/vedio-networks.
———. "Video Nights and Dispersed Pleasures," in *The Public Is Watching: Sex, Laws and Videotapes*, New Delhi: PSBT and the Ford Foundation, 2007, 105–120.
"Tale of 3 Films," *Times of India*, 11 December 1978, 8.
Tanvir, Kuhu. "Pirate Histories: Rethinking the Indian Film Archive," *BioScope: South Asian Screen Studies* 4. no. 2 (2013), 115–136.
Tarlo, Emma. *Unsettling Memories: Narratives of the Emergency in Delhi*, Berkeley and Los Angeles: University of California Press, 2003.
Tarratt, Margaret. "Monsters from the Id," in *Film Genre Reader*, ed. Barry Keith Grant, Austin: University of Texas Press, 1986, 258–277.
Tashiro, Charles S. *Pretty Pictures: Production Design and the History of Film*, Austin: University of Texas Press, 2010.
"Theater Gutted," *Screen*, 13 February 1981.
"Theatre Owners Warned," *Times of India*, 22 August 1981.
Theophanidis, Philippe. "Scratches in Kubrick's *2001: A Space Odyssey*," 3 September 2018, https://aphelis.net/scratches-kubrick-2001-space-odyssey/.
Thielemans, Veerle. "Beyond Visuality: Review on Materiality and Affect," *Perspective* 2 (2015), 1–7.
Thomas, Rosie. *Bombay before Bollywood: Film City Fantasies*, Albany: State University of New York Press, 2013.
———. "Indian Cinema: Pleasures and Popularity," *Screen* 26, nos. 3–4 (1 May 1985), 116–131.
Thompson, Kristin. "The Concept of Cinematic Excess" (1986), in *Narrative, Apparatus, Ideology: A Film Theory Reader*, ed. Philip Rosen, New York: Columbia University Press, 1986.
"3-D Creates Havoc in Bombay Suburbs," *Trade Guide*, 16 November 1985.
Thrift, Nigel. "Movement-Space: The Changing Domain of Thinking Resulting from the Development of New Kinds of Spatial Awareness," *Economy and Society* 33, no. 4 (November 2004), 582–604.
Timpone, Anthony. *Men, Makeup, and Monsters: Hollywood's Masters of Illusion and FX*, New York: St. Martin's Press, 1996.

Tiwary, Ishita. "Screening Conjugality: The Affective Infrastructure of the Marriage Video," in "Home Video and Media Texts," special issue, *PostScript: Essays in Film and Humanities* 35, no. 3 (Summer 2016), 21–36.

———. "Unsettling News: Newstrack and the Video Event," in "Media Populism," special issue, *Culture Machine* 19 (November 2020).

———. "What Is Video?" in *Acts of Media: Law and Media in Contemporary India*, ed. Siddharth Narain, Delhi: Sage Publications, 2022.

Todorov, Tzvetan. *The Fantastic: A Structural Approach to a Literary Genre*, Cleveland and London: Case Western Reserve University Press, 1973.

Tombs, Pete. "The Beast from Bollywood: A History of the Indian Horror Film," in *Fear without Frontiers: Horror Cinema across the Globe*, ed. S. J. Schneider, Godalming, UK: FAB Press, 2003, 243–253.

———. *Mondo Macabro: Weird and Wonderful Cinema around the World*, New York: St Martin's Griffin, 1997.

Tompkins, Kayla. "Crude Matter, Queer Form," *ASAP/Journal* 2, no. 2 (2017), 264–268.

Torre, Dan. *Animation—Process, Cognition and Actuality*, London: Bloomsbury Academic, 2017.

"Trade Delegation Meets CM," *Screen*, 1 April 1983.

"Trade Leaders Flay Working Group's Superficial Report," *Screen*, 19 September 1980.

Tralli, Lucia. "Layers of Film, Encrusted Images: Editing Practices in Cecile Fontaine's Cinema," *Feminist Media Histories* 2, no. 3 (2016), 73–89.

Tronzo, William. *The Fragment: An Incomplete History*, Los Angeles: Getty Research Institute, 2009.

Tsivian, Yuri. *Early Cinema in Russia and Its Cultural Reception*, trans. Alan Bodger, London and New York: Routledge, 1994.

Tuchman, Gaye. "Women's Depiction by the Mass Media," *Signs* 4, no. 3 (1979), 528–542.

Tuli, A. C., letter, "Shocking Condition of Theaters," *Screen*, 2 May 1980.

"Tune to Vividh Bharati Today & Every Saturday at 9.45 pm for the Radio Programme of India's First Horror Film," *Times of India*, 11 February 1978.

Turnock, Julie. "The Auteur Renaissance, 1968–1980: Special/Visual Effects," in *Editing and Special/Visual Effects*, ed. Charlie Keil and Kristen Whissel, New Brunswick, NJ: Rutgers University Press, 2016.

———. *Plastic Reality: Special Effects, Technology, and the Emergence of 1970s Blockbuster Aesthetics*, New York: Columbia University Press, 2015.

"UP Govt Warned of Closure of Cinemas," *Patriot* (New Delhi), 14 April 1978.

Usai, Paolo Cherchi. *The Death of Cinema: History, Cultural Memory, and the Digital Dark Age*, London: British Film Institute, 2001.

———. *Silent Cinema: An Introduction*, London: BFI, 2009.

Valančiūnas, Deimantas. "Indian Horror: The Western Monstrosity and the Fears of the Nation in the Ramsay Brothers' *Bandh Darwaza*," *Acta Orientalia Vilnensia* 12, no. 2 (2011), 47–60.
Van Hollen, Cecilia. *Birth on the Threshold: Childbirth and Modernity in South India*, Berkeley: University of California Press, 2003.
Vasudev, Aruna. *Liberty and License in the Indian Cinema*, New Delhi: Vikas Publishing House Pvt. Ltd., 1978.
Vasudevan, Ravi. "In the Centrifuge of History," *Cinema Journal* 50, no. 1 (Fall 2010), 135–140.
———. *The Melodramatic Public: Film Form and Spectatorship in Indian Cinema*, Ranikhet: Permanent Black, 2010.
Veerana, Certificate Number 872, Central Board of Film Certification, Mumbai.
Vesuna, Sheila. "Sarosh Modi: I Have Done for Make-Up Men What Salim-Javed Did for Writers," *Star & Style*, 1–14 August 1986, 52–53.
"Video Fever," *Screen*, 23 November 1983.
"Video Parlors Raided," *Times of India*, 30 December 1987, 3.
"Video Will Extinguish Exhibition Trade," *Screen*, 18 March 1983.
"Videotape," *Screen*, 6 February 1981.
Vismann, Cornelia. *Files: Law and Media Technology*, trans. Geoffrey Winthrop-Young, Stanford, CA: Stanford University Press, 2008.
Vitali, Valentina. *Hindi Action Cinema: Industries, Narratives, Bodies*, Bloomington and Indianapolis: Indiana University Press, 2008.
———. "The Hindi Horror Film: Notes on the Realism of a Marginal Film Genre," in *Genre in Asian Film and Television: New Approaches*, ed. Felicia Chan, Angelina Karpovich, and Xin Zhang, New York, Palgrave Macmillan, 2011, 130–148.
———. "The Hindi Horror Films of the Ramsay Brothers," in *Capital and Popular Cinema: The Dollars Are Coming!*, Manchester, UK: Manchester University Press, 2017, 122–157.
Vohra, Gautam. "Film City May Remain Only Paper Plan," *Times of India*, 18 December 1973.
Wadia, Dinaz "Video Zombies," *Times of India*, 18 May 1984.
Warner, Michael. "Publics and Counterpublics," *Public Culture* 14, no. 1 (2002), 49–90.
Wasser, Frederick. *Veni, Vidi, Video: The Hollywood Empire and the VCR*, Austin: University of Texas Press, 2001.
Wasserman, Sarah. *The Death of Things: Ephemera and the American Novel*, Minneapolis: University of Minnesota Press, 2020.
Watkins, Elizabeth. "*Don't Look Now*: Transience and Text," *Screen* 56, no. 4 (Winter 2015), 436–449.
Weber, Max. "Bureaucracy," in *From Max Weber: Essays in Sociology*, trans. and ed. H. H. Gerth and C. Wright Mills, Oxon: Routledge, 1991.

Weinstock, Jeffrey. "Introduction: The Spectral Turn," in *The Spectralities Reader: Ghosts and Haunting in Contemporary Cultural Theory*, ed. Maria del Pilar Blanco and Esther Peeren, London: Bloomsbury Publishing, 2013.

Weld, Kirsten. *Paper Cadavers: The Archives of Dictatorship in Guatemala*, Durham, NC: Duke University Press, 2014.

Westmore, Michael. *From "Rocky" to "Star Trek": The Amazing Creations of Hollywood's Michael Westmore*. Guilford: Lyons Press, 2017.

Whissel, Kristen, in conversation with Regina Longo, "Review: Kristen Whissel Talks about Spectacular Digital Effects; CGI and Contemporary Cinema," *Film Quarterly* 68, no. 1 (Fall 2014), 83–86.

Wilkinson-Weber, Clare. *Fashioning Bollywood: Costume and Culture in the Hindi Film Industry*, London: Bloomsbury Academic. 2013.

Wilkinson-Weber, Clare M., and Alicia Ory DeNicola, *Critical Craft: Technology, Globalization, and Capitalism*, London: Bloomsbury Publishing, 2016.

Willemen, Paul. *Looks and Frictions: Essays in Cultural Studies and Film Theory*, Bloomington: Indiana University Press, 1994.

Williams, Linda. "Film Bodies: Gender, Genre, and Excess," *Film Quarterly* 44, no. 4 (1991).

Williams, Raymond. "Violence," in *Keywords*, Oxford: Oxford University Press, 1976, 329–331.

"Woman Killed," *Screen*, 19 June 1981.

Wollen, Peter. *Signs and Meaning in the Cinema* (1969), London: Bloomsbury Publishing, 2019.

Wood, Robin. "An Introduction to the American Horror Film," in *American Nightmare: Essays on the Horror Film*, Toronto: Festival of Festivals, 1979, 7–28.

"Writ Petition against Ban on Film," *Times of India*, 28 December 1978, 4.

"Written Answers to Questions" (1973), Minister of Information and Broadcasting I. K. Gujral, Rajya Sabha, 27 August 1973, https://rsdebate.nic.in/.

"Written Answers to Questions" (1977), Rajya Sabha, 15 December 1977, https://rsdebate.nic.in/.

Yadav, Vijay Kumar. "2 Members of Affluent Sindhi Family Held for Cheating 166 Investors of Rs. 30 Crores," *Hindustan Times*, 23 August 2019.

Young, Damon. "In Defense of Psychoanalytic Film Theory," in *The Oxford Handbook of Film Theory*, ed. Kyle Stevens, New York: Oxford University Press, 2022, 117–148.

Yue, Genevieve. *Girl Head: Feminism and Film Materiality*, New York: Fordham University Press, 2020.

Yumibe, Joshua. "Colour as Performance in Visual Music, Film Tinting, and Digital Painting," in *Performing New Media 1890–1915*, New Barnet, UK: John Libbey Publishing, 2014, 293–302.

Zhou, Chenshu. *Cinema Off Screen: Moviegoing in Socialist China*, Oakland: University of California Press, 2021.

Zinman, Gregory. *Making Images Move*: *Handmade Cinema and the Other Arts*, Oakland: University of California Press, 2020.

Index

Aakhri Cheekh, 11
Abbott, Stacey, 21–22
accidents, 28, 35–37, 172–74, 176–77, 186
Advani, L.K., 53
aesthetics: bootleg, 184; counter-, 28; of the grotesque, 170; of horror, 212; high-modernist, 147; materialist, 16–20, 41; of video, 216
Agent Vinod, 6, 12
Alien, 57, 161
All India Film Producers Council (AIFPC), 193–96, 206
Alucarda, 13, 57
Andhera, 56, 133
Apostolidis, Paul, 138
archive, 28–29, 42, 66, 77–78, 83, 93, 175, 208, 211–18; pirate, 215–18. *See also* National Film Archive of India
Askari, Kaveh, 218
atmosphere, 2, 19, 32, 35–36, 111–48, 158, 164, 191, 205–6. *See also* mise-en-scène; production design.
Aur Kaun, 8, 9

Bajirao Mastani, 115
Baker, Rick, 154
Bali, Yogeeta, 86

Bandh Darwaza, 1–42, 123–24, 133, 211–12, 218; accidents in, 40; atmosphere in, 19; consumption of, 38–39, 211–12; things in, 23, 27; transnational aspects of, 13–14
Barjatya, Sooraj, 12
Barsaat, 119
Barthes, Roland, 26, 53, 84
Bartlett, Becky, 25, 140
Bees Saal Baad (1962), 60
Bees Saal Baad (1988), 8, 12
Benson-Allot, Caetlin, 20, 183
Besharam, 90
Bhakri, Mohan, 8, 11, 13, 29, 38, 124, 134, 158, 160, 181–210, 215–16
Bhogal, Avtar, 12
Bhola Bhala, 90
Bhosle, D.R., 59
Birje, Hermant, 13
Bite Me Once Already, 106
body horror, 154–56
Bollywood, 1, 15–16, 29, 115–16
Bombay (magazine), 175
Bombay cinema, 8, 15, 22; crises of, 114, 134; and film reception, 186; genres of, 151; golden age of, 8, 114; history of, 119, 192; studio system, 16, 116; and video, 183

277

278 INDEX

Bombay horror, 1–42; atmosphere of, 113–18, 144; and censorship, 110; and circulation,
Bombay horror (*continued*)
  210, 218; and failure, 38–41; materialist aesthetics of, 17–21; materialist historiography of, 27–31; origins of, 31–33; prosthetic effects in, 150–58, 163, 170–80, 213; spectral materialities of, 5, 212; and video, 218
Bombay Talkies (studio), 6, 120, 122
Bride of Frankenstein, 77
Brinkema, Eugenie, 19, 176
Britton, Andrew, 60
Brown, Bill, 38
Bruno, Giuliana, 115
bureaucracy, 49–54, 62–77, 85–98; and cinematic time, 54; post-Emergency, 53; temporality of, 49. *See also* paperwork
Buscombe, Edward, 22–23

Carroll, Noël, 152
camp, 25, 155
Cannibal Holocaust, 57
casting, 60, 135, 165. *See also* extras
Cavell, Stanley, 128
censorship, 12, 16–17, 29, 33–34, 45–78, 80–110, 112, 150, 197, 226n1; censor script, 69–78; certificates of, 44–54, 64, 69, 76–77, 80, 82, 86, 92, 98, 100, 107, 197, 226n1; code, 12, 45, 47–48, 51–54, 63, 75–77, 110; and color, 103–6; and *Darwaza*, 43–78; and the *Gazette of India*, 62–69; and *Jaani Dushman*, 79–110; and *Veerana*, 151; spectrality of, 105–6; temporality of, 48–55, 77
Chakraborty, Mithun, 12–13, 121, 200
Cheekh, 8, 11, 13, 82, 160, 184–92, 197–98, 215
Chehre Pe Chehra, 158–59, 161
Chopra, Aditya, 12
Chopra, B.R., 12
Cinematograph Act, (1952), 48, 63, 64, 90, 93,
circulation, 5, 15, 16, 17, 20, 28, 31, 34, 37, 57, 78, 96, 106, 108–9, 120, 180–98, 205–18; of paperwork, 53; subaltern, 28, 208. *See also* video
Cities of Sleep, 242n84
class, 15, 37, 51, 53–54, 136, 182–209, 217, 228n38
Clover, Carol, 99
color film, 22, 34, 57, 93–108; Eastmancolor, 102–8
Comolli, Jean Louis, 177

continuity errors, 3, 26, 118–21, 140–44
convention, 116–19
corporeal history, 31
corporeality, 31–39, 47, 62, 74, 85, 107, 136, 151, 156, 171, 173, 176; and extras, 136; of filmmaking, 31, 33, 62, 171, 176; of handiwork, 107; and history, 31; of images, 85, 156; and labor, 136–37; of prosthetic effects, 176. *See also* spectral materiality; things
Curse of Frankenstein, The, 56, 59, 230n85
Curse of the Swamp Creature, 25
curses, 6, 8, 22; in *Darwaza*, 117–18; in *Purana Mandir*, 129–30, 138–39
cuts, 21, 32, 33, 36, 69–71, 78–110, 165, 178; and censorship, 32, 36, 69–71, 91, 100, 107, 109; and *Darwaza*, 69–71; in *Jaani Dushman*, 81, 109–10; in *Veerana*, 165, 178

Dahshat, 117, 127, 160–63; special effects in, 160, 163
dance film, 6
darkness, 2–3, 18, 22, 84, 98, 132, 144, 149, 205, 211
Darwaza, 1, 6–8, 11, 33, 43–77, 94, 117, 123, 133, 165, 226n1; booklet design of, 60–62; censor script of, 69–76; censorship of, 44–45; temporality in, 47–48
day-for-night shooting, 22
Demons (1985), 171
Desai, Manmohan, 189, 208
Dhawan, Anil, 43
digital cinema, 156, 179, 214
Dilwale Dulhania Le Jayenge, 12
Disco Dancer, 6, 12
disgust, 151–53, 168–79; in *Dahshat*, 162; ideology of, 36; and *Jaani Dushman*, 152
Doane, Mary Ann, 21
Do Gaz Zameen Ke Neeche, 56, 226n100
Doordarshan (television network), 195–96
Dracula (1931), 13, 22, 56, 159
Dumas, Chris, 140
Dutt, Aloke, 157–58, 159, 178
Dutt, Sunil, 86
Dwyer, Rachel, 23

Elephant Man, The, 154, 159
Ek Nanhi Munhi Ladki Thi, 56, 133
Emergency, The (1975–77), 33–34, 52–53, 91, 98, 145–47
Entity, The, 209
Ernst, Wolfgang, 217

Evil Dead, 13
excess, 24–26, 37, 83–84, 96, 104, 151–63, 171–74
exhibition, 35, 38, 51–52, 64, 181,183–88, 194, 201–4; crisis of, 191
Exorcist, The, 46, 56, 81, 164, 173
extras, 134–45, 232n22

failure, 20–30, 32, 37, 38–42, 83, 114, 140–48, 186, 203– 218; fertility of, 25; temporality of, 38–39
Fay, Jennifer, 114
Filmalaya Studio, 121–23
Film hi Film, 121, 232n21
film phenomenology, 41, 176, 240n40
Film Studio Setting and Allied Mazdoor Union (FSS&AMU), 123
finance, 31, 35–36, 119–21, 125, 183, 189–90, 197
Flueckiger, Barbara, 108
Flusser, Vilém, 93
Frank, Hannah, 20
Frankenstein (1934), 56
Friday the 13th, 13
Frith, Paul, 230n85

Gandhi, Indira, 33, 52, 196
gangster film, 6, 23, 59
Ganti, Tejaswini, 15
genre, 17–18, 21– 27, 34– 47, 56–58, 89, 112, 116, 127, 162–63, 170, 171, 183, 203, 213; body, 39, 41, 163, 171; and Bombay horror, 17–18, 37; and Hindi cinema, 14; and horror, 24, 34, 116, 162, 213. *See also* Bombay horror; gangster film; heist film; melodrama; spy thriller
Ghai, Tina, 13
ghost stories, 5, 8
Gopal, Sangita, 14–15, 23
Gopal Krishna, 12
Gopalan, Lalitha, 82
Govil, Nitin, 29, 116, 229n71
Groo, Katherine, 41, 84
Grover, Gulshan, 179
Gupta, Akhil, 65
Gupta, Arti, 126

Haiwan, 8
Halloween (1978), 57, 99
Hanich, Julian, 152
Hantke, Steffen, 156
Hart, Adam Charles, 21

Hatyarin, 22, 151, 157
heist film, 56
Herbert, Daniel, 204
Hilderbrand, Lucas, 184
Hills Have Eyes, The (1977), 57
Hochschild, Arlie, 65
Hoek, Lotte, 29
horror film: 1–8; and censorship, 33–34, 43–110, 112, 150, 151, 197; contemporary, 213; and failure, 17, 20–30, 37–41, 83, 114, 140–48, 185, 203, 211–12; financing of, 31, 34–35, 56, 120–21, 125, 183, 189–90, 197; Indian, 6, 11, 33, 45, 47, 55–62, 69, 70, 72, 151, 158, 200; repetition in, 117–18; and temporality, 55; theories of, 39; and video, 183. *See also* Bombay horror
Horror of Dracula, 13, 56, 59, 94
House, 57
Huang, Erin, 41
Hum Aapke Hain Koun!, 12

imitation, 1, 13, 199–200, 218
Indian Federation Against Copyright (INFACT), 206–7
Indian Motion Picture Distributors Association, 194
Insaf Ka Tarazu, 12
intertextuality, 117–18
I Spit on Your Grave, 57
Iyer, Usha, 13, 31

Jaani Dushman, 8, 11, 22, 33, 46, 69, 78, 79–110, 152, 159, 182, 218, 230n38; censorship of, 80–110; color in, 93, 95–96, 108–9; damage to, 99–103; and the frame, 83–86; and melodrama, 97–89, 90; violence against women in, 87–88
Jaaved, Jaaferi, 229n72
Jadu Tona, 5, 8, 46,
Jaikumar, Priya, 5, 117, 229n70
Jain, Kajri, 139
Jeetendra, 86
Jhoota Kahin Ka, 90

Kabrastan, 11, 13, 124, 151, 181–82, 184, 200–3, 215, 218
Kapoor, Raj, 159, 160
Kapoor, Sheila, 172, 174, 175
Kapoor, Trilok, 74
Karaganis, Joe, 217
Kasam Paida Karne Wale Ki, 200
Kermode, Mark, 34

Khan, Imitaz, 74
Khan, Saroj, 172
Khandpur, K.L., 52, 91–92
Khooni Mahal, 8, 23, 121, 124, 134, 157, 199, 201
Khooni Murdaa, 134, 158, 178, 184, 192–93, 195, 198–99, 209–10
Khooni Panja, 5
Khosla, Raj, 6, 59
kitsch, 16, 23, 139
Kohli, Rajkumar, 8, 46, 79, 91, 182
Kohraa, 6, 59, 60
Kolnai, Aurel, 170
Korde, Bal, 74
Korsmeyer, Carolyn, 151
Kristeva, Julia, 152

labor, 28, 31, 55, 65–66, 123–24, 135, 137, 142–45, 148, 158, 171, 177, 179, 186, 214, 231n68
landscape, 5, 59, 116, 195. *See also* atmosphere
Larkin, Brian, 203
Leary, Charles, 138
Liang, Lawrence, 45
Lim, Bliss Cua, 3, 48
London, Christopher, 130
Lowenstein, Adam, 147

MacDowell, James, 142
Madhumati, 6, 57, 59
Mahadevan, Sudhir, 37, 232n21
Mahal, 6, 57, 59
Mahila Kalakar Sangh (MKS), 135
Maine Pyar Kiya, 12
makeup, 55, 150–80, 213. *See also* prosthetics effects
Malhotra, Madhu, 13
Mard, 189
Martin, Adrian, 18–19
Mask of Satan, 13, 164
masks, 56, 58, 149–80, 236n80.
Masood, Iqbal, 16, 191
Masque of the Red Death, 94
materiality, 18–20, 39–44, 76–85, 114–15, 151–73, 179–80, 213–14, 215; bodily, 151; cinematic, 20, 21, 24, 26, 36, 39–40, 54, 91, 107, 213; historical, 28, 114–15, 180; of light, 168; turn to, 19–20. *See also* prosthetic effects; spectral materiality
Maut, 121
Mazumdar, Ranjani, 82, 115
Mazzarella, William, 47

Meden, Jurij, 106
media archaeology, 216
Mehta, Monika, 143
melodrama, 2, 12, 14, 15, 17, 87–89, 90, 145, 189, 200, 209
Miller, D.A., 141
Miller, William Ian, 165
Ministry of Information and Broadcasting, 12, 32, 51, 64, 89, 91, 197. *See also* censorship
mise-en-scène, 30, 35, 41, 47–48, 84, 88, 113–15, 128, 138, 142–43, 147, 171
Mishra, Vijay, 59
Mohamed, Khalid, 12, 81, 127
Mohan Studios, 122
monsters, 6, 8, 11, 15–25; in *Dahshat*, 161; in *Darwaza*, 8, 11, 43, 47, 54–60, 62–77; in *Jaani Dushman*, 22, 79–99, 101–9; in *Veerana*, 149, 157, 161
montage, 30, 45, 47, 79
moral panic, 28, 31–32, 208
Mughal E Azam, 115, 122
Mukherjee, Debashree, 30, 119

Nandy, Pritish, 114
Natraj Studios, 135
Ndalianis, Angela, 40
Neale, Steve, 155–56
Nightmare on Elm Street: Dream Warriors, 13
Night of the Living Dead, 24
Nosferatu, 13, 21

obsolescence, 21, 28, 59, 106, 124, 216
Omen, The (1976), 56, 121
Onibaba, 171

Pandian, Anand, 25
paperwork, 32–34, 47–49, 51–54, 65, 76–78. *See also* bureaucracy; things
Parinda, 6
Peeren, Esther, 28
Pemgirikar, Pradeep, 159, 236n80
Pilar Blanco, Maria del, 28
Pinney, Christopher, 85
piracy, 184, 206–9, 217–18,
possession, 43, 57, 151, 164
Prasad, Madhava, 228n38
Pregnancy and Childbirth, 145
Prince, Stephen, 69, 82
production design, 35, 62, 114–19, 124–28, 139–43, 178, 212, 214
Profondo Rosso, 94

props, 5, 11, 20, 31–40, 113–19, 128–32, 141–45. *See also* masks; things
prosthetic effects, 36, 57, 157–59, 168, 170, 174–79, 213–14. *See also* makeup
Psycho (1960), 60, 99
psychogeography, 115
Purana Mandir, 8, 14, 22, 34, 36, 111–48, 151, 183–88, 207–8, 218; atmosphere in, 112–13; continuity errors in, 140–42; flashback in, 139–47; forbidden places in, 124–29, 133; mise-en-scène in, 128, 138, 142–43; tactility of, 114
Purani Haveli, 117, 124, 127, 130–33
Pyaar Jhukta Nahin, 145–48
Pyasa Shaitan, 8, 13, 188

Raat, 14
Raat Ke Andhere Mein, 82–83, 185, 196
Rabid, 57
Raj Kapoor Studios, 119, 122
Ram, Kalpana, 146
Ramsay Brothers, 1, 8, 12; as studio, 118–23
Ramsay, Fatehchand Uttamchand, 56
Ramsay, Gangu, 11
Ramsay, Keshu, 74
Ramsay, Kiran, 11
Ramsay, Shyam, 11
Ramsay, Tulsi, 11, 13, 29, 37, 43, 56, 59, 62, 77, 111, 115, 121, 124–27, 132, 139, 151, 172, 188, 201
Rani, Devika, 120
Ranjan, Dinesh, 135–36
Rathore, Manohar, 232n44
Ray, Satyajit, 12, 108
Reanimator, 154
reception, 19, 30, 86, 182, 186
regulation, 32–34, 54, 82–83, 91–110, 182, 212. *See also* censorship
remediation, 210
Richards, Rashna Wadia, 27
R.K. Studios, 119
Roy, Reena, 86, 136
Roy, Srinivas, 127, 159, 164, 172

Saamri, 8, 117, 188, 200–2
Saaransh, 12
Saat Saal Baad, 8, 12, 121
Sannata, 117, 127, 129, 133
Sarab Sanjhi Gurbani, 195
Sarkar, Kobita, 50, 96
Sau Saal Baad, 11, 13, 199
Savini, Tom, 154

Schuppli, Susan, 83
Sconce, Jeffrey, 25
Sedgwick, Eve, 116
Seeing, 3–5, 39, 41, 96, 212; vision and, 83–84
Sen, Meheli, 17, 23, 33, 117, 151
Sen, Shaunak, 239n84
Sex Vigyaan, 145
Sharma, Vijay, 12
Shaviro, Steven, 18, 155
Shining, The, 57
Sholay, 6, 125, 206
Singer, Ben, 88
Sinha, Shatrugan, 86
Sipos, Thomas, 25
Smith, Dick, 154
Sobchack, Vivian, 176, 216
Sofer, Andrew, 142
Son of Frankenstein, 56
Spadoni, Robert, 22
special effects, 151–63, 170–76. *See also* prosthetic effects
spectrality 3, 5; turn to, 28
spectral materiality, 5, 28, 31, 33, 48, 78
spy thriller, 6
Srinivas, S.V., 189
Stevens, Kyle, 39
Steyerl, Hito, 216
streaming media, 15, 22, 38, 109, 213–18
Subhash, Babbar, 6, 13, 200, 209
Sundaram, Ravi, 205, 217
Suresh, Mayur, 197
Syed, M. K., 122

Tagore, Sharmila, 12–13
Tahkhana, 8, 117, 123, 124, 127–28, 131, 133, 172
Talwar, Vinod, 5, 8, 11, 22, 29, 37, 82, 182, 185, 196–97, 198
Tanvir, Kuhu, 215, 218
television, 11, 13, 38, 48, 183–84, 192, 194–96, 198, 200, 204, 209–10, 213; death by, 209
Texas Chainsaw Massacre, The (1974), 24, 99
Theophanidis, Philippe, 102
Thing, The, 154–55, 156, 157, 180
things, 20–21, 38–40, 114–15, 156–57, 170–74, 213; celluloid, 20–22, 33–38, 67, 78, 80, 93, 98, 100, 103, 107, 108, 217; latex, 5, 20, 36, 40, 150, 155, 157, 159, 162, 165–66, 171, 172–74, 175, 176, 178, 200, 214; paper, 20, 33, 43–44, 45, 49, 50, 53–55, 63, 64–65, 72, 77, 98, 107, 128, 192; plastic, 20, 93, 106, 127, 135, 150. *See also* makeup; masks; materiality; props; prosthetic effects

Thomas, Rosie, 14, 188, 229n70
Thriller, 200–2
Tiwari, Anjani, 127–28
Tombs, Pete, 87
Tucker, Christopher, 154, 159

uncanny, the, 21–22
undead, the, 12, 181, 200, 202. *See also* zombies
Usai, Paolo Cherchi, 86

vampires, 1–2, 13–14, 19, 21–23, 27, 36, 40, 133, 175, 182, 211
Vasudev, Aruna, 52, 90
Veerana, 13, 36, 82, 121, 124, 131, 133, 149–80, 218; and disgust, 153–57, 162, 164–71, 175, 178–80
video, 37–38, 183–84, 192–209, 215, 217
video parlors, 31, 184, 204–8, 212
violence, 1, 5, 8, 82–83, 89–99, 102–7, 136, 147, 154, 208–9; ancestral, 6, 184; and censorship, 34, 46, 54, 76, 82–83, 110, 112, 150–51
visual damage, 3, 33, 37, 78–82, 86, 99–100, 102–9, 191, 213

Vitali, Valentina, 35–36, 119

Walas, Chris, 154
Walking Dead, The (1936), 56
Weber, Max, 50
Westmore, Michael, 159
Whissel, Kristen, 214
Wilkinson, Clare, 36
Williams, Linda, 40, 154
Williams, Raymond, 91
witches, 1, 11, 18, 20, 36, 153, 168, 177–82, 202
Woh Kaun Thi?, 6, 59
Wood, Robin, 17, 41

Yue, Genevieve, 105
Yumibe, Joshua, 95

Zakhmi Aurat, 12
Zborowski, James, 142
Zee Horror Show, 11
Zinda Laash, 13
Zinman, Gregory, 108
zombies, 153, 181, 200. *See also* undead, the

South Asia Across the Disciplines is a series devoted to publishing across a wide range of South Asian studies, including art, history, philology or textual studies, philosophy, religion, and the interpretive social sciences. Series authors all share the goal of opening up new archives and suggesting new methods and approaches, while demonstrating that South Asian scholarship can be at once deep in expertise and broad in appeal.

Extreme Poetry: The South Asian Movement of Simultaneous Narration, by Yigal Bronner (Columbia)

The Social Space of Language: Vernacular Culture in British Colonial Punjab, by Farina Mir (UC Press)

Unifying Hinduism: Philosophy and Identity in Indian Intellectual History, by Andrew J. Nicholson (Columbia)

The Powerful Ephemeral: Everyday Healing in an Ambiguously Islamic Place, by Carla Bellamy (UC Press)

Secularizing Islamists? Jama'at-e-Islami and Jama'at-ud-Da'wa in Urban Pakistan, by Humeira Iqtidar (Chicago)

Islam Translated: Literature, Conversion, and the Arabic Cosmopolis of South and Southeast Asia, by Ronit Ricci (Chicago)

Conjugations: Marriage and Form in New Bollywood Cinema, by Sangita Gopal (Chicago)

Unfinished Gestures: Devadāsīs, Memory, and Modernity in South India, by Davesh Soneji (Chicago)

Document Raj: Writing and Scribes in Early Colonial South India, by Bhavani Raman (Chicago)

The Millennial Sovereign: Sacred Kingship and Sainthood in Islam, by A. Azfar Moin (Columbia)

Making Sense of Tantric Buddhism: History, Semiology, and Transgression in the Indian Traditions, by Christian K. Wedemeyer (Columbia)

The Yogin and the Madman: Reading the Biographical Corpus of Tibet's Great Saint Milarepa, by Andrew Quintman (Columbia)

Body of Victim, Body of Warrior: Refugee Families and the Making of Kashmiri Jihadists, by Cabeiri deBergh Robinson (UC Press)

Receptacle of the Sacred: Illustrated Manuscripts and the Buddhist Book Cult in South Asia, by Jinah Kim (UC Press)

Cut-Pieces: Celluloid Obscenity and Popular Cinema in Bangladesh, by Lotte Hoek (Columbia)

From Text to Tradition: The Naisadhīyacarita and Literary Community in South Asia, by Deven M. Patel (Columbia)

Democracy against Development: Lower Caste Politics and Political Modernity in Postcolonial India, by Jeffrey Witsoe (Chicago)

Into the Twilight of Sanskrit Poetry: The Sena Salon of Bengal and Beyond, by Jesse Ross Knutson (UC Press)

Voicing Subjects: Public Intimacy and Mediation in Kathmandu, by Laura Kunreuther (UC Press)

Writing Resistance: The Rhetorical Imagination of Hindi Dalit Literature, by Laura R. Brueck (Columbia)

Wombs in Labor: Transnational Commercial Surrogacy in India, by Amrita Pande (Columbia)

I Too Have Some Dreams: N.M. Rashed and Modernism in Urdu Poetry, by A. Sean Pue (UC Press)

The Place of Devotion: Siting and Experiencing Divinity in Bengal-Vaishnavism, by Sukanya Sarbadhikary (UC Press)

We Were Adivasis: Aspiration in an Indian Scheduled Tribe, by Megan Moodie (Chicago)

Writing Self, Writing Empire: Chandar Bhan Brahman and the Cultural World of the Indo-Persian State Secretary, by Rajeev Kinra (UC Press)

Landscapes of Accumulation: Real Estate and the Neoliberal Imagination in Contemporary India, by Llerena Searle (Chicago)

Polemics and Patronage in the City of Victory: Vyasatirtha, Hindu Sectarianism, and the Sixteenth-Century Vijayanagara Court, by Valerie Stoker (UC Press)

Hindu Pluralism: Religion and the Public Sphere in Early Modern South India, by Elaine M. Fisher (UC Press)

Negotiating Languages: Urdu, Hindi, and the Definition of Modern South Asia, by Walter N. Hakala (Columbia)

Building Histories: The Archival and Affective Lives of Five Monuments in Modern Delhi, by Mrinalini Rajagopalan (Chicago)

Reading the Mahavamsa: The Literary Aims of a Theravada Buddhist History, by Kristin Scheible (Columbia)

Modernizing Composition: Sinhala Song, Poetry, and Politics in Twentieth-Century Sri Lanka, by Garrett Field (UC Press)

Language of the Snakes: Prakrit, Sanskrit, and the Language Order of Premodern India, by Andrew Ollett (UC Press)

The Hegemony of Heritage: Ritual and the Record in Stone, by Deborah L. Stein (UC Press)

The Monastery Rules: Buddhist Monastic Organization in Pre-Modern Tibet, by Berthe Jansen (UC Press)

Merchants of Virtue: Hindus, Muslims, and Untouchables in Eighteenth-Century South Asia, by Divya Cherian (UC Press)

Seeing Things: Spectral Materialities of Bombay Horror, by Kartik Nair (UC Press)

Founded in 1893,
UNIVERSITY OF CALIFORNIA PRESS
publishes bold, progressive books and journals
on topics in the arts, humanities, social sciences,
and natural sciences—with a focus on social
justice issues—that inspire thought and action
among readers worldwide.

The UC PRESS FOUNDATION
raises funds to uphold the press's vital role
as an independent, nonprofit publisher, and
receives philanthropic support from a wide
range of individuals and institutions—and from
committed readers like you. To learn more, visit
ucpress.edu/supportus.

www.ingramcontent.com/pod-product-compliance
Lightning Source LLC
Chambersburg PA
CBHW021339230426
43666CB00006B/344